Lives of
Young Koreans
in Japan

JAPANESE SOCIETY SERIES

General Editor: Yoshio Sugimoto

Lives of Young Koreans in Japan

Yasunori Fukuoka

Translated by Tom Gill

Trans Pacific Press

Melbourne

First published in 2000 by
Trans Pacific Press
PO Box 164, Balwyn North, Melbourne, Victoria 3104, Australia
Telephone: +61 3 9859 1112

E-mail: tpp.mail@gmail.com
Website: http://www.transpacificpress.com

Set in CJR Times New Roman by digital environs Melbourne
enquiries@digitalenvirons.com

Printed in Melbourne by BPA Print Group

ISBN 1–8768–4300–4 hardback
ISBN 0–6463–9165–8 paperback

National Library of Australia Cataloging in Publication Data

A catalogue record for this book is available from the National Library of Australia.

British Library Cataloging in Publication Data

A catalogue record for this book is available from the British Library.

US Library of Congress Cataloging in Publication Data

A catalogue record for this book is available from the Library of Congress.

Contents

Tables

Figures

East Asia, showing principal places mentioned in the text.

The Korean peninsula, showing principal places mentioned in the text.

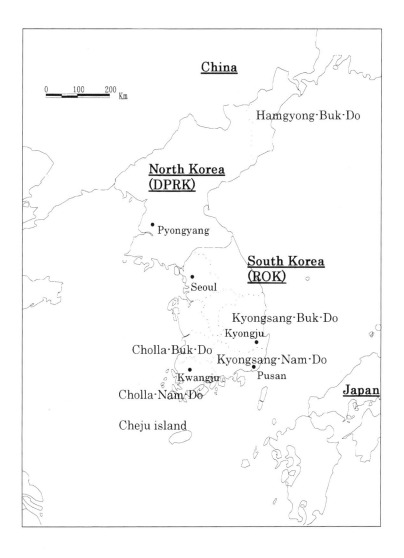

Japan, showing principal places mentioned in the text. Broad districts are in large type, prefectures in medium type and cities in small type.

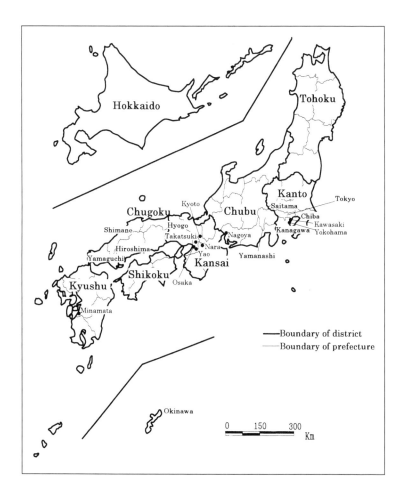

Preface

The life-history method

In this book I have attempted to gain an understanding of the ethnic identity of younger[1] members of Japan's ethnic Korean community, known in Japan as *Zainichi*[2] Koreans, chiefly by means of the life-history method.

This method, entailing the compilation of detailed life histories on the basis of in-depth interviews, has been criticized on the grounds that practical limitations prevent it from being applied to more than a small number of people, making it difficult to see the big picture. It is argued by many Japanese sociologists that the only way to grasp the overall scale and nature of a social problem is through a quantitative method based on the use of questionnaires.

I do not deny that statistical analysis of quantitative data has much value in establishing an overall profile of a social group, in identifying the distribution of specific opinions and attitudes, and discovering cause-and-effect relations between a number of variables. However, the statistical approach will only work if certain preconditions are fulfilled. One requires a list of members of the overall population to be studied, and one must be able to generate random samples from that list. In the case of the Japan-resident Koreans who are the topic of this book, these conditions are impossible to meet.

Since I define the target population very broadly, as 'ethnic Koreans permanently residing in Japan,' it naturally includes many people who have acquired Japanese nationality, for whom there is no official published list. Local authorities do keep lists of Koreans who are nationals of the Republic of Korea (ROK; South Korea) or of the Democratic People's Republic of Korea (DPRK; North Korea), as part of larger records covering all foreign nationals who stay in Japan for more than ninety days, but these are not made available for mere academic surveys.[3] *Mindan*[4] and *Chongryun*,[5] the residents' associations for South and North Koreans respectively, hold lists of names that while not complete, do cover most of the South- and North-affiliated Koreans in Japan. However, the political antagonism between these two bodies makes it virtually impossible to gain the wholehearted cooperation of one without alienating the other.[6]

It follows from all this that questionnaire surveys are not really feasible if one wishes to study the whole spectrum of the ethnic Korean population. Hence I decided to use the life-history method, making up for methodological weaknesses of the approach by interviewing as many people as possible and by seeking out people with as wide a range as possible of life experiences, opinions, etc.

In a two-year period (1988–89) I and my assistant, Tsujiyama Yukiko, interviewed about 120 young Zainichi Koreans, including some with Japanese nationality. By 1993 I had added a supplementary survey of some thirty more interviewees for a total of 150 in-depth interviews.

I started off by interviewing ethnic Korean students and graduates of Chiba College of Health Science, where I was working at the time. They were all female, and every single one of them was using an assumed Japanese name. However, in the essays they wrote for me they revealed their Korean identity and expressed some of the bitter experiences they had undergone because of it. In addition, Kim Haeng-Yi, one of my few ethnic Korean friends at the time when I commenced this project, kindly introduced me to many of his friends and relations.

In these ways I gradually developed a network of Korean contacts. Some of them did not just agree to be interviewed themselves, but actually introduced many of their friends as well. Thus I was able to conduct concentrated interviews with young members of Chongryun, of the Mindan-affiliated Korean Youth Association in Japan (KYAJ), and of *Mintōren*,[7] a Zainichi organization that supports neither Seoul nor Pyongyang. I also interviewed many young people who had practically no organizational affiliation: people using Japanese aliases and hiding their Korean identity in their everyday lives, people working for big Japanese corporations, people who had been to the USA for lengthy periods of study, people holding Japanese nationality because they or their parents had naturalized or because they were born of a mixed marriage.

Around the time I passed the 100-interview mark, I started to feel that a picture of the overall situation of Korean youths in Japan was emerging. The quantitative approach defines the nature of the whole subject of analysis in advance, by attempting to select random samples that form a faithful miniature version of the target population. With a more qualitative approach like my own in this book, the whole emerges slowly from the data as it accumulates. The whole that emerges will not be quite the same as the whole revealed in quantitative surveys, but I do not think it is in any sense an inferior form of sociology. Rather, the two images are like a pair of two-dimensional perspectives of the same three-dimensional object, seen from different angles.

The miniature version of the total population that a quantitative method attempts to produce has both strengths and weaknesses. It is effective in establishing broad trends, but tends to overlook or undervalue those minority elements in the population that do not conform to the broad trends. With a qualitative approach, even minority groups within the whole can be properly investigated through intensive selection of interview subjects. If the image of the whole that emerges from the quantitative approach is a miniature version of it, perhaps with the details blurred, then the image generated by the qualitative approach is like a stage with a spotlight that falls first on one group of actors, then on another. Its weakness is that it cannot accurately establish the relative size and importance of each group of actors in the play as a whole;[8] its strength is that it can convey the detailed differences between the actors as well as the broad similarities.

Theoretically speaking, the image of the whole produced by this life-history method can never be a really complete or comprehensive one, however many interviews one may conduct. All the researcher can do is make the most of the time and resources available, and avoid putting an end to the survey until professional instinct suggests that something like a true picture has been produced.

I honestly believe that the intensive interview method adopted has enabled me to cast light on aspects of reality that would elude a quantitative survey, and that I have been able to reproduce something not too far away from the rich variety of the overall subject. I leave it to the reader to decide whether I have in fact succeeded in presenting a total picture of the circumstances and problems of ethnic Korean youths living in Japan.

Notes on methodology

As far as individual circumstances would allow, I tried to make each interview last for three to four hours. The longest ones took over six hours. They were not formal question and answer sessions; rather, I would briefly make an inquiry and allow the interviewee to respond in any way and at any length he or she wished to. I did attempt to maintain a loose structure to the interviews, by carrying a short list of themes to ask about. These were broadly as follows:

(a) Basic facts: Korean name; assumed Japanese name where used; time and place where each name used; date of birth; nationality; grandparents' place of origin in Korea; their *bonkwan* (ancestral place of origin, indicating clan affiliation); affiliation to any ethnic organization; family composition; etc.

(b) Personal background: Circumstances under which grandparents came to Japan; occupation, lifestyle and attitudes of grandparents and parents; situation of siblings and relatives.

(c) Own life history: Experiences of discrimination; thoughts and feelings; self-identity. For example, first awareness of Korean ethnicity; experiences at school; degree to which natal household maintained Korean culture; problems encountered in securing employment or in love and marriage; etc. Basically I tried to follow the chronological course of events. I made a special point of always asking interviewees how they felt, or what they thought, about the various events they described. Even more than the facts, what interested me were their meanings to the individual.

(d) Opinions on issues: Use of real and assumed names; suitability of non-Koreans etc. as marriage partners; inability of many young Koreans to speak the Korean language; reluctance of Japanese government to grant various human rights to ethnic

Koreans; etc. I also asked about their feelings toward Korea and Japan. Some of these matters almost invariably cropped up in personal connections earlier in the interview, but I tried to confirm the subject's opinions on them in general terms towards the end.

I always kept two tape-recorders running during the interview, starting the second tape a few minutes after the first. This way there was no risk of data loss in the event of mechanical failure, and also the interviewee was free to carry on talking while I was changing tapes.

I did all the transcription work myself. I preferred not to employ assistants, for fear that they might fail to pick up certain nuances in the speech, either for lack of knowledge of the issues, or simply because they had not been present at the original interview. Doing the transcribing myself also had tremendous advantages for the research. To make a perfect transcript I would have to play back the tape three or four times. In the process I would mentally absorb the data. Later, when I came to produce case studies based on the taped data, this would prove invaluable.

Research ethics

In the United States, interview-based research such as this can only legally be conducted if a consent form is signed in advance by the interviewee. Typically there is a confidentiality clause along the following lines: 'The records of this study will be kept private. In any sort of report we might publish, we will not include any information that will make it possible to identify a subject....' Personally I am doubtful as to whether a single signed piece of paper can really solve all the ethical problems that arise in the course of conducting fieldwork and publishing the results. In the worst case, such a document can end up being no more than a piece of protection for the researcher against possible legal action from informants.

In any case, there is as yet no such established code of ethics for the social sciences here in Japan. Moreover, in a study like the present one, virtually all the material gathered is more or less private in nature. Failure to be aware of this leads inevitably to hurtful violations of privacy. Accordingly I have drawn up my own personal set of ethical rules as follows:

Before publishing a case study based on any interview, I must show the manuscript to the interviewee and obtain his or her consent

To date I have published thirty-seven interview-based case studies of Zainichi Koreans in Japanese. However, there were two other case studies that I wanted to publish, but for which I could not get the subjects' permission. I did not publish those studies, nor will I publish any study without the subject's consent, however interesting I may consider it to be.[9]

In many other cases, showing the text to my subjects has been of great benefit. They have often been able to correct errors made by themselves in recalling events, and inaccuracies made by myself in recording their stories.

Before publishing any interview-based material, I decide in consultation with the subject whether to use the subject's real name or not

One naturally hesitates to publish the real names and dwelling places of people who are subject to discrimination, since there is always the possibility that it may expose them or people connected to them to further discrimination. At the same time one cannot deny having a feeling that these case studies have a more immediate impact on the reader when all the details are real. This is a genuine issue in Japan, where the usual mainstream response to problems of discrimination, whether against Koreans, *Burakumin*[10] or some other group of people, has been to deny the existence of those problems. The great majority of mainstream Japanese are ignorant and apathetic concerning discrimination issues and would like to keep it that way. Even if such people happen to read an account of Japanese discrimination against minorities, they will tend to view it as an abstract problem that doesn't affect them directly so long as all the personal and geographical details have been air-brushed out.

Hence my personal rule: If the subject gives consent, I generally use the real name. If the subject prefers not to be identified, I respect his or her wishes. In several cases I have actually suggested that it might be advisable not to use the real name, only for subjects to tell me that since they are making the effort to live under their own name in Japanese society, they do not want a false name used in the published version of their life stories.

I delete any passages that the subject does not want published

Many of my subjects tell me that while they do not mind having their life stories published, there are certain passages that they would like deleted or altered because they pose a problem for their families or associates. Often these problems also relate to the use of real names, and appear to reflect concern to avoid causing bad feelings among people close to the subject.

In many cases I delete particularly sensitive passages myself, before I show the text to the subject. In particular I usually delete references to sexual relationships, divorces and the like, unless those references strike me as absolutely essential to bringing out the present-day identity of the subject. Likewise I delete passages that may be shocking or disturbing to other informants. Since I sometimes interview several people who are friends or relations of one another, sometimes I hear something about an informant from somebody else that was not mentioned when I interviewed the informant. I assume that such matters are better left out.

In the end, however conscientious I may be about observing these three rules, I cannot get away from the fact that it is in the nature of the genre that interview-based life histories will constantly impinge on the subject's privacy. Even if one conceals their real name, it will not stop anyone who knows the subject from recognizing them if they happen to read the book. I am acutely aware that no code of practice, however well intentioned, will ever amount to total protection of privacy. In the end all I can do is stick to the basic principle of respecting the informant's view of the matter.

Outline of the present work

In the Introduction I attempt to problematize the simplistic dichotomy between 'Japanese' and 'foreigner' that pervades thinking on ethnic identity in Japan. This I do by isolating three variables – blood lineage, culture and nationality – and permutating them against each other to generate eight theoretical types into which members of Japanese society might fall. I try to demonstrate that people resembling each of these theoretical types do actually exist in Japan today. My aim is to show that the notion of Japan as mono-ethnic society is a mere illusion; and to expose the intolerance implicit in the way the majority categorizes the various minorities.

Part One consists of eight chapters. Chapter 1 is a brief historical sketch of the formation of Japan's Korean minority, starting from the pre-war colonial period and showing how the rights of the Koreans have continued to be trampled on in the supposedly democratic society of post-war Japan. Chapter 2 summarizes the present-day circumstances of the younger generation of Zainichi Koreans, with special reference to the issues of language, names and marriage.

With Chapter 3 we come to the kernel of my argument. From my interview material, I deduce five types of orientation among the subject population. These are the pluralist, nationalist, individualist, naturalizing and ethnic solidarity types.

In the five chapters that follow (Chapters 4–8), I present case histories of ten young Zainichi Koreans – two examples each of the five types. I hope that by reading their stories, the reader will gain a concrete understanding of the range of life-orientations identified in Chapter 3.

Part Two consists of twelve case studies of second- and third-generation Zainichi Korean women. I hope it will supply a more vivid impression of the sheer horror of discrimination against the Korean minority than was possible within the theoretical constraints of Part One. Real-life people seldom fit neatly into the categories that we academics build for them, of course, and I hope the stress on unvarnished reality in Part Two will counterbalance the more theoretical approach of Part One.

Finally, in the Conclusion I discuss some recent, generally positive, developments in the political and legal treatment of Zainichi Koreans. I analyze the consciousness of young Japanese people regarding the Zainichi Korean question. And I make suggestions at the personal and political level as to how Japanese society might one day develop into one in which people of different ethnic origins can live together peacefully on the basis of mutual respect for each other's differences.

The Introduction and the eight chapters making up Part One are closely based on an earlier Japanese-language work of mine, *Zainichi Kankoku-Chōsenjin: Wakai Sedai no Aidentiti (Japan-Resident Koreans: The Identity of the Younger Generation)* (Tokyo: Chūōkōron-sha, 1993). Part Two is based on a slightly earlier Japanese-language book that I co-authored with Tsujiyama Yukiko, *Hontō no Watashi wo Motomete: 'Zainichi' Nisei Sansei no Josei-tachi (In Search of My Real Self: Japan-Resident Korean Women of the Second and Third Generations)* (Tokyo: Shinkan-sha, 1991).

In preparing this text for English-language publication, I have modified substantially the Introduction and Chapters 1–3, while the Conclusion is entirely new. The discussion of methodology and research methods contained in this Preface is also new, as are the notes at the end of the text, which have been added to make the text more accessible to an English-reading audience. Some readers may feel that there are too many notes, or that some of them cover unnecessarily obvious points. However, I discussed the matter with my translator, Tom Gill, and we decided to try and create a book that could be read with profit by people with no specialist knowledge of Japanese society or the role of the Korean minority within it. I hope that readers who have such knowledge will feel free to press on with the main text and ignore the notes.

However, the case studies that make up Chapters 4–20, though slightly edited, have not been updated. Some readers will no doubt be left wondering what actually happened to each subject after the period described in each case study – particularly in cases where the narrative breaks off with the subject at a critical crossroads in his or her life. As a matter of fact I do know 'what happened next' to my subjects, and what they are doing today. However, that information was acquired through personal correspondence and not through survey interviewing. Accordingly it would not be appropriate for me to discuss the matter here. This, too, is a question of research ethics.

There is another reason why I do not consider it necessary to describe what happened next. If I were a storyteller by profession, I might have been interested in continuing the narrative to present something as close as possible to a smoothly rounded life story. However, I am not a storyteller but a sociologist. To a sociologist the real question of 'what happens next' is not about what each individual informant is doing today. These interviews were conducted around the end of the 1980s and start of the 1990s. It is clear enough from them that young Koreans living in Japan at that time were troubled by various kinds of internal conflict. Would a similar survey, conducted for example around 2010, twenty years later, reveal similar kinds of identity conflict among young Zainichi Koreans? Or would it find that they had become able to live their lives freely, untroubled by such conflict? To a sociologist, that is the real question of 'what happens next.' I hope that I may one day have the opportunity to conduct that follow-up survey myself; alternatively, I would be delighted if some young researcher were to take up the challenge.

Writing style

It has always been a principle of mine to write my sociological works in a straightforward style accessible to the general reader. The English of the present translated volume faithfully reflects that style. One reason why I try to write without technical jargon or elaborate grammatical structures is because I always hope that my books will be read by the people who are their subjects. I view them as my most important readers.

I am pleased to say that the Japanese-language works on which this book is based have found many readers in Japan, including some who are themselves Zainichi Koreans. The following is an extract from a letter I received from a female Zainichi Korean reader who was one of my interview subjects:

I was recently approached by the mother of a girl who has been having difficulty getting on in Japanese society since graduating from a Korean high school last year. We talked of all sorts of things, and when we parted, I gave her a copy of your book with the suggestion that she give it to her daughter to read. Later I received a telephone call from the mother, saying that your book had greatly encouraged her daughter.

To a sociologist like myself, there can be no more pleasing compliment than to be told that my works have given somebody new heart to carry on the daily struggle that is life for so many members of Japan's ethnic Korean minority. I hope this first publication of my work in English will play its own part, however small, in improving worldwide understanding of the reality of life for Japan's minorities. If in so doing it can contribute, however indirectly, to social reform in Japan, then it will have done its job.

Note to the reader

In this book, Japanese and Korean names are written with the family name first, as is customary in East Asia. Korean people mostly have monosyllabic family names and disyllabic personal names; I hyphenate the personal name, as in 'Kim Dae-Won,' a boy called Dae-Won from the Kim family. The sole exception I have made is that of the late North Korean leader Kim Il Sung, in whose case I have adhered to the established practice of writing his name without a hyphen. Japanese and Korean have a shared system of Chinese pictographic writing, but pronunciation of the same character is often very different between the two languages. Where Korean names are given a Japanese reading (quite a common practice in Japan), I romanize without the hyphen, as in 'Kin Daigen,' the Japanese reading of 'Kim Dae-Won.'

Romanization of Japanese words has been based on the Hepburn system. In accordance with common Japanese practice, I have refrained from using macrons to indicate long vowels in names of people and places. For names of organizations and other nouns, however, long vowels are indicated by macrons thus: ō (oh), ū (oo), etc. I have romanized Korean words by attempting to reproduce the pronunciation of the original as faithfully as possible, without reference to any particular system. Only in the case of personal names, where the person has an established spelling, such as that used in their passport, I have adhered to that spelling.

I have not italicized Japanese and Korean names of individuals and places. However, I have in principle italicized all other Japanese and Korean nouns, with the following exceptions: (1) words that are familiar in the English language (e.g., 'kimono'); (2) names of organizations (Mindan, Chongryun, etc.) and the frequently appearing terms 'Zainichi' and 'Burakumin,' which are italicized on first reference only.

Where informants have asked for their identities to be protected, I have made up names for them and indicated this fact in the text. I have attempted to give them names with a similar atmosphere to their real names, however, especially with the regard to the question of whether the style of the name is Korean, Japanese or a bit of both.

In describing people as first-, second-, third- or fourth-generation migrants, I have adhered to the Korean custom of counting through the paternal line. Thus, for example, where someone is the offspring of a first-generation father and a second-generation mother, I describe that person as a second-generation migrant, rather than as a third-generation migrant.

Many informants talk about their schooldays. Note here that the Japanese school education system is based on the American one, with six years of primary school (ages 6–12) followed by three each of junior high school (12–15) and senior high school (15–18). However, the school year starts in April and ends in March. For the benefit of non-American readers, I have used terms such as 'second year of senior high school' rather than 'eleventh grade.' It may seem strange to use such cumbersome terms rather than simply stating the person's age. But the fact is that year groups at school are important conceptual units in Japan and are automatically used by my subjects. So I have tended to keep the terminology rather than converting year groups to ages, something that cannot be done precisely in any case.

Acknowledgments

It was a series of chance personal encounters that led to the publication in English of this book.

In 1995 I happened to be put in charge of negotiations on an academic exchange agreement between Saitama University, where I work, and Monash University, Australia. I thus became acquainted with Professor Ross Mouer, who was kind enough to read some of my works in Japanese and who subsequently introduced me to Professor Yoshio Sugimoto of La Trobe University.

The first time I met Professor Sugimoto in Tokyo, he invited me to publish some of my sociological work on Japanese minority problems in English-language book form. Much though I appreciated the invitation, I initially hesitated to take it up. The Japanese-language discourse on Zainichi Koreans is full of specialized jargon, which I knew I would struggle to translate into suitable English. To convey the meaning of my works as in the original Japanese, I needed to find a translator who was not just a native speaker of English with an excellent command of Japanese, but also had some understanding of Japanese minority problems.

Eventually, with the help of Professor Komai Hiroshi of Tsukuba University and Ms Yamaka Junko of Lingua Guild, Inc., I managed to get matched up with Dr Tom Gill. Tom is a social anthropologist, whose doctoral thesis at the London School of Economics was entitled *Men of Uncertainty: The Social Organization of Day Labourers in Contemporary Japan*. Like the present work, his writings are based on fieldwork and interview methods; and since June 1997, he had been working in Japan at Kyoto Bunkyo University. While living in Japan during the 1980s he refused fingerprinting in support of the Zainichi Korean movement against this notorious piece of bureaucratic harassment. In short, he is the ideal person to translate a work of this nature.

I have spent a most interesting year working with Tom on this translation. We have corrected each other's errors, adapted the content for an English-reading audience, and I am confident that the end result is a book that conveys what I have to say every bit as well as the Japanese originals on which it is based.

I am deeply honored that my book will be the first published by Trans Pacific Press and most appreciative of their efforts to publish a suitably priced book that can be easily obtained by those who have an interest in this important problem.

Although the bulk of the English manuscript of this book was completed in March 1998, I am pleased that I was able to include in the final version the latest situation surrounding the Zainichi Koreans during the last two years. Two changes are particularly noteworthy. Firstly, the opportunities for graduates of Korean ethnic schools to sit entrance examinations for Japanese national universities have increased. Secondly, a bill enabling foreign citizens who have permanent residency (of which a majority are Zainichi Koreans) to vote in local elections has been presented to the Diet.

I would like to thank Mr Bradley Williams (Ph.D. Candidate at Monash University who is conducting research in Japan at Saitama University) for his assistance in adding these changes to the book. I am also glad that the translator of this book, Dr Tom Gill, has been able to find suitable employment as an Assistant Professor at the Institute of Social Science, University of Tokyo.

Many, many people helped me over the years it took to create this book. First of all I would like to thank each and every one of the Zainichi Korean people who permitted me to interview them while I was doing the research. Many were kind enough to introduce me to friends and relatives who were also willing to be interviewed. I would also like to thank a number of Korean friends who supplied me with various research materials. In particular, my thanks go to Mr Kim Heang-Yi, Mr Bae Jung-Do and his wife, Ms Chung Wol-Soon (now sadly deceased), Mr Lee Kyung-Jae, Mr Suh Jung-Woo, Ms Suh Ok-Ja, Mr Chong Yang-I, Ms Yoon Cho-Ja, Mr Kim Kyung-Pil, Mr Choi Hee-Sub, Mr Lim Sam-Ho, Mr Lee Yang-Soo, Ms Park Hwa-Mi, Mr Kim Chul-Soo, Professor Park Sam-Seok and Professor Suh Yong-Dal.

I owe an especially deep debt of gratitude to Ms Tsujiyama Yukiko, who was my research assistant for most of the project. It is largely thanks to her that the project did not break down half way, but continued all the way to completion. The second of the two Japanese-language books on which this volume is based, *Hontō no Watashi wo Motomete*, was co-authored by Ms Tsujiyama and myself, and I owe her further thanks for permitting me to publish the present work under just my own name.

Another collaborator to whom I send special thanks is Dr Kim Myung-Soo. As I mentioned in the Preface, the quantitative data generated by our 1993 joint survey of young South Koreans has provided valuable supplementary data for the present volume. It is largely thanks to Dr Kim's expertise that the survey produced such useful data.

Many researchers offered me valuable advice and intellectual stimulation while I was working on this book. I would like to thank all of them, and particularly Professor Sofue Takao, Professor Ishida Takeshi, Professor Hirowatari Seigo, Professor Ejima Shusaku, Professor Jeffrey Broadbent, Professor Tanaka Hiroshi, Professor Amino Yoshihiko, Mr Kim Chan-Jung, Mr Yamawaki Keizo, Dr Masiko Hidenori, Dr Sonia Ryang, Mr Fukudome Noriaki, Dr Tai Eika, Professor Tanaka Kazuko, Dr John G. Russell, Ms Lim Young-Mi, Professor Momiyama Akira and Professor Takagi Eiji. Several young friends of mine assisted in various ways with the gathering of information, and here my thanks go to Ms Kubo Kazuyo, Ms Cho Kyong-Hee, Mr Takenoshita Hirohisa, Mr Hyun Moo-Am, Ms Toma Miyuki and Mr Uchino Takashi.

At the translation stage, I was greatly helped by Dr Kwon Soon-Chul, my colleague at Saitama University, on whom I relied for advice on English readings of Korean words, especially personal and place names. Another of my colleagues at Saitama University, Professor Yamamoto Mitsuru, was kind enough to draw up the maps showing the place-names that appear in the text.

Ms Seo Akwi (a Zainichi Korean who studied at Toronto University), Ms Jackie Kim (a Korean American student who is studying at Sophia University in Japan), Ms Erin A. Chung (Ph.D. Candidate at Northwestern University who is conducting research in Japan as a Japan Foundation Fellow), Mr Jeffrey Bayliss (Ph.D. Candidate at Harvard University who is also conducting research in Japan as a Fulbright Fellow) and Ms Elise Foxworth (Ph.D. Candidate at the University of Melbourne who is also conducting research in Japan as a Japan Foundation Fellow) gave up some of their valuable time to read the text for careless errors. Needless to say, I alone remain responsible for any errors that may remain.

My thanks go also to five Monash University students who came to me on the exchange program and encouraged me to publish my work in English after studying Japanese minority problems with me: Mr Paul Larsen, Ms Martha Howard, Ms Kate Phipps, Ms Jodi Robertson and Mr David McMahon.

I am particularly grateful to Mr Kimura Fumihiko of Chūōkōron-sha and Mr Ko I-Sam of Shinkan-sha. These two gentlemen oversaw publication of the two Japanese books that would later form the basis of the present volume. Without the skills of these two excellent editors, the Japanese material might never have been good enough to warrant translating into English for a wider audience.

The cover illustration for this book is a photograph taken from the 1988 Ikuno Korea Festival in Osaka. This photograph was graciously provided by Mr Kim Sung-Woong, a second generation Zainichi Korean.

Work on this book was facilitated by two grants from the Japanese Ministry of Education, Science, Sports and Culture. A Grant-in-Aid for Scientific Research (1988–89) helped finance the original survey and a Grant-in-Aid for Publication of Scientific Research Results (1997) helped finance the English translation. Herewith, my thanks in writing.

Finally, I would like to express my gratitude to my former supervisor at the University of Tokyo, Professor Mita Munesuke. Professor Mita taught me the pleasures of practicing sociology. Without his guidance, I would not be where I am today. Also, I would like to thank my wife Machiko and my daughters Shima and Chie, for their unflagging spiritual support during the lengthy period it took to complete this book.

Fukuoka Yasunori
Urawa, Japan
February, 2000

Introduction:
'Japanese' and 'Non-Japanese'

'Japanese' – An undefined term

It is widely believed, especially among Japanese people themselves, that Japan is a 'homogeneous' society. The government itself has repeatedly declared that there is no problem with minorities in this country.[1]

This is not true, of course, and never has been. In many parts of Japan there are still communities of Burakumin, the descendants of people defined as outcastes during the feudal Middle Ages (see Preface, Note 10). The Ainu, a distinctively different ethnic group who inhabited Japan long before the formation of the Yamato[2] Japanese who came to dominate the archipelago, are still to be found, living mainly in Hokkaido and struggling to maintain their distinctive and long-suppressed culture. The people of Okinawa, formerly the citizens of an independent Ryukyuan kingdom, were subject to persecution by their Japanese conquerors until well into the post-war period. Even today the Japanese government's willingness to allow a heavy concentration of US military facilities on the Okinawan islands surely reflects a discriminatory consciousness towards the Ryukyuan people.

And then there are the Koreans – people brought to Japan before and during the war by circumstances beyond their control, and their descendants. Today, the great majority of them are second-, third- or fourth-generation migrants, born and raised in Japan. These people, whose human rights are still not fully recognized in Japan, are the subject of this book. The 1980s and 1990s have brought new waves of immigration to Japan, from Asia and South America, and the new migrants have generally met with the same ingrained prejudice that their predecessors suffered on their arrival in Japanese society.

Admittedly Japan's minority population is relatively small, but that does not mean there is no problem. On the contrary, the overwhelming numerical dominance of the majority makes it all the easier to ignore or isolate the minorities. In that sense, it may be that Japan's minorities inhabit an even more severe environment than their counterparts in societies that recognize themselves to be multiethnic. I wish to stress that Japan is nowhere near achieving the kind of tolerance that will allow the majority and the minorities to live together in a spirit of mutual acceptance of difference.

However, although the homogeneous society is no more than a myth, it remains a particularly powerful myth with enduring influence over the identity-formation of Japanese people. So rather than simply denouncing it, I think there is a need for us to very carefully analyze precisely what people mean when they say that Japanese society is homogeneous.

Claims to that effect are based on the assumption that Japanese society is made up of a single ethnic group, 'the Japanese.' The concept is generally taken for granted, but I wish to suggest that it is not as unproblematic as people make out.

Hirowatari Seigo (personal communication) has pointed out that nowhere in Japanese law is there any definition of what precisely is meant by the word 'Japanese.'[3] This may seem like a questionable assertion, considering that Japan's Nationality Law[4] clearly states in Article 1 that: 'The conditions necessary for being a Japanese national (*Nihon kokumin*) shall be determined by the provisions of this Law.' The law states that Japanese nationality may be acquired through birth or naturalization. Any 'person who is not a Japanese national' is defined as an 'alien.'

But although the law defines 'a Japanese national,' note that it does not define 'a Japanese.' This is not mere nitpicking. Nationality is no more than an artificial concept that can be changed to include or exclude different groups of people by legal reform. As is well known, some countries determine nationality by place of birth; others, including Japan, determine it by blood inheritance. Even within that broad principle, however, the definition of Japanese nationality can vary and indeed has done so.

Until 1984 only a child whose father had Japanese nationality could acquire nationality in turn; but the reform of that year extended the right of nationality to the offspring of mothers with Japanese nationality.[5]

The fact is that there is a considerable gap between what the law defines as a Japanese national and what the average 'Japanese' believes to be a Japanese in terms of 'common sense.'

Eight degrees of Japaneseness and non-Japaneseness

Very well: What exactly is a 'Japanese'? Or to put it a little more specifically, what are the defining features of the image of Japaneseness in the minds of most 'Japanese' people?

It is customary to define 'where people are from' in terms of two elements: ethnicity and nationality. Hence bipartite labels such as 'Chinese American' or 'African American,' where the first term of the label denotes ethnicity and the second half nationality.

However, it is my contention here that 'ethnicity' should in turn be broken down into two components: 'blood lineage' and 'culture.' Adding in 'nationality' thus gives us a set of three variables, and enables us to draw up the kind of typological framework shown in *Figure 0.1* below. I believe that if we reconstruct the concept of Japaneseness by looking at the various permutations of these three variables, we will arrive at a picture of what Japaneseness really means that is not too far removed from the 'common-sense' view itself.

Definitions:

'Lineage'
I put this term, and 'culture,' in inverted commas to indicate that we are talking about 'lineage' and 'culture' as constructs conceived in Japanese society, not in any absolute sense of the word.[6] A plus sign indicates that a person has 'Japanese blood'; a minus sign indicates blood of a different ethnic group.

'Culture'
Here a plus sign indicates that a person has internalized 'Japanese culture.' That is, the person speaks Japanese, and has the kind of

Figure 0.1 Typological framework of 'Japanese' and 'non-Japanese' attributes

Types	1	2	3	4	5	6	7	8
'Lineage'	+	+	+	-	+	-	-	-
'Culture'	+	+	-	+	-	+	-	-
Nationality	+	-	+	+	-	-	+	-

values, customs and lifestyle generally thought of as 'Japanese.' A minus sign indicates that the person has internalized a different culture.

Nationality
Here a plus sign indicates that a person holds Japanese nationality under the Nationality Law discussed above. A minus sign indicates that the person does not hold Japanese nationality, or is an 'alien' under the law.

Varying these three terms against each other produces eight possible permutations, as shown in *Figure 0.1*.

Now let me make it perfectly clear that this is a theoretical construction. It does not attempt to faithfully reproduce the tremendous complexities of actual social phenomena. It is a gross simplification, with only a very limited degree of applicability to reality.

For example, I freely admit that my framework glosses over the question of how to classify people of mixed blood, mixed culture or multiple nationality.[7] Rather than dealing with these problems in depth at this point, allow me to simply acknowledge them and hope that the reader will still find some heuristic value in this construction of mine.

I also freely admit that there may well be no one on earth that fits neatly into one of my eight categories. The typology is an attempt to strike a balance between the infinite variety of real life and the crude dualism of the common conceptualization of 'Japanese' and 'foreigner.' Its value, I believe, lies in giving us some kind of a conceptual handle on Japanese society. Moreover, it is striking that all eight of the types generated by this theoretical model can in fact be identified in real-life Japan.

Having issued these caveats, let me now consider the kinds of people to whom these eight different labels might apply.

1 'Pure Japanese'

Type one covers people who are of 'Japanese lineage,' have internalized 'Japanese culture' and hold Japanese nationality.

In other words, this is the widely-held image of a 'pure Japanese,' the kind of person that most people in Japanese society believe themselves to be.

2 First-generation Japanese migrants etc.

Type two covers people who are of 'Japanese lineage' and have internalized 'Japanese culture,' but hold foreign nationality.

First-generation migrants from Japan to North or South America, or to Hawaii, the so-called *issei*, would fall into this category. In recent years a few of these people have returned to Japan, along with far greater numbers of second- and third-generation emigrants, as so-called 'workers of Japanese descent' (*Nikkeijin rōdōsha*).[8] Most Japanese think of these people as 'Japanese,' although they are foreign nationals and may have largely forgotten the Japanese language.

Another case in point would be that of Japanese women who married Korean husbands during the period from 1910, when Japan annexed Korea, to 1952, when the San Francisco peace treaty came into force. Under the prevailing nationality law, they were reclassified from 'domestic registration' (*naichi koseki*) to 'Korean registration' (*Chōsen koseki*) upon marriage.[9] After 1952 these women became foreigners to Japan, holding Korean nationality. They could not regain their Japanese nationality except by applying for naturalization like any other kind of foreigner.

3 Japanese raised abroad

Type three covers people who are of 'Japanese lineage' and hold Japanese nationality, but have internalized a foreign culture.

This rare combination may be observed in a few of the so-called 'returnee children' (*kikoku shijo*). This term denotes Japanese children who spend several years abroad in connection with their parents' employment and then return to Japan; in some cases, they are actually born in the foreign country, and grow up and go to school there, so that by the time they return to Japan they have internalized the other country's culture more than Japan's.

These cases are very exceptional, however. Usually these children are inculcated with Japanese culture, and especially the language, in the household. Again, many of them attend special Japanese schools.

Accordingly people of Japanese lineage and nationality who have been raised abroad are thought of by most Japanese as regular members of Japanese society. Their categorization as such implies pressure to 'behave like a Japanese.' Tales of these children being bullied at school are commonplace. Sadly, too, in their efforts to fit in with those around them, they tend to forget the foreign language they have previously acquired.

4 Naturalized Japanese

Type four covers people who have internalized 'Japanese culture' and hold Japanese nationality, but are of foreign lineage.

Some of the ethnic Koreans living in Japan called *Zainichi* (see Preface, Note 2), who are the subject of this book, fall into this category – those who have been born in Japan, raised in an environment that does not stress their Korean ethnic identity, educated in Japanese schools, and who have acquired Japanese nationality through naturalization.

In legal terms, these people are no different from any other Japanese. But they cannot conceal their ethnic origins when it comes, for example, to marriage. It is a fact that many members of Japanese society still define these people as 'non-Japanese' and tend to feel an aversion to them as potential marriage partners.

5 Third-generation Japanese emigrants and war orphans abroad

Type five covers people who are of 'Japanese lineage,' but have internalized foreign culture and hold foreign nationality.

This would apply to many *nisei* and *sansei* (second- and third-generation Japanese emigrants), especially the latter. Most Japanese have the feeling that, by and large, these people are basically Japanese – a feeling that tends to last only until they actually meet one of them. For reasons explained in Note 8 (p. 276), *nisei* and *sansei* are accounting for a growing proportion of the foreign workers coming to Japan, and so these encounters are becoming more frequent. Then comes the discovery that although these people may look very Japanese, they cannot necessarily speak the language. This realization produces a vague feeling of uneasiness that will not be dispelled until it is realized that despite their appearance, these people have been brought up abroad.

Another case in point would be the so-called 'war orphans' and their offspring. These were ethnic Japanese children who lived with their parents, mainly in Manchuria and other parts of China, during Japan's colonial adventure. They were abandoned by their parents as they fled from the advancing Soviet forces and subsequently brought up by adoptive Chinese parents. All these people speak Chinese and have absorbed Chinese culture. They have Chinese nationality unless and until they settle permanently in Japan and regain their Japanese nationality. Normal usage would describe them as 'Japanese Chinese' (*Nikkei Chūgokujin*). But this kind of cool, objective language has never been used by the Japanese media when discussing these people. They are invariably described as *Chūgoku zanryū koji* (orphans abandoned in China) and viewed as objects of sympathy and collective national guilt as victims of war. It is probably fair to say that most Japanese people view the war orphans as 'Japanese.'

It is well known, however, that those war orphans who have actually moved back to Japan under the Japanese government repatriation programs, after half a lifetime spent in China, often experience agonies of conflict in their engagement with what is for them an alien culture. To put it bluntly, once they arrive in Japan they cease to be fellow countrymen who are sentimentalized objects of pity – 'poor Japanese' – and instead come to be viewed simply as grown-up Japanese people who cannot speak the language – 'stupid Japanese.' This set of attitudes has greatly obstructed the attempts of the war orphans to join Japanese society.

6 Zainichi Koreans with Japanese upbringing

Type six covers people who have internalized 'Japanese culture,' but hold foreign nationality and are of different ethnic lineage.

Another sub-section of the young Zainichi Koreans who are the subject of this book fall into this category – those who have been brought up in Japanese-speaking households and attended regular Japanese schools, but have not naturalized. Such people usually use a Japanese alias rather than their original Korean name, and can pass for Japanese if they conceal their ethnic identity. However, the day their Japanese associates discover that they are of Korean extraction is the day they cease to be viewed as fellow Japanese.

7 The Ainu

Type seven covers people who hold Japanese nationality, but are of different ethnic lineage and have internalized an independent culture.

Part of Japan's Ainu ethnic minority would fit in this category. Only a part, because the fact is that very few Ainu can still speak the Ainu language these days. This is the outcome of Japanese government policy from the Meiji era (1868–1912) onwards, under which the Ainu homeland, *Ainu-Moshiri*[10] was renamed 'Hokkaido' and subjected to intense programs of colonialism and assimilation. Even so, Ainu are clearly categorized as 'non-Japanese' by most mainstream Japanese today. This is the main reason why many Ainu strive desperately to conceal their Ainu identity, even while others attempt to assert aboriginal rights through such organizations as the Utari Association.[11]

8 'Pure non-Japanese'

Type eight covers people who are of non-Japanese lineage, have internalized non-Japanese culture and hold foreign nationality.

In short, we are talking about foreigners – not in the sense in which the word is used in Japan's Nationality Law, under which people in groups two, five and six above are also classified as foreigners, but as understood by most members of Japanese society.

That means 'pure foreigners,' an image of unambiguous foreignness to place in mental counterpoint opposite the image of unambiguous Japaneseness with which most Japanese identify themselves.

The Japanese word used to describe these 'pure foreigners' is *gaijin*, an abbreviation of *gaikokujin*, literally a 'person from an outside country.' The term always used to be associated with Caucasians who came to Japan from Europe and North America. In recent years, however, Japan has become one of the principal centers of the global economic system, and has attracted large numbers of migrant workers from various Asian countries. These days it is common enough to meet these people while walking the streets or riding the trains.

The myth of the 'homogeneous society'

Three points emerge from the above intellectual experiment.

First, it is quite clear that the concept of 'Japanese' and 'non-Japanese' is by no means a simple dichotomy with a distinct borderline. There is a whole spectrum of intermediate identities between the two conceptual poles of 'pure Japanese' and 'pure foreigner.' The typological style adopted above is of course no more than a crude conceptual device: in reality, varying degrees of ethnic blood-mixing and of Japanese/foreign cultural internalization generate a seamless continuum of subtly contrasting ethnic identities.

Take for example the remarkably difficult question of how Ryukyuans should be classified. These are the contemporary inhabitants of the Ryukyu islands, now known as Okinawa prefecture. In recent years it has become customary in Japanese society to think of Ryukyuans as 'Japanese.' But the Ryukyu islands used to be an independent kingdom. In cultural terms, too, the islands have developed very differently from mainland Japan, albeit on shared prehistoric origins (Takara 1993). It is clear that the various languages spoken on the Ryukyus are of the same linguistic family as Japanese, but they are so distinctive that it is debatable whether or not they can properly be considered dialects of Japanese (Masiko, personal communication). At the very least it is a fact that most mainstream Japanese cannot understand the Ryukyuan languages in their spoken form.

Whether the Ryukyuan people should be thought of as Japanese or as a separate ethnic grouping is an equally fine point. However, Tomiyama Ichiro has convincingly shown that the Ryukyuan people have a history of being coerced into 'turning Japanese' (Tomiyama 1990).

A second point that arises from the theoretical framework outlined above is that the three elements of lineage, culture and nationality do not carry equal weight in the formation of percept-ions of Japaneseness and non-Japaneseness. Quite clearly lineage is the dominant element.

Types two, three and four all carry two pluses and one minus. Type two (first-generation Japanese emigrants etc.) and type three (Japanese brought up abroad), both feature Japanese lineage, and tend to be pulled into the 'Japanese' category. But type four (naturalized Japanese) do not have Japanese lineage and tend to be pushed out to the 'non-Japanese' category despite their Japanese culture and nationality.

Likewise types five, six and seven all carry one plus and two minuses, but only type five people (third-generation Japanese emigrants, war orphans, etc.) are generally pulled into the 'Japanese' category. The ethnic Koreans of type six and the Ainu of type seven both tend to be classified as 'non-Japanese.'

Third, and here we come to my main conclusion, Japan is definitely not a homogeneous society. However numerous or scarce the eight types described above may be, the sheer fact of their existence testifies to that. The persistence of the myth of Japanese homogeneity in the face of the facts speaks only to an exceedingly low level of tolerance on the part of the majority toward elements differing from it.

It may be objected that Japan, if not entirely ethnically homogeneous, is at least considerably more homogeneous than most countries. Certainly if one compares Japan to the USA, built on the persecution of the Native Americans and subsequently populated by immigrants, or with China, a country which officially recognizes fifty-six different ethnic groups within its borders, it is obviously a relatively ethnically homogeneous nation.

Note, however, that when people speak of Japan as a homo-geneous society, the description nearly always comes with the unstated implication that this is a good thing.[12] The trouble is that when discourse mixes factual description with tacit value judgments, it is all too easy for unconscious intolerance to come into play.

Japanese society will not tolerate ambiguous identity. Faced with a person who shows certain characteristics that differ from the mainstream, Japanese society will respond in one of two ways: either the ambiguous person will be forced to abandon those characteristics and become as much like a 'pure' Japanese as possible; or the person will be classified simply as 'non-Japanese.' Further, the full members of Japanese society are defined as 'Japanese,' and the 'non-Japanese' are only permitted to reside in Japan on the sufferance of the majority. Thus those who are defined as 'non-Japanese' are effectively deprived of membership rights in Japanese society. And so the myth of Japan as a mono-ethnic society continues to persist in the realm of ideas, however far removed it may be from lived reality.[13]

Are 'Zainichis' temporary residents?

I stated earlier that in expressions such as 'Chinese American' or 'African American,' the first term of the label denotes ethnicity and the second half nationality. I put it that way for the sake of simplicity, but ground-level reality is not always so simple. Since I have identified culture, alongside lineage and nationality, as a third key component, the question arises of how culture is conveyed in these two-part terms. The fact is that sometimes it is included in the former term and sometimes in the latter. Thus when a second-generation Chinese immigrant to the USA, born and raised in Chinatown and fluent in Chinese, calls herself a 'Chinese American,' she may well mean that although she is a citizen of the USA, she has thoroughly mastered her own, Chinese, culture. By contrast, when a black American refers to himself as 'African American,' the emphasis may in some cases be on the second part of the term – although Africa may be the land of his ancestors, he has acquired American culture and is proud to be a full-fledged citizen of the USA.

In the case of Zainichi Koreans, it is striking that although some English-speaking sociologists refer to them as 'Korean Japanese,' within Japanese society they are never referred to as *Chōsen-kei*

Nihonjin, *Kankoku-kei Nihonjin* or *Koria-kei Nihonjin*, the various Japanese equivalents of 'Korean Japanese' – this despite the fact that first-generation migrants are forming a dwindling proportion of the total, and the great majority are second-, third- or fourth-generation migrants, born and raised in Japan. Instead they are invariably described as *Zainichi Chōsenjin* or *Zainichi Kankokujin*.

Now the *zai* in *Zainichi* implies 'temporary' residence,[14] as in expressions such as *zai-Bei* (staying in America) or *zai-Rio* (staying in Rio). The terminology is quite distinct from that used to describe people who are living in a country permanently and hold nationality and rights of citizenship, such as *Nikkei Amerikajin* (Japanese Americans) or *Nikkei Burajirujin* (Japanese Brazilians).

The terminology is symbolic. Whatever the legal status of each member of the Korean minority, and however permanently they may in fact be living in Japan, at the conceptual level they are still viewed as mere temporary residents by most members of Japanese society, whether unconsciously or by some mechanism of collective subjectivity.

Even ethnic Koreans who have acquired Japanese nationality by naturalization, and people who are the offspring of mixed Korean-Japanese marriages, are not referred to as 'Korean Japanese.' Legally these people may be citizens of Japan, but in social terms they are still thought of as 'non-Japanese' and are subject to avoidance behavior. This is especially so in the field of marriage, where Korean ethnicity is frequently a problem. Thus it happens that many ethnic Koreans feel obliged to constantly conceal their identity and act as Japanese throughout their lives.

In short, not only has the concept of the 'Korean Japanese' failed to take root in the Japanese language, but the reality to which such a term would refer cannot at present be observed in Japanese society.

Amid this culture of intolerance toward difference, what sort of life experiences are young ethnic Koreans having, and what thoughts are running through their minds?

In this book I hope to answer these questions and explore the identity of what is a very distinctive ethnic minority.

Part One

Identity Formation in Japan's Korean Minority

1 The History of Japan's Korean Minority

Migration to Japan by Korean workers in the pre-colonial period

A certain amount of historical background is necessary to any full understanding of the issue of ethnic identity among young Koreans in Japan. The histories of Japan and Korea have been intimately related since ancient times. Until the early nineteenth century Korea was the more advanced of the two countries, responsible for introducing Japan to numerous aspects of civilization.

However, I propose to start this brief historical sketch with events of the more recent past, which had a direct effect on the formation of the Korean minority in Japan. Specifically, let us begin in the year 1876, when the Treaty of Kanghwa was signed between Japan and Korea. This was an unequal treaty, forced upon Korea, under which Japan helped herself to consular jurisdiction over her near neighbor.

Until recently it has been widely believed that before Japan formally annexed Korea in 1910, there were very few Koreans in Japan. A figure of 790, most of them exchange students, has been extracted from government records for the period immediately before annexation. However, recent research by Yamawaki Keizo has disproved this, showing that in fact from the late 1890s onward, there were numerous unrecorded Koreans working in Japan in the coalmines, on the railways, and as traveling peddlers of Korean candy. Numbers are impossible to establish because the main sources are contemporary newspaper articles, but were probably in the thousands (Yamawaki 1994:73–88).

The Treaty of Kanghwa set Japan on the road to the annexation of Korea. Given this fact, and the close geographical proximity of the two countries, it is hardly surprising to find that there were considerable numbers of Korean workers coming to Japan in the pre-colonial period. There is no doubt that annexation was the decisive event in the history of Japan's Korean minority; I would merely like to point out that the historical origins of Japan's ethnic Korean minority go back a good deal further than 1910.

Economic refugees and forced migrant labor

Japan's 1910 annexation of Korea was the cue for a series of repressive colonial measures. From 1910 to 1918, Japan confiscated large tracts of Korean land in the name of 'Land Survey Enterprises' (*Tochi Chōsa Jigyō*), while the 'Rice Production Increase Plan' (*Sanmai Zōshoku Keikaku*; 1920–34) certainly succeeded in boosting rice production, only to transfer so much of the crop to Japan that Korea was left even poorer than before, especially in the rural districts.

The destruction of their livelihoods forced many Koreans to leave their homes and seek work elsewhere in a desperate bid to escape from poverty. Those in the southern provinces, especially Kyongsang-Do, Cholla-Do and Cheju island, fled to Japan, while those in the northern provinces tended to head for Manchuria, in what is now Northeast China.[1]

Forced against their will to become 'citizens of the Japanese Empire,' and with their livelihoods destroyed by Japanese colonialism, many Koreans had no choice but to seek some kind of living in Japan. Theirs was a cold reception, marked by contempt, discrimination and hostility from the Japanese population. When the Great Kanto Earthquake struck in 1923, Koreans were made scapegoats, falsely accused by the police of starting fires and poisoning wells. More than 6,000 of them were killed in the ensuing witch-hunt, some by the police, others by ordinary Japanese citizens stirred up by the police (Hatada ed. 1987:174).

Despite all this, the numbers of Koreans coming to Japan in search of work continued to rise steadily. The migration pattern showed two distinct phases. First individuals, mostly men, would come on their own as temporary migrant workers. Despite the many hardships caused by oppression and discrimination, they would eventually manage to establish a livelihood. In the second phase, married male migrants would bring their families over from Korea, while unmarried migrants would return to their hometowns in Korea, find themselves a spouse, and come back to Japan to commence family life. This shift from single male migrant labor to permanent family residence was already happening at the start of the Showa period (the late 1920s). Both phases were marked by chain migration, as information flowed through local and familial networks and more Koreans came out to join friends and relatives already established. By 1938, there were some 800,000 Koreans living in Japan.

Then came the war, and with it a wave of involuntary migration as the Japanese government subjected its Korean colonial subjects to forced labor in mines, munitions factories, etc. (Park 1965). As is now well known, many Korean women were rounded up and forced into prostitution as 'comfort women' to the imperial army (Takagi 1992, Yoshimi 1995). There are varying estimates of how many Koreans were in Japan when the surrender finally came in 1945, but a figure of 2.3 million would probably be close to the mark.[2]

Colonial assimilation policies

Japan's colonial rule over Korea, especially during the war period, showed an obsessive concern with thoroughgoing, comprehensive assimilation. Under slogans such as *Naisen yūwa* ('Domestic-Korean harmony,' the 'domestic' meaning Japan of course) and *Naisen ittai* ('The homeland and Korea as one'), the Japanese authorities sought to turn the people of Korea into loyal subjects of the Japanese emperor, to whom they were made to swear allegiance on numerous occasions. They were also obliged to attend acts of worship at Shinto shrines, and to use the Japanese language. Thus did assimilation policies extend to every aspect of life – political, religious and cultural. The objective was to make it possible to draft the Koreans into the 'sacred war' in Asia and the Pacific.

A striking instance of cultural assimilation policy was the forced use of Japanese names under the Korean Civil Affairs Ordinance as revised in 1939. The frequent use of Japanese names by Koreans living in Japan today stems from this pre-war policy, known as

Sōshi-Kaimei. The term literally means 'make a surname and change one's forename.' The cultural implications of this policy ran very deep. As well as changing one's personal name to a Japanese-sounding one, each Korean was supposed to adopt a family name – a fundamentally different concept to the traditional Korean system of clan names. The ultimate aim of the policy was to transform the Korean kinship system into a Japanese one (Miyata *et al.* 1992).

The two systems are radically different. Japanese kinship is based on the concept of *ie* or 'house.' The *ie* basically covers family members who live in the same household. Maintaining the *ie* across generations has been considered so important that a male heir has traditionally been adopted in cases where there is no son to inherit. The father of the household used to have absolute authority over all other members, including servants, who would be members of the *ie* even in the absence of any blood connection. Since the *ie* was the basic unit of kinship, sons who left home to set up their own households would be viewed as relatives rather than members of the *ie*, with the same applying to daughters who married into another *ie*. Adopted sons would usually come from a related family, but adoptions with no family connection were also acceptable – something unthinkable in the traditional Korean system.

In Japan some people are particularly proud of their *ie* and maintain a family tree, but Koreans tend to maintain a much fatter set of documents, sometimes running to several volumes, called a *chokbo.* This is an attempt to document the births, deaths and notable exploits of all male descendants of a single ancestor said to have lived several hundred, or even more than a thousand years ago.

This reflects the fact that Korean kinship is based on the principle of *dongseong-dongbon.* The term literally means 'same surname, same ancestral land,' and as that implies, the idea is that people with the same surname and hailing from the same ancestral land (*bonkwan*) belong to the same clan and accordingly have their lives documented in the same *chokbo.* Clans are in principle exogamous, meaning that marriage partners must be sought from other clans. Thus people with the same surname, such as 'Kim,' may only marry if their ancestors hail from different parts of the country. The Kim of Kimhae and the Kim of Kyongju are different clans and hence intermarriage is permitted, but fellow Kimhae Kims may not marry. The result is that marriage is forbidden between people whose blood relationship is so remote as to be virtually non-existent.[3] Those people would have no problem getting married under Japanese law.

The *dongseong-dongbon* system includes rules governing the choice of names. Surnames usually consist of a single character – Kim, Park, Lee, etc. – though a few surnames have two characters, such as Nam-Gung or Che-Gal. Forenames, by contrast, usually have two characters but occasionally just one. When a newly-born boy is named, one of the characters in the forename will be dictated by rules designed to show how many generations from the common ancestor the boy is. Thus one can tell just by looking at the forename which generation a male Korean is in, irrespective of his age. For example, the Osaka-based campaigner for ethnic Korean rights, Lee Kyung-Jae, is considerably older than his fellow activist Lee Chang-Jae, but the shared character 'Jae' shows that both men are in the same generation of the Lee clan of Chonju.

The Korean kinship system is founded on Confucianism, from which it derives its patrilineal aspect. Children take the paternal surname, and it never changes even on marriage. Under the *Sōshi-Kaimei* policy, however, women were obliged to take their husband's surname when they got married. Thus the Japanese authorities were imposing not just a name, but a whole system of kinship, upon the Koreans.

Korean youths living in Japan today are divided on the issues of kinship and marriage. Some of these third-generation migrants have absorbed Japanese values to the extent that they reject the *dongseong-dongbon* system and insist that so long as there is no close blood relationship with a potential marriage partner, they will go ahead and marry. But the first generation and most members of the second generation still believe the *dongseong-dongbon* marriage rules should be observed.

These differences reflect the fact that first- and second-generation Koreans feel a closer affiliation to their clan than do the young third-generation migrants. Regional associations of members of the same clan exist in Japan just as in Korea, and their leaders are generally first-generation migrants.

Ethnic origins preserved in 'Japanese' names

The Japanese 'Government-General of Korea' issued an order for all Koreans to register Japanese surnames during a six-month period starting in February 1940. After initial attempts at resistance and sabotage, eventually some 80 percent of the population complied with the directive. In the remaining 20 percent of cases, the surname of the household head was automatically designated as the surname of other family members – including women who had married in from other clans and would therefore have different surnames under the Korean system.

It may well be, however, that this outward show of compliance concealed a considerable degree of passive resistance. Many people selected Japanese names that encoded their Korean roots and even the particular clan to which they belonged. Thus people with the Korean surname Kim would choose Japanese surnames that incorporated the character for 'Kim' (meaning 'gold' and pronounced 'kane' in its ethnic Japanese reading): names like Kaneda, Kaneyama or Kanemoto. Similarly 'Chang' would be incorporated in 'Harimoto,' 'Kwon' in 'Gonda,' 'Chon' in 'Senda,' 'Moon' in 'Fumimoto' and 'Yang/Ryang' in 'Harimoto.' In each of these cases, the first of the two characters in the Japanese name is the one used to write the Korean name, although the reading has been Japanized.

Likewise, some Koreans simply used Japanese readings for their own *bonkwan* (ancestral land) as their new surname. Thus people hailing from Andong would use the surname 'Ando,' and those from Shinchon would use 'Nobukawa.' Similar transformations included Sangsan becoming 'Shioyama,' Sachon 'Hanakawa,' and Hadong 'Kato.' These are simply Japanese readings of the same characters. In other cases just the first character of the *bonkwan* was used, with some generic character meaning 'field,' 'river' or 'mountain' being stuck on the end. Examples would include 'Koda' (Kwangju) and 'Tatsukawa' (Talsong).

Another strategy sometimes adopted was to choose a Japanese name that included a reference to the tribal history recorded in the *chokbo*. I lack the space to detail these more elaborate transformations, but suffice to say that the names 'Takayasu' and 'Kunimoto' used by the Lee of Chonju, 'Arai' by the Park of

Milyang, and 'Takemoto' by the Bae of Bunsong, stem from this strategy.

It may well be that there were some Koreans who had Japanese names thrust upon them by the Japanese authorities. Still, as the above examples show, many Koreans managed to stay in touch with their roots through the name they chose. Obviously there was widespread prior consultation among relatives spread over quite a wide area before they registered their Japanese names.

However, the determination to defend ethnic pride revealed by these names has not always been communicated to the younger generation of Zainichi Koreans. It gradually dawned upon me in the course of interviewing my informants that the migrant family history starting with the grandparents' generation had hardly been passed on to the third generation at all. One instance of this was that many of them had no idea of the origins of the Japanese names that they were still using for convenience in Japanese society. Some of them did not even know where their own *bonkwan* was.[4] It would appear that the true significance of these artificially constructed Japanese names is becoming gradually obscured with the passing years.

Who stayed on after the war?

Let me return now to the history of the formation of Japan's ethnic Korean community.

On August 15, 1945, Japan's unconditional surrender was announced to the people in a historic radio broadcast by Emperor Hirohito, and the Korean people were liberated from the chains of Japanese colonialism. Most of those who were residing in Japan when the war ended soon headed back to their homeland. However, some 600,000 stayed behind.

What sort of people stayed on in Japan after the war?

It is widely believed in Japan that most of the Koreans living here today are people forcibly brought here during the forced migrant labor period and their descendants. However, when I was research-ing this book I was struck by the fact that not one of my 150 informants said that their parents or grandparents had been press-ganged to Japan under the forced migrant labor policy. Just one informant mentioned an uncle who died while doing forced labor in a Hokkaido coalmine. While my survey population was certainly not generated by random sampling, it nonetheless provides strong suggestive evidence that most of the Koreans who were forced to come to Japan during the war left shortly after, while those who stayed behind were largely people who had come to Japan of their own will, before the start of the forced migrant labor policy.

This makes intuitive good sense. To the Koreans forced to work as slaves in the mines, factories and construction sites of a colonial oppressor, many of whom had seen their fellow countrymen worked to death, starved or murdered as an example to the others, life in the hated Japan could have held few attractions. Besides, most of them had been abruptly separated from their families and hometown communities when the press gangs came for them, and must have yearned to go home and be re-united with them.

For those Koreans who had chosen to come over to Japan in search of work, albeit under extreme economic duress, the decision whether or not to repatriate must have been a more complex one. In many cases they had been living in Japan for ten or twenty years, and their immediate families were living with them in Japan, not in Korea.[5] They had no land and no house in Korea. Going home would mean restarting their lives from zero. In Japan they would certainly have experienced systematic discrimination, such as being paid lower wages than their Japanese workmates, and would have felt the racist contempt of many individual Japanese. But many first-generation Koreans have stories of more positive encounters as well. Some even tell of Japanese friends who sheltered them from the lynch mobs after the Great Kanto Earthquake.[6]

And so, when the war came to an end, many of these earlier, longer-established migrants must have seen continued residence in Japan as the lesser of two evils. Indeed, several of my informants told me how their parents originally planned to return to Korea after the war, only to change their minds when they heard from acquaintances who had departed immediately that conditions in Korea were so bad that things were actually better in Japan.

It is my belief, then, that people from the phase of migration pre-dating the forced migrant labor program made up the great majority of Japan's post-war ethnic Korean population.

Among them were some who did in fact go home, only to return to Japan after finding that they were unable to make a living in their home districts in Korea. Others came from Korea for the first time after the war, relying on relatives to help them get established. These people were treated as illegal entrants and were subject to deportation if discovered. Fear of deportation drove many of them to take cover in the ethnic Korean districts of Osaka and other major cities. There are thought to have been several tens of thousands of these unregistered residents, but most of them declared themselves at their local Immigration Bureau at the time when their children reached school age, received 'special residence' permits, and became able to join the society of legal Korean residents in Japan.

Denied the rights of Japanese and foreigner alike

How did the Japanese government treat those Koreans who stayed on in Japan after the war?

Regrettably enough, there was not the slightest improvement on the treatment meted out during the pre-war colonial period. The post-war Japanese government denied Korean residents both the rights of nationals and those of foreigners.

Consider for example the fate of the ethnic Korean schools. These were set up after the war in various parts of Japan by first-generation Korean migrants who still hoped to one day return to their motherland and to whom it was therefore imperative that their children be educated in the Korean language, history and culture. The Japanese government, however, suppressed these schools, on the grounds that it was unthinkable for Japanese nationals to receive a non-Japanese education. In the immediate post-war period, when Japan had yet to sign peace treaties with the Allied Powers, Koreans still technically held Japanese nationality from the Japanese government's point of view.

But in striking contrast to this position, in December 1945 the government deprived Japan-resident Koreans of the right to vote, and in May 1947 it made them subject to the Alien Registration Ordinance. Clearly the implication of this was that the Koreans, who were Japanese nationals but did not hold family registration on Japanese territory, were not 'real' Japanese.[7]

After 1952, when the allied occupation ended and Japan regained full control of her domestic affairs, the same flagrant abuse of ethnic Koreans' human rights continued. The San Francisco Peace Treaty took effect on April 28, 1952. On that very day, the government of Japan stripped the Japan-resident Koreans of Japanese nationality without allowing them to choose between Korean or Japanese nationality.

Freed from the restraints of the allied occupation, the government of Japan rapidly passed a series of legal measures to provide aid and support to those who had suffered losses or damage during the war. But the Koreans who had been forced to fight for the imperial army or to support the war effort as civilians were excluded from the provisions along with the surviving family members of those who had died in the Japanese cause. They may have been Japanese nationals when they made their great sacrifices, but they were not Japanese nationals at the time when the compensation arrangements were legally established – so ran the shabby logic of the Japanese authorities.[8]

In striking contrast again, those ethnic Koreans who had been press-ganged into the Japanese imperial army, had been involved in atrocities against the allied prisoners of war on the orders of their Japanese superiors, and had been found guilty of war crimes by the allied tribunals, were not given remission of their sentences once they lost their Japanese nationality. Article 11 of the Peace Treaty between Japan and the Allied Powers stated that Japan could not quash convictions or reduce sentences imposed on Japanese nationals by allied military tribunals. In 1952, twenty-nine Korean nationals and one Taiwanese appealed to the Supreme Court for remission of sentences on the grounds that they were no longer Japanese nationals. They lost the case, after just three hearings over a six-week period. The supreme court sided with the Japanese government's view that as the men had been convicted of crimes committed when they were Japanese nationals, they should not have their sentences commuted (Utsumi 1982:213–46).

Four policy models

It is often argued that the Japanese government has consistently adopted a policy of assimilation toward the Korean minority. But is it correct?

George Eaton Simpson and J. Milton Yinger outline six main types of policy that may be adopted by a dominant group toward a minority, each of which may be applied on its own or in combination with one or more of the others. They are as follows (Simpson and Yinger 1972:17–24):

1 *Assimilation.* A policy that demands the minority group to abandon its distinctive culture, language and customs and merge with the dominant group. Aims to remove the problem of how to deal with the minority by absorbing it.

2 *Pluralism.* A policy that allows the minority group to maintain its independent culture and distinct ethnic identity. If this policy is rigorously carried out, ethnic differences can cease to give rise to discriminatory relationships, leading to equitable coexistence on the basis of acceptance of difference.

3 *Legal protection of minorities.* This is one aspect of the pluralist approach, applied where the concept of equal rights for minorities meets with strong opposition.

4 *Population transfer.* A policy that attempts to remove friction between majority and minority groups by physically moving the latter away from the former – specifically by sending the minority to its homeland or by shutting it up in reservations. Though sometimes implemented out of honorable motives, this policy essentially entails getting rid of an unwanted irritation. It can be expressed as 'ethnic cleansing,' and may have extremely sinister implications.

5 *Continued subjugation.* A policy that attempts neither to absorb the minority group nor to expel it, but rather to maintain its inferior social status and subject it to oppression and exploitation.

6 *Extermination.* A policy of genocide, adopted in cases of extreme hostility.

Using Simpson and Yinger's minority policy framework as a tool, I would now like to conduct another experiment. Excluding extermination, which happily has not been a feature of post-war Japanese minorities policy, and combining 'pluralism' and 'legal protection' into the single category, 'respect for human rights,'[9] gives four models that the Japanese government *could* have followed in its treatment of the Korean minority. Let me now attempt to outline imaginary scenarios of how postwar Japanese treatment of the Korean minority might have developed in the case of each one of these models being adopted.[10]

Scenario 1: Respect for human rights

This scenario assumes that based on due awareness of the wrongs done by Japan during the colonial period, the government respects the wishes of each individual Korean, whether that individual desires to stay in Japan or return to Korea:

The first step is to gather and conserve materials for a thorough investigation of the practices of forced migrant labor, sex slavery and other abuses that occurred during the colonial period. This is followed by a sincere apology and the payment of compensation. Those who had been forced to labor without payment are paid appropriate back-wages.

Those who wish to return to Korea are swiftly repatriated, with the Japanese government taking responsibility and bearing all costs. The Koreans on Sakhalin are repatriated or taken back to Japan, as they wish.

Those who choose to remain in Japan have their basic human rights respected. The ethnic schools are officially recognized and accorded financial support from the public purse. Up to 1952 the holding of Japanese nationality is formally permitted and voting rights are accordingly guaranteed. The Koreans are not subject to alien registration, of course.

Free choice of nationality is permitted in 1952. Those who do not choose Japanese nationality are granted permanent residence and unlimited rights to re-entry after traveling outside Japan. There are no deportations, no fingerprinting of aliens, and no obligation to carry one's alien registration certificate with one 'at all times.'[11] Voting rights are granted to non-nationals, and non-Japanese enjoy the same rights as Japanese to social welfare etc. Discrimination, whether in marriage, employment or residence, is outlawed. With the exception of the diplomatic service, non-Japanese are allowed to take on all forms of public office, rather than being excluded as an 'indisputable legal principle'...[12]

This is, of course, just a scenario. None of the above policies has, in fact, been adopted by the government. Clearly, 'respect for human rights' has not been the dominant theme of Japanese government policy.

Scenario 2: Assimilation

A thoroughgoing assimilation policy would reflect an institutional unease with the idea of people from different ethnic backgrounds living in Japanese society with their ethnic identity unchanged. The policy would be to turn these people into Japanese by means of universal naturalization. If it had any reasoning ability, the government would recognize that the Korean minority in Japan was an outcome of Japan's pre-war colonialism, and would accordingly seek to accomplish assimilation by instilling a positive image of Japan in the Korean minority rather than by the brutal assimilation policies of the colonial period:

This means first the payment of adequate wages for forced labor carried out by Koreans during the war. Up to 1952, the Koreans do not have their rights as foreigners respected, but they *are* granted the rights of any holder of Japanese nationality. They are not made subject to alien registration and they keep their voting rights. However, since ethnic consciousness is a barrier to assimilation, they are not allowed to run ethnic schools.

In 1952, free choice of nationality is allowed. Those who choose to take Japanese nationality are encouraged to 'Japanize' as fast as possible; the rest will be made to naturalize in the fullness of time. Making life too difficult for these people might provoke protest movements; on the other hand, making life too easy for them might make naturalization lose its attraction. As a compromise, the government allows permanent residence but maintains troublesome institutions such as the need to obtain a re-entry permit when traveling outside Japan. Foreigners are not allowed to become civil servants, nor to vote in elections. Distinctions between Japanese nationals and foreigners are also maintained in eligibility for social welfare etc. Only measures provoking particularly powerful objections from the Korean community, such as fingerprinting and the obligation to carry the alien registration certificate at all times, are avoided.

Conversely, the government takes measures to encourage 'Japanization.' As a public service, non-nationals are sent information on Japanese schooling when their children reach school age.[13] People hailing from the pre-war Japanese colonies are given a special incentive to adopt Japanese nationality in the form of a simplified application procedure for them and their offspring. There is relatively little form-filling, and there are no intrusive personal inquisitions. Naturalization is granted more or less automatically on application. However, the use of a Japanese-sounding name after naturalization is compulsory...

As this scenario suggests, the real Japanese government has only implemented one half of an assimilation policy. The various forms of harassment designed to deter people from maintaining their ethnic identity are all part of government policy, but the carrot to go with the stick, i.e., the positive inducements to become Japanese, are missing. On the contrary, the government has passed all sorts of measures that might have been designed to arouse anti-Japanese feeling among ethnic Koreans. Thus one cannot say that the Japanese government has carried out a consistent policy of assimilation.

Scenario 3: Expulsion

This is my slight simplification of Simpson and Yinger's 'population transfer.' Since conditions at the time did not really give the Japanese government the option of corralling the ethnic Koreans into reservations, I restrict the concept to that of getting rid of the minority by sending its members back to their original homeland. An expulsion policy would imply that the Japanese government felt absolutely no responsibility for the pre-war colonial policies that created the Japan-resident Korean minority. The Koreans would be viewed as no more than an irritation to Japanese society, to be removed by repatriation. Government policy would seek to make it difficult for the Koreans to live in Japan and easy for them to return to North or South Korea.

Once the war is over, the first step is to create conditions that will enable those Koreans who wish to leave to do so as quickly as possible. Thus the government refrains from placing any restrictions on the repatriation of assets acquired by Koreans during their period in Japan.

Those Koreans who do stay on in Japan are obliged to undergo alien registration and are subjected to strict controls. However, the ethnic schools are tolerated because it will be easier for Koreans to return to their motherland if their Japan-born children can still use the Korean language. The schools cannot be formally recognized, but ways are found to provide them with state assistance.

In 1952, the government naturally removes Japanese nationality from ethnic Koreans and erects stiff bureaucratic obstacles to any Korean seeking naturalization. Misdemeanors by Koreans are often punished by deportation. As big a gap as possible is opened up between the human rights of Japanese and those of Koreans, and the procedure for gaining a re-entry permit when traveling abroad is hedged about with difficult legal procedures. In these and other ways, the Korean minority is made to taste the sheer inconvenience of living in Japan.

On the principle that the Japanese government has no responsibility for the education of foreigners, the children of Japan-resident Koreans are excluded from publicly-run Japanese schools as far as possible. Where Korean parents are absolutely determined to send their children to those schools, they are made to pay special entrance and tuition fees to encourage more Korean families to use their own ethnic schools. Pressure is exerted upon the ethnic schools to instill in their students the importance of going home to the motherland – for example, teaching along those lines is one of the conditions for acquiring state funding for the schools...

Once again, the policies adopted by the real government of Japan only half fit the scenario. It is true that it has been made difficult for Koreans to live in Japan, but it has not been made particularly easy to return to Korea. Specifically, the government did place restrictions on Korean asset repatriation after the war; has not provided state assistance for the Korean schools in Japan, although Japan-resident Koreans are obliged to pay taxes; and whilst the government certainly dragged its heels over issuing schooling information to ethnic Korean parents (see Note 13), it has made no particular attempt to remove Korean children from publicly-run schools. So from a strictly objective viewpoint, one would have to say that the government has not followed an expulsion policy, at least not with any consistency.

Scenario 4: Subjugation

The government betrays the human rights of the Korean minority at every turn, and takes measures to ensure that life in Japan is as difficult as possible for its members. They are denied Japanese citizenship, but also denied the rights of foreigners. At the same time, no measures are taken to ease the return to the mother country. Some policies show elements of the assimilation principle, others show the expulsion principle. Both principles are at times adopted when it suits the government. But in both cases, the punitive side of the principle is maintained and the more positive, incentive side discarded. The net effect is neither to assimilate nor expel the Korean minority, but to maintain its inferior social status and subject it to oppression and victimization.

This time, we are not talking about a hypothetical scenario. This is reality. For once, abstract theory fits concrete actuality like a glove. Having created the Korean minority by its own irrespon-sible actions before and during the war, the government has viewed it as no more than a potential threat to public order, to be controlled by any means possible. I hope this intellectual exercise has shown that it is not mere rhetoric to speak of Japanese government policy toward the Korean minority as one of oppression or subjugation, but a simple, sober statement of fact.

Grudging reforms

It is fair to say that the government of Japan has not once taken a positive step, on its own initiative, to promote the rights and interests of Japan-resident Koreans. Reforms have been implemented slowly, grudgingly, and only when unavoidable in the face of intense political pressure.[14] Thus the 1965 Agreement on the Legal Status and Treatment of the Nationals of the Republic of Korea, which granted 'treaty-based permanent residence' to South Korean nationals,[15] was no more than a necessary appendage to the normalization of Japan-ROK relations. Two other reforms – the granting of 'exceptional permanent residence' to North Korean nationals under a revision of the Immigration Control Act made in 1981,[16] and the extension of the social welfare system to cover permanently resident foreign nationals under the same legal revision, were measures required to demonstrate Japan's compliance with the United Nations Convention Relating to the Status of Refugees.

In 1991 a new law was passed, cumbersomely entitled the Special Law for the Handling of Immigration Affairs of Persons Who Have Divested Themselves of Japanese Nationality on the Basis of Peace Treaties with Japan. This unified all the various treaties under which residents of former Japanese colonies were treated, giving them uniform status as 'special permanent residents.' Then in 1992 a partial reform of the Alien Registration Law removed from permanent residents and special permanent residents the hated obligation to put a fingerprint on their alien registration cards. The principal beneficiaries of this reform were of course Zainichi Koreans.

Though these moves do represent improvements, they would never have come about without a high-profile Zainichi movement against fingerprinting peaking in the mid-1980s, a heightening of international concern over human rights issues, and the need to maintain good diplomatic relations with the ROK. None of these reforms were thought up by the government out of concern for the welfare of Zainichi Koreans.

Even today, the government continues to deny non-Japanese nationals the right to employment in public administrative positions without any legal justification (see Note 12), and strives to shackle those local authorities who ignore its recommendations and make a positive effort to employ non-Japanese. Since 1992 the Ministry of Education has allowed foreign nationals to be employed as teachers in publicly-run schools, but only with a special contract that does not allow them to take any post with administrative authority, such as principal or vice-principal, or to participate in staff meetings.[17] They are thus excluded from all forms of power and decision-making.

Clearly, then, Koreans in Japan still have a long way to go before they can fully overcome their history of subjugation.[18]

2   Japan's Korean Minority Today

A rough sketch of the Zainichi Korean population

At the end of 1996 there were 657,159 registered foreigners in Japan with North or South Korean nationality. They accounted for 46.4 percent of the total of 1,415,136 foreigners registered in Japan. The large number of so-called 'newcomer' migrants from Asia and Latin America has recently reduced the Korean percentage in the non-Japanese population, but even so Koreans are by far the biggest ethnic minority in the land. The Chinese are second with 16.6 percent of the registered total, followed by the Brazilians with 14.3 percent.

However, when people talk about Zainichi Koreans, they are usually referring to those who came over to Japan during her period of colonial rule over Korea, and their descendants. The figure of 657,159 just cited includes Korean newcomers who have come to Japan for business, study, marriage, etc. A truer figure for the Zainichi population would probably be in the region of 550,000.[1] However, in the forty-five years from 1952, when the San Francisco Peace Treaty came into effect, until the end of 1996, just over 200,000 Koreans acquired Japanese nationality. In addition many people with Japanese nationality have been born of mixed Japanese-Korean marriages. These people and their offspring make up another large population bloc that is at least partially Korean in identity.

Korean newcomers all hold South Korean nationality, it being virtually impossible for North Koreans to travel to Japan. Among the Zainichi population, however, there are nationals of North and South Korea.[2] Nationality has very little to do with geographical place of origin and very much to do with political allegiance. Nearly all Zainichi families hail from South Korea, mainly from the provinces of Kyongsang-Do and Cholla-Do, and from Cheju island, but in the first two decades after the partition of Korea they overwhelmingly supported North Korea. The experience of poverty, racism and cruel working conditions in Japan gave them a strong working-class identity and a natural sympathy for the workers' state in the North. Many were also strongly influenced by the Japan Communist Party and had an admiration for North Korean leader Kim Il Sung, based on his reputation as a leader of guerilla warfare against the Japanese during the colonial period.

In his interesting book on the Korean diaspora, Nomura Susumu estimates that in 1955 North Koreans outnumbered South Koreans by a ratio of 3:1 in the Zainichi population. However, as the Japanese and South Korean governments steadily strengthened the inducements to take out South Korean nationality, as the balance of power on the Korean peninsula shifted in favor of the South, and as some Zainichi Koreans started to achieve a measure of prosperity in Japan, a growing number of Zainichi Koreans switched allegiance from North to South. Nomura estimates that South Koreans became a majority in 1969, and that by 1992 the ratio was 2:7 in favor of ROK nationality (Nomura 1996:266–7). However, there may well be some people sympathetic toward North Korea despite holding South Korean nationality for practical purposes.

Most Zainichi Koreans belong to one of two representative organizations: Mindan (the Korean Residents Union in Japan) or Chongryun (the General Association of Korean Residents in Japan) (cf. Preface, Notes 4 and 5). The former supports South Korea, the latter North Korea. In recent years growing numbers of Zainichi Koreans have left both organizations, however, sometimes in favor of new groupings that do not always reflect mainland Korean politics.

Koreans who look Japanese in Korea

In March 1990, I made my first visit to South Korea. I was taking part in a 'South Korean Historical Journey' organized by the Osaka-based Research Center for Koreans & Minorities in Japan. Many of the participants were from the Takatsuki Mukuge Society, an influential element within Mintōren.[3] Our party had ten members including myself: four ethnic Korean and six Japanese. We were looked after in South Korea by a professional guide named Yang Hee-Jeong and by Lee Bok-Mi, a Zainichi woman who had gone from Japan to Korea for study purposes.

In Seoul we ate out with a young Korean woman called Lee Ki-Nam, who was a friend of Bok-Mi. Wanting to know how mainland Koreans viewed their compatriots who were second- and third-generation migrants in Japan, I asked Ki-Nam to guess which members of our party were Koreans and which were Japanese. She correctly identified all six Japanese, but was also convinced that three out of the four young Zainichi Koreans were Japanese as well. Only Hong In-Sung, a second-generation Zainichi in his thirties, struck her as Korean. Kim Pak-Myung, Kim Chol-Nyon and Han Ah-Shin, all third-generation Zainichis, struck her as 'absolutely Japanese.'

The one Zainichi Korean whom she identified happened also to be the only one who could speak any Korean, but the table conversation had all been in Japanese, which Ki-Nam had learned at university. When I asked her how she made her judgment, she replied 'hair style, clothing, expression and general atmosphere.'

It seems that when viewed by mainland Koreans, third-generation Zainichi Koreans appear no different from Japanese. They are seen as non-Koreans in Korean society, just as they are seen as non-Japanese in Japanese society. This phenomenon symbolizes the broader circumstances in which they are placed.

The general trend in the lives and consciousness of young Koreans in Japan is moving steadily toward assimilation with Japanese society. In contrast, as I showed in the previous chapter, the post-war policy of the Japanese government toward the Korean minority has been one of subjugation, and has not been marked by any consistent policy of assimilation. How are we to read this apparent contradiction?

The question of how assimilation proceeds must be seen not only in terms of government policy but also in terms of majority-minority relations at the level of everyday social life. We must also distinguish between the assimilation imposed by brute force upon the first-generation migrants who came to Japan after growing up in Korea and naturally absorbing Korean culture, and the meaning of assimilation to the second- and third-generation migrants born and raised in Japan.

In the period of colonial domination, Japan's official public policy was one of assimilation – the Koreans were to be turned into loyal servants of the emperor. Nevertheless, when the first generation of migrants arrived, they were met by discrimination and oppression at the level of everyday life. They responded by learning Japanese as fast as they could in order to better fit in with Japanese society.

However, the degree to which the first-generation migrants could assimilate was naturally limited. Although they have no problem conversing in Japanese, it is a language learned in adulthood and as such there is a certain amount of interference from their native Korean. Many of them also have difficulty with reading and writing. Several times I have heard of first-generation Korean migrants who spoke only Japanese in the household, only to suddenly shift into Korean when hospitalized in old age. This would embarrass their families, who had generally checked them into hospital under an assumed Japanese name and had not planned on their Korean identity being revealed.

I did not meet very many first-generation migrants in the course of my research, but those I did meet had a certain distinctive atmosphere about them. The expressions on their old faces, etched with long years of hardship, and the body language informing every casual gesture, made one aware that they were Koreans.

Things are very different for members of the second and third generations. I would now like to look at the nature of the assimilatory forces enveloping the younger generations, with particular reference to three crucial issues: education/language; names; and marriage/nationality.

Majority speak only Japanese

Until May 1992 I taught sociology at Chiba College of Health Science. Since my own research has always focused on discrimination issues, I used to cover gender, ethnic and Burakumin[4] discrimination in the course. Before commencing the course I would get the students to write essays on topics designed to see just how much understanding they had of these issues. For example, I would ask them 'If there were a Zainichi Korean in this class, how do you think you would behave toward that person?' A number of students gave answers to the effect that they would bestow their friendship upon such a person 'if the person could speak Japanese.'

This kind of naive response is frequently encountered by young ethnic Koreans themselves. If they tell new Japanese acquaintances of their ethnic identity, they are more than likely to be asked where on earth they picked up such fluent Japanese.

As a matter of fact, no second- or third-generation migrant, born and raised in Japan, has any difficulty in speaking, reading or writing Japanese. Conversely, the majority of them cannot communicate in Korean (see Note 14). A minority go to special Korean schools in childhood, but most of them attend ordinary Japanese schools and Japanese is generally the language spoken in the household as well.[5] They are surrounded by a welter of Japanese-language information – radio, television, comics, magazines, everything is in Japanese. To all intents and purposes, Japanese is their 'mother tongue.' Korean, if you like, is their 'mother country's tongue.' Brought up in a linguistic environment that is over-whelmingly Japanese, they naturally absorb the language and with it, the culture. It is no different from the air they breathe.

The real question, then, is which young ethnic Koreans have managed to master the *Korean* language.

The biggest category is of course those who attend ethnic Korean schools. As of 1993 there were 81 ethnic Korean elementary schools, 57 middle schools, 12 high schools and one university, located at Kodaira city on the western outskirts of Tokyo. In all these cases 'Korean' means 'North' Korean, since these schools are run by Chongryun, the ethnic organization that supports Pyongyang. In addition, there are just four schools run by the 'South' Korean community – two in Osaka and one each in Tokyo and Kyoto. These schools combine elementary, middle and high school education.

As of 1986,[6] out of about 150,000 school-age Zainichi Koreans, some 130,500 (86%) were attending Japanese schools, 19,500 (13%) 'North' Korean schools, and 1,600 (1%) 'South' Korean schools. Even the very small figure for Zainichi Koreans attending 'South' Korean schools is an exaggeration, for it includes the children of South Korean businessmen, diplomats, etc. stationed in Japan. This group has been growing rapidly in recent years and now constitutes a majority in the 'South' Korean schools.[7]

The 'North' Korean schools conduct education entirely in Korean except for lessons where Japanese is taught as a foreign language. This has profound legal implications, for it prevents the Japanese Ministry of Education from recognizing the schools as 'Article 1 schools' under the 1947 Japanese School Education Law. Until April 2000 (see Conclusion, pp. 255), this meant that graduating from a Korean school *did not* entitle one to apply for admission to Japanese universities unless special recognition of qualifications was obtained from each university applied to. In practice, over half of all prefectural, municipal and private universities *did allow* graduates of Korean schools to take their entrance exams, but none of the national universities did so.[8]

Until very recently, Korean schools also suffered various other petty discriminatory handicaps officially justified by their lack of Article 1 status. Their pupils would not qualify for a school student discount when buying a Japan Railways train pass, for instance, and they would not be allowed to field teams in the national sporting events such as the annual athletics and baseball tournaments. Only in the 1990s did these unpleasant practices start to disappear. On the other hand, not being Article 1 schools does enable the schools to draw up their own curriculum without interference from the Ministry of Education.

Students educated at these 'North' Korean schools emerge with a more or less perfect command of Korean, and are well capable of communicating with their countrymen in North Korea. Over the last fifty years, North and South Korea have developed quite distinct versions of the Korean language, and graduates of these schools speak a distinctively 'Northern' version.[9] At the same time, however, they cannot entirely overcome the interference of their mother tongue, Japanese. For example, they may use turns of phrase that are rather direct translations of Japanese expressions, or speak with an intonation that faintly echoes their regional Japanese dialect.[10]

By contrast, the 'South' Korean schools conduct lessons in Japanese, only teaching Korean for four hours a week or so. The two schools in Osaka have acquired Article 1 designation, and the

Kyoto school is working toward that goal. Zainichi students attending these schools – especially the one in Tokyo – have the advantage of hearing authentic Southern-style Korean spoken by their friends who have come over from the ROK. Even so, I understand that even very enthusiastic linguists find it hard to entirely master the Korean language at these schools.

A second group of Zainichi Koreans who can speak Korean is composed of those who go to South Korea to study the language at language schools or universities. In recent years just under 200 students a year have been taking up this option.[11]

A third group is those who develop an intense desire to know their own ethnic language and study it in Japan, whether by attending language schools, following lessons on television,[12] or any other means that comes to hand.

A fourth group consists of those second-generation migrants who picked up the language by hearing it spoken about the household by their first-generation parents. Their listening skills tend to be good, but they have various problems with speaking. They may only know the dialect of the district of Korea where their parents were brought up, and find it hard to get their ideas across to Koreans who live in mainland Korea, where the Northern and Southern versions of the language have become far more standardized over the years. They may also struggle to use the polite forms of speech required on certain occasions.[13]

It is impossible to put an authoritative figure to the proportion of young Zainichi Koreans who can speak the Korean language, but estimating mainly from the numbers attending ethnic Korean schools, it is unlikely to exceed 20 percent. The rest know just a few odd words and everyday greetings, if that.[14]

Majority use assumed Japanese names

'Kimura Mayumi.' 'Ryo Mayumi.' Both of them are me.
But I prefer 'Kimura Mayumi.'

This is a line from an essay written for me by one of my students who was an ethnic Korean. 'Ryo' is the Japanese reading of the Korean surname under which she is legally registered. At the time, she did not know the Korean reading. Like the overwhelming majority of Zainichi Koreans, she had a Japanese alias ('Kimura'), which she used in most everyday situations.

The aliases used by Zainichi Koreans are fundamentally different from aliases such as pen names, stage-names, etc., which are arbitrarily chosen by individuals for their own reasons. These aliases are semi-formal. Although the legal name must be used on important legal documents such as passports, driving licenses, and certificates of competence to practice medicine, nursing, etc., the alias may be used when registering at school, for employment, in commercial transactions. The assumed surname is passed on through the generations, while the forename is chosen not by the individual but by his or her parents. Reflecting its semi-formal status, the alias is printed on the alien registration form, in brackets next to the legal name. Zainichi Koreans who decide to express their ethnic pride by discarding their Japanese alias sometimes apply to their local authority to have the alias deleted from the registration documents.

According to a 1984 survey of foreign nationals living in Kanagawa prefecture (Kimpara *et al.* 1986), over 90 percent of ethnic Koreans living there have a Japanese-sounding alias in addition to their Korean names. Adding together those who use only the Japanese name and those who use both, some 80 percent of Koreans in the survey were using Japanese names at least when in Japanese company.[15] My own research confirms this finding: in the 1993 KYAJ survey of 800 young ethnic Koreans with South Korean nationality, 83.8 percent said that they used their alias at least as often as their real name, including 35.3 percent saying they used the alias 'exclusively,' and another 30.3 percent saying they used it 'almost exclusively' (Fukuoka and Kim 1997:78).

Only a small minority of ethnic Koreans use their Korean names all or most of the time. Among the younger generation, that minority appears to be composed of three distinct groups: those who have attended Korean schools, where Korean names are used as a matter of course; those who are involved in campaigning against discrimination or over Japan's responsibility for the 'comfort women' and other wartime abuses, many of whom abandon their Japanese aliases as they become more politically aware; and those who had parents with a strong ethnic consciousness who only gave them a Korean name and brought them up with it, even if isolated from Zainichi networks.

However, the big question is why the great majority of Zainichi Koreans *do* use aliases even today.

It has long been believed that the biggest factor is simply avoidance of discrimination from the Japanese – and indeed, first- and second-generation Koreans have vivid memories of failing to get work when using their ethnic names. Until the late 1970s it was virtually impossible for ethnic Koreans to get employment with Japanese companies even if they had graduated from university. Only specialist qualifications in professions such as medicine or dentistry would lead to jobs. Many Koreans had little option but to carry on small family businesses such as *yakiniku* restaurants or *pachinko* parlors.[16]

Important though this factor is, my own research suggests that the most fundamental reason for the use of aliases lies elsewhere. Over long years of using their Japanese alias, many ethnic Koreans find that they get used to the name, or even come to like it. The survey mentioned above asked respondents if they felt that they 'had to use an alias to avoid discrimination.' Only 10.2 percent agreed strongly with the statement, with another 16.0 percent agreeing tentatively. In contrast, the proposition 'It is only natural to live with the name you are used to, whether it is your real name or an alias' registered 48.0 percent strong agreement and 23.3 percent tentative agreement (Fukuoka and Kim 1997:85–7).

This may well be an indication of just how far assimilation has advanced within the community. In districts with large ethnic Korean populations it is not uncommon for fellow Koreans to greet one another by their Japanese names. In most households, too, it has become established practice for parents to address children by their Japanese names.[17] I have mentioned that in recent years a growing number of young Koreans, politicized through involvement in the anti-discrimination movement, have returned to using their Korean names. While that is true, it is also true that their parents rarely make much effort to call them by their unfamiliar Korean names even if asked to do so. Some of my young informants told me that their parents objected to receiving mail addressed to their children by their Korean names as this would reveal their own Korean identity to the post office.

My own conclusion on the subject of aliases is broadly thus. The first generation of Korean migrants used Japanese names simply because they were forced to by the government under the assimilation policy of the colonial period. The second generation, living in post-war Japanese society, were not legally obliged to use Japanese names but felt the need to do so in order to avoid discrimination. Their children, the members of the third generation, are now so used to Japanese names that they appear more 'natural' than their Korean names. Even if they develop a political awareness of the significance of using the Korean name once they reach adulthood, they hesitate to do so – partly because they fear discrimination but also partly because the Korean name no longer has that feeling of familiarity.

'Real name' not always 'Korean name'

Another great change that may be observed in ethnic Korean naming practices also bears eloquent testimony to the progress of assimilation. While it is commonly assumed that Zainichi Koreans have an 'official' Korean name, entered on their alien registration certificate, and an unofficial Japanese alias that they use in everyday life, this is by no means always the case. The truth is that nowadays the relationship between the two oppositions, Real Name/Alias and Korean Name/Japanese Name takes many different forms. Let me give a few examples based on my own interview data.

1 Legal name = Korean name = only name

Kim Cheol-Soo (male) and Moon Yi-Ryoung (female) were two interviewees of mine who had been through Korean school and had no Japanese-style name. A slightly different case was that of Suh Young-Soon, who went through the Japanese education system all the way to university, using the name 'Jo Eijun,' which is a Japanese reading of the characters in his Korean name. Even with the Japanese reading, the name was obviously non-Japanese. Once he completed his education, he decided to start using the Korean reading of his name.

2 Legal name = Korean name; alias = Japanese-style surname + Japanese reading of Korean forename

Lee Kyung-Jae used to go by the name of 'Takayasu Keisai.' 'Takayasu' is a surname adopted long ago by the Lee clan of Chonju (cf. Chapter 4, Note 2), while 'Keisai' is the Japanese reading of 'Kyung-Jae.' While both names are just about plausible as Japanese names, together they sound slightly non-Japanese.[18] Likewise, Kim Sung-Ok used to call herself 'Ueda Seigyoku.' 'Ueda' is a common Japanese surname, but the forename 'Seigyoku' is the Japanese reading of 'Sung-Ok' and would never be given to an ethnic Japanese female. This case often arises when the parents have a strong ethnic Korean identity that prevents them from giving their children Japanese aliases, but where the children themselves prefer to use Japanese names as they grow up.

3 Legal name = Korean name; alias = Japanese-style surname + Japanese forename

This is the most familiar case, believed by some to be virtually universal among Zainichi Koreans. The alias is totally different from the Korean name, not just a different reading of the same characters, and is designed to sound Japanese. Thus one of the Mintōren leaders, Suh Jung-Woo, used to be known as 'Tatsukawa Kazuaki.' Lee Kyung-Hee, one of my students in Chiba, had 'Takeda Hitomi' as her alias.

4 Legal name = Korean surname + Korean reading of Japanese forename; alias = Japanese-style surname + Japanese forename

I have an old friend called Kim Haeng-Yi. He used to go by the Japanese alias of 'Kaneda Koji.' 'Kaneda' is written with the same character as 'Kim' (read *kane* in Japanese), but with an extra character (*da*) added. 'Koji' and 'Haeng-Yi' are written with exactly the same characters, but in this case the name is rare in Korean but common in Japanese. Kim's parents had deliberately given him a Japanese-style forename. A similar case is that of Kim Soo-Il, a Korean community activist in Kawasaki (a town with a big Korean population). His Japanese alias was

'Kaneyama Hidekazu.' Again the Korean surname had one character added to it to give the Japanese version, while the personal name used the same characters – characters that form a very familiar Japanese name (Hidekazu) and a less familiar Korean name (Soo-Il).

I earlier mentioned the case of a Korean student who called herself 'Kimura Mayumi.' Her official name is Yang Jin-Yoo-Mi, which would read 'Ryo Mayumi' in Japanese style. But 'Mayumi/Jin-Yoo-Mi' is written with three characters and real Korean names never have more than two. Her second-generation parents had deliberately given her a Japanese-style name on her official documents, not just for use as an alias.

Nor is this case particularly unusual. I know quite a few cases of young Zainichi Korean women with three-character names, such as 'Mieko' (Korean reading: Sam-Young-Ja), 'Yukiko' (Yoo-Ki-Ja) and 'Emiko' (Hye-Mi-Ja). I have also come across one male case, a man called 'Yujiro' (Ung-Chi-Rang). None of these are plausible as Korean names.

Overall, there is a clearly observable trend in ethnic Korean naming practices toward more Japanese names, reflecting the increasingly permanent residence intentions among the community. The use of Korean names based on traditional *chokbo* principles (see last chapter, p. 6) is becoming rare, while conversely, the use of names that are more Japanese than Korean (case 4 above), naturally unheard-of among first-generation migrants, is becoming more prevalent with each succeeding generation, especially among women.

If that is the main trend, recently there has been also a clearly discernible counter-trend, as young parents who have graduated from Korean schools, people working for ethnic Korean organizations, and others involved in the anti-discrimination movement, give their children names that reflect their heightened ethnic awareness.

Sometimes those names are authentically Korean. Thus Kawasaki-based Mintōren leader Bae Jung-Do and his wife Chung Wol-Soon have named their two daughters Byung-Soon and Jung-Soon, and their son Byung-Joo. They have no Japanese-sounding aliases.

In other cases, the names chosen contain special meaning grounded in the experience of the Zainichi Korean community. Thus Lee Kyung-Jae (mentioned in case 2 above) has three daughters, called Soo-Ryo, Mi-Yoon and Yi-Hwa, and a son called Young-Hwa. They are written with characters that read pleasantly to the Japanese eye – the characters for Yi-Hwa, for instance, mean 'pear-blossom.' Lee Kyung-Jae explains the choice of names thus: 'We thought that as the children were Korean, they probably ought to have Korean names…but at the same time we wanted names that would sound pleasant to a Japanese ear when pronounced with the Korean reading – Korean names that Japanese could easily get along with.'

Or consider the case of Kim Soo-Il (mentioned in case 4 above). He has named his daughter Rin-Yi. 'The character *Rin* means "neighbor,"' he explains. 'I wanted her to grow up as a child who was good to her neighbors. The character *Yi* is often used in Korean female names, and we chose it for its pleasant sound.'

Korean-Japanese marriage: numbers increasing, but barriers still strong

The following is an extract from a letter written to me by a Japanese woman who had read a couple of interview-based books on Japan's ethnic Koreans co-written by myself and Tsujiyama Yukiko (Fukuoka and Tsujiyama 1991a, 1991b).

> Reading the two books based on your fieldwork, I feel as if I am receiving direct, personal counseling, and am experiencing a sense of liberation that I have not tasted for a very long time.
>
> My relationship with K, a Zainichi Korean man, came to such a terrible end that until this year I have not been able to talk about it to my sister or my close friends.
>
> I can now honestly admit that I wounded him with a single casual remark uttered out of ignorance. However, I also think that he never realized that there was reverse discrimination in what *he* said to *me*.
>
> The course of true love is never smooth, but when it is bound up with social issues such as legal deprivation of

rights and refusal of employment, things become complicated and almost tragic.

For a long time I have been wondering what went wrong with my relationship with K.

Because I had never once heard the word 'Korea' from his own lips, I did not know how best to approach the matter to gain understanding without wounding his heart. Looking back, I think my vague sense of uneasiness came from my inability to grasp precisely where his identity lay. Since he himself was still groping towards it, I had no chance of understanding...but I got it into my head that it was somehow 'the right thing' for people to use their own name rather than an alias.

It all happened eight years ago – a whole series of happenings that actually seemed to have been designed to put me to the test. Although so much time has passed, it makes me slightly sad to find how vividly I can still recall those events when there is something to trigger the memory. I think I will continue to read books about the Korean minority in Japan for some time yet.

As this letter suggests, there remain barriers to marriage between Koreans and Japanese here in Japan.

Some young Japanese are still trapped in a deep-seated loathing of the very idea of marrying a Korean. Even if they are free of such prejudice, they may well find their parents strongly opposed to any match that brings the two ethnic groups together. There may be objections from the Korean parents, too. Again, there are many cases like the one hinted at in the letter above, where there is a mutual attraction across the ethnic divide between two young people, but inability to understand each other's position, experience and thought leads to a breakdown in the relationship.

What then, is the big picture of Korean-Japanese intermarriage? *Table 2.1* tabulates intermarriage trends since 1960, based on marriages reported to the Japanese government. Data is given at five-year intervals for 1960 to 1990 and at one-year intervals thereafter.

It has to be said that this kind of official data must be treated with extreme caution. For a start, it naturally does not cover

Table 2.1 Marriages involving Koreans in Japan

Year	A Husband: K* Wife: J**	B Wife: K Husband: J	C K-J marriages (A+B)	D All-K marriages	Total (C+D+others) Cases (%)
1960	862 (24.5)	310 (8.8)	1,172 (33.3)	2,315 (65.7)	3,524 (100.0)
1965	1,128 (19.8)	843 (14.8)	1,971 (34.6)	3,681 (64.7)	5,693 (100.0)
1970	1,386 (20.1)	1,536 (22.3)	2,922 (42.4)	3,879 (56.3)	6,892 (100.0)
1975	1,554 (21.4)	1,994 (27.5)	3,584 (48.9)	3,618 (49.9)	7,249 (100.0)
1980	1,651 (22.8)	2,458 (33.9)	4,109 (56.6)	3,061 (42.2)	7,255 (100.0)
1985	2,525 (29.3)	3,622 (42.0)	6,147 (71.3)	2,404 (27.9)	8,627 (100.0)
1990	2,721 (19.5)	8,940 (64.2)	11,661 (83.7)	2,195 (15.8)	13,934 (100.0)
1991	2,666 (22.8)	6,969 (59.7)	9,635 (82.5)	1,961 (16.8)	11,677 (100.0)
1992	2,804 (27.4)	5,537 (54.1)	8,341 (81.4)	1,805 (17.6)	10,242 (100.0)
1993	2,762 (28.5)	5,068 (52.2)	7,830 (80.7)	1,781 (18.4)	9,700 (100.0)
1994	2,686 (29.1)	4,851 (52.6)	7,537 (81.7)	1,616 (17.5)	9,228 (100.0)
1995	2,842 (31.7)	4,521 (50.5)	7,363 (82.2)	1,485 (16.6)	8,953 (100.0)

* K is an abbreviation of Korean.
** J is an abbreviation of Japanese.

Source: Ministry of Health and Welfare (ed.), *Jinkō Dōtai Tōkei (Vital Statistics of Japan)*. Compiled from two sections: 'Trends in marriages by nationality of bride and groom: Japan' and 'Foreigners in Japan: Marriages by nationality of bride and groom.'

unreported marriages. Second, among those 'Japanese' reported as having married Koreans there are quite a few people who are in fact ethnic Koreans themselves but have acquired Japanese nationality, or who are themselves the offspring of mixed Japanese-Korean marriages. Third, the 'Korean' category includes Koreans born and raised in Korea as well as Zainichi Koreans. It is difficult, therefore, to gain an accurate impression of what is actually going on. The best one can do is compare different sets of official data to confirm each other as far as possible.

Thus migration data shows that the number of Koreans entering Japan with visas granted to them as 'the spouse of a Japanese national' was 578 in 1990, rising to 1,080 in 1991, steadying at 1,081 in 1993 and then falling back to 916 in 1995 and 845 in 1996. This figure probably approximates to the number of Korean-resident Koreans marrying Japanese each year. However, there are doubtless some cases of mainland

Koreans entering Japan in other visa categories and subsequently marrying Japanese nationals. Again, the total number of Koreans living in Japan with the 'spouse of Japanese national' qualification was 15,810 in 1989, rising to 19,999 in 1990. The rise of just over 4,000 in one year would approximate to the number of new marriages between Japanese and Koreans lacking the special residence status of the Zainichis. I have heard that the overwhelming majority of marriages between Japanese and mainland Koreans are between Japanese men and Korean women,[19] and such cases probably account for most of the increase in this category.

Another relevant migration statistic covers people entering the country as the 'spouse or child of a permanent resident,' which would account for most cases of mainland Koreans marrying Zainichi Koreans. The numbers are very small: 42 in 1990, 151 in 1991. As before, there must also be cases of people entering the country on some other class of visa and subsequently marrying Zainichi Koreans with permanent residence status.

With the above-mentioned caveats in mind, it seems possible to draw the following two conclusions from the data in *Table 2.1*:

(a) Marriages between Zainichi Koreans and Japanese have been steadily increasing in recent years. The figures in column C include marriages between Japanese and mainland Koreans, which could account for a maximum of just over 4,000 marriages in 1990. Even if that maximum figure is deducted, however, Japanese-Zainichi marriages appear to outnumber all-Zainichi marriages by a ratio of about 7:2. Switching the unit of calculation from marriages to individual people, it would appear that out of every 11 Zainichi Koreans who get married, 7 marry Japanese against 4 who marry fellow Zainichis.

(b) Marriages between Zainichi women and Japanese men are much more frequent than those between Zainichi men and Japanese women. Even if we assume that all 4,000 of the marriages in 1990 between Japanese and mainland Koreans involved Japanese men and Korean women, that would still leave marriages between Japanese men and Zainichi women outnumbering the reverse case by about 5,000 to under 3,000.

This implies that there are many ethnic Korean men who cannot find marriage partners.

Except for the minority who live in ethnic Korean quarters or attend Korean schools, young Zainichi Koreans tend to live in relative isolation within dominantly Japanese communities.[20] It is not uncommon for them to know no other Koreans except for their own relatives.[21] That being so, ethnic Korean women have increasingly managed to get over the ethnic divide and set up love marriages with Japanese men. Love marriages and arranged marriages between fellow Koreans have shown a concomitant decline. But ethnic Korean men have found it much harder than their countrywomen to make love-marriages with Japanese. This is the picture that emerges from the data.

How can we account for this striking gender difference in marriage prospects? Let us consider two hypotheses: one that finds the main cause on the Korean side, and one that finds it on the Japanese side.

If the cause lies on the Korean side, it most probably has to do with differing parental expectations for male and female children: in short, could it be that Korean parents are relatively willing to allow their daughters to marry Japanese, but much less willing to let their sons do the same?

The possibility cannot entirely be ruled out. However, my own experience indicates that attitudes to intermarriage among Korean parents are highly variable with respect to gender, with no dominant themes. Thus some take the view that the son's bride must be a fellow Korean in order for her to be able to properly conduct the *Jesa*, a Korean rite of ancestor-worship.[22] Others say that the bride will get on so long as she gets to know the family customs, and have no objection to a Japanese girl marrying in. In the reverse case, some object to their daughters marrying Japanese because they will adopt their husband's nationality and 'become Japanese,' while others say that since a daughter leaves her family anyway upon marriage, it does not matter if her new husband is Japanese.[23]

Given this complex variety of attitudes, it seems unlikely that the main factor for the low incidence of Korean male-Japanese female marriages lies on the Korean side. That would appear to lend some credence to the reverse hypothesis, that the main factor is on the Japanese side. It appears to be generally true that Japanese women are less likely than Japanese men to marry people subject to social discrimination.[24]

This probably reflects the dominant status of the male in Japanese society. Even today it remains the case, in Japan at least, that a woman's social status is determined by that of the man she marries. Moreover, Japanese still tend to practice virilocal marriage, so that a woman who marries a husband from a minority group will often be expected to live with or close to her husband's family, often in an area with a concentration of the minority group. Mainstream Japanese men, by contrast, can take a minority bride out of her minority environment and expect her to adjust to his own family and community. Hence the implications of minority marriage are far bigger for women than for men. This may reduce the enthusiasm of Japanese women for minority marriage, or strengthen the opposition of their parents, relative to the male case. Finally, it may be that since unmarried daughters tend to be in a weaker position than their brothers *vis-à-vis* their parents, they are less able to overcome parental opposition to unconventional marriage.

Increase of Koreans with Japanese nationality

In 1947, just after the war, 598,507 Koreans underwent the newly established process of 'alien registration,' accounting for 93.6 percent of all registered foreigners. At the end of 1996, as mentioned above, that figure stood at 657,159, of whom 548,968 had 'special permanent residence status.' These were Koreans who had settled in Japan long-term under the historical circumstances described in the previous chapter. The remaining 100,000 or so were so-called 'newcomers' – mainland Koreans who had come to Japan for work, marriage, or temporarily for study, training, etc., plus their families.

These figures give the impression that the Korean population in Japan has barely changed in the fifty years since the war. This is counter-intuitive, since the overall population of Japan has risen roughly from 72 million to 126 million in the same period. Repatriation is a factor, of course, particularly the 93,339 people, mostly ethnic Koreans with a few Japanese spouses, who were sent to the DPRK during two repatriation programs run by the Japanese and North Korean Red Cross (1959–67; 1971–84).

However, the main factor preventing a greater rise in the ethnic Korean population statistics has been large-scale naturalization. As mentioned above, over 200,000 Koreans were naturalized between 1952 (when Japan stripped the Korean minority of Japanese citizenship; see last chapter) and 1996.[25] Obviously some of these people will have died over the years; on the other hand, children and grandchildren of these naturalized Koreans, born with Japanese nationality, also account for a substantial number of people.

In addition, many people born of mixed Japanese-Korean marriages also have Japanese nationality. Until the 1984 revision of the Nationality Law, children born to a Japanese father and Korean mother would be designated as Japanese nationals. Where the father was Korean and the mother Japanese, the children would be Korean nationals, but some couples who were keen for their children to have Japanese nationality got around the law by not registering their marriage, in which case the children would be defined as 'born out of wedlock' and thereby take their mother's nationality.

Since the 1984 revision, all children of mixed marriages have been able to hold Japanese nationality. Moreover, the 1984 revision also included interim measures, under which children of mixed marriages aged under 20 on the day the law came into force were enabled to acquire Japanese nationality simply by notifying the authorities of their wish to do so. Under these measures some 16,000 North and South Korean nationals switched to Japanese nationality during a three-year period from 1985 to 1987.

There is no way of arriving at a precise figure for the number of people of entirely or partially Korean ethnicity who have become Japanese nationals through the methods just described. However, if we add to the long-term resident Korean nationals those who have acquired Japanese nationality, plus 'newcomers' legally registered and otherwise, then people of Korean or partly Korean descent must account for at least 1 percent of Japan's overall population.

Japanese nationality law permits the children of mixed marriages to hold dual nationality until the age of 22. Of course, however, this only applies where dual nationality is also recognized under the nationality law of the other country involved in the marriage. This has some profound implications.

The Republic of Korea is currently working on legal reforms that would recognize nationality through either parent, but at present ROK law only recognizes the paternal line.[26] This means that where the father is Japanese and the mother is 'South' Korean, the child is not eligible for Korean nationality and must be Japanese; whereas if the mother is Japanese and the father Korean, the child can hold dual nationality with the Korean claim recognized through the father and the Japanese claim through the mother.

The Democratic People's Republic of Korea bases its nationality law on blood inheritance, but includes a provision – Article 5 – under which the nationality of children born in marriages between foreign-resident DPRK nationals and foreign nationals may be decided by mutual agreement between the parents. However, the government of Japan has never extended diplomatic recognition to the DPRK. The government bases its treatment of North Korean nationals resident in Japan on South Korean, not North Korean, nationality law.

Thus although dual nationality is legally permitted until the age of 22, in practice when a mixed-marriage birth is registered in Japan, the child is given the Japanese parent's surname and is entered in the Japanese parent's family register. In legal terms and everyday life alike, the child is likely to grow up using just one, Japanese, name. It is highly unlikely that such a person will renounce Japanese citizenship on reaching the age of 22.[27]

As I mentioned earlier, marriages in Japan between Korean and Japanese nationals are rapidly increasing. If one includes cases of Japanese nationals marrying mainland Korean brides, then Japanese-Korean matches account for over 80 percent of all marriages in Japan involving at least one Korean national. Unless the parents take special measures to remove their children's Japanese nationality, the children will effectively become Japanese nationals. Nor will this be a mere quirk of nationality law: as time goes by the offspring of these marriages will become Japanese in fact as well as on paper.

Ultimately, these trends will probably lead to the Korean minority being absorbed into Japanese society, a prospect that probably pleases those who believe in Japan as a 'homogeneous society.' At the same time, it may ultimately be the only way for the ethnic Koreans themselves to escape from discrimination.

However, from the standpoint of people like myself, who wish to see Japan become a tolerant society, in which people of different ethnic backgrounds can live together peacefully on the basis of acceptance of each other's differences, the present trends have a disturbing aspect as well. There is nothing wrong with the increase in 'Korean Japanese,' with Korean ethnic origins but Japanese nationality. One still hopes, however, for a society in which such people will not feel obliged to conceal their Korean background, and will see no contradiction in maintaining their Korean cultural identity while living as full members of Japanese society.

3   A Typology of Zainichi Identities

Life-history interviews

From 1988 to 1993 I conducted interviews with over 150 Zainichi Koreans, most of them of the younger generation. The interviews focused on life histories, with particular reference to ethnic identity.

My interviewing style was not particularly subtle: it quite simply consisted of asking whatever I wanted to know. I generally started by asking how the subject's grandparents came to arrive in Japan, and then went on to inquire about the lives of his or her parents and immediate family, before focusing on the subject's own various experiences and thoughts from infancy to the present day. The interviews generally lasted three or four hours.

I believe I asked questions about quite a number of topics that my subjects would not normally like to discuss with an outsider. I also believe that by discussing these topics with them, I brought back painful memories of the experience of discrimination and the bitter thoughts associated with it.

Even so, I often received letters of thanks from young Koreans who were the subjects of interviews a few days afterwards, thanking me for listening to their troubles, apologizing for accepting hospitality from me and so on. One of these letters reads as follows:

> If you are still researching the problem of discrimination
> in twenty years' time, we sincerely hope you will listen to
> what our children have to say. It is a pleasure just to
> imagine how our children will feel about us, and what sort
> of life we might be leading then.

When the interviews were at the planning stage, I was warned by a young female ethnic Korean academic that Koreans would not easily open their hearts to a Japanese researcher. However, once I commenced the project I found that although a few people did indeed refuse to be interviewed, the vast majority were extremely cooperative in discussing even strictly private matters.

Caught between assimilation and differentiation

The findings obtained from these interviews may be condensed into two simple themes.

First, my findings dramatically problematize Japanese conventional wisdom regarding young Zainichi Koreans, which has it that with two or three generations of forebears already living in Japan they feel relatively little conflict in their lives within Japanese society. My study shows that the great majority of them have, in fact, experienced suffering and conflict.

Japanese conventional wisdom has tended to divide the Zainichi Korean population roughly along the following lines: first generation, resentful of Japan and nostalgic for the motherland; second generation, disheartened by experiences of discrimination and poverty, and determined to establish the foundations for a successful life in Japan; third generation, well enough adjusted to Japanese society to get by without too many problems.

I do not deny that there are some young Koreans who are well enough adjusted to get along both in Japanese society and with fellow Koreans, and who live their lives without experiencing very serious conflicts. For example, one young Korean woman who routinely uses her Japanese alias in everyday life confidently told me that 'to date I have had absolutely no experience of discrimination.' She went on: 'I somehow seem to have two selves. When I'm with my Japanese friends I feel as if I'm Japanese myself, or at least I don't feel that I'm at all different. When I'm with people like my cousins…well, in the end Koreans are Koreans. I seem to have drawn a dividing line between the two selves.' Asked if this division was a conscious process, she said no – 'it feels as if I just naturally respond to the atmosphere in each situation.' She would appear to have developed a kind of switching mechanism.

However, closer questioning revealed that this woman did think it possible that she might suffer discrimination if her Japanese friends found out that she was ethnically Korean: a certain sense of threat had been internalized. She was not unaware of racial discrimination in Japanese society; rather, one discerns an unwillingness to think deeply about her own position within it. One might call it an unconscious refusal to confront the problem. In this sense it seems fair to classify this case as one of 'conflict avoidance' rather than one where conflict is absent (Fukuoka and Tsujiyama 1991a:187–215).

As a straightforward matter of fact, the great majority of young Koreans in Japan do experience discrimination to greater or lesser degree; do feel the sting of the contemptuous gaze of the Japanese; and do have experiences that subject them to conflicts of identity. Uncertain how to go about their lives, they are in a state of confusion with no way out. Conflict is the experience of the great majority of Zainichi Koreans, not just one part of the population.[1] This is the thrust of my first set of findings.

My second main point is that the casually used term *Zainichi Kankoku-Chōsenjin* (Japan-resident Koreans) conceals a great variety of realities and forms of consciousness among young ethnic Koreans. Most Japanese, however well-educated, have merely distinguished between those Koreans who determinedly maintain their ethnic identity and those who tend to assimilate into Japanese society. In fact, however, the ways in which young Koreans grope toward their identity in Japan show far greater variety than this crude distinction would imply. I will discuss this second set of findings later in this chapter.

Conflicts of identity; diversity of identity. Why has this state of affairs arisen?

The identity that young Zainichi Koreans are 'given' is composed of two main sets of elements. One set is Japanese: they grow up within Japanese society, using Japanese as their mother tongue, and acquire Japanese culture through a sort of natural process. Aspects of their lives such as ways of thinking, ways of feeling, values and lifestyles, have much in common with those of the Japanese people around them. This set of elements may be called the 'assimilated self' – assimilated to Japanese society, that is.

But however deeply these people may be submerged in Japanese society, a second set of elements, based on the ethnic Korean inheritance, will always be present. The strength of ethnic awareness varies greatly according to each individual's living environment: the degree to which ethnic culture is maintained within the household; whether or not one has attended a Korean school; and degree of involvement with ethnic organizations or groups. It remains correct to say that in ways of thinking, ways of feeling, values and lifestyles, Zainichi Koreans always have something about them that differs from the surrounding Japanese population. This something may be called the 'differentiated self' – again in relation to Japanese society.

A similar dichotomy may be observed in the way young Zainichi Koreans express their aspirations for the future. Some wish to be the same as those around them (i.e. the Japanese), and may be said to 'aspire to assimilation.' Others do not mind being different from those around them, or wish to be different from those around them, or even feel they have to be different, and may be said to 'aspire to differentiation.'

The reason I use this cumbersome turn of phrase, as I will explain in detail later, is to make the point that opposition to assimilatory aspirations takes several forms, and does not necessarily imply the kind of raised ethnic consciousness *vis-à-vis* the mother country that is often described simply as 'ethnic pride.' Hence my use of the more widely encompassing expression, 'aspiring to differentiation.'

Feelings of contempt, avoidance and discrimination toward ethnic Koreans remain deeply ingrained in Japanese society. In the course of their personal development, most young ethnic Koreans are made to internalize the negative image that Japanese people hold toward them. This negative image constitutes a powerful magnetic field around which contradictory self-images of assimilation and differentiation co-exist, creating an intricate mixture of assimilatory and differential aspirations. It is here that we may locate the basis of their identity conflicts.

Let me explain in a little more detail.

In the case of the great majority of third-generation Zainichi Koreans, who attend Japanese schools and use Japanese names, those who are free from identity conflict are very much the exception. During childhood, when they are first told by parents or relatives that 'although you are living in Japan, you are not Japanese but Korean,' they do not have any negative feelings about it. But around the time that they reach the final years of elementary school and move on to junior high school, just when they are entering puberty, many young Koreans have exceedingly painful experiences that make them unbearably ashamed of their own ethnic identity.

This is when the impact of discrimination and prejudice from Japanese people experienced from preschool age onward begins to be keenly felt. For instance, one of my female informants recalled telling a good friend of her ethnic identity and finding that from the very next day the friend would no longer talk to her (Fukuoka and Tsujiyama 1991a:107). Another recalled overhearing her best friend's mother saying 'That child's Korean, so you mustn't play together' (Fukuoka and Tsujiyama 1991a:152). A third reported the experience of being shamed before the whole class by another child who revealed that 'She isn't Japanese, she's Korean' (Fukuoka and Tsujiyama 1991a:20–1). Through a succession of incidents like these, the negative image of ethnic Koreans held by Japanese ends up being internalized by the Koreans themselves.

Rendered unable to have confidence in themselves as they are, they become more desperate than ever to be the same as the Japanese people around them. They make up their minds that no one must ever know that they are not Japanese, and conclude that they must keep the shameful fact a deadly secret. However, the more strongly they yearn to assimilate, the higher the wall preventing their assimilation becomes. Until recently, ethnic Koreans had to submit to being fingerprinted on reaching their sixteenth birthday, under the Alien Registration Law[2] – a humiliation that none of their friends had to endure. It was a painful reminder that they were different from all those around them (Fukuoka and Tsujiyama 1991a:22, 110–11, 156).

Those who respond to all this by recognizing that they can never be the same as those around them, and decide to pay more heed to their own ethnic roots, face another wall. It is a wall that they find within themselves. Brought up in Japan, they do not know their own people's language. They have not acquired their own people's culture. The perception that they have 'lost their identity' inflicts further suffering upon them (Fukuoka and Tsujiyama 1991a:83–98, 134–48).

As they grow up, ethnic Korean youths find themselves torn between the powerful and conflicting desires to assimilate to

Japanese society and to maintain their Korean identity. As they waver between the two, they inevitably encounter a host of conflicts and troubles.

Conflicting impulses

I would now like to add a few words of explanation toward defining the opposition I have outlined between the 'assimilatory impulse' and the 'differential impulse.'

In scholarly discourse on ethnic identity, the meaning and usage of the term 'assimilation,' and its Japanese equivalent, *dōka*, is already well established. It denotes the process by which individuals or groups of people obliged to deal with a dominant alien culture, whether by migration or conquest, adopt the dominant culture and learn to conform to it.

I too define 'assimilation' in the conventional way, as the process by which members of an ethnic group living as a minority in a host society come to conform to the dominant culture. When the dominant authorities of the host society develop policies to promote the assimilation of ethnic minorities, I define those policies as 'assimilatory policies.' The pressure stemming from behavior and attitudes on the part of members of the majority that consciously or otherwise encourage members of a minority group to assimilate, I define as 'assimilatory pressure.'

In contrast, I define the 'assimilatory impulse' as a form of consciousness among members of the minority group by which they positively hope to become homogeneous with the majority culture. Whether the assimilatory impulse is in fact a straightforward response to assimilatory policies and assimilatory pressure is a question that I will put to one side for the present.

Turning now to the 'differential impulse,'[3] this I define as a subjective consciousness on the part of minority group members that does not desire homogeneity with the majority culture. In other words, I define it only as the *absence* of the impulse to homogenization with the majority group. Note that I do not intend any strong definition, such as 'possession of firm ethnic consciousness' or 'affirmation of the undisguised self.' In which direction the differential impulse becomes oriented is an open question.

A typology of identity formation

When people experience conflicts of identity, they start to look around for ways to overcome conflict and reconstruct their own lifestyle and identity in ways that will enable them to get on with life. Sometimes the process starts with the subject's parents, who anticipate conflict and attempt to pre-empt it by socializing their children in ways that will eliminate conflict.

Let us ask, then, what kind of identity young Zainichi Koreans are searching for or constructing.

As I mentioned earlier, it will not do to define the options confronting them as a simple dichotomy between tenaciously clinging to their ethnic identity or assimilating to Japanese society and 'turning Japanese.' The quest for identity among the young Koreans whom I met took on a far greater variety of forms. My honest impression was that every single one of them was truly individual in his or her approach. However, that will not suffice to depict the consciousness of young Zainichi Koreans as a whole. Only by establishing certain broad categories can we begin to sketch a profile of the overall group.

In my mind's eye, the faces of each and every one of the young Koreans I interviewed floats before me. And as I recall them, they form groups – groups differing from each other in the ways they pursue their identity. I will now attempt to draw up categories of identity derived from the lived reality of the actual people in question – a somewhat different organizational style to that used in the Introduction, where I prioritized theoretical consistency.

I believe that four identity types can be deduced from character-istics observable in lifestyle choices, and that they can be arranged in a quadrant schema. I propose to label the two axes 'Interest in the history of Korean subjugation' and 'Attachment to a Japanese hometown.' I further propose to label the four types generated by these two axes the pluralist, nationalist, individualist and naturalizing types, respectively.[4]

I do not deny that these labels are short on theoretical abstraction and have little analytical power as patterned variables. They are merely attempts to clarify impressions that emerged in the course of a gradual accumulation of interview material. I thought of organizing my data in terms of all sorts of different variables, but at present this four-part taxonomy is the only one that comes to mind into which the data will fit without being forced. (Even so, one sizeable group within the population dose not fit into the schema. The character of this fifth group places it in between the pluralist and nationalist tendencies. I will label it the 'ethnic solidarity' tendency.)

This paradigm of young Zainichi Korean identity may be expressed by the diagram given in *Figure 3.1.*

Figure 3.1   Classificatory framework for the construction of identity by young Zainichi Koreans

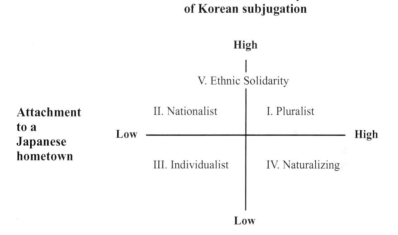

Although as I say this paradigm emphasizes observed reality rather than theoretical consistency, the fact remains that like any diagram, it simplifies the chaos of reality as far as possible. Similarities among types have been played down and differences made much of. Naturally I do not claim that each individual, with their own unique personality, will fit neatly into one of the four quadrants. That would be impossible.

Nevertheless, I believe that this kind of categorizing procedure does help us to see the overall distribution of young Zainichi

Koreans' positions on the identity question. The characteristics of each type are as follows.

The pluralist type

'Living together while respecting mutual differences' is the key phrase expressing the nature of the pluralist type. Their overriding concern is to rid Japanese society of ethnic discrimination and thereby create a society in which people of different ethnic origins can live together on the basis of respect for differences among their respective positions. In short, they look to social reform for a solution to the problem of social discrimination. They have a strong tendency to put down roots in the district of their birth and upbringing, and seek to change society starting with their own immediate surroundings.

The pluralist tendency may chiefly be observed in the members of an organization called Mintōren. Mintōren was founded in 1975, growing out of the movement focused on the Hitachi Employment Discrimination Trial of the early 1970s.[5] It was a networking organization modeled on citizens' movements (see Preface, Note 7).

Looking at the life histories of the original Mintōren leaders, who were in their late thirties when interviewed, most of them used Japanese names, attended Japanese schools, and came up against Japanese discrimination and prejudice in their childhood. These experiences gave them a negative image of themselves as Zainichi Koreans. At some point in later life, however, the opportunity arose to study the history of the Korean minority in Japan, and they came to the realization that the conflicts they were experiencing stemmed not from their own Korean identity but from the discrimination inherent in Japanese society. They went on to shape a new identity as Zainichi Koreans who could live with pride in Japanese society.

Among the second generation of Mintōren members, in their twenties when interviewed, some may be observed who are relatively free of internalized negative images compared to the leadership generation. This may well reflect the fact that they have been brought up from childhood with positive examples of ethnic Korean lifestyles from which to learn.

There is a strong tendency among these younger pluralists to replace the idea that they have no mother country to call their own with new thinking that views their place of birth and upbringing in Japan as their hometown. They do not predicate their identity on affiliation to a state, whether by clinging to the Korean 'motherland' or attempting to merge with the host country, Japan. Instead they show a powerful affiliation to the regional society of their upbringing.

Their choice of a lifestyle that combats racism implies the attachment of great importance to using their original ethnic Korean name. Using a Japanese alias may afford some temporary relief from discrimination, but it will not solve the problem of discrimination itself. Using the alias has the effect – whether intended or not – of concealing one's ethnic origins, and also rules out any meeting of minds with Japanese who show some under-standing of the Zainichi Korean problem. Pluralists place great weight on relations with people who will share their anti-racist struggle, irrespective of whether such people be ethnic Koreans or Japanese.

Factors in their educational history mean that many of these people cannot speak Korean. Likewise many have inherited relatively little Korean ethnic culture. They do not usually feel any shame at their inability to speak their own mother country's tongue. As they see it, this is no more than a condition left to them by their personal history. However, Korean-speaking ability and understanding of ethnic culture are viewed as desirable attributes, and many pluralists are making efforts to pick up the language and culture, however slowly.

To sum up, young pluralists have no pre-existing model on which to base their lives. They do not identify themselves with 'Koreans in Korea,' or with Japanese. Instead it would appear that they are trying to forge a distinctive new lifestyle for themselves as 'Zainichi' – 'ethnic Koreans in Japan.'

The nationalist type

Nationalist types view themselves as 'overseas nationals,' typically of North Korea that they hope will eventually be reunified with the South. Key issues for them are the development and reunification of the motherland. Consequently they have no

51

wish to assimilate with the Japanese society in which they live, and are concerned rather to maintain the society of Japan-resident Koreans in the spirit of an expatriate community.

They also show a fierce determination to defend themselves and their organizations from assaults by the Japanese government on their rights as overseas nationals of North Korea. This determination gives rise to a number of issues. However, it is rather difficult for this group to make demands that go beyond the position they have adopted as overseas nationals of North Korea. For example, pluralist-type Koreans sometimes demand that foreigners permanently resident in Japan should be given the right to participate in politics, at least at the local level. But nationalist types have arrived at a critical interpretation of this demand, regarding it as 'interference in the domestic affairs of a foreign country' and 'a step toward assimilation.'

Similarly their stance toward racism in Japanese society places heavy emphasis on the principle of mutual assistance within the Chongryun community (see Preface, Note 5). On the issue of housing discrimination, for instance, a test case in Osaka[6] was supported by Mintōren, but nationalist types took little interest in the case. Generally their view is that there is no point in trying to get a fair deal out of a Japanese landlord in the first place. Instead, they prefer to avoid the problem by activating networks of mutual assistance among fellow Koreans when looking for housing.

The nationalist tendency is chiefly to be observed among Korean youths who locate themselves within a social sphere centered on Chongryun. A look at their life histories shows that typically they have attended Chongryun-affiliated ethnic Korean educational institutions, at their parents' behest, all the way from elementary school to high school or university. There they have learned the language, history and culture of Korea – and internalized ethnic pride in their Korean identity.

To that extent they have not experienced the conflict of ethnic identity suffered by most other Koreans in Japan. They may be subjected to harassment by Japanese on their way to school, but they have the strength to resist it. No amount of harassment will make them ashamed of their Korean identity.

They refer to their motherland or homeland as 'One Korea.' They have learned all about Japan's invasion of Korea and as such have a powerfully critical view of Japan. Accordingly they feel little sense of attachment to the country of their birth and upbringing. Some of them even feel that Japan is 'just another foreign country.' They try to live their lives upon the principles of Kim Il Sung to the extent possible in their very different environment, and some speak of returning to the motherland once reunification has been achieved.

These youths are nearly all bilingual, picking up Japanese from their everyday surroundings and Korean from school. To them it is only natural that Koreans should speak Korean; those who cannot are viewed as pathetic specimens that hardly qualify as Koreans at all.

In principle they use only their ethnic Korean name. In practice, they will occasionally use a Japanese name simply to avoid trouble in their transactions with Japanese society. Imbued as they are with ethnic pride, they do not feel their identity in any way threatened by the use of a Japanese name for the sake of convenience.

They also display a strong tendency to restrict their living space to the confines of ethnic Korean society. It is not rare for their entire circle of intimate associates to be fellow Koreans. In employment likewise, they tend to work for one of the various bodies associated with Chongryun, or to take over a family business from their parents. In many cases they will not even consider seeking employment with a Japanese company, believing that they have no chance of being taken on anyway.

Thus the young nationalists separate themselves from Japanese society, with the result that although in objective terms they are surrounded by discrimination just like other Zainichi Koreans, they nonetheless tend to experience less discrimination than most.

The individualist type

The key phrase summing up Koreans of this type, though it is not one they use themselves, is 'self-expression.' Their chief concern is to get themselves established, in a strictly individualist sense. They are often after personal success, which in effect means escaping from discrimination under their own steam, through upward social mobility. This is the way they have chosen to respond to social discrimination.

Individualists are often to be found among the ranks of young Koreans whose aim is to study abroad – often in America – or graduate from a high-ranking Japanese university, and then to gain employment with a foreign company or a prestigious Japanese one.

The common thread running through their life histories is an upbringing that has given them a degree of confidence in their own ability. This means that even if they do experience the discomfort and conflict of living as ethnic Koreans in Japan, they are spared the trauma that might otherwise result from those experiences. They do not hold a negative image of themselves; rather they take the view that any problems they experience pertain purely to the circumstances in which they have been placed. Accordingly they attempt to change those circumstances, either by going abroad or by rising to a higher position in Japanese society. Their ideal is the cosmopolitan lifestyle.

Their desire for mobility means that they feel relatively little attachment toward the region of Japan where they had their own upbringing; on the national level, too, they seldom feel much devotion to Japan or to any version of Korea. Similarly their emphasis on the individual precludes any deep interest in the history of the Korean ethnic group in Japan. It matters little to them whether they use a Korean or Japanese name, and they would rather learn English than Korean as they believe the former will work to their advantage in career terms.

In personal relations they pay little attention to ethnicity or nationality, but feel a sense of liberation in relations with people who share their respect for individual achievement.

The naturalizing type

These are Koreans whose basic desire is to 'become Japanese.' They attempt to become the same as Japanese in any way possible, hoping that by identifying with the host people they can escape from ethnic discrimination. This attitude is chiefly to be found among those young Koreans who actually do take on Japanese nationality.

Their life histories often start with a childhood in which theirs was the only Korean family in an otherwise wholly Japanese neighborhood. Members of their own family would use Japanese aliases and conceal their ethnic origins. Few elements of Korean ethnic culture would be maintained in family life. Consequently many of them did not even discover that they were not Japanese until quite a late stage in their personal development.

Moreover, they would internalize the negative image of Koreans held by Japanese people in the course of development. Hence the discovery that they were Korean themselves tended to come as a great blow. Thus they chose to try and expunge the discomfort of ethnic minority status by 'adapting' to the surrounding Japanese society.

The circumstances of their upbringing tend to mean that their closest friends are all Japanese. In their desire to become the same as their friends, they increasingly distance themselves from their Korean ethnic identity. They often say that their own country is Japan, not Korea. They feel a powerful attachment to the region of their upbringing. They do not feel comfortable with their Korean surname, though on paper at least it is their official name,[7] and they feel that their Japanese name is much more their own. Born and raised in Japan, they see their inability to speak Korean as something that can't be helped and doesn't much matter anyway. Likewise they see no point in making a fuss about Japan's history of colonialism in Korea – to them, it's all water under the bridge.

Thus in all sorts of ways, people of this type seek to dissolve conflict through an individual response that deals with social discrimination by adjusting to their surroundings.

The ethnic solidarity type

I have now outlined the basic characteristics of the four types defined by the quadrants in *Figure 3.1*. However, there is one other group which has a degree of influence among young ethnic Koreans that is not covered by any of these types. I refer to those youths who join the Mindan-affiliated *Zainichi Kankoku Seinen-kai*, officially translated as the Korean Youth Association in Japan (KYAJ) and usually known by its Japanese acronym, *Seinenkai* (see Preface, Note 4).

It is hard to place the principal members running the KYAJ anywhere on the four quadrants in *Figure 3.1*. Their identity appears to lie somewhere between the pluralist and nationalist types. Let us call them the 'ethnic solidarity type.'

The key concern of these people is mutual assistance among Zainichi Koreans. They aim to defend the rights and improve the treatment of their fellow Zainichis, and thereby win recognition of the Korean minority as a legitimate entity. They also seek to improve Korean language skills, increase awareness of Korean culture and encourage the use of Korean names.

As I mentioned, pluralist types see neither Japan nor Korea as a homeland, but are attached to their place of upbringing within Japan; while nationalist types pay respect to Korea they hope to see reunified and see Japan as merely a foreign country. Ethnic solidarity types often feel an attachment both to South Korea, as the motherland, and to Japan, as the country of residence.

Pluralist types value relations with people of any ethnic background, Korean or Japanese, who will join them in the struggle against racism. Nationalist types construct a living space that has almost no room for relationships with anyone other than fellow Koreans. It is not uncommon for them to have no Japanese friends at all, though they may have a few Japanese acquaintances. In the case of ethnic solidarity types, their principal relationships before becoming involved in KYAJ activities were with Japanese friends. But whereas Mintōren carries out various activities in consort with Japanese sympathizers, the KYAJ only allows Korean youths to take a central role in its activities. As they take a bigger part in those activities, KYAJ members tend to find relationships with fellow ethnic Koreans gradually taking on more importance in their personal lives.

At this point, allow me to add a couple of extra points regarding *Figure 3.1* above.

Styles of resistance

The first concerns the various styles with which people respond to the various problems that impinge upon their lives as Zainichi Koreans. The three types in the top half of the diagram – the pluralist, nationalist and ethnic solidarity types – all take part in organized, collective movements to campaign against discrimination, defend human rights, and demand payment of war reparations from Japan. There are, however, striking differences among the three types in their stance toward the various problems and campaigning styles adopted.

Pluralists define the various issues as problems of Japanese society, and often campaign in partnership with Japanese activists. Ethnic solidarity types define them as problems for the Korean community to sort out, and rarely engage in joint action with Japanese. In effect they tend to rely upon government-level negotiation between the Republic of Korea and Japan for solutions to problems. Nationalist types view the problems of the Korean minority as diplomatic issues between the governments of the Democratic People's Republic of Korea and Japan. They take their cue from Pyongyang in organizing movements, and the main roles in them are invariably taken by fellow Koreans rather than Japanese.[8]

Despite these very significant differences, the three types just discussed have in common a tendency to undertake a *group* response to the various problems confronting Zainichi Koreans. In contrast, the two types on the bottom half of *Figure 3.1* – the individualist and naturalizing types – adopt an *individual* response to those problems. Individualists seek to escape from the stigma of 'alien ethnicity' via achievements that will win them a positive reputation on meritocratic terms. The naturalizers seek the same end by approximating as closely as possible to the Japanese majority in hopes that their ethnicity will pass entirely unnoticed.

Definitions of ethnicity and nationality

My second point relates to definitions of ethnicity and nationality. Nationalist types have a very strong awareness that their identity is founded on ethnic pride. They also have a strong belief that ethnicity and nationality should be coterminous. They would not dream of applying for Japanese nationality. Their attitude is shared, to a somewhat milder degree, by the ethnic solidarity types.

Naturalizing types take exactly the opposite view to the nationalist types. To them Korea is no more than a country where their grandparents happened to be born. Having been born and raised in Japan, they see it as a desirable thing to adopt Japanese nationality. In so doing, they believe that they can 'become Japanese.'

Individualists differ from both nationalists and naturalizers in that they reject the whole principle of affiliation in favor of individual meritocracy. They long to cast off the chains of ethnicity and nationality alike; they long to soar above these mundane affiliations, and achieve personal freedom on their own terms.

Pluralists also show a relativistic view of ethnicity and nationality, but whereas individualists would like to be *above* ethnicity and nationality, pluralists aim to operate *within* these constructs. In a sense, ethnic origins do matter to pluralists. They seek to acknowledge difference and use it as the basis for harmonious multicultural life rather than ethnic strife. The concept that 'ethnicity = nationality,' once accepted as an objective truth, is also starting to be relativized. Pluralists do not aspire to Japanese nationality under the present Japanese naturalization system. They are, however, beginning to think that the right to choose one's nationality freely should be recognized – that the Japanese government should ease naturalization procedures and admit the concept of the Japanese national who is distinctively Korean in ethnic terms. Mintōren used to have a sub-group called the *Minzoku-mei wo Torimodosu Kai* (Society for Winning Back Ethnic Names) whose members included people who had become Japanese nationals through naturalization or being the offspring of mixed marriages.[9]

The magnetic field of minority status

As I shall now demonstrate, it is possible to reduce the two-dimensional diagram of *Figure 3.1* to a one-dimensional diagram laid out in terms of the inversely proportional factors of ethnic consciousness and assimilatory consciousness.

Imagine a diagonal line running through the second and fourth quadrants of *Figure 3.1*. Label the top-left pole 'Koreans in Korea.' Label the bottom-right pole 'Japanese.' Note that these terms are in inverted commas because they refer not to actual people but to the images of those people in the minds of Zainichi Koreans – the imagined Korean admired by nationalists and

Figure 3.2   Types of young Zainichi Koreans related to ethnic consciousness

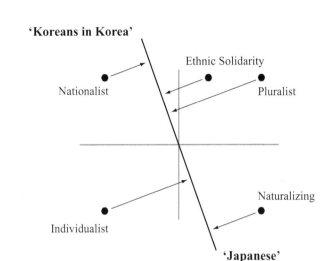

despised by naturalizers, the imagined Japanese despised by nationalists and admired by naturalizers.

The diagonal then signifies the spectrum of ethnic/assimilatory consciousness, and the five types I have described may be ranged along it as shown in *Figure 3.2.*

Reducing the picture to one dimension reminds us of one very important point: namely, that for all their attitudinal variety, all these young people live in a sort of magnetic field defined by their status as Zainichi Koreans. All of them are branded, if you like, as 'marginal people.'

Admittedly, as the graph shows, in varying degrees these youths have internalized ethnic consciousness or assimilatory conscious-ness. The fact remains, though, that even the most fervently nationalist types can never attain their ideal of 'being Korean' in the way they imagine the people of North Korea to be. Because of their upbringing in Japan, they have inevitably assimilated to a foreign culture to some degree. At the other extreme, even those who yearn for naturalization can never quite succeed in 'being

Japanese' in total conformity to their conceptual model. Even if they succeed in acquiring Japanese nationality, the pervasive discriminatory consciousness of Japanese society will always classify people of different ethnic origins as 'non-Japanese.' As they move through Japanese society, they will always have within them some awareness of being different.

In this chapter I have attempted to map out the overall range of responses by young ethnic Koreans in Japan to the problem of their identity, based on material gathered through personal interviews. I have divided those responses into five broad 'types' – pluralist, ethnic solidarity, nationalist, individualist and naturalizing.

In the following chapters I will present concrete examples of each of these types. It is of course impossible to fit real living human beings precisely into neat conceptual boxes. It is far more normal for each individual to have a unique mix of elements related to several of the different types I have outlined. I merely hope that by giving examples of informants who were particularly close to each of the types, I will be able to give the reader some idea of the multiplicity of identities to be found among young Zainichi Koreans today.

4   Learning to Live with the Japanese

The two case studies in this chapter concern active members of Mintōren (see Preface Note 7). Among all the various kinds of Zainichi Korean, these people are the most typical instances of internalization of the 'pluralist orientation' (see Chapter 3, pp. 50–1).

Case study 1: Lee Kyung-Jae

Lee Kyung-Jae was born on March 7, 1954, in Nariai-Kitanomachi, an all-Korean settlement of some thirty-five households located at Takatsuki city, in between Kyoto and Osaka. Kyung-Jae is a second-generation immigrant and holds South Korean nationality. He is the third-born of four siblings, and when interviewed (December 18, 1989) was 35 years old. After graduating from high school he founded the Takatsuki Mukuge Society (see Chapter 2, Note 3). Since then he has devoted himself to building networks to further the struggle against ethnic discrimination. Today he is still the representative of the Mukuge Society, while he makes his living working for a real estate agency.

His father, Lee Kang-Chae, was born in Cholla-Nam-Do,[1] in what is now South Korea, back in 1917. He was the oldest son of his family, a position that gave him special responsibility for inheriting the household and maintaining the family line. At around the age of eighteen, he came to Japan on his own and found employment in Osaka. He used to say the reason he came was 'because you couldn't make enough to put food on the table over there' in Korea. Lee senior adopted the Japanese surname 'Takayasu.'[2]

Kyung-Jae's mother, Chung Soon-Nam, was born in 1929, also in Cholla-Nam-Do. She was brought to Japan at the age of three by her mother, to join her father who was already there. Chung Soon-Nam never went to school. Instead she helped with the housework and worked in a factory. To this day she has difficulty reading and writing in Japanese and Korean alike.

Lee Kang-Chae and Chung Soon-Nam got married around 1947. Unable to make a living in Osaka, the couple moved to a deserted labor camp at Nariai a year or two later. Like many other camps where Koreans had been made to work constructing secret munitions factories for the Japanese war effort, the one at Nariai had plenty of empty barracks as the workers had gone back to Korea or moved to other parts of Japan, typically Osaka. Here Lee Kyung-Jae's parents scraped a living, his father working as a day laborer and junkman, while his mother took on a decidedly dangerous job operating a stone-crushing machine at a quarry.

Despised own ethnic identity

Born and raised in a Korean community, Kyung-Jae naturally became aware of the fact that he was Korean from an early age. He attended the local elementary school using the Japanese reading of his Korean name: 'Ri Keisai.'

'I suppose it was around the third grade that I got to thinking that I hated being Korean. Korean girls were getting terribly bullied, and we Koreans started getting into fights with Japanese kids who told us to piss off back to Korea when they saw us on the way to and from school. I reckon that's when it all started.

'I couldn't stand being Korean, and I couldn't stand being poor. It all got mixed in my mind with the image of my drunk and violent dad. I blamed everything on him.'

When Kyung-Jae was in fifth grade, some money disappeared from his classroom. 'We were all questioned by the teacher, but the Korean kids were kept back much longer than the others. Actually the thief wasn't one of us. Anyway, I thought to myself, it's because I'm Korean that I have to go through all this – so let's stop being Korean. I asked my mother if I could change to a Japanese alias.'

And so when Kyung-Jae moved on to the Takatsuki No.6 middle school, he did so under the name of Takayasu Keisai. 'There weren't many people who knew I was Korean, so I thought this would be a really good chance to hide the fact. I was absolutely determined to carefully conceal my Korean identity and live just like a Japanese. That meant I stopped playing with my Korean mates. Not easy, considering we all cycled to school together from Nariai. I used to peel off from the group when we reached the school's main entrance, and go bustling into the classroom on my own. I guess it would have been totally obvious to any observer what I was up to, but I actually thought I'd come up with the perfect scheme.'

In March of his first year of junior high, Kyung-Jae's troubled relationship with his ethnicity took a new turn, as he persuaded a couple of his Korean mates to join him in running away from home. 'The three of us ran away together. We just thought school was a drag. We jumped a freight train and made it as far as Hamamatsu' – 280 kilometers away – 'before we were caught and sent home. The teachers made quite a fuss about it – three Korean kids running away, you know. They figured they had to do something about it.'

Progressive teaching at middle school

At the time, the school was experimenting with 'liberation education' – trying to re-engineer classroom relations so that children subject to discrimination would be at the center of activities rather than being banished to the periphery. This entailed teaching the victims of discrimination to defend their rights and improve their self-image, as well as teaching the children in the majority group the importance of human rights. A female teacher in her twenties, Yoshioka Haruko, was given special responsibility for Kyung-Jae. He explained to me how his self-awareness changed while he was attending her class.

'I was still trying to conceal my Korean identity in my second year at junior high. One of my classmates was a Japanese kid called Y, who was relatively well trusted by the Korean kids. He wrote an item in the class journal saying "Takayasu is Korean, but he keeps trying to hide the fact. I think there's something wrong with that kind of way of life." When Mrs Yoshioka read the piece she had a word with me in private. "You!" she said, "I want you to say that you're Korean, right in front of the whole class. Or haven't you got the guts? That's kind of pathetic." I blurted out that I wasn't afraid at all…and so I was trapped into declaring my Korean identity in front of the whole class.

'All my classmates said things like "Good luck to you," and "Please live your life with pride." That really pissed me off. What was all this stuff about pride? What the hell did I have to be proud of? I was poor, I was no good at studying, I was wearing tatty clothes. "How am I supposed to live my life with pride?" I said. The whole class went really quiet. "Well then, don't say such garbage!" I shouted at them, and ran out of the class. After that I went back to my old ways: showing up late, sneaking off early, skipping classes – it was like that every day.

'While I was away, the class had a talk and decided that since I'd been made to expose my little secret like that, everyone else should do the same. So everyone in the class wrote a piece about their secrets, you know, and they were all put together in a collection called *Butchaketa Hanashi (The Truth Revealed)*. One of the Japanese kids, a boy named T, wrote a piece that went like this: "My dad makes his living as a charcoal burner. But there's not much call for charcoal these days, and so there's hardly any money coming in. My dad got drunk and got wild. Once he tried to kill the whole family. My dad's life hasn't changed since then. I hate my dad." When I read it, I realized something. It wasn't just us Koreans who were having a tough time. With friends like this, maybe I could go to school again.

'Had a few chats with my class teacher as well. I told her I hated being Korean. She said, "There's nothing wrong with being Korean. It's discrimination that's wrong." I said, "You've got it all wrong. It's because my dad's lazy that we're poor." She said, "No, no, you've got to think about this discrimination problem." That kind of thing. In the end, I did start thinking about discrimination. And from that time I somehow lost that feeling of having to hide. I felt better inside. Because I didn't have to hide.'

When Kyung-Jae graduated from Takatsuki No.6 middle school, the name called out at the graduation ceremony was his own Korean name. 'Graduating with my own name was a big thing for me. I prepared for it. I made posters, explaining that Koreans have three names – their Japanese alias, their real name, and the Japanese reading of their real name. Me and my mates went on about it in class, too, telling everyone about it.'

Kyung-Jae proceeded to a private senior high school. In another abrupt change of course, he went back to calling himself 'Takayasu Keisai.' 'In those days I had no thought of ethnic pride and all that. I just wanted to be free from discrimination, that's all, and I guess I didn't really have much awareness about my real name.'

Compared to Takatsuki No.6 middle school, the environment at senior high was totally different. There was no attempt to deal with the discrimination issue. 'In senior high, I hid and I got through undetected. The only reason I'd been able to declare my real name in junior high was because I got support from the people around me. There was no such thing at senior high. I just had this very strong feeling that I'd hate it if my identity were known, that I was frightened. My classmates often said insulting things about Koreans. "If you get into a fight with the guys from the North Korean school, they'll gang up and come after you. They're a scary bunch...eh, Takayasu?" And I'd go, "Err...guess so..." I didn't have any friends at senior high.'

Kyung-Jae says that what kept him going through school were the monthly meetings of a club that Mrs Yoshioka organized for graduates of Takatsuki No.6 middle school.

Launch of the Mukuge Society

Kyung-Jae graduated from senior high without any particular employment prospects. It is customary in Japanese senior high schools for teachers to help graduating students to find jobs or university places, but Kyung-Jae was excluded from this service because of his ethnicity.

While working at various part-time jobs, he launched the Mukuge Society in August of his graduation year. 'Here's how I saw things at the time. My younger Korean mates were in junior high, smoking cigarettes, skipping classes, and getting into trouble with the police. My older mates were a bad lot too. And then there was my lot. Things were just carrying on the same, generation after generation. So I figured that although some of the Japanese teachers were doing their best, we needed to make a place where Korean kids could get together and educate each other.'

The Mukuge Society's activities included studying the history of Japan's invasion of Korea, and interviewing local first-generation immigrants about their experiences. The interviews were compiled in a pamphlet entitled *Kon'nan-shite Ikite-kitan'ya (This Is How We've Been Living)*. However, it was no easy matter getting the society established. There were endless setbacks and fresh starts. 'Attendances gradually got smaller and smaller and smaller, until it reached the point where I'd go to meetings and no one else would come. Often I'd just pass the time reading a book all on my own, and come home feeling pretty lonely.'

In the course of overcoming these obstacles, Kyung-Jae acquired an acute awareness of the importance of rooting the movement firmly in the local community and basing the struggle on self-help principles.

'Thinking about how to liberate myself from discrimination in my own way of life, I came to realize that I would be untrue to myself if I didn't base my thinking on Nariai. Since I'd been born and raised in Nariai, you see, I would be a pretty funny sort of activist if I didn't pay special attention to the people there. At the time, Nariai had no kind of infrastructure worth mentioning. The houses were jerry-built and the whole place was insanitary. I wanted to do something for that village. When I got downhearted with campaigning alone, I went to Mindan and to Chongryun. I'd say: "I want to do something about the public utilities in Nariai. Won't you work with me?" I got the same answer from both places: "Mr Lee, it's no use bothering about little problems like that. We don't need the government of Japan to look after our local environment, because we've got a magnificent country all of our own." At last the scales fell from my eyes. It was no good relying on somebody else. I would simply have to do it myself.'

And so Kyung-Jae battled on, sometimes all on his own. I asked him where on earth he got the energy from. Kyung-Jae said he didn't really know himself, but he mentioned a couple of possibilities.

'Maybe it came from guilt feelings over the grudge I had against my parents. I always hated them for giving birth to me as a Korean. I hated being Korean, I hid the fact as well as I could, and I hated my parents for making me Korean. It would have been a bit more understandable if I'd hated my parents for beating me, but the real thing I had against them was making me a Korean – absolutely ridiculous from their point of view. The realization that I was wrong about that was one of the things that made me tick.

'Another thing was my sense of responsibility toward my younger Korean friends. I kept telling them not to give in to discrimination, and I felt that gave me a certain responsibility not to give in myself. It would be one thing for *them* to say, "We can't do it, so that's it," but quite another for *me* to throw in the towel after all that talk about fighting the good fight...well, I'd have been a laughing stock. I said that after I went on to senior high the next generation of Korean kids at middle school were all bad boys, right? Well, Mrs Yoshioka came and asked me if I couldn't say something to them. I wrote a letter, saying that bad behavior by Koreans only made Japanese happy, because it confirmed their prejudices...something like that. You know what? She just said to me: "I'm sending these words straight back to you." How could I play the high and mighty like in that letter, when I wasn't even taking the cause seriously in my own life? That was her point. The way my words came back to me like that – well, let's say it had an impact.'

In June 1978, Kyung-Jae started a club for the Korean children living in the Nariai region. 'At the time I was working at the quarry, loading stones onto a dump truck and driving them off. The moment work finished, I'd rush home, get my supper down as fast as I could, and then go off to the children's club at half-past-six. Then from January 1979 I quit the quarry job to devote more time to the Mukuge Society. Mornings I worked at a factory run by another Korean. From lunchtime onward I was an activist. The following year I quit the morning job and worked full-time for the Mukuge Society.'

From this time on, his circle of fellow activists started growing, with Japanese as well as Korean youths getting involved. The Mukuge Society took on projects ranging from children's clubs at schools and in ethnic Korean communities, through classes in Korean language and ethnic music and dance, to classes in reading and writing Japanese for first-generation immigrants who had never mastered the skill.

Having thus established its credentials, the Mukuge Society took to engaging in negotiations with the local authorities, winning several concessions. In 1979 the nationality clause was struck off the official list of employment conditions for public officials working for Takatsuki city. Four years later, in 1983, Takatsuki employed its first non-Japanese nationals, when two Koreans working at Mukuge-sponsored children's clubs were put on the town payroll as public employees. Then in 1985, the Mukuge Society's ethnic education section (one branch of its multifaceted activities) was officially recognized by the local Education Committee as an Educational Project for Zainichi Koreans in Takatsuki, and was granted a degree of financial support. By 1989 the Mukuge Society had seven full-time workers. As well as the two full-time public employees, two more (one Korean and one Japanese) had part-time public employee status. Thus the Society's activities had shifted from being purely voluntary to being partially government-sponsored.

Doing business as a Korean

After all these years campaigning against discrimination, what sort of identity has Kyung-Jae formed for himself today? I asked him for his thoughts on such matters as the ethnic name and language issues and national affiliation.

Ever since he launched the Mukuge Society, Kyung-Jae has strictly gone by his own name. 'It wasn't something I wanted to do as a fundamental matter of principle. But I knew I had to fight against discrimination. And I figured it wouldn't look good – a Korean activist using a Japanese name! People in general just wouldn't think I was Korean.' Nowadays, however, Kyung-Jae is thoroughly committed to his Korean name.

In 1988 Kyung-Jae ceased full-time activism and got a job at a real estate agency run by a fellow Korean where he still works today.[3] Many Koreans, even those who are strongly committed to their Korean name, still use an alias for business purposes, simply because it is much harder to do business if one is known to be Korean. But not Kyung-Jae.

'When I show my business card to a client, you should see the way their face changes. They're really surprised. Well...the company has managed to build up a bit of a reputation, so it doesn't damage business too much if there happens to be a Korean guy called Lee Kyung-Jae sitting next to the Japanese president. What the clients don't know is that in fact the president is *also* Korean – unlike myself, he insists on using a Japanese name! His kids are members of the Mukuge children's club...

'Anyway, there are times when I wonder whether it's really OK to hand over a card with a Korean name on it. If some deal worth hundreds of millions of yen fell through because of it and the firm lost out on some major profits, there'd be hell to pay. So I always feel kind of nervous when I get out my business card. Still, I wouldn't think of going back to my alias. I want to create the kind of business environment where people realize that if you're honest enough to use your own name, there's all the more reason to trust you.'

On national affiliation, Kyung-Jae has this to say: 'If you ask me about my fatherland, or motherland or what have you, I guess I'd have to say that for me, it's Japan. Korea is a foreign country. I go there as a tourist. My hometown is Nariai. I'm not really interested in the question of Korean reunification. I'm not saying it isn't necessary. I just mean it doesn't much matter that much to me personally. I think it's because the Koreans in Japan have spent so much time and effort arguing about that kind of thing that they're still so deprived of rights here in this country. I think the question of Korean reunification should be left to people actually living in Korea – the people who've been separated from each other. The Koreans here in Japan haven't been separated. They go on about Mindan and Chongryun and all that, but the fact is they all go out drinking together. OK, so they may have differences of opinion – Japanese people disagree with each other about all sorts of things too. But no one talks about Japanese people being "divided," eh?'[4]

On the language issue, Kyung-Jae's feelings have changed over the years. 'The first time I went to South Korea, I didn't feel the slightest bit embarrassed about being unable to speak the language. To me it was a foreign language, so why should I be able to speak it? But now I *do* want to get good at Korean. Right now, even if I do go to South Korea, I just go around reading the Japanese guidebook wherever I go. I feel I'd like to do better than that...learn a lot of Korean and explore the country from off the beaten track a bit. These days I can speak a bit of Korean, but if you think that's turned me into a raving Korean nationalist, you're quite wrong. I just think it's kind of classy to be able to speak another language besides Japanese.'

Japanese nationality as right, not privilege

In 1982, Lee Kyung-Jae refused fingerprinting. This led to his being arrested and charged in 1985. On November 2, 1989, the Supreme Court dismissed the charges against him as part of an amnesty for people accused of minor offenses, following the death of Emperor Hirohito. For Kyung-Jae, who is still campaigning against discrimination, the next step is to win a full set of citizens' rights for Zainichi Koreans.

'I've never considered naturalization myself. But these days I'm thinking it would be good to campaign for Japanese nationality to be made available as a right to all permanent residents. It should be something that the individual can choose if he or she wishes. Not something that you have to grovel for, as if it were a special favor. I took part in the human rights movement against finger-printing. If as an extension of that movement we managed to get Japanese nationality offered to us as a right, I guess I'd say Yeah – give it to me, too. If you could get your human rights by getting nationality, I'd agree to it. But I've got my pride, you see, and if I'm told to bow my head to get through the gate that leads to Japanese nationality – well, that makes me angry. It also makes me angry if we all have to go through the gate together. People who want to go through that gate should go through; people who don't want to shouldn't have to. I'm calling on Japanese society to become that sort of place.'

Kyung-Jae naturally wants political rights that include partic-ipation in national elections. 'At Mintōren meetings, I sometimes say, "Why shouldn't Japan have a prime minister called Lee Kyung-Jae?" People become members of parliament through elections, right? And elections are expressions of the will of the people. So who's to say there's anything outrageous about a foreigner becoming a member of parliament or prime minister? Winning an election means that the voters believe you're the right person for the job, so what's wrong with that?'[5]

Case study 2: Lee Chang-Jae

I interviewed Lee Chang-Jae on September 23, 1989, the day before his twenty-fourth birthday. He was born on September 24, 1965, in Yasunaka, a predominantly Burakumin district of Yao city, Osaka prefecture. Out of 1,200 households in Yasunaka, just over 100 were ethnic Korean.

Chang-Jae is a third-generation Korean, holding South Korean nationality. His grandparents migrated to Japan from the southern Korean province of Kyongsang-Buk-Do, but he knows little of the circumstances surrounding the move. His paternal grandfather died when Chang-Jae was in the first grade, and his grandmother returned to North Korea with one of her granddaughters, and subsequently died there.[6]

Nor did Chang-Jae learn anything about the migration from his father. 'My *abeoji* (father) is a man of few words. He has nothing to say when he's around the house. Only "I'm home," "Give me some supper" and "I'm going to bed." It's always been like that.'

His father was born in Yamaguchi prefecture in 1933. 'So I guess my grandfather must have come over on his own initiative; it can't have been forced migrant labor.'[7] Chang-Jae's grandfather started off as a coalminer, later becoming a woodcutter. His son, Chang-Jae's father, initially followed him into the latter line of work. Today Chang-Jae's father is a casual construction worker.

Chang-Jae knows equally little about how his maternal grandparents came to Japan. His mother was born in Shimane prefecture in 1941. Her parents were already on the elderly side when she was born, so from an early age she had to cook for the family and generally look after her parents. She ended up going to elementary school a year late, and even when she did start going to school her absences were frequent.

Chang-Jae's parents were brought together by an arranged marriage.[8] After the birth of their first child, a daughter, they fell into debt and had to leave their home in Yamaguchi prefecture, fleeing to Osaka. There were many more moves to come. 'Apparently they moved a dozen times or more. And I've heard from my mother that because it wouldn't do for the Japanese living around them to discover that they were Korean, they couldn't even let my grandfather out of the house. They just kept moving from one rented house to another, until they finally settled in Yasunaka, where I was born. Here the jobs were badly paid but at least there were plenty of them, besides which it was easy to borrow rice. I think it was a convenient place to live for them.'[9]

The Tokebi Children's Club

Until the fifth grade, Chang-Jae went by the Japanese pseudonym of Murata Katsuo. Indeed, his whole family was living under the Murata pseudonym.

He was aware of his Korean identity at least by the first grade. When school lunch was served, he casually used the word *sudkarak* to refer to a spoon, only to find that no one understood him. It used to be quite common for ethnic Korean families to mix in a few words of Korean with the Japanese spoken in the household, especially where the first-generation grandparents were living with the family. Chang-Jae had simply not realized that *sudkarak* was not a Japanese word.

'When I saw that no one understood the word I thought, "I mustn't use this word,"' he recalls. 'Before that, I really thought I was Japanese. People used to call me "Katchan,"[10] just as if I were a little Japanese boy. There was one difference, though – the ceremony we used to worship our ancestors was a Korean-style *Jesa*.[11] So I felt that there was something kind of different in the atmosphere.'

Chang-Jae's people were poor. 'When I was in the second grade, I went to play with a friend from an ordinary district outside the buraku. What amazed me was the house. It had a gate. I was also surprised to find that the mother was at home all day. And I vividly remember the cake she gave us.'

Chang-Jae has three sisters, two older than him and one younger. At the time of our interview, one of his older sisters, Bok-Mi, was studying in South Korea; later she would serve as guide on the trip to South Korea described at the start of Chapter 2. The other older sister, Chung-Mi, was an instructor at the Tokebi Children's Club, a local group teaching Korean children their ethnic language and culture (see below). Chang-Jae's younger sister, Jik-Mi, was at university.

'Looking back on our childhood, I think my two older sisters really hated being Korean. I myself wasn't bothered about it that much. I came along just as a great generational change was happening. The forerunner of the present Tokebi Children's Club was started when I was in third grade. Every day straight after class, I would go to the Buraku Children's Club, and then I'd go to Tokebi in the evening. There I was taught not to be ashamed of being Korean. My older sisters never had the benefit of that, and they desperately tried to escape from anti-Korean bullying at school. Even so, there were a lot of tears.

'My feelings and those of my older sisters were fundamentally different. They started out different. For my sisters there was a long, heavy period of darkness. When we were at elementary school, there was this atmosphere that you sensed right from the first year, that you mustn't let anyone find out that you're Korean. My second-oldest sister was two grades above me, so she was in the fifth grade when the Tokebi Club was started. I was still in the third grade, and those two years made all the difference. I think those five years she went through before the Club started were really hard to bear – because you just wouldn't hear people saying things like "It's OK to be Korean." You'd only hear negative stuff. There was discrimination absolutely everywhere in those days. It was thought perfectly natural at school. Even the teachers were at it.

'The sister immediately above me didn't learn to live with pride in her Korean blood until she went to senior high school. That was when she started using her real name. And my oldest sister only changed when she went to university.'

The Buraku Children's Club, which Chang-Jae mentions, was run by the *Buraku Kaihō Dōmei*. (Buraku Liberation League),[12] in an attempt to inculcate the ability to resist discrimination in Burakumin children. The Tokebi Children's Club, which made such an impact on Chang-Jae and his sisters, was founded in 1974 by a group lead by a 20-year-old man called Suh Jung-Woo, who today is chairman of the Human Rights Association for Koreans in Japan (see Preface, Note 7). It was a move based on awareness of the acute need for ethnic education for Korean children in Yasunaka. The Club started off meeting in a single room in an old tumbledown tenement. It is still being run today, in an old hall that it inherited from a local youth club run by the Buraku liberation movement. The name *Tokebi* comes from a creature of Korean mythology, described by Suh Jung-Woo as 'playful, possessed of superhuman power and with an impish tendency to make trouble for those in authority.'

'At the Buraku Children's Club, I was just another Burakumin kid. People called me "Murata." When I went to the Tokebi Club, people called me "Chang-Jae." I was always stuck between the two…but you get used to it, you know. "Chang-Jae" here…"Murata" there. Korean here…Japanese there. But I felt most relaxed at the Tokebi Club. In the end I guess I just felt more open when all the other kids were Korean too.'

Chang-Jae's friends from the Tokebi Club took care to call him 'Murata' when they saw him at school. 'There was an unspoken understanding. Everyone understood very well that it wouldn't do to call each other by our real names at school.' Even so, word did get out eventually. 'When I was in fourth grade, a couple of kids from outside the buraku – kids I didn't know at all – came up to me and started taunting me for being Korean – "*Chōsen, Chōsen.*" I just said, "Yeah well, what about it?" The bullying didn't work on me, so they lost interest, I guess. But there was another girl in my class who got it real bad. "*Chōsen, Chōsen.*" It cut me up. She was crying, see, but I couldn't do anything to help. I was only just strong enough to look after myself.'

When Chang-Jae told one of the instructors at the Tokebi Club about his failure to intervene in the bullying incident at the school, the instructor bombarded him with challenging questions. 'He said, "Are you a Burakumin? Or are you a Korean? When you go to that Burakumin Children's Club, just what are you? What kind of discrimination are you getting? Anti-Burakumin discrimination? Or anti-Korean discrimination?" After that, I remember being sat down on a *tatami* mat in front of the Burakumin kids and saying, "From today, I'm using my real name. Please call me Lee Chang-Jae." Crying, you know. I declared my real name through the tears.'[13]

Chang-Jae subsequently made a similar announcement at his elementary school. In the fifth grade he and a classmate, Son Soo-Gil, declared their Korean identity and asked to be called by their Korean names in a declaration that was shown all round the school on closed-circuit television.[14] 'We did feel anxious that we might lose friends, but we had made up our minds that come what may, we would insist on using our real names from now on.'

Even among the Korean children attending the Tokebi Children's Club, Chang-Jae and Soo-Gil were in a minority. Most of them did not use their real names at school. 'For one thing, their parents wouldn't approve. They'd say, "That kind of thing'll only get you into trouble. You'll do much better for yourself if you use a Japanese name and make like a Japanese." For the parents, who knew what it was like living in a discriminatory society, the idea of using one's real name was quite ridiculous. My friend Son's parents were opposed, too. But mine weren't. They were kind of unusual parents, and they just said, "It's your life, so live it the way you want to. If you want to use your real name, why shouldn't you?" And that was that.'

The two boys' resolve was strengthened by the support they received from the Burakumin children among whom they lived. 'I think I've become what I am today because I've always lived as a Korean among Japanese. If I'd lived in an all-Korean environment, I rather doubt I'd ever have got out of it. I might have got on OK in Korean company, but I reckon I'd have carried on concealing my identity whenever I emerged into the outside world.

'When we were in junior high school, we used to talk things over with the Burakumin kids. By day, we'd play our hearts out together. By night, we'd talk. I can remember saying to them, sometime around midnight, "You guys don't have a clue what it's like being Korean!" And they'd say the same kind of thing back to us. Everyone crying, you know. They had their troubles, we had ours, and between us we kind of stimulated each other, you know.'

Trying times

To Lee Chang-Jae today, his old Japanese pseudonym is no more than a relic of the past. 'I've forgotten it,' he says. 'I've completely forgotten it.' But forgetting was not something that came to him easily.

In junior high, dating Japanese girls was a problem. 'I wanted to ring up a Japanese girl at her house, but I just couldn't. I couldn't bear to imagine saying "It's Lee here" on the phone, and someone from her family saying "There's some strange kid on the phone," or something like that. They definitely would have said something like that, you know.'

Another stressful occasion for Chang-Jae was when the subject of Korea was raised in school social studies classes. 'I don't know if it was shyness or what, but several times when the teacher mentioned "Korea," I suddenly felt my stomach tightening …knowing that everybody would turn and stare at me. In my heart I knew that Koreans were despised. I also knew that because I'd declared my real name I had to stand up and fight against discrimination…and yet somehow the pressure seemed to be more intense than if it were just about that. If at the time I'd really felt proud to be a Korean, I guess I could have held my head up high. But the fact was we *were* despised, we *were* poor, and I really had not the slightest idea as to what I was supposed to be proud of.'

Chang-Jae proceeded to a public senior high school. He was separated from his Korean and Burakumin friends alike, and was suddenly on his own. 'The pressure that came from using my real name was intense. When we introduced ourselves on the first day, I said, "I am Lee Chang-Jae" – and I suddenly felt these cold stares coming at me from all directions.

'One time someone from another class, I'd no idea who, threw a little balloon full of water from an upper story, and I got covered in water. "Lee, come here!" someone said. I was scared stiff. Still, I went up the stairs, determined to somehow put my man down if it came to a fight. I opened the door and said, "Who did that? Who was it? Come on, step forward!" Out came this pretty tough looking guy. He looked like he could knock me out with his first punch. I thought uh-oh, I've really blown it this time. But I got lucky. There was a kid in that class who kind of liked me and he calmed things down. "Hey, hey, cool it fellahs…" Yep. I was real lucky.'

Hard to be a postman

When he reached the third year of senior high school, Chang-Jae came up against the barrier of employment discrimination.

'At the start of my third year, I asked my class teacher if there was any chance of a job for an ethnic Korean like myself. He just shook his head and said, "Hmm, it's kind of tough for Koreans…"

So I thought: I'm in trouble here, I've got to do something about it. As it happened, a mate of mine from the buraku, admittedly a Japanese, had just got a job with the post office. I thought that was a pretty good job and I wouldn't have minded going for it myself, but postal workers were public servants and I knew you had to be a Japanese national to get that kind of job, so I figured it was a non-starter. I thought I might try and go to vocational school to learn a skill, or just go and work on a building site like my old man.

'But then Suh Jung-Woo (founder of the Tokebi Club, see above) said to me, "You want to be a postman, right? Well, why don't you give it a try?" I told him there was no point, because of the nationality clause. I told him I didn't want to fight some battle that I could never win. I told him there was no knowing how many years it might take before the nationality clause was removed.

'At the time, my family was up to its neck in debts, and I needed to start earning as fast as possible. Then it turned out that Suh Jung-Woo had been talking to my friend Son Soo-Gil about becoming a postman, too, and Son had agreed that he would go for it. I told him he was an idiot. "There's a nationality clause," I said. "It's all very well wanting to be a postman, but they'll never let you!" He disagreed. "It'll be OK," he said. "They'll scrap the nationality clause." "I'm damned if I'll wait for that to happen," I said. "I'm getting straight down to work." That's how I felt in those days, you see.

'The toughest thing to bear was when one of the girls in the buraku started asking me why I didn't apply to be a postman. "There's a nationality clause," I said, yet again. "But I thought you'd been fighting against discrimination all this time," she said. "Who else is going to fight for the scrapping of the post office nationality clause if you won't?" The words came to me like a tolling bell. "We'll support you," she said. "We won't just abandon you." Well...being spoken to like that by a Japanese, what could I do? At last a kind of resolve started to harden within me. After all, I would have to give it a try. Another thing that helped make up my mind was thinking about the kind of lives my parents were living. The lives of Koreans in the settlement were just all wrong. Why? Because of these regulations banning them from public employment. Add in the fact that private enterprises wouldn't employ Koreans either, and what's left? Only this: that the way things stood, the children of the Tokebi Club would end up facing exactly the same discrimination as my parents' generation. And the thought really did hurt.'

When Chang-Jae and Soo-Gil tried to take the post office exam in the fall of their final year at senior high, the examiners refused to even process their applications. 'So we started a petition campaign in the school, for the scrapping of the nationality clause. The response was incredible. I was moved to tears by the support from the Japanese kids. Out of about 1,000 students in the whole school, 800 or so signed the petition. Some girl that I didn't know at all went around persuading her friends to sign up. "You know that kid called Lee," she'd say, "well, he can't get a job at the post office because of the nationality clause. That won't do, right?" My fellow third years signed up in no time. Son and myself raised funds for the campaign by selling ballpoint pens with "Association Embracing Lee and Son" written on them. A hundred yen each. Everyone bought them.'

After graduating from senior high, Chang-Jae and Soo-Gil worked at the post office as part-timers (to which the nationality clause did not apply), while continuing their campaign against the nationality clause.

'We didn't make much progress. We thought of giving up. But then the Japanese kids from the buraku would get us fired up again with their encouragement. In the end, one of my friends from the buraku went with us all the way to Tokyo. He said to this person from the Ministry of Posts and Telecommunications, "I was brought up together with these guys, so what's the difference between me and them?" He was weeping as he spoke. I was so happy. I'm pretty sure I'd have lost that battle if I'd been on my own.'

The two friends graduated from senior high in March 1984. On May 24 that same year, the nationality clause was abolished nationwide.[15] The two young men commenced intense preparations for the post office exam to be held in October, with the assistance of teachers from their old school. 'We were desperate to pass. If we failed the exam after all that, we'd have been so embarrassed we'd have had to leave town. Honestly, I've never studied so hard. Memorizing characters, writing compositions, brushing up my reading skills … I hated reading books, but I went all out for it.'

Chang-Jae and Soo-Gil both passed.

Solidarity within the post office

In April 1985, Lee Chang-Jae and Son Soo-Gil started work at the post office in Sakai, a large city just south of Osaka. 'At first, the other workers were excessively polite to us. They called us "Mr Lee" and "Mr Son."[16] Among themselves the Japanese staff never called younger workers "Mister," they just used the name on its own. It was like we were a kind of boil or swelling, that had to be handled with extra caution. I asked around among the boys, and learned that indeed, the management had ordered them to call me and Son "Mister." I raised the matter at the union. I said it felt strange being called "Mr Lee." I asked them to stop it and call me "Chang-Jae" instead. These days everyone calls me "Chang-Jae."

'In that first year, out of 200-odd delivery men taken on by the Kinki Bureau of Post and Telecommunications, there were five Koreans including ourselves. The others were people who'd seen flyers advertising the fact that foreign nationals were now allowed to apply for delivery jobs. We went to see them. They said it was kind of a relief to think that there were other Korean kids beside themselves, out there delivering the mail. We felt that way too, so we suggested we might as well get together once a month or so. And that was the start of the "Association of Korean Postal Workers to Consider the Problems of Zainichi Koreans." I became the group's representative.

'Members of the Association have to work hard at their jobs, and on that basis, speak their minds. A person's words carry far more weight if that person is working to the best of his ability. If you don't work properly, and just laze around and complain all the time, your words end up working against you. On the basis of that principle, we work toward creating a workplace where we can work under our own names without fear of discrimination. We welcome any Korean who wants to join so long as they support this basic principle.

'Because you know, there were a couple of discrimination incidents at the post office in August 1984, just before we sat the exam. Graffiti saying "Koreans go home!" appeared on the lavatory walls at two post offices, at Kadoma and Moriguchi, the same slogan in both places. The workers' response was incredible. About 200 of them went to lobby the management. "How come this has happened when you've just abolished the nationality clause?" they asked. "It's because you've been shutting out foreign residents all this time, right? Scrapping the clause has just brought that racist consciousness to the surface!"

'It was a shock to hear of a discrimination incident at the post office, the very place where we were trying to get employed. But when we saw the struggle of the Japanese workers with our own eyes, we were more moved by that than dismayed by the original incidents.'

Chang-Jae sees two main challenges now facing him. One is to increase the number of Koreans working for the post office. With cooperation from high-school teachers, the Association of Korean Postal Workers holds study meetings to help Korean youths prepare for the exam for mail delivery staff. As of 1992 there were twenty-six foreign permanent residents working for the Kinki Bureau of Post and Telecommunications, out of just thirty-one employed by the post office nationwide. As of April 1993 the Association of Korean Postal Workers had nineteen members, including one Korean who had acquired Japanese nationality. Fifteen of them were using their ethnic Korean names in the workplace.

The other big challenge for Chang-Jae is to get rid of the nationality clause that still applies to clerical jobs inside the post office, as opposed to mail delivery jobs (see Note 15). Post office regulations allow holders of delivery jobs to take an exam to enable them to transfer to internal jobs after three years' service. To date, however, Chang-Jae has yet to win permission to take this exam.

'Together with the Japanese'

How does Lee Chang-Jae view his own identity today?

On the name issue, he says, 'Using your real name means telling everyone that you're Korean, right? So there is a certain tension there. I don't deny that, but in another sense, it's kind of easy to live under your own name. You get a straight response from other people. I think people who hide their identity actually end up on the receiving end of more discrimination. They get to hear people close to them bad-mouthing Koreans, or they live in fear of being exposed by some particularly racist person. Hiding your identity doesn't free you from discrimination.

'In the end, hiding your identity is very stressful, and leaves you vulnerable to attack. Someone comes up to a Korean kid who's hiding the fact and whispers in their ear, "You're Korean, right? I'm gonna tell everyone!" – and the kid runs a mile. And when a racist person sees that, oh what fun he has. But if a racist tries to hurt someone who openly displays their Zainichi identity, it's not nearly so much fun. They resist, and they're much harder to bully. If someone at school had said to me, "Chang-Jae, you're Korean, I'm gonna tell everyone," I would just have said, "You don't have to tell everyone, 'cause they already know. I'm gonna get you back by telling everyone that you've been trying to threaten me."'

On the nationality issue, Chang-Jae has this to say. 'No way will I naturalize. Then again, if the system changed, if Japan had a government that would let me take Japanese nationality with no limitations, with no fingerprinting, no personal investigation, with my name unchanged, on the basis that "this Korean kid called Lee Chang-Jae is a citizen of Japan"…well, I might go for it. After all, I'm here for the duration. I've got nowhere else to go. I don't even know how I'd make a living if I went to South Korea.' And Lee Chang-Jae laughs out loud.

'My mother country? That's a tough one. I guess Korea, since my grandparents were born there? If you ask me what my own country is, though, I'd say Japan. Yasunaka, in Yao, is my hometown.'

Lee Chang-Jae has many Japanese friends. 'I like the slogan "Together with the Japanese." All this time, Japanese and Koreans have been living together, working together, building society together, and it's that society that we've built from which us Koreans have been excluded. We want to turn that society into one of genuine togetherness among equals. What I'm saying is, let's proceed on the basis of mutual acceptance, including acceptance of our differences. After all, the Japanese themselves are only made to think that they're "all the same" at a superficial level. In reality, each of them is different from the others. In the process of building a society out of a disparate bunch of individuals, they've been bewitched by the concept of sameness and lost awareness of their own position. I hope that by making them aware of our presence in their society we Koreans will help them to gain a realization of that. I'm taking on the Korean issue because it's a struggle to enable myself to be myself. That's where it all starts from, don't you think?'

5 For the Sake of Our Fellow Zainichis

The most representative examples of Zainichi Koreans who have internalized the 'ethnic solidarity orientation' are to be found among members of the Korean Youth Association in Japan (KYAJ), known in Japanese as *Zai-Nihon Daikanminkoku Seinen-kai* (*Zainichi Kankoku Seinenkai* for short, or just *Seinenkai*: see Chapter 3, pp. 55–6).

Case study 3: Kim Dae-Won

Kim Dae-Won was born on February 13, 1967, in Tokyo's Sumida ward. He is a third-generation Zainichi Korean, holding South Korean nationality. When I interviewed him, on August 11, 1991, he was 24 years of age and working as head of the Publicity Department at the Tokyo Regional Headquarters of the KYAJ. He was subsequently promoted to chairperson of the Tokyo Regional HQ in the spring of 1993.

Dae-Won says he has heard that his paternal grandfather came over to Japan immediately after Japan annexed Korea. 'He was living in a village on Cheju island, working as a teacher of Chinese classics and as a sort of judicial scrivener. But he found he couldn't make a basic survival income that way, so he came over to Osaka in hopes of making some money. After the war he moved to Tokyo and opened a shop selling *jeogori* (ethnic Korean dresses) in Asakusa. Then he got into money-lending, land-leasing and so on, and he seems to have done pretty well for himself. He was a real stern, feudalistic, old *halabeoji* (grandfather).[1] He was a great believer in tradition and he taught his grandchildren manners very strictly indeed.

'It was the same with my *abeoji* (father). He didn't react to anti-Korean discrimination by trying to hide in a corner – no way. His attitude is "Yes, I'm Korean. Want to make something of it?" He's always boasting about how he's made his way through life with his head held high. Back in the late fifties and early sixties he was a money-lender on the Ginza[2] and got to be quite an influential man, but after a while he got into trouble with too many defaulters. Later he went into coffee shops, cabarets, etc., but those businesses flopped too. These days he's running a small plastics factory. He's pretty feudalistic as well. A real stern defender of tradition. Enough to make you wonder whether he really is a second-generation Zainichi. He's more like a first-generation type, really.

'My *eomeoni* (mother) was brought up in a wealthy household, and had things pretty easy compared to the hardship other Korean migrants had to endure. She graduated from the senior high section of the Tokyo South Korean School. The marriage with my father was an arranged one. Again, she's a person to whom manners and education really matter. She's a traditional wife-and-mother type, who sees a woman's role as being to set up a household, support her menfolk, and defend the family at all costs. If you ask me, she's a typical Cheju woman.'[3]

Dae-Won's family sets great store by its lineage. *Jesa* ceremonies of respect for the ancestors are held fifteen or sixteen times a year (see Chapter 2, Note 22). Dae-Won is the first-born son among three siblings and therefore will inherit responsibility for maintaining the *Jesa*. 'I've been taught about the importance of maintaining the *Jesa* since I was small, and I am determined to firmly defend that tradition.'

Bullied at school

There were no other Koreans in the region of Tokyo where Dae-Won was born and brought up. Although his grandfather was an enthusiastic member of Chongryun, Dae-Won and his brothers were sent to a Japanese school rather than a Chongryun-affiliated Korean school. 'My father figured that since we were living in Japan, it would be better for us to go to a Japanese school and try to get into a good university. But I recall that when I was around the third or fourth year of elementary school we had a home tutor from the North Korean school who came to teach the *uri mal* (Korean: literally 'our language') to me and my younger brother.

My father said that one must learn the *uri mal*. "A Korean who doesn't know the language is not a true Korean."'

But then one day the teacher from the Korean school suddenly stopped coming. The reason was that Dae-Won's father had switched allegiance from Chongryun to Mindan.[4]

Dae-Won's Japanese pseudonym was 'Miyata Masayuki.' He used this name until fall of his first year at university. But he first became clearly aware of his Korean identity much earlier, in his second year at elementary school. 'Before that, I had this vague feeling that there was something different about me, but I hadn't actually realized that I wasn't Japanese. Then one day my mother took me aside and said, "I've got something to say to you, so listen carefully." I sat there, stiffly upright and really nervous, while she said: "You are not Japanese. You are Korean. From now on, you must live your life with the pride of a true Korean. Japanese kids may wander around, drinking juice in the street and showing off their bad manners, but you must under no circumstances do such things. If you do, people will point at you and say you're doing it because you're Korean. Come what may, you must spend your days in ways that do not bring shame upon you."

'So the next day, I just innocently went up to my Japanese classmates and said, "Excuse me, I'm not Japanese. I'm Korean. Please carry on being my friend." Alas, this raised the curtain on a tragedy. I was bullied unremittingly until about the fifth grade of elementary school. I took physical blows, I took wounding insults, every day was a bitter struggle for me. It would start in the morning, the moment I got to school. "Oy, Korean!" I'd be surrounded, I'd be beaten up. I had some pride, so I did my very best not to cry, but in the end I couldn't bear it and I just cried and cried. Couldn't stop the quivering lip, you know. It was like that every morning.

'My mother was furious. She rang up the parents of the kids who were bullying me, time and again. "What kind of education are you giving your child, that he picks on people just because they've got different nationality!" She spoke to the teachers at school about it, too.'

For Dae-Won himself, this was a period when being Korean was a hateful thing. 'I used to have fights with my mother about it. I'd say, "It's all very well telling me to take pride in being Korean, but how can I be proud when I'm in a state like this?" She'd get angry with me. She'd say "Well you *are* Korean, whether you like it or not, so you'll just *have* to take pride in it!"'

Sympathy from Korean seniors

'My class teacher in the fifth and sixth years of elementary school was an elderly lady who looked out for me a bit. When the subject of the Korean peninsula came up in social studies classes, she'd say, "This is Miyata's country, but it's quite wrong to discriminate against someone just because they're from a different country." After that I didn't get picked on so much, and I started to have more self-confidence. I also started to express opinions positively in class. When we did drama in class, I got to write the script and direct the play myself, telling all the other kids what to do like I was running the whole show.

'I used to go to the library, hunting around for adult-type books. I was learning my history. The annexation of Korea, the forced migrant labor program, the campaign to change Korean people's names, and so on. Even while I was still in elementary school, I could already debate those matters as well as the next man.'

When Dae-Won had finished fifth grade, his father started taking him to Korean-language lessons organized by Mindan. 'There were some older boys from the Korean Youth Association in Japan there, and they really made a fuss over me. I only went there once a week, but I really looked forward to it – not so much because of learning the language, but because of being spoiled silly by the older boys. Some of them were 27 or 28 years old. They'd come to the language class after work, and they'd say, "Hey, it's Dae-Won. Glad you came, little guy. Let's go and have something good to eat, eh?" As well as the weekly classes, I was always sure to be there when the KYAJ held a summer-camp or a baseball game or whatever. I carried on with the KYAJ until the first year of senior high. By then I was going with the big boys on home visits to recruit new members, helping man the telephones and so on.

'But all this time, I was still going by the name of "Miyata Masayuki" and wearing the protective armor of Japanese identity at school. I just didn't want the subject of Korea even mentioned. When the history teacher started going on about "Shiragi" and

"Kudara,"⁵ I was just sitting there with my heart in my mouth, praying for the lesson to end.'

Dae-Won also concealed his identity in his relations with a Japanese girlfriend. 'I dated her as "Miyata Masayuki." She didn't know I was Korean. I kept telling myself to face up to the fact that she'd dump me the moment she found out…it was a sort of weird obsession that had me in its grip.

'The way things were, the times I spent with the big boys from the KYAJ were like an oasis for me. The times when I could be Kim Dae-Won. All the big boys called each other by their Japanese pseudonyms, but I was always called "Dae-Won."'

However, Dae-Won drifted away from the KYAJ during the course of his first year at senior high school, not to return until his freshman year at university. 'I got to feel kind of disappointed. Gradually fewer and fewer people came to the Sumida ward branch of the KYAJ. By the time I woke up to it, I was letting myself into the office with my own key, sitting around there waiting on my own, and cycling around passing out flyers for the summer-camp, also on my own. People from the Tokyo headquarters offered to help me out, but I would always turn them away. I'd say "Our branch can look after itself." Still and all, people just would not get involved. In the end I felt I just couldn't carry on any more.'

Back in the fold at nineteen

'In November of my first year at university, the KYAJ organized a thing called the "Youth Boat." This was a ride in a boat called the *Sunflower*, all the way from Kobe to Okinawa. It was planned as a real big event, with workshops on ethnic education, and with Zainichi Chinese youths and foreign exchange students among the participants.

'The chairperson of the Tokyo HQ asked if I'd like to join in, just for old times' sake, and I thought "Why not?" At least it would be a chance for a bit of travel.

'Going on that trip was what brought me back into the KYAJ fold. One thing really surprised me. I had more or less known I was Korean since I was a kid, and that my real name was Kim Dae-Won, and I could speak the language at least a little. I'd also been taught a certain amount about the *Jesa*, and Korean etiquette. I thought that was only natural. But you know, there were about 300 people on that Youth Boat, and when the participants were divided up into discussion groups, people were saying things like "I don't know my Korean name," "I can't even say hello in Korean," and even, "I couldn't care less whether I'm Korean or not." I thought, this won't do at all. I was also very impressed by a speech made by Professor Kim Yang-Ki.[6] He was arguing that ethnic Koreans should make much more use of their Korean names while living in Japan. And the sight of the Korean youths somewhat older than myself working so hard for the cause made me think I'd like to do the same myself.'

When he returned from his cruise aboard the *Sunflower*, Dae-Won finally threw away his Japanese name for good, though in Japanese company he used the Japanese reading of his Korean name – 'Kin Daigen.' 'Exposing myself by using only my real name meant that I could see who my real friends were, and also that I could live my life free of fear at last. When I was a freshman, before I went on the Youth Boat, I recall I joined some club or other, and one of the older girls there said, "Korean people are all kind of square-jawed, you know…" My heart missed a beat. She turned and looked at me. "Miyata, you've got a big face, so I reckon you could be one of them, right?" I couldn't admit it – I just shrugged my shoulders. When I started using my real name, that all changed. Someone would say, "You can't be Japanese with a name like Kin Daigen," and I'd say, "You're dead right. I'm Korean." And they'd say, "Oh, I see." True, some people did stop socializing with me when they found out, but I just thought good riddance. It spared me unnecessary trouble.'

In his sophomore year at university, Dae-Won reopened the Sumida branch of the KYAJ and became its chairperson. 'Then someone from the Tokyo HQ asked if I would do some work there as well. I immediately said I would. Pretty soon I was doing two jobs at once, working at headquarters and at the branch as well. I was at it every day. I would skip classes at university. From the age of nineteen to the present day, I have devoted myself body and soul to the KYAJ. If you took this organization away from me, I don't think I'd have anything left.'

As a schoolboy, Dae-Won wanted to become a lawyer – he was influenced by his father, who saw it as a sure route to success in life. When he got to university, Dae-Won was more interested in becoming a fashion designer, and started studying the techniques. But his activism has swept such ambitions aside. 'When I graduated from university, I knew that because I'd been so immersed in KYAJ affairs, I would probably end up simply taking over the plastics factory from my father. Even so, I just wanted to carry on organizing.'

Dae-Won's father was not pleased about his son's immersion in the affairs of the KYAJ. '"You can do all the organizing you like after you've made some money," he used to say. "You're only being used, so get out quick. Mindan and the KYAJ get hold of people with time on their hands just so that they can use them." I would argue back. "Mindan may be like that, but the KYAJ is different!" When I was 22, we had a thing about whether or not I should become a full-time KYAJ official. I was determined to do it; he wouldn't have it. In the end, I ran away from home. I didn't go home for about two months. And then, typically enough, my dad finally gave in.'

Dae-Won's activities as a full-time worker at the KYAJ's Tokyo HQ keep him very busy indeed. 'Being an activist isn't a nine to five job, you know. Even on ordinary days I have meetings from eight p.m. until ten-thirty or eleven. When there's some big event coming up, I often stay up all night, hammering away at the word processor. Last year, what with the protest over the 1991 question, I would be up all night standing guard over the hunger-strikers at Sukiyabashi.[7] Sometimes I don't get home for a week or a fortnight at a stretch.'

Dae-Won describes the meaning of his work for the KYAJ thus: 'What initially made me get back into the KYAJ was the thought that it just wasn't right for Korean kids to be going around not even knowing what their Korean names were. We have to create a living environment where ethnic Koreans can live in an ordinary, natural way. That is firstly a problem that has to do with the Alien Registration Law, and it was also bound up with the 1991 revision of the Agreement on Legal Status. That's why we took the initiative, handing out leaflets, organizing demonstrations, etc. And in our club activities, what we're saying to Koreans living here in Japan is: "We will change the environment for you, so you do your bit, too: don't be ashamed of being Korean, use your

Korean name openly and boldly, and do your best to get ahead in Japanese society.'"

However, all Dae-Won's self-sacrificing activities have not led to quite the results he would like. 'Ironically enough, the better the environment for Koreans becomes, the fewer people take part in KYAJ activities. If we go skiing, or to the seaside, we can get about eighty people together. Well...the Korean Youth Association in Japan has an image of being terribly political and kind of grim, right? So that kind of recreational activity is necessary to get people to come along the first time, and get rid of that grim image. But if we try and really get down to business with a serious study group, we can only get about twenty people to show up. And as for the evening socials – well, we'd like to have some serious discussion, some wider debate on organizational issues, but all we get is idle gossip. These days I'm always asking myself what the purpose of the KYAJ really is.'

One of the biggest obstacles confronting Dac-Won is the difference in thinking between himself and his parents, who still have the mindset of the Korean aristocracy or *yangban*. 'At the KYAJ culture circle we sometimes dance the *samul nori*,[8] and being a leader I naturally have to get the thing started. So I dance, and I play the *jang-gu* – a kind of drum – a little as well. Once my mother happened to see a photo of me wearing the special clothing of the *samul nori* and I really can't tell you how angry she was. "We are *yangban*!" she shouted. "You shouldn't be performing that kind of thing, you should be watching! The people who do that are *sangnom* (commoners) – it's beneath you!" I argued back: "What are you saying! In this day and age, can you still not think of human beings as equals?" A waste of breath.'

Another problem for Dae-Won is that the more deeply he becomes involved in the KYAJ, the more his personal relations tend to be limited to fellow ethnic Koreans and the fewer opportunities he has to socialize with Japanese people. 'Inevitably, the more activism I do, the less time I have to spare. These days I have hardly any Japanese friends. So I myself sometimes think I've become a rather weird kind of person. What's happened is that my field of vision has narrowed. But there's really no way of avoiding it, is there?'

What's in a name?

What about Kim Dae-Won's identity today? His experiences as a Korean activist in Japan have led him to attach particular importance to the issue of names.

'As far as I'm concerned, using one's real name counts for everything. I'd even go so far as to say that you don't need knowledge of Korean history and language, so long as you use your real name. Of course I *do* try to learn my own language and history. But none of that stuff has any meaning if you don't use your own name. Given the choice between going under a pseudonym and speaking fluent Korean, or not knowing the language but using your own Korean name, I'd say the latter was far better. I think that what shows you've got Korean blood isn't your nationality, it's your name. The name is the one issue where I won't compromise. When I was at university I used to use the Japanese reading of my name – "Kin Daigen" – in Japanese company and "Kim Dae-Won" with fellow Koreans. Not any more. These days, nobody gets to call me "Daigen"...nobody at all.'

Since May 1991, Dae-Won has been working at his father's factory by day and carrying on his KYAJ activities in the evenings. His name remains an issue. 'I want to take on the challenge of using my real name at work, too,' he says. 'My dad says I should at least use a pseudonym when doing business. He says it's in my own interests. But I won't have that. I always tell him that you have to at least try to use you own name. I've had business cards printed with my own name on them. So far the main contractor we've been supplying has been a company run by a naturalized Korean, so there hasn't been a problem, but one day I would like to do business more widely under my own name.'

Dae-Won's view of South Korea has changed over the years. 'I first went to South Korea when I was in the sixth grade at elementary school. I was taken there by the people from the Sumida KYAJ. That was the only time I was reduced to tears. When we arrived at Kimpo Airport in Seoul, I shouted "Kim Dae-Won sets foot on the soil of his mother country!" and I cried my eyes out. I think that was probably because I had a kind of image of Korea from hearing my parents speak about it. The next time I went I was in my third year at university, when I was one of nearly 700 people taking part in a Mindan-sponsored jamboree. Since then I've gone there more or less every year, as a group leader for ethnic Korean youths. But I've become disillusioned. To put it lightly, I feel like a tourist in a foreign country. A tourist who just happens to have Korean nationality. And because there are some youngsters who want to see South Korea, I take them there, that being my job. That's all. It may be the land of my *halabeoji* and *haleomeoni* (grandfather and grandmother), but it isn't my country. That's how it feels.

'Japan is the country where I was born and grew up. On the whole I like Japan. With exceptions. Such as the rather closed nature of the society. Basically what I'm doing as an activist is taking on those aspects of Japan that I dislike. So it really bugs me when problems like the legal status of Zainichi Koreans is treated as a diplomatic issue to be sorted out between the governments of Japan and the ROK. To me, problems involving Zainichi Koreans are to be counted among Japan's domestic problems and should be solved by us ethnic Koreans ourselves.

'I happen to think that nationality and ethnicity are two different things. Personally, I've never felt the slightest urge to naturalize, because there's no need for it. But if people do naturalize because of some overriding force of circumstance, and then later decide to live as ethnic Koreans, and revert to using their Korean name – or, well, I suppose even if they *don't* revert to using their Korean name – I don't want to reject those people. Even within the KYAJ there's talk of admitting naturalized Koreans these days.'[9]

Ever since he was at elementary school, Dae-Won has had two principles drummed into him by his parents: 'Don't naturalize,' and 'Marry a countrywoman.' He adds: '"Countrywoman" means a fellow Korean, of course, but just being Korean isn't enough for them. It mustn't be a girl from the mainland, she's got to be from Cheju island, the same as my family. And even within Cheju, she's got to be from the right village, and she mustn't be from the Ko or Ha clans, because women from those clans are supposed to be strong-willed and allegedly don't look after their menfolk properly. The other day it suddenly occurred to me that my own grandmother was a Ko. I pointed this out, but my father said, "Yes, and she turned out to be just the kind of grandmother you'd expect."'

On the finer points of geographical and social background, Dae-Won rejects his father's opinions. But Dae-Won himself admits that he wants to marry a fellow Korean. 'If I get married, I'd like it to be with a Korean who lives in Japan, like me. I'd like to restrict the field to Zainichi. I wonder why. Maybe my parents' brain-washing has worked. When all's said and done, I would like to bring my children up as Koreans. I want to pass on the ways of behaving that I was taught by my own parents. So I want a woman who will defend the household, and I think it just wouldn't work with a Japanese. I don't think I'd hit it off with a mainland Korean, either. I don't think either a Japanese woman or a mainland Korean woman would understand the feelings and ways of thinking of this Zainichi Korean, Kim Dae-Won.'

Case study 4: Park Kong-Ja

Park Kong-Ja was born in Tokyo on August 3, 1967. She is a third-generation migrant, holding South Korean nationality, and is the third of four siblings. She was 25 on May 25, 1993, the day I interviewed her at the Central Headquarters of the KYAJ, where she was working as deputy head of the Planning Division. Central HQ is located in Tokyo's upmarket Minami-Azabu district, inside the same building that houses the South Korean consulate. She would later quit this job to make a study of traditional Korean dance forms.

Kong-Ja was never told about the circumstances that brought her paternal grandparents to Japan. Her grandfather died before she was born; her grandmother was still alive at the time of our interview, and given to reflecting on the hardness of life in a mixture of Japanese and Korean. 'She seems to have had some extremely bitter experiences, and I have the feeling that she doesn't want to talk about them.'

Her father is a stone dealer. 'He flies to Korea, collects stones from the mountains there, and brings them back to Japan. Mostly my father is just someone I'm scared of. Ever since I was little, he's often been away from home on business, and I haven't really known how to talk to him. He does liven up after a few drinks, though.'

Her mother was the oldest daughter of her family. 'That meant she was always having to look after the younger kids in the family when they were still infants. She even had to carry them on her back when she went to school. She talks about those times. She's a pretty lively, active, straightforward kind of person.'

Koreans are the ones who get bullied

Until the age of nineteen, Kong-Ja went by the Japanese pseudonym of 'Matsui Kyoko.' [10] She says the process of realizing that she was an ethnic Korean went through four stages, which she describes thus:

'At the first stage, I just knew I was Korean without having any idea what that meant. As soon as I was aware of my surroundings, I would hear two things from my *eomeoni* (mother) – that our family had another name, "Boku," and that this was because we were Korean.' At the time, Kong-Ja did not know that in fact, 'Boku' was the Japanese reading of her real Korean surname, 'Park.'

When Kong-Ja was in her first year of elementary school, the whole family moved to a little town on the outskirts of Kofu, the prefectural capital of Yamanashi, a rural prefecture two hours west of Tokyo by train. 'My father had acquired a kind of directorship at a big stone masonry. We lived very well, and I remember thinking how rich we were. But ours was the only Korean household in the area, and within two or three days of our arrival everyone knew we were Korean. I was bullied, of course, and I had this very powerful awareness that Koreans get bullied and that I hated being Korean. But that was all I knew about Koreans – that they got bullied.

'My most vivid memory concerns my brother. He's two years younger than I. When he was in the second grade or thereabouts, he didn't come home from school one day. We went looking for him, and found him stripped naked and buried up to his neck in a sandpit in the grounds of a local temple…crying.

'I myself had sliced oranges left over from school meals thrown at me on my way home from school. Then there was an incident with a friend of mine who lived over a little police box where her dad worked. One day I had a fight with her. A typical girls' fight. The kind where you don't speak to each other for ages. We had a joint diary where we took it in turns to write the entries, but we hadn't written anything in it for a couple of weeks because of the fight. Anyway, one day she came to my house with the diary and tried to say sorry. I told her to buzz off home, but afterwards, when I read what she'd written in the diary, I realized that I needed to apologize to her. So I went to the police box, but the policeman – my friend's dad – said to me, "You Koreans should go home to Korea!" I went home in tears.

'Until I reached junior high school, I didn't know what it was I disliked about Koreans, only that I did dislike them, so that being one myself, it was only natural that I should be bullied and there was nothing I could do but put up with it.'

A casual revelation

'It was when I went up to senior high school that I casually told everyone I was Korean.' This was the second stage of Kong-Ja's journey to ethnic awareness.

She went to a prefectural commercial high school. Since the fourth year of elementary school she had been attending evening classes in the use of the *soroban* (the Japanese abacus), and had ideas of parlaying her skill with figures into a career as a tax accountant. Accordingly she chose to attend a local commercial senior high school.[11] She acquired a new set of friends, and school life suddenly became much more enjoyable:

'No one was bullying me, no one was muttering things about me in the shadows, school life was suddenly full of hope. It was fun. I joined the *soroban* club, and got to enter national competitions and stuff like that.' Encouraged by this supportive environment, Kong-Ja revealed her identity to her friends.

'In the summer of my first year at senior high, I passed the test to get a license to ride a motor scooter. In the section of the license for name and nationality I entered "Boku Kyoko" (the characters of Kong-Ja's Korean name, with their Japanese reading), and "Republic of Korea." I showed the license to all my friends. Since the third year of junior high I'd started to get the feeling that maybe one reason why I got bullied for my ethnicity was because I didn't talk about it myself, so this time I took the bold approach: "Look, look, look," I said, "I'm a foreigner. I'm different from you lot!" In my excitement about getting the license I told everyone that I was Korean.

'I was briefly nervous about what I'd do if I got ostracized for saying all that, but luckily the kids around me showed no change toward me at all. At the time I had the feeling that yes, I was Korean and therefore had another name – "Boku" – but apart from that I was a "perfectly normal Japanese."'

The masonry where Kong-Ja's father worked went bankrupt when she was in the fifth year of elementary school. Her father continued to have difficulties at work after that, and in the summer of her second year at senior high, the family moved to Saitama prefecture, just to the north of Tokyo.

'I didn't want to change schools. I had this dream of becoming a tax accountant, you see. I told my father. He gave me a great big slap in the face and said, "What do you think you're talking about? I think you're forgetting you're just a school kid!" I transferred to a private high school in Tokyo, and at that point I was thinking this way: "My dream's gone. I'll just graduate in the ordinary way, get a job in the ordinary way, and then get married in the ordinary way." That was the tone of my thinking.

'Before graduation I was thinking that I'd like to get some kind of job in computers, so I had a look at the recruitment literature that had been sent to the school and sent off my résumé to four computer companies. I gave my name as "Matsui Kyoko" and my legal domicile as the "Republic of Korea." Not one of them even gave me the chance to sit their recruitment exam. It was a shock to me: after all, it was no good being Korean. Then one of the teachers called me over and said, 'Look here, Matsui, there's this financial institution that's run by South Koreans living here in Japan, which would probably be glad to have someone of your ability, so why don't you give it a try?' – and he introduced me to Tokyo Shōgin Bank.'[12]

Plenty of fellow Koreans

'When I started work at Tokyo Shōgin, I finally got a clear view of what it meant to be a Korean, or to be precise, what it meant to be a Korean in Japan.' This was the third stage on Kong-Ja's road to ethnic awareness.

'When I went to the orientation meeting which the bank held for new recruits, I found myself in the presence of Koreans of my own generation for the first time. Somehow I felt terribly happy…they all had names with three characters![13] There were about thirty girls and ten boys. There were a couple of Japanese kids as well. When I started working there, it was fun right from the start. The older employees were nice to me, and everyone had stories to tell about their lives as Zainichis. Everything I saw and heard was new and pleasing to me. I used my own name, though with its Japanese reading – "Boku Kyoko." At first it felt kind of funny with everyone calling me "Miss Boku," but once I got used to it I started to think that maybe this was, after all, my real name.

'In training, the first thing I learned was that there were lots of other Koreans like myself living in Japan. That gave me the comforting feeling that I had lots of friends. At morning assembly we would practice three simple Korean phrases every day – like *eoseo osipsiyo* (welcome), for instance.'

Abandonment of self-loathing

'Then I joined the KYAJ, put all my effort into activism, and got to understand a lot more things.' This was the fourth stage.

Kong-Ja first came across the KYAJ in the fall of her twentieth year. On a company trip organized by the bank, she got into conversation with an older employee who was in the Arakawa ward branch of the KYAJ. She told her that after their regular meetings they all went out to eat *monja*,[14] and invited her along. When Kong-Ja visited the Arakawa branch, she got a warm welcome from everyone there.

'I introduced myself as "Boku Kyoko." "Wrong," they said. "Your name is read Park Kong-Ja." Up till then I actually didn't know the Korean reading of my own name. Somehow I was ridiculously pleased to hear it pronounced that way.'

After that, Kong-Ja took to putting in an appearance at the Arakawa branch once a week after work. The workmate who had first invited her was a graduate of a North Korean school, and taught her the Korean language.

At this stage, Kong-Ja was actually using three different names. 'To the outside world, I was "Matsui Kyoko." At work in the bank

I was "Boku Kyoko." And at the KYAJ I was "Park Kong-Ja." For a while I felt quite natural using my three names, but one day I was doing some shopping with my credit card, and I accidentally wrote the character *Park* instead of the *Matsu* in *Matsui* on the transaction slip. I thought "oops," and I added a couple of strokes to change the *Park* into *Matsu*. Just then I felt kind of funny. I thought, after all, Park Kong-Ja is my real name, so why don't I just use it all the time?

'After that, I started to refer to myself by my full name, "Park Kong-Ja," in everyday conversation. Young Japanese women often refer to themselves by their forename rather than "I," right?[15] It was a bit like that. So the people around me got to calling me "Park Kong-Ja" as well. That was kind of relaxing for me.'

Kong-Ja enjoyed her activities with the KYAJ and got more and more involved. After four-and-a-half years she quit her job at Tokyo Shōgin Bank and took on a new post working for Mindan's Chamber of Commerce and Industry. At the same time she was serving as head of the women's section of the KYAJ's Saitama branch. Then in January 1991 she left home, set up an independent lifestyle for herself in her own apartment, and took on a full-time post at the KYAJ's Central Headquarters.

Her father bitterly opposed her decision to fly the nest. 'I explained the situation to my mother first. It was like lifting a veil covering my heart, and I broke down in tears. She said she would support me, but that I'd have to get my father's consent. I went to him and said, "Father, I'm thinking of taking on a job at the KYAJ head office in Tokyo. It will be tough to commute from Saitama, and besides I think it's about time I stopped depending on you and mother for everything." He kept saying 'You're not old enough, you're not old enough." At last he gave in and said, "All right then, please yourself!" It was a breakdown in our relationship that took me half a year to repair.

'What I wanted from the job at KYAJ head office was knowledge – answers to a lot of questions I had in my head. Just by sitting here I get to hear all sorts of information about Korean communities throughout Japan. Enough to make my head spin. The first thing I learned was the historical process that created those communities. I realized that the old me, who had hated being Korean, was all wrong. Knowing so much about Japan, and nothing whatever about

Korea, I was in no position to form such an opinion. I would have to know as much about Korea as I knew about Japan before I could make an informed judgment. Perhaps it was beyond me to attain the same level of knowledge, but at any rate I wanted to get as close as possible to people from my own country in order to get my knowledge of Korea even a little closer to my knowledge of Japan.'

Kong-Ja's first visit to South Korea came when she was twenty, when she took part in a KYAJ training trip there. 'I thought: "This is the place where we originally came from!" I was incredibly moved, and the tears were flowing.' But a visit to a Seoul amusement district brought a rather different experience: 'We got mixed up with a drunk, and a friend of mine was injured. He was shouting at us: "Take your damn moneybags back to Japan, you bunch of no-good *ban-chokbali*!" I had really complicated feelings about that.'

Chokbali originally means 'cloven-hooves.' It is a traditional Korean term of abuse directed at Japanese, comparing them to cows or pigs and deriving from the Japanese custom of wearing *tabi*, felt socks dividing the big toe from the others. *Ban* means 'half,' and thus *ban-chokbali* means 'half-Japanese' and is a term of abuse signifying Japan-resident Koreans.[16]

When interviewed, Kong-Ja had been to South Korea some fifteen times. Half her visits had been as a leader of KYAJ excursions, the other half private travel.

'I've taken to finding some free time and heading over there when I'm feeling emotionally drained, when I feel like clearing my mind of everything just for once, you know? Sitting on a bench at the Kyongbok Palace in Seoul just makes me feel so relaxed and at ease.'

Life as a Zainichi

Park Kong-Ja says she feels 'on fire' with enthusiasm for her work for the KYAJ, and as we have heard she makes frequent trips to South Korea. How does she see her identity today?

'Even now I feel that I'd like to become a "Korean Korean," and say that "I am a Korean," but in the end I have to say that I am a "Zainichi Korean." As I see it, the difference isn't just in the language. Compared to mainland Koreans, I walk with a different rhythm, I breathe differently, I have a different atmosphere about me. These are the things that make me think yes, I am a Zainichi.'

Kong-Ja also sees herself as fundamentally different from the Japanese with whom she grew up and with whom she identified until she completed high school. 'Zainichis are always navel-gazing. Always asking themselves what their origins are, what their culture is, always looking for something. Japanese just stroll through life without bothering about that kind of thing.'

Ever since she started working for the KYAJ, Kong-Ja has insisted on using only her Korean name with its Korean reading. Today she has become wholly accustomed to it. 'If I happen to bump into some old friend, who says "It's Matsui, isn't it?" I honestly don't understand. I say, "What? Are you talking to me?"' Kong-Ja had a hard time finding a landlord who would rent an apartment to her under her Korean name, but even so she uses it in every situation.

'There's a beauty parlor I go to near here. The people there know that my surname is pronounced "Park," but they used to have trouble reading my personal name. So when it was my turn to be seen, they looked at the waiting list and said, "Park Kyoko, this way please." I said: "You've got it wrong. My name is pronounced *Park Kong-Ja*. Go on, say it out loud. Remember it." And they did – just like that.'

Japanese people are not entirely absent from Kong-Ja's social life, but she has far more important relationships with fellow Koreans. 'I do think I've become overly absorbed in the world of Zainichi Koreans. I have some Japanese friends, but they're light-hearted friendships, just for having a laugh. Serious friends, that I tell my true feelings to…well, they're all Zainichi Koreans. Marriage? I want to spend my time with someone who understands my feelings and with whom I can feel at ease. I don't insist that he's got to be a fellow Korean, but I have a feeling that he will be.'

6 Living as Overseas Nationals

Young Koreans who have internalized the 'nationalist orientation' (Chapter 3, pp. 51–53) tend to be those who have received ethnic education at North Korean schools. Many of them go on to work for bodies related to Chongryun after graduation.

Case study 5: Lee Jae-Soo

Lee Jae-Soo was born in Hiroshima prefecture on January 12, 1961. When interviewed, on August 29, 1989, he was 28 years old. He holds North Korean nationality. He attended North Korean schools throughout his education, and went on to work for the Chongryun-affiliated Chōgin Bank.[1] He has a Japanese pseudonym, Kimura Tadashi. His wife is also Korean and at the time of our interview they had one son.

Jae-Soo's father was born in 1928, in the southern Korean province of Kyongsang-Nam-Do, and was brought to Japan at the age of three. His own father – Jae-Soo's grandfather – had been struggling to make a living in Korea; he went over to Japan to work, later having his wife and child come over to join him. Jae-Soo's father went to work himself after finishing element-ary school, and did a wide variety of jobs. Now he drives construction trucks. One of his younger brothers, Jae-Soo's uncle, went to live in North Korea under one of the 'repatriation programs.'[2]

Jae-Soo's mother is Korean but was born in Japan, in 1928. She never went to school and cannot read or write Japanese. Many of her relatives died in the atomic bombing of Hiroshima, 1945.

No feeling of discrimination

Jae-Soo was born and raised in a Korean settlement of a few dozen dwellings. His playmates were Korean, the home cooking was mostly Korean, he was called by his Korean name at home, and thus became vaguely aware of his Korean identity from an early age. The issue snapped into focus when he was sent to the local North Korean school. 'When you're a little kid, you don't really think about nationality much, do you? But when I went up to school I thought "Hmm...so, I'm in Japan but I'm going to a Korean school. I see!"'

He enjoyed himself at school. 'It was fun playing with my mates and all that. The school rules said you must always speak in Korean once you got through the front gate, but we did use Japanese as well. Once you start playing, the Japanese words just pop out naturally, you know? We used to play baseball speaking a crazy mixture of the two languages.

'We often used to get into fights with the Japanese kids. We'd get off the train and head for the school, and on the way we'd pass groups of Japanese schoolkids. They'd shout out, "Oy! Koreans," and we'd shout back, "Yeah, what about it?!"'

Despite these violent encounters, Jae-Soo insists that he did not feel aware of discrimination at this stage. 'I didn't fight because of any grudge toward them, it was just youthful high spirits. But looking back, I suppose there was always a sense on our part that they had to be kept in their place. I'm sure we were kind of scared that if we didn't keep them down like that, we might lose control over them. After all, they outnumbered us by far. The only reason we never lost in those fights was that we had spirit and guts.

'A specific example of discrimination against me? Well, I can't really think of one. Perhaps we just didn't get that sense of being discriminated against as strongly as our Korean mates who went to Japanese schools. I don't think we were persecuted at all really. That's because we were living among Koreans all the time, as we still do today.'[3]

Jae-Soo also showed a detached attitude toward the finger-printing system in the Alien Registration Law, a topic that infuriates many other Zainichi Koreans. 'My friends all went along to be fingerprinted, so I thought I might as well do the same. I just felt that since we were foreigners the authorities would naturally want to be sure of our whereabouts, which was why they did this kind of thing. Besides, these were rules made by the Japanese government, so nothing I might say would change anything. And anyway, one little fingerprint wasn't going to do me any harm.

'I think it's actually Koreans who've been to Japanese schools who tend to get angry about that kind of thing. They put up with discrimination all the time in their daily lives, and the resentment just piles up higher and higher, until it bursts out over something like fingerprinting. Those of us who've been to Korean schools haven't sensed that everyday discrimination, so we don't have that big pile of accumulated resentment, and I think most of us aren't really bothered too much about that kind of thing.'

After graduating from a North Korean senior high school, Jae-Soo went to work for Hiroshima Chōgin Bank. He says the issue of employment discrimination didn't bother him that much either. 'I had lots of friends in the same position, so I didn't feel particularly anxious. I think all of us had an awareness that we *Chosun-saram* (Koreans) wouldn't be able to get jobs with Japanese companies, so that we'd have to fix something up for ourselves. We were told about it by our parents, and we knew about it from what was going on around us.'[4]

Reflecting his education and working circumstances, Jae-Soo's friends are overwhelmingly Korean. 'I don't have any close Japanese friends. I know a few Japanese people, but they're not really friends. I tend to feel that it's only natural, since I've been so deeply immersed in Korean society all this time. At bottom I cling to this feeling that "friends" means "Koreans." I've never really been in a position to make friends with Japanese. I never got to know them in my schooldays, and here at Chōgin all the people around me are Korean, too.'

Jae-Soo got married in 1987. His Korean wife also graduated from a North Korean high school, and also worked at Chōgin. This was an office romance.

Understated ethnic pride

Jae-Soo insists that he has never once felt bad about being Korean. He has never worried about it and has never felt that it caused him loss. 'It's not that I feel I'm something special because of being Korean, I just happen to think it's a perfectly natural state of affairs.' For Jae-Soo, ethnic pride takes an understated yet powerful form. It is axiomatic that he is Korean; there is no need to make a big fuss about it. Whereas many young Koreans in Japan describe themselves specifically as 'Zainichi' Koreans, Jae-Soo calls himself simply 'Korean' (using the 'North Korean' term, *Chōsenjin*).

However, he does sometimes use his pseudonym. At work he is Lee Jae-Soo, just as he was at school. But in his neighborhood his family are known as the Kimuras. 'The neighbors all call me "Kimura," whether they happen to be Japanese or Korean themselves. Again, suppose for instance I'm out shopping in a department store, I tend to call myself "Kimura Tadashi," not because I'm ashamed of being Korean or anything, but simply because it's easier that way. Easier than having everyone turn round and stare at me when they hear me announce my name as "Lee."'

It seems that the way Jae-Soo sees it, it is precisely because of the strength of his ethnic pride that he does not feel any conflict of identity when using his alias.

Again in sharp contrast to many Koreans who have been to Japanese schools, Jae-Soo has no doubt as to where he is from. Whichever way you put the question – 'homeland,' 'motherland,' 'own country' – the answer is always the same: Korea, or *Chōsen*, defined as the whole Korean peninsula. More specifically, he considers his father's province of Kyongsang-Nam-Do as the location of his own roots. As for Japan, 'Well…it's the place where I happen to be living.'

So far Jae-Soo has made two visits to North Korea. 'What the people over there say is that they had everything destroyed in the Korean War, and they've rebuilt it with their own hands, so the activities of overseas nationals like myself hardly seem worthy of comparison.'

Believing as he does that it is only natural for Koreans to hold Korean nationality, Jae-Soo is critical of those who choose to apply for Japanese nationality. 'Basically people naturalize because they haven't got any confidence in themselves, right? I don't like that kind of thing. It's sort of like running away from yourself.'

Jae-Soo is distressed that so many young ethnic Koreans cannot speak their own language. He himself is fluent in Korean and Japanese alike. 'What makes a person Korean?' he rhetorically asks. 'In the end I reckon it's blood and language. I don't see how you can call yourself Korean if you don't have one of those two vital things, the language. You may be Korean by blood and nationality, but people won't recognize you as Korean if you can't speak the language.'

For reunification

To Lee Jae-Soo, reunification of his motherland is the biggest single issue there is. 'I'm not just saying that. I really mean it. You see, the country got divided in the first place because of interference by the Americans and Soviets. These great powers turned Korea into a battleground, killed lots of Korean people, and divided the country. What could be more tragic than that? The way things are now, I really do think there's a risk of war. And if that happens, everything that's been achieved, in North and South alike, will all go for nothing. That's why reunification just has to be achieved.'

As a national of the DPRK living abroad, Jae-Soo sees himself as having a special responsibility to contribute to reunification. 'As we see it, international opinion is important. The job of us overseas nationals is to create the right climate of opinion. So we're engaged in PR activities. Here at Chōgin Bank we're playing a major role in strengthening the Korean community overseas. We provide financing for Korean enterprises. That naturally helps those Korean enterprises to get bigger. When they get bigger, they also get more powerful. That in turn gives them more influence over the Japanese government. I think that strengthening the overseas Korean community will have much to do with achieving reunification of the homeland.'

Case study 6: Han Il-Hun

Han Il-Hun (not his real name) was born in Tokyo in 1965. When interviewed, on February 18, 1990, he was 24 years old. He holds North Korean nationality. He graduated from a North Korean high school, went on to work for Tokyo Chōgin Bank and then moved to an estate agency. He has a Japanese alias that he uses at work. He is married to a fellow Korean and has two children.

Il-Hun's father was born in Kyongsang-Buk-Do in 1938, and was brought to Japan by his parents at the age of one. He dropped out of Japanese high school and started work, helping out his father (Il-Hun's grandfather) with his shoe-making business. He soon got married, and Il-Hun was born shortly after, but when Il-Hun was one year old, he divorced his wife, remarrying when Il-Hun was five. Il-Hun's stepmother was a second-generation Zainichi Korean.

Il-Hun's father went on to do various jobs, including a spell in the scrap metal trade, and later operated his own mah-jongg[5] parlor. Today he and his wife are running a *yakiniku* restaurant (see Chapter 2, Note 16). 'My *abeoji* (father) has a pretty slovenly image. Once he's cleaned up the restaurant, he just goes to sleep or slopes off to play mah-jongg. But for some reason it's kind of hard to dislike the guy.'

Il-Hun instinctively refers to his stepmother as *eomeoni* (mother). 'She's a very straightforward person. Speaks her mind. She wouldn't make a big fuss about little things when she was bringing me up, and I really liked her. I have no recollection at all of being given a hard time because I was only her stepson.'

Fighting lad

Il-Hun knew he was Korean before he went to elementary school. 'For a start my *halme* (grandma) was hard of hearing, and she never picked up Japanese. She always spoke in Korean. I also knew that I had two names, "Il-Hun" and "Kazunori" (the Japanese reading of the characters in the Korean name). My uncle and aunt, who lived with us, were both teachers at a North Korean school, and we had a great big photo of "Kim Il Sung, the Great Leader" displayed in the home.'

During his childhood Il-Hun used to play with the local Japanese children, but they all knew he was Korean. 'I did get into a few fights because of their tendency to leave me out of things for being Korean. I always won the fights, which was a sure way to make them shut up about it.'

When Il-Hun's father remarried, the family moved to his stepmother's house. 'I went to a Japanese kindergarten there for about six months. I started off going to Japanese elementary school, too, as there was no Korean school in the neighborhood. I used the Japanese reading of my name, "Kan Kazunori." Sure enough I got straight into fights – and again, that stopped them from bad-mouthing me pretty sharp.'

Halfway through his first year at elementary school, the family moved back to the old house and Il-Hun switched to a Korean school. 'My aunt was teaching at that school, so I was delighted to go there. I still got into lots of fights, though. I always wanted to be boss of the playground, and didn't like being ordered around by anyone. But I never managed to be top dog at the Korean school. I often wondered what made those boys so tough. I can remember that I had to lower my sights and scrap to make number three in the pecking order.

'As for studying, I got top grades in my first report after moving to the Korean school. I got the impression that Korean was kind of easy as languages go.' Il-Hun was helped by the fact that he had been brought up in an environment where a fair bit of Korean was spoken. 'Only Korean was spoken at the school. You'd get told off if you were caught speaking Japanese. I soon got the message. Within a month of arriving from the Japanese school, I'd stopped using Japanese. But that changed. By junior high, just about everyone was using Japanese – myself included. In the end I suppose Japanese is sort of easy to use.'

One of the changes that accompanied Il-Hun's move to the Korean school was that he stopped playing with the local Japanese children. 'I really did start looking at Japanese people in a different light. I thought they were a bunch of bastards, as a matter of fact. I think they do lay on the anti-Japanese education a bit thick at Korean schools. Looking back, I reckon they did tend to exaggerate the truth quite a lot, even with the very young kids.'

Midway through elementary school, Il-Hun stopped fighting. He became something of a favorite with the teachers. 'I was a star pupil at elementary school and at junior high, though I say it myself. I wanted to become a teacher at a Korean school – that was my ambition. As I saw it, in the third and fourth generations there would be more and more Korean children who couldn't speak the language and wouldn't know the customs. That struck me as a shame, and I had this idealistic image of myself doing what I could to teach these kids their culture.'

At junior high school Il-Hun rarely had trouble with the Japanese youths he encountered in the street. 'Basically the students at the Korean school were tougher, so there was no trouble unless we stirred it up ourselves. Every now and then a bunch of us would decide that the Japanese kids had been getting kind of cheeky, and we'd go and beat up on them a bit. I didn't get into that sort of thing very often, though. I was a conscientious student – and besides, the school would come down on you like a ton of bricks if they got to hear of it.'

Il-Hun proceeded to Korean senior high school. 'In my first summer at senior high I had slightly too much of a good time, and when school reopened I hardly went near the place. I played *pachinko* all day long. An older boy had taught me how to bring up the triple seven. I could clean out a *pachinko* machine and walk off with 10,000 yen in my back pocket.[6] I used the winnings to treat all my pals to eats and drinks.'

Il-Hun's teacher told him he couldn't go up to the second year, and he was faced with expulsion. However, his uncle used his influence to persuade the school to allow him to progress to the second year, and finally prevailed upon Il-Hun to return to the path of good behavior and hard study.

Even during his all-day *pachinko* phase, Il-Hun never lost his sense of ethnic pride. 'I was really proud to have been born Korean. I wonder why. Looking back at it now, there was nothing particularly good about being Korean. Part of my positive feeling came from all the good friends I made while I was at Korean school. There were a few dropouts among us, but we all tried to help them. Like we'd go along to their houses, and say, "Look, we're all waiting for you, so why don't you come on back to school?" Or we'd teach them the stuff they'd missed. That kind of thing.'

Though he had returned to his studies, Il-Hun was still getting into fights with Japanese. 'Strange to say, the teachers at the Korean high school tended to encourage us. They'd been in plenty of fights during their own schooldays – in fact things had been much rougher in their time. So they didn't give us a hard time about fighting. On special patriotic occasions such as National Foundation Day or the Emperor's Birthday, right-wing groups and bad students would lie in wait for us at the railway stations we were known to use to get to the Korean school. The teachers knew what to expect, and they'd tell us "Don't you dare let them beat you." Or they'd say, "Club activities are off today, so you can go straight home. Only make sure that you don't get arrested if you get into a fight."'

Quitting and marrying

Il-Hun toyed with the idea of applying for Korea University and becoming a teacher, but eventually one of his cousins persuaded him to join him working at Tokyo Chōgin Bank. He quit just under three years later at 21, having acquired a qualification for dealing in residential land and buildings. 'I just wanted to get some kind of qualification and put my own capabilities to the test,' he says.

At the same time he got married, to a Korean woman who had been in the same year-group at Korean high school. He had never had a relationship with a Japanese woman. 'My parents never hassled me to marry a Korean, but I have to say I'd already made the decision myself. Being Korean, I had to marry a fellow-Korean and leave Korean descendants. After all, I was the eldest son of the Han family.'

Having quit work and married, Il-Hun went looking for a new job. A rude awakening followed. 'I started off looking at Japanese companies. I picked out a few estate agencies with around thirty employees, and applied for work. I was pretty confident, because the qualification I'd acquired counted for quite a lot in the industry. I was blissfully unaware of the harsh social realities. I went to my first job interview, they told me I'd hear from them in a few days, and then they told me I hadn't got the job. When I asked why, they said, "Oh, no particular reason, we just don't think you'd fit in here." I tried somewhere else and the same thing happened again. By the time of my third interview I was a lot less confident. Sure enough, they turned me down as well. I started to panic…I'd already quit from the bank, you see. I finally got lucky at the fourth attempt. The boss of this company told me he'd had a Korean friend at the place he worked before he set up his own business, so he didn't have any problem with the ethnic thing. So he took me on. Pure luck. Boy was I happy. That round of job-hunting was the first direct experience of discrimination I'd had in my life. I'd heard the word, but I never thought it would happen to me. It was the first time I'd ever really felt down.'

Il-Hun joined the company under his Japanese alias, 'Nishihara Kazunori.' 'I didn't even bother asking to be allowed to use my real name. It would just have been inconvenient in the workplace. The customers were all Japanese, you see. In that environment "Han Il-Hun" just doesn't sound right. The boss asked me which name I'd like to use. I said, "It's alright, 'Nishihara' will be fine." He said, "Well, I suppose it will be easier to do your job that way."'

Il-Hun told the whole staff that he was Korean. 'I told them of my own accord. I just said, "Hello, I'm Korean, but I hope we can be friends anyway. My real name's Han Il-Hun, but please call me Nishihara while we're at work." They didn't react too badly. The guys in the same sales team as me all treated me pretty straight. So I think that discrimination isn't that strong on the individual level – when it's just one person getting on with another.'

Il-Hun quit the company after one year. He had found that the company's overriding concern with profit made work very demanding. He moved to a new estate agency that a Korean friend was just starting up. 'There were four of us. Me and the boss were Korean. The other manager and the secretary were Japanese. We mostly handled sites for *pachinko* halls.'

Il-Hun still works for this company today. Though he is now working for a Korean concern, he still uses his Japanese alias. 'Nearly all the clients looking to buy land for *pachinko* halls are Korean, but the kind of land they're looking for – prime commercial sites close to railway stations – is invariably owned by Japanese. So I have to carry on with the "Nishihara" thing or it would be kind of hard to get the job done.'

In his school days Il-Hun always used his Korean name, but nowadays he uses his Japanese name at work and his Korean name in his everyday home life. 'At first it didn't come naturally,' he admits. 'I used to stammer when I introduced myself as "Nishihara." But it doesn't bother me any more now. Even so, however far you go in pretending to be Japanese, a Korean is still a Korean.'

A secret revealed

Il-Hun grew up knowing nothing about his biological mother. 'Even if I asked, no one would tell me anything about her. I've never seen a photo of her, and I haven't got a single thing to remind me of her. For some years I was brought up by my grandparents, because I had no mother and my father was hardly ever in.'

At the age of 23, Il-Hun's aunt told him a crucial fact: that his real mother was Japanese. 'I was only told very, very recently, having already grown up and set up my own household. Until then the whole family had kept it secret. Everyone was under orders not to mention it to me. My aunt quietly told me about it once the family had judged that I was emotionally mature enough to take it.'

The news aroused complex emotions in Il-Hun, but he says it did not shake his Korean identity – something that may be put down to the ethnic pride inculcated in him at Korean school. 'It's only very recently that it's fully sunk in that I'm half-Japanese. The possibility had never occurred to me. I'd always thought of myself as purely Korean, and I'd got a Korean education at Korean schools, and I'd always lived my life as a Korean…Basically, nothing has changed. I just think, "Oh, so I've got that kind of blood in me…" That's about the size of it. I'm quite an optimist, really, though I say it myself. I'd always felt glad to be Korean, you see…'

Il-Hun says that language is the key to his Korean identity. 'You've got to learn the language. I mean, you're born in Japan, you look just like a Japanese, and if you can't speak the language, what else have you got to establish your ethnic identity? I'm planning to send my own kids to Korean school. Even if they say they want to go to a Japanese school, I think I'll put my foot down and insist…at least until they've picked up the language.'

Orders from above

Han Il-Hun has yet to visit North Korea. His class wasn't selected for the high school graduation trip to Pyongyang,[7] and Il-Hun is still waiting for an opportunity.

'My homeland, my motherland, my own country – call it what you will, it's Korea. My home province, unfortunately, is Kyongsang-Buk-Do.[8] As for Japan, it's just my country of birth. I like Japan, basically. Frankly, it's probably easier to live here than in any other country. Even if you told me to go back to my home country, I wouldn't. This is where I like it best, honestly.'

As Il-Hun sees it, responsibility for Japan's history of colonial oppression in Korea lies with the state rather than with Japanese people as individuals. 'It was all down to the system they had in Japan at the time. If you asked me whether I thought all the Japanese people oppressed the Koreans in those days, I'd say no. It wasn't as if anyone had a grudge against Koreans. It was just state orders. I don't think people are to blame for actions carried out under orders from the state, which wields overwhelming power. It's not the fault of a single individual, you see.'

7   Going It Alone

The 'individualist orientation' (Chapter 3, pp. 53–4) is not of course associated with any particular group. Rather one finds it internalized by young Koreans who seek self-fulfillment on their own terms. They tend to be highly motivated, aiming perhaps for academic and career excellence, and in some cases the search for fulfillment takes them away from Japan, often to the United States.

Case Study 7: Kwon Dae-Soon

Kwon Dae-Soon (not his real name) was born in the Kansai district of western Japan in 1965. He was 23 when interviewed, on July 8, 1989. He is a second-generation Zainichi Korean holding South Korean nationality. He attended Japanese schools throughout his education, which culminated in graduation from the Faculty of Law at the University of Tokyo: the most prestigious degree attainable in Japan. He found employment at a major high-street bank, where he was still working at the time of our interview.

His paternal grandfather came to Japan 'around 1932 or 33.' Dae-Soon has heard that this was not a case of forced migrant labor. His father was born in 1933, but did not come to Japan until 1942 when he came over to visit his father (Dae-Soon's grandfather). In the end Dae-Soon's grandfather and father ended up living together in Japan, leaving the rest of the family in their hometown of Pusan. Despite difficult economic circumstances, Dae-Soon's father worked his way through school and graduated from a Japanese university. After repeated rejections, from a bank, a steel company and a trading house, he went into graduate school after which he finally succeeded in securing professional employment. He speaks perfect Korean, of the southern variety.

Dae-Soon's mother was born in Osaka in 1937. She graduated from one of the few ethnic Korean high schools affiliated with Mindan, and went on to Japanese junior college. Her marriage to

Dae-Soon's father was an arranged one. She speaks enough Korean to travel solo in South Korea without inconvenience.

Korean name, Japanese reading

Dae-Soon grew up within Japanese society, isolated from Korean culture. However, his entire family used Korean names, so that Dae-Soon was aware of his Korean ethnic identity from an early age. His father only gave his children Korean names, so he had no Japanese alias. However, all the way from kindergarten to university he used his Korean name with its Japanese reading, Gon Daijun.

'My name was different from the other kids', right? For a start my surname only had one character instead of the usual two. And even a kid can sense that "Daijun" is a pretty rare name. So I think I had this feeling that I was different from the other kids around me even before I went to a kindergarten.' Some time around the fourth year of elementary school he became aware that the difference lay in his Korean ethnicity. 'I think it may have been because I started to notice my parents explaining things by saying, "It's because we're South Korean." I suppose I just got used to it in the course of everyday life.'

When Dae-Soon was going to the local elementary school, all his classmates knew about his ethnicity, since he himself respond-ed to comments about his unusual name simply by saying 'It's because I'm Korean.' However, he feels he was rarely bullied over his ethnicity as such. 'It seldom went beyond a bit of silly teasing over my funny-sounding name. Unfortunately, though, I was also fat in those days, not great at sports, and good at studying. With three strikes against me like that, I did, of course, get bullied. Still, I really do feel that it had nothing whatever to do with being Korean.'

Looking back on his schooldays, Dae-Soon believes that his openness about his ethnic identity actually made it more difficult for his classmates to bully him for it – however merciless they may have been about his other personal attributes. 'I happen to think that you're more likely to get bullied for it if you try to hide it. So I reckon my parents' strategy of giving me only a Korean name was an exceedingly wise one.'

Dae-Soon went on to a private high school,[1] at which he announced the fact that he was Korean when introducing himself on the first day. 'When it was time for self-introductions, I said something like "I'm Gon Daijun. I know it's a funny-sounding name, but I'm Korean, you see." Well, it would just be a bore if I had lots of people coming up to me and saying "That's a rare sort of name – Chinese, are you?" Better to tell everyone at the same time. I also had this image of being a big boy now, even though I was only twelve at the time, and mature enough to handle the situation. If anything it would do me more harm than good to hide my identity, so I just spat it straight out. A kind of pre-emptive strike if you like. Hmm...I meant to be really casual about it, but yeah, I guess it was a pretty tense moment for me.'

Dae-Soon says that he never encountered any barriers stemming from his Korean identity up to this point. Still, the anticipation of barriers did affect his view of the future. 'All the way from elementary school, I had never thought of getting employment with a company. My father was a strong influence. We had a really serious talk about it when I was in my second year at senior high. He told me to forget about getting a job with a Japanese company – hardly any of them would have me. Although there was a thirty-year gap between his experience and mine, I still thought he probably knew what he was talking about. So I thought, right: I'll try and become a professor.'

A job at the bank

Dae-Soon passed the entrance exam to the University of Tokyo Faculty of Law at the second attempt. His decision to take on the toughest examination in the land was connected to his ethnicity. 'It did weigh on my mind, yes. I tried for Tokyo University because I thought the name would help me when I emerged into society. Personally I fancied going into the Literature Department and reading a few good novels, but that wasn't going to put rice on the table. I also thought of becoming a doctor, but my father was against it. He told me to steer clear of the Medical Department and go for something in the humanities. So I chose Law. I must admit I'd heard quite a few times that a Tokyo University law degree could come in handy in the employment stakes too.'

Dae-Soon enjoyed life at university and took an active part in club activities. In his fourth year, however, the need to make a final decision on his career direction began to weigh upon him. 'I only started thinking about jobs in my final year, and it was all a bit sudden. Until then I'd just drifted along, thinking I'd probably be OK if I went into academia, but I finally started to wonder whether I really fancied the idea of scholarly research. I got to thinking that I might not be cut out for it. So I thought that perhaps I would, after all, go for a job, rather than pursuing my studies further. I couldn't entirely discount my father's experience of discrimination in the job market. It did occur to me, though, that so far I had tended to uncritically accept everything my father told me and that maybe it was time to get out of that habit. I decided it was about time I started to think for myself, putting a little distance between myself and my parents. And not just think for myself, but act on my own account too. Because after all, if I didn't act now, I really might end up regretting it for the rest of my life.'

From mid-June onwards, Dae-Soon started paying visits to companies that rang him up to sound out his job intentions on tip-offs from friends of his who had joined the staff previously.[2] Dae-Soon made a point of mentioning his ethnicity on the first telephone inquiry, and only visited companies that didn't show any change in tone on learning of it. He visited twelve companies. Three withdrew their expression of interest after interviewing Dae-Soon, and six more he turned down himself. The other three offered him jobs. He finally accepted the offer from his current employer – a leading city bank.

When Dae-Soon started work, he took the opportunity to stop using the Japanese reading of his name. 'Gon Daijun' became 'Kwon Dae-Soon.' 'When they offered me the job, I told them that I might use the Korean reading, and asked if that would bother them. I thought it could be a problem, but they said it would be fine with them. Then at the end of March the time came to register my name on the company payroll, and I suddenly remembered the matter of the reading. I hadn't quite made up my own mind on whether to call myself Kwon Dae-Soon, and I actually asked them to wait a little, while I talked the matter over with my parents. The person in charge of registration said, "It's you who'll be using this name. We'll put 'Kwon Dae-Soon' under the characters of your name when we print your business cards, so in a sense you'll be using it forever. So do please decide the matter for yourself." He seemed pretty laid-back about it, so that night I just rang up my father and asked him which reading he thought I should use. "Well, it's got to be Kwon Dae-Soon," he said. "All right, that's what it will be," I replied.

'I reckoned that now I was a full member of society, people would notice my ethnicity more than when I was a student, in which case I might as well be bold about it and use the Korean reading. Banking involves meeting a lot of people, and I thought I should show them that an obviously Korean person was doing a good job of work. I reckoned that if I created this precedent, many others would follow. I had the rather conceited idea that this would be my little contribution to solving the ethnic Korean problem in Japan.'

Having started at work, Dae-Soon has found the atmosphere very favorable. 'Nobody looks on me as some kind of alien element, no one has treated me any differently from the rest. I think my promotion chances are good. When they offered me the job they told me that they saw me as potential management material. I believe that so far I've been treated absolutely fairly at work.'

Name and nationality outweigh language

Kwon Dae-Soon has never had any negative feelings about his Korean ethnicity; nor has he ever felt any urge to be the same as the Japanese people around him. 'I've always thought there's not that much difference between us anyway. The lifestyle's pretty much the same. OK, so the food's a little bit different. And some Japanese people are kind of surprised when I tell them about the *Jesa* rituals we have to commemorate the dead and honor the ancestors.'

Dae-Soon's belief that there is little difference between him and the Japanese around him may in part be related to the fact that he cannot speak Korean. 'I'm embarrassed that I can't speak Korean. Well I say that, but I could always study it, of course. I suppose the reason why I don't actually push myself that far stems from the fact that, to tell the honest truth, I can get by quite well enough without it. Since I don't intend to return to Korea, I don't need to learn the language. Though I probably should try and pick it up anyway. I guess I have to admit I've been lazy about this.

'I've been to South Korea, and I wasn't treated like a Korean. "Can't speak the language! Who is this guy?" I know it sounds rather pathetic, but if truth be told I kind of resented that attitude…as I'd made the effort to go over and all that, you know? Anyway I did feel that there was no place for me there, at least not now.'

Even so, Dae-Soon's ethnic identity is firmly Korean, probably reflecting his family's openness on the subject. He sees his nationality and name as outweighing the language issue in the formation of his identity. This very attitude, however, is causing Dae-Soon heartache over the question of marriage – his biggest problem at the time of our interview.

Ever since he was at elementary school, Dae-Soon has had it drummed into him by his parents that he must not marry a Japanese woman under any circumstances. Until he got into university he never stopped to think about it – he was a serious student at high school and did not get involved with girls. But there is a Japanese woman he has been seeing since he was at university. He naturally told her that he was Korean when they first got to know each other, and it didn't seem to bother her in the slightest.

'If I were Japanese, or if she were Korean, one or the other, sure I'd like to marry her. But as things stand, it's difficult. My father would be furious. There's no way he'd say "Do as you please!" and let it go at that. I have to be aware of that when I decide what to do. Because of the discrimination he experienced himself, he'd see it as a kind of betrayal if I married a Japanese. And then there's the change in the Japanese Nationality Law. It used to be that if the wife was Japanese and the husband Korean, their children would automatically have Korean nationality, but nowadays even if a Korean man marries a Japanese woman the children become Japanese unless you take deliberate legal steps to give them Korean nationality. To be honest, I wouldn't want my wife telling me she wanted them to have Japanese nationality. The question is whether she'd understand that.'

Even if Dae-Soon does end up marrying a Japanese, he still hopes to raise his children with Korean nationality and solely Korean names. His attitude is a response to the conflation of nationality and ethnicity that he sees as being the prevalent view within Japanese society. 'It's not like being in America. Here, I think there's a feeling that once you cut yourself away from your nationality, you lose your ethnicity as well. I just can't imagine someone naturalizing and yet still carrying out the *Jesa* ceremonies. Besides, in the end it's the Minister of Justice who decides whether you can naturalize or not. Whether he'll be kind enough to let you become Japanese. The Japanese effectively tell you to dump your ethnic identity if you want to become one of them. They make a special issue out of the name. They want you to use a Japanese one. And ultimately I think it's your name that really determines your ethnic identity.'

Case Study 8: Yu Hwa-Mi

Yu Hwa-Mi (not her real name) was born in Tokyo in 1964. She was 28 when interviewed, on January 13, 1993. She is a third-generation Zainichi Korean holding South Korean nationality. After attending Japanese schools throughout her education, she graduated from university and worked for a foreign-owned bank in Tokyo. She subsequently traveled to the United States to attend graduate school there. Our interview took place while she was home for the winter holidays.

Hwa-Mi's paternal grandparents passed away while she was still in the early years of elementary school, and she has not been told the full details of how they came to Japan. Her father graduated from a Japanese university and became qualified for the profession that he now practices.

A childhood spent in hiding

Although Yu Hwa-Mi has only one name, its characters can be read as 'Yanagi Kazumi,' a convincing Japanese name. Throughout her childhood and early adulthood, Hwa-Mi used the Japanese reading. She did not even realize that she was Korean until the second year of elementary school. 'I was looking forward to my *Shichigosan* ceremony,[3] but my grandfather and grandmother both died shortly before that time of year, and it never happened. I was upset about it, and assumed it had been canceled because we were in mourning. But then someone, I think it was my older sister, said, "I don't think we'd have done it anyway, since we're Korean." Until then I'd had no idea. I even thought my grandparents were using some Japanese dialect when I heard them speaking Korean.

'In my third and fourth years at elementary school, I was teased by a boy who said, "Oy, you're a foreigner!" "How come?" I said. "My mom said you were," he replied. In those days I would hotly deny the suggestion. But once I got into the fifth and sixth years, I realized that this only made me seem more suspicious, and I learned to be a little more subtle in my performance. I'd say, "Hmm, you might be right. Maybe my ancestors got naturalized in the Nara era⁴ or something." That way the other person could never think of anything to say, and they lost interest. I hid myself really thoroughly, and that kind of trickery was all in a day's work. I couldn't see anything good about being different to the people around me. My ethnicity was something I must never tell anyone about – that was the idea I had in my head.'

Hwa-Mi's parents encouraged her to enter the medical profession, and she started attending cram schools while still at elementary school. She attended private all-female establishments for her junior and senior high-school education. At junior high school she came to look upon her ethnicity almost as a curse: 'With 100 million people living in Japan, and only 600,000 Koreans, why, oh why, did I have to be one of them? It felt like a piece of random misfortune, as if I'd been in a traffic accident or something. So I didn't want to investigate the matter too deeply…in fact I didn't want to think about it at all. We used to get a Korean newspaper – I always threw it in the bin the moment it came through the door.'

In her second year at senior high, Hwa-Mi rebelled against her parents, who were still pushing for her to study medicine while she favored something in the humanities. As she saw it, their insistence reflected the small number of career options available to Zainichi Koreans, and the answer was not to accept the limitations but to get rid of them by naturalizing. She got into arguments about it with her father, who did not see naturalization as the solution to the family's problems. In the end, Hwa-Mi got her way and studied humanities rather than medicine at a private university.

Being a real foreigner

Hwa-Mi made her first trip abroad in her third year at university. 'I'd never had a passport until then. I didn't like it either, getting the passport that confirmed my Korean nationality. But my mother insisted that it would be good for me to see a bit of the world, so I got to go and study English in Britain during the summer holidays of my third year. When I went, I discovered that it was actually very relaxing to be a really obvious foreigner. All the people walking in the streets were speaking a totally different language from mine, and I thought, "Hey! Different language! This is what it's like to be a *real* foreigner." I really liked it. Part of it was that it didn't matter whether I was Japanese or Korean or whatever – I was just another Oriental. It felt great…I was hooked.'

Even at university, Hwa-Mi made no particular effort to tell her friends about her ethnic identity. She only told one older student, who had chosen to write his graduation thesis on the problem of ethnic Koreans in Japan. But then, as she prepared to make a second visit to Britain during the spring holidays before her final year, she told quite a few more friends.

'I was in the skiing club, and I had to tell my friends in the club that I wouldn't be joining them for their skiing camp because I was going to Britain. "Why do you have to go to Britain now?" they asked. "Couldn't you go next year?" I said, "I'll have trouble getting a job if I don't pick up a bit of English. Getting employed is going to be tough for me." "Why?" "It's going to be tough because I'm not Japanese." "What?! Well what are you, then?" "I'm Korean." "So were you born there?" "I certainly wasn't!" They didn't have a clue. Well, it was partly my own fault for passing so casually as Japanese all that time. "How can it be?" they said. "We can't believe it! You seemed just the same as us!" That kind of thing.'

When the time came to look for work, Hwa-Mi surprised herself by getting the job at the foreign-owned bank. 'I didn't think I stood much chance of getting a job, because of my Korean nationality. So I didn't really put much effort into job-hunting. But I slightly fancied my chances with foreign-owned companies, so they were the only ones where I really gave it a go.' The strategy paid off – eventually.

'I know I wasn't trying as hard as I might, but even so I feel I got turned down an awful lot of times. Though I say it myself, I was from the law department of a pretty well-known university, and this was just a couple of years after the Equal Employment Opportunity Law[5] came in. Plus the economy was in good shape, so the circumstances were favorable all round. Students from the same department at the same university were getting job offers just like that, as early as July. I had to wait until September before I got fixed up, and it was quite obvious that I only got the offer because someone else had run off to another company after initially accepting it. OK, so I didn't have a particularly great academic record, but kids with similar records would show up at employment seminars[6] run by companies, send off their résumés at the same time as me, and get invited to interviews within three days, or a week at most. For me it might take two whole months before I even got called to interview. Even the bank that finally did employ me took exactly a month to offer me an interview after I took their written test. Usually there's no way it would take that long. I could see they only called me when they'd nearly finished recruiting and had been turned down by some more attractive prospect. I don't want to put it all down to my nationality, but at the time I couldn't help thinking that it must have had something to do with it.

'When I started work at this foreign bank, they asked me whether I wanted to use the Korean or Japanese reading of my name. I thought people would never catch it if I called myself "Yu," and I'd wind up having to repeat it four or five times, so I said I'd stick with "Yanagi." So I'm afraid I passed up a valuable opportunity there, and carried on passing as "Yanagi Kazumi."'

Hwa-Mi had learned the Korean reading of her name when she was in junior high school, but no one had ever called her by it and so it didn't quite feel natural to her. The bank may have been foreign-owned, but her immediate superiors and colleagues were all Japanese. She herself spent her working life as 'an ordinary Japanese – or a fake Japanese, if you like.'

'About a year after I started work, I started to feel really suffocated. I felt this powerful urge to get out of Japan again, and went through a very difficult period of agonizing over whether to go and study abroad again or what. I talked about it to one of my old college friends. "How come you don't like Japan?" she asked. I said something about how it seemed like such a closed society, and of course I ended up sounding critical of Japan. At this point she said, "Well, if you hate it here so much, why don't you go back to Korea?" She was a nice kid, you know, but this was the response of a pure and simple Japanese. Oh no, I thought, I should have known I'd get this sooner or later. "It's all very well telling me to go home," I said, "but how can I? I don't even speak the language." "How come?" she asked. "Oh, never mind," I said. "Just forget it, alright?"'

Among her college friends, Hwa-Mi gets on particularly well with a young Japanese woman who lived abroad for over fifteen years and got into the university via a special exam for long-term overseas residents returning to Japan. 'She always says that inside she feels two-thirds non-Japanese. But she looks entirely Japanese, and she says it always troubles her that the Japanese people around her don't understand her. They get at her, saying things like, "You're Japanese, right? So how come you don't understand this or that thing about Japanese people?" I'm just the opposite to her – born and raised in Japan, and I guess you could say Japanese in outlook, but I just happen to have different nationality. It's amazing how well we get on together. We love swapping stories about how Japanese society cramps our style.'

Off to America

In the end Hwa-Mi quit her job at the bank after two years and three months. In the fall of 1990 she enrolled in a degree course at a university in the United States, studying sociology. 'At the time I didn't consciously feel that I wanted to study the Zainichi Korean problem. I didn't yet have the strength to tackle the issue head on. I just felt I'd like to take another look at sociology. I was interested in things like refugee problems and foreign migrant workers – things that probably wouldn't have engaged me if I'd been born an ordinary Japanese.'

Hwa-Mi's long-standing concern with the importance of English had made her an enthusiastic student of the language. By the time she got to the US she had mastered it to the point where she did not need to attend the special language classes laid on by the university prior to the new term. Once classes started, 'I worked so hard that I'm proud of it myself – and I got straight As.' Her honors essay dealt with the occupational problems of ethnic Koreans living in North America. 'Since there were so many Korean-run groceries, dry goods stores and mini-marts, I did a survey to find out why so many Koreans were doing the same kind of work. Nearly all of them were first-generation immigrants, and they were all well educated. Even so, they were all running these small businesses.'

In the fall of 1992,[7] Hwa-Mi moved on to graduate school, planning to specialize in the study of minority groups. Determined to move on to a doctorate after getting her masters, she threw herself into her studies.

Hwa-Mi compares her identity in the US and on returning to Japan as follows: 'When I come back to Japan, I'm afraid I tend to revert to being a fake Japanese. When I'm in America there's this atmosphere where I can do whatever I like and say whatever I like. Maybe it's just me, but when I'm in Japan I have these fears in the back of my mind that I might appear to be biased or self-obsessed, studying Zainichi problems when I happen to be one myself. I really feel constrained psychologically. In America they have this thing about letting people do and say what they want, and it doesn't seem to matter much.'

Hwa-Mi says it always takes her ten minutes or so just to explain to Americans what a Zainichi Korean is. 'First they ask me where I come from, and I say Tokyo. Right away they think I'm Japanese. I explain that I'm not, and that involves going into a lot of detail about differences in nationality law, perceptions of civil rights, and so on. It takes them a while to get the picture. But once they do, they're really interested. By and large Americans don't make much of a distinction between one Oriental and another. After all, on the domestic scene there, there are moves toward ethnic solidarity among all Asian-Americans – whether they're ethnically Japanese, Korean, Filipino, Indian or whatever. So I guess "Asian" is a good enough description for me.

'I suppose I'm never quite at home, wherever I go. America has its enjoyable aspects and Japan its restrictive aspects, but America also has its tiring aspects. Like, you've got to express yourself even if you haven't got anything to say. That can be quite mentally exhausting.'

Hwa-Mi started using her Korean name when she commenced her studies abroad. 'The name on my enrollment form had to match the name on my passport, so I called myself "Hwa-Mi Yu."[8] I've got quite used to using that name when I'm speaking English. But when I'm talking in Japanese, I must admit I do still go back to "Yanagi Kazumi." A funny thing happened once. There was this Korean American movie director who was working on a documentary comparing the problems of Koreans in Japan and black people in America. I had the opportunity to be interviewed by him. Neither of us spoke Korean, so he said, "I'll ask the questions in English, and you answer in Japanese." The first thing he asked me was my name. I came straight out with "My name is Yanagi Kazumi," in Japanese, and then I realized with a shock that after using "Hwa-Mi Yu" all that time in America, I'd naturally switched back to "Yanagi Kazumi" the moment I start speaking Japanese again.'

Stateless defiance

Asked about her native country, motherland and 'own country,' Hwa-Mi bluntly answers 'none' on all three counts. When she was working at the bank she made a fleeting three-day visit to Seoul with her father. 'It was interesting, as a foreign country that is. I think my features still look more Korean than Japanese, but I was still looked upon as Japanese, as you'd imagine. I wasn't shocked. To me it seems perfectly natural. The fact that I'm different from the Koreans living in South Korea is only to be expected, and I don't have any sense of inferiority over my inability to speak Korean. I just have the kind of interest in Korea that you might feel toward a distant relative. Long ago I had such an intense psychological rejection of all things Korean that I couldn't even eat *kimchi*, but nowadays I'll eat anything, and I suppose I get along well enough with the Koreans from Korea whom I have dealings with in America. As for Japan, I don't think there's anywhere else in the world that's as safe and as easy to live in, but I do sometimes get the feeling that this idea that everyone's got to do everything together is kind of constricting, that it's hard to breath freely in Japan.

'These days I'm challenging the whole notion of ethnic identity. Going to grad school in America, I often meet people from Korea who are in the States. Some of them think it's an absolute disgrace that I can't speak Korean, and that I'm kind of inferior because I'm already three generations away from the motherland. My view is "So what if I can't speak Korean? What does it matter if there are some Koreans who can't speak the language?" I've decided I really have to take these people on. My resistance is based on the premise that it's not very progressive to make all that fuss about ethnic identity in the first place, and that I'd be in such a mess that I really wouldn't be able to get along at all if I couldn't enjoy my own half-and-half sort of identity, and see it as another way of having fun.

'The fact that I'm a Korean in Japan has certainly held me back in some respects, and it's been a great influence on the formation of my personality, but on the other hand this chance circumstance of birth has brought me blessings, too. There's no way I will ever fall into set ways of seeing things, and in that sense I have absolute confidence in myself. I think I understand myself well enough to know that if I'd been born as an ordinary Japanese in Japan, I'd have been just like any other useless Japanese, full of prejudices, so in that sense I'm glad I was born the way I was. It's because I've turned to resistance that I think that way.

'On the nationality issue, I am now in complete agreement with my father. The thing is that within Japanese society as a whole it is not possible for me to cheerfully and casually mention that my ancestors are Korean...so I have the feeling that if I did adopt Japanese nationality, I would become much too sensitive to the reactions of people around me, and I'd surely be carried along in the direction of concealment. And since I see a fundamental problem with that, I no longer have the slightest intention of humbly requesting the honor of being granted Japanese nationality. Nor do I feel like acquiring American citizenship. Even if I were to end up living permanently in America, I'd be perfectly happy to stay as a "Zainichi Korean." I feel a certain suspicion toward America, the way the people go on about how strong and great their country is, how it's the best in the world and all that. There's something wrong with the way they justify their own country's actions so easily. All that stuff about America's special role in maintaining world peace really sticks in the throat when you look at all the trouble they've caused by poking their noses into the affairs of the little countries around them.

'This is just a personal opinion, but if you ask me, the reason why the problem of ethnic Koreans in Japan has got so strikingly out of hand is because the Japanese are so stubbornly Japanese and the Koreans are so stubbornly Korean. The issue has just got stuck between the national characters of these two peoples, and that's why it's in such an awful mess. I want to see a new way of thinking, which concentrates on people instead of getting tangled up in these trivialities of nation and race. I think it's nonsense to talk about doing things for the Korean people, or making contributions to the development of Japan, and all that. Lately in particular I've been wondering why we can't all just live together peacefully on earth as human beings.'

Postscript

A few months later, in August 1993, I received a letter from Yu Hwa-Mi. Writing from the United States, and having just completed three years of study there, she showed a marked change of attitude on the nationality issue:

If one takes the view that nationality has no meaning above what is written on the documents, then there is no particular need to make a big deal out of Korean nationality. If I return to Japan to live there in the future, I shall acquire Japanese nationality. Having left Japan, and had dealings with mainland Koreans, I have had many opportunities to be made aware of how close I feel to Japan and how far I feel from Korea. In my case, to put it frankly, my lifestyle, my culture, my language – whichever one you look at, they're all Japanese. At the very least, my first twenty-five years, during which I lived an ordinary life in Japan, are an ineradicable fact of my life, no less so than the Korean blood in my veins. So I don't see why I shouldn't have my say on things that concern me, as a respectable citizen holding Japanese nationality. I also think it's just a simpler way of going about things. If I don't do this thing, I feel I'll always be a sort of 'moratorium person,' or to put it more drastically, that I'll never become an adult as long as I live.

Having said that, even if I do become a Japanese person, I no longer have the slightest intention of acting out some kind of unnatural performance of undefined 'Japaneseness.' That's because, irrespective of nationality, I will, come what may, be myself.

8 Turning Japanese

The 'naturalizing orientation' (Chapter 3, pp. 54–5) tends of course to be found at its strongest among young ethnic Koreans who do in fact choose to naturalize.

Case Study 9: Tokumizu Mitsuo

Tokumizu Mitsuo (not his real name) was born in Tokyo in 1963, the family moving to neighboring Saitama prefecture shortly after his birth. When interviewed, on June 25, 1989, he was 26. He has one older brother. Since graduating from high school he has been working at his father's printing company. In 1987 the entire family naturalized, switching from North Korean to Japanese nationality.

Mitsuo's father was born in 1934, in the southern Korean province of Cholla-Nam-Do. He was brought to Japan by his family in 1943, at the age of nine. Mitsuo's father, whom I was also able to interview, explained the circumstances thus:

'The first thing that happened was my big brother getting carried off to Japan under the forced migrant labor program, and then dying here in Japan. The rest of us came over to take possession of his remains. But this all happened when the war was getting very intense, and in the end we just couldn't make it back to Korea.'

Despite the loss of his older brother, who in all probability was worked to death in a Japanese labor camp, Mitsuo's father insists that he feels no hostility toward Japan. 'In a way, his death saved all our lives. I think we would have died if we'd gone back to Korea...we'd all have been killed in the Korean War. So I don't bear any grudge against Japan. I wasn't subjected to any cruel treatment myself, you see – not personally.'

Despite many hardships, Mitsuo's father worked his way through part-time commercial high school. Today he owns his own small printing company. He accepted the idea of naturalization partly for convenience at work, and partly for the sake of his sons, who both wanted to become Japanese nationals. He himself continues to refer to himself as a 'naturalized Korean' and makes no attempt to hide the fact from those around him.

Mitsuo's mother is a second-generation Zainichi Korean, born in Tokyo in 1941. She too endured great hardship and the constant need to help out at home prevented her from getting a satisfactory education even at elementary level. Again like her husband, she applied for naturalization because she felt it was in the interests of her sons, who had become acculturated to Japan. Like her husband, she makes no attempt to conceal her Korean ancestry. She still wears her *jeogori* when attending Korean weddings, *kimchi* is still a staple part of the family diet, and the rice cakes eaten to celebrate the New Year are Korean-style *dduk*, not Japanese-style *mochi*.

Her biggest concern at present is for her sons' marriage prospects. 'You know, Japanese people don't like our sort. They really seem to hate us. It's different if you've got lots of money, then they'll let you marry their daughters all right. But people like us have got nothing. We couldn't even dream of having a Japanese bride marry into the family. But on the other hand, once you've naturalized, some Korean girls also get put off joining the family. That's the problem. The fact that people like us are sort of stuck in the middle. It's no good just rashly changing your nationality. It's all very well if the boys can find girls to marry them by their own efforts, but if they can't, well…At least our younger son has found a steady girlfriend. A Japanese girl.'

Late realization

Mitsuo describes himself in his schooldays as follows: 'I think they thought I was pretty dumb – dumb but cheerful…I didn't really take the lead in anything much, but if someone else had a good idea I wouldn't mind hopping on the bandwagon…I was kind of in-offensive, I just happened to be good at getting along with people…something like that.' To all outward appearances, Mitsuo was a robust young man. He worked industriously at the part-time job he got while at senior high school, making deliveries for a sushi restaurant, and put his earnings into customizing his 50cc moped.

Apart from the occasional meeting with relatives on his mother's side, Mitsuo was brought up in an environment where he never had any contact with fellow Koreans. The entire family went by Japanese pseudonyms on all occasions. As far as he was concerned he had just one name, 'Tokumizu Mitsuo.' 'Chang Kwang-Ung,' the name on his alien registration card, was an irrelevance. He also recalls that Korea was never mentioned in the home – no one ever told him how the family came to migrate to Japan. Even at the time of our interview Mitsuo did not know that his family's *bonkwan* (ancestral homeland) was in the district of Deoksu, nor that his Japanese surname, 'Tokumizu,' was in fact written with the same characters as 'Deoksu,' only read the Japanese way. He didn't even know how to read his own Korean surname, Chang, and his knowledge of the Korean language was virtually non-existent.

Mitsuo only became aware of his Korean identity in his last years at elementary school. 'My big brother was at junior high, and he already knew about it. I think it was him who told me about it. I think he just said, "We aren't Japanese, you know" – something along those lines. But it only really struck me that I was Korean when I started at junior high school myself and had to start carrying the alien registration card.'

As our interview proceeded, however, Mitsuo started to recall other Korean details of his childhood. 'Like, when we visited some relatives' house, I noticed they had this rather unusual wardrobe. It was a black, lacquered wardrobe with mother-of-pearl inlay or something. Plus they had dolls dressed in *jeogori* and all that. Quite a lot of that sort of stuff, actually. I think I may have felt a bit funny about it.'

Mitsuo also attended just one Korean-style wedding. 'All the female guests were wearing *jeogori*, and I thought, "Wow! This is incredible."'

But these experiences did not make Mitsuo feel any closer to Korea. 'I felt dimly aware of the connection, but basically I tried to deny it. Yeah…there was no such thing for me!'

When Mitsuo was nearing the end of elementary school, his paternal grandmother came to live with his family. 'My grandma only spoke Korean, so I didn't understand what she was going on about – not a word. My mother didn't understand either. Only my father could follow her.' It was at about this time, with this compelling new evidence of the family's Korean ethnicity, that Mitsuo recalls hearing from his brother that they were 'not Japanese.'

Going underground

'As soon as I was really clear that I was Korean, I did my level best to hide the fact. Since everyone around me was Japanese, I didn't want to be thought of as different. There might be no danger in being known as Korean by one's Japanese friends, but even so, you do tend to think that way inside yourself, know what I mean? At the time I really hated being Korean. Especially after I got the alien registration card and went to senior high school...that's when I really started hating it.

'I was never directly bullied during my schooldays, but just once a friend said to me, "They say you're Korean." I didn't feel good about that at all. My friends seemed to have a vague awareness of it, but they all avoided mentioning it.' Mitsuo does not recall feeling uncomfortable about this state of affairs, except when the general topic of Koreans came up in his friends' conversation. 'That did put me on edge.'

In particular, Mitsuo often heard talk about fights with boys from the nearby North Korean school. He felt a sense of allegiance with his Japanese friends, but also a desire to escape from the whole situation, to avoid being there in the first place. 'When I heard my mates going about how scared they were of the *Chon*,[1] I just avoided getting into the conversation. I pretended I wasn't listening, hoping they'd soon move on to some other subject.'

Despite all his negative feelings and attempts to conceal his Korean identity at senior high school, Mitsuo did reveal the fact to five or six of his friends. 'As they were friends, I thought I'd better let them know. After all, you can't conceal that kind of thing forever. And I didn't want to keep things hidden from my friends. I knew they already had a pretty good idea about it, but I told the guys I could trust anyway...sort of confirming it, if you like. They just said, "Is that so?" and carried on being friends with me as before.'

Naturalization

While Mitsuo was still at senior high, he and his brother started telling their parents that they wanted to naturalize during conversations at home. He explains the reasoning thus:

'Well, we'd been living all that time in Japanese society. We didn't have any Korean consciousness. So we thought that if it were possible to become Japanese, maybe we might as well go for Japanese nationality. It would just be kind of convenient. Since we had absolutely no intention of going back to Korea. We'd be living in Japan, so it would just be more convenient to get Japanese nationality and become Japanese.'

The brothers' request met with different reactions from their two parents. 'My father didn't really like that kind of talk. He didn't say much about it, but we had the feeling that he wasn't too keen. I guess he feels proud of being Korean. My mother wasn't particularly opposed. She seemed to think that if that was how we felt about, we might as well do it.'

The family finally converted to Japanese nationality when Mitsuo was 24 years old. 'I felt really great about it. Because I'd been wanting to become Japanese myself.'

However, Mitsuo says the transformation is not quite complete. 'I suppose I feel closer to being a Japanese now that I've changed my nationality, but I'm still not entirely Japanese. I suppose I've become 90 percent Japanese, but there's still that other 10 percent. My Korean past, that still remains. The past that I've lived in up to now.'

Carefree living

Asked about which country he views as his native country, motherland and 'own country,' here is what Tokumizu Mitsuo says: 'Korea just doesn't come into it. I suppose I might feel a slight partiality for Korea when watching sports. That's about the limit of it.' He describes Japan as his native country and his homeland. 'I don't want to leave this place. I really don't want to leave. All my friends are here.'

Mitsuo says he has no interest in the issue of Korean reunification, which he sees as having nothing to do with him. As for

Japan's history of invasion, domination and discrimination *vis-à-vis* the Korean people, he says it feels 'unreal' (*esoragoto*) to him. 'I haven't experienced it myself, you see. I know about it, but since no such thing has happened in our generation, it seems unreal. Something that happened a long time ago...no more than that. So I actually tend to feel that it's wrong to make a fuss about it. Since that kind of thing doesn't happen anymore. There may still be something like it going on behind the scenes, but there's no way it'll come out in the open, the way it used to in the old days.'

Even so, Mitsuo sees the circumstances of his birth as 'basically unfortunate.' 'Well, if I'd been born over there everything would have been easy. If I'd been over there from the beginning I wouldn't have felt out of place at all. Being born here in Japan ...well, it just can't be helped, that's how I feel. I just try to live my life without offending anyone. It's not a problem that I lose sleep over, and I don't look on it as such a big problem either.'

Like his parents, Mitsuo does not attempt to conceal the fact that he is a naturalized Korean. He has a Japanese girlfriend, whom he met because a friend of hers was going out with a friend of his. Mitsuo told her about his Korean ethnicity about a month or two after the start of their relationship. She said it made no difference to her.

One of the characters in the film *Yoon's Town*[2] is a Japanese woman who abruptly changes her attitude toward her boyfriend when she discovers that he is a Zainichi Korean. 'There may be a few women like that,' says Mitsuo, 'but they'd be no more than one in ten thousand or thereabouts. People just aren't that sad.'

Case Study 10: Ogawa Yoko

Ogawa Yoko (not her real name) was born in Tokyo in 1967. She was 25 at the time of our interview, on August 30, 1992. Her father is a second-generation Zainichi Korean with South Korean nationality and her mother is Japanese. After attending commercial high school, she went on to train as a nurse. In 1986, at the age of nineteen, she and her younger sister took Japanese nationality under the special measures included in the 1984 revision of the Nationality Law.

Her paternal grandfather, a first-generation migrant, died in the same year Yoko was born and she knows him 'only from photographs.' Her grandmother is still alive in her seventies, but has never talked to Yoko about the circumstances of her arrival in Japan.

Yoko's father, a second-generation Zainichi, was born in the Tohoku district of north-eastern Japan in 1943, at the height of the war. He completed junior high school and then moved to Tokyo where he worked in a *yakiniku* restaurant (see Chapter 2, Note 16). Today he runs his own *yakiniku* restaurant. Yoko's mother, though Japanese, had a rather similar background. She too was born in Tohoku, leaving her farming family to go to Tokyo after completing junior high school. She worked in the same *yakiniku* restaurant as Yoko's father, and ended up marrying him.

'Apparently they both had trouble with their parents. My father's parents told him it was out of the question to go and marry a Japanese, and my mother's parents told her it was out of the question to go and marry a Korean.'

Self-discovery at junior high

Although I happen to know from my own research that the area where Yoko lived from elementary-school age to twenty was one with many Korean families, she was not aware of this at the time of our interview. Moreover, she says she did not become aware of her own ethnic identity until rather late in childhood.

There must have been other Zainichi children in her class at elementary school, but Yoko says she was completely unaware of it. 'Everyone used ordinary Japanese names, you see, and at the time I just thought everyone was Japanese.' The only children that she knew were Korean were those attending the local North Korean school. 'There was a Korean junior high school nearby, and I must say we were scared of those children. Nothing frightening ever happened to me personally, but I used to hear from friends about how the Koreans would start a fight at the drop of a hat and so on, and yes, I was scared. When I was out on my bicycle I always steered well clear of them.'

It may seem almost incredible that Yoko could live for years in a neighborhood with a large Korean population without realizing that she was a Korean national herself. However, the family always went by the name of 'Sugiyama,' the Japanese alias adopted by Yoko's father, and Korean topics were never raised in household conversation.

When Yoko was still too young to go to school, her parents sometimes used to take her to *Jesa* memorial services for the family's deceased ancestors at her paternal grandmother's house. On these occasions she noticed that her uncles and aunts would 'speak in a language that I hadn't heard before.' No doubt the mysterious language was Korean, but Yoko was very young, and did not draw the conclusion that her father, and to a degree herself, were not Japanese. She carried on going to the services until she was around her second year at elementary school, but after that her father took to attending them by himself – partly, says Yoko, because of the unfriendly attitude shown to his Japanese wife by his Korean relatives.

Yoko recalls being very happy at elementary school, while under the illusion that she was Japanese. 'I was really lively – the kind of kid who volunteers to be leader of her year group, that kind of thing. I had the best of my school days at elementary school. I did everything in a positive spirit.'

Yoko was finally woken from her illusion just before starting junior high school. 'I saw some kind of document that had to do with going up to junior high from which I realized that I wasn't Japanese. Until then I had noticed that my relatives spoke a different language when they got together, but I never wanted to find out the truth of the matter. When I looked at this document, though, I knew the truth all right. I said to my mother, "Is this right? Am I...different?" She said, "Yes, as a matter of fact you aren't Japanese." It was a terrific shock. I was devastated by it...there was a wave of regret as I realized I wasn't Japanese. I decided I'd have to hide it. I thought I'd get bullied, or at least that I might lose my friends because of being different from everyone else.'

Yoko hid her identity right through junior high school. 'I didn't tell a soul. I even tried to hide the fact that my parents were running a *yakiniku* restaurant, since inside me I had this image that "*yakiniku* equals Korean."' She hated having to fill in the section on 'official domicile' (*honseki*) in official documents such as those required to register for senior high school entrance examinations.

'You have to fill in the documents and take them to school, right? I was extra careful not to let anybody get a look at them.'

At the time, Yoko 'really hated' her Korean identity. Up to then her total assumption of Japanese identity had spared her from discrimination, but it had also caused her to absorb the negative images of Korean people prevalent among Japanese. She says she has 'no idea' as to whether there were other Koreans in her class at junior high. 'I really didn't want to think about it, I didn't feel like touching the subject in any way.' The vitality went out of her and she became a quiet, subdued pupil.

Yoko went on to commercial senior high school, still unable to find anything positive in her Korean identity. 'I had never thought of naturalization or anything. I just thought I'd have to live the rest of my life as a Korean. I felt trapped. I once asked my mother why she hadn't given birth to me as a Japanese. She said, "It can't be helped. I just got married to your father." Then I think I said something terrible to her. "That was all very well for you, but what about us?" Something like that. You see, I'd heard from my cousin that however brainy and hard-working we might be, we'd never be able to get jobs like Japanese kids could, our employment chances would be limited.'

Even at senior high school, Yoko never told any of her friends that she was Korean. Her father never discussed the matter with his daughters. On the other hand, around the time Yoko graduated from senior high school, her mother started telling her about the troubles she had suffered as a result of marrying a Korean husband. 'For instance, there was a time when the restaurant was struggling, when the business was kind of shaky, and my father's relatives blamed it on my mother. They'd say she was too tough on him, that she'd make a fool of him when she was supposed to be supporting him, and stuff like that.'

Becoming Japanese solves nothing

In 1984 the Japanese Nationality Law was revised to recognize inheritance of Japanese nationality through either parent, rather than only through the paternal line (see Chapter 2, pp. 39–40). Interim measures included in the reform enabled the children of mixed marriages who were minors (under the age of 20) on January

1, 1985, to automatically acquire Japanese nationality simply by notifying the authorities of their wish to do so during the three-year period 1985–87.

'I was nineteen. I'd just graduated from senior high school. Just at this sort of crossroads in my life, it suddenly happened that you could get Japanese nationality if you had one Japanese parent, just by switching your registration from one parent to the other. I was really hurried into it. My parents were telling me that if I didn't do it now, I'd have a real hard time going through all the hassle of the ordinary naturalization process later on. They said I wasn't going to go and live in South Korea in the future, and if I was going to live here in Japan, it was obviously going to be better for me if I had Japanese nationality.'

In the end, Yoko went along to her ward office with her mother and younger sister to make the change. 'All we had to do was hand over the documents. There were no hard questions or anything like that.'

Yoko may have been strongly urged to acquire Japanese nationality by her parents, but she was also decidedly in favor of the move herself. However, as it turned out, changing nationality only served to deepen Yoko's sense of internal conflict.

'I looked at the registration document. It said, "Japanese nationality acquired, such-and-such a day, such-and-such a month, such-and-such a year." My Korean family name, Kang, was written there as my original name as well. When I saw all this I got another shock. If these things remained on my family register, it meant that I'd only changed my nationality, and that – obvious though it was, of course – I still wasn't really Japanese.'

Yoko's case differed importantly from those where entire families naturalize. Her father still held South Korean nationality. When she and her sister took Japanese nationality, they were transferred from their father's register to their mother's. This meant that their surname also changed, from 'Sugiyama' – their father's Japanese alias – to 'Ogawa,' their mother's maiden name. Only their father retained the 'Sugiyama' surname.

'Before, the surname on my father's national insurance card was "Sugiyama," and the names of my mother, my sister and me just went underneath his. But now only my father had that surname, while my mother was listed as "Ogawa Mitsuko," and the two of us were listed under her name, so it was worse. I hated showing that card on visits to the doctor or dentist. It was better before, because at least everyone in the family had the same name.'

Although Yoko's father encouraged his daughters to take Japanese nationality, today it appears that he is unsure as to whether it was really the best choice. 'When we did it, he was saying that he'd get himself naturalized, too. But he still hasn't done it, so I guess he doesn't really want to. Now he says he feels lonely about it. When he's alone with my mother, he goes on about not having any children registered as his, and not having any children to carry on his name.'

A caring career

Yoko had no job lined up when she graduated from senior high school. During her school career she had not come across any teachers with an interest in the Zainichi problem who might have helped her approach the job market. 'I think I might have got a job in the ordinary way if I'd been Japanese, but as it was I had nothing arranged by the time I graduated. The teachers made plenty of effort to help kids who were making plenty of effort themselves to get jobs, but if you didn't approach them, well, they'd have a word with you about it, but that was about it. Personally I preferred to look after myself anyway, so I didn't really think of asking the teachers for help. There were about forty in my class, and I think there were just two of us that didn't have jobs to go to.'

Eventually Yoko found a job as a dentist's assistant. 'I planned to work for a year and then use the money I saved to go back to school.'

A year later, she passed the entrance examination for a nursing school[3] attached to a local hospital. She chose the hospital for its convenient location, not knowing that its principal happened to be a Zainichi Korean and member of Chongryun.

'I got quite a surprise. When I went along to take the exam, about thirty of the candidates were wearing *jeogori* uniform.[4] There was only one class for each year-group at the school, and about a third of the students in each class were completely Korean. They all used their real names. It didn't bother me particularly, but some kids who'd come in from the countryside, and hadn't had any kind of contact with that kind of person before, did have a funny feeling about the Koreans, and some of them didn't have a very good image of them.'

During her two years at the nursing school, Yoko told no one of her own Korean ancestry. But she worked at the hospital for two-and-a-half years after acquiring her auxiliary nursing qualification, and it was during this period that she first mentioned it to a close friend who was herself a graduate of a North Korean school.

'She also had a kind of complicated background. Her real mother was Japanese, apparently, and she'd been put in her mother's family register so that she had Japanese nationality, but she used her father's Korean surname. I liked her, and I knew about her complicated situation, so I figured she'd understand if I talked to her about it.'

It was from this friend that Yoko first learned how to pronounce her own Korean name – 'Kang Yang-Ja.' Although she had known that her official name was Korean right through high school, she never knew how to pronounce it until after she had taken Japanese nationality and it had ceased to be her official name.

Nowadays Yoko makes a point of telling her closest friends about her ethnic identity. 'I only tell people I can trust – people who I feel absolutely certain will say it doesn't matter and that they'll carry on being friends with me. I suppose in the end you don't want to keep secrets from your friends.'

A racist rejection

While she was working as an auxiliary nurse at the hospital, Yoko struck up a relationship with a Japanese doctor, who eventually proposed marriage to her. However, when she told him of her father's nationality, the proposal was abruptly withdrawn.

'When he proposed to me, I thought uh-oh, I suppose I'll have to tell him. I asked my mother for advice, and she said, "He's bound to find out sooner or later, so it's probably better to tell him now." So I did. When I got home from seeing him, I didn't say anything, so she didn't ask me how it went. She knew what had happened anyway, from the atmosphere. Later she told me that my father had talked to her about it, going on as if it was all his fault for being Korean.

'I told my cousin, who'd married a Japanese and naturalized, what had happened. He tried to console me. He said, "If he really loved you, that kind of thing wouldn't matter. He only makes a fuss about your old man being Korean and all that because he doesn't really love you." He also said that the man's attitude was an insult to my parents, and it would be no good marrying a guy like him anyway.'

The relationship dragged on for a while after that, but the couple finally drifted apart. 'He kept saying we couldn't get married. So, well, the gap between us just widened. Because we couldn't get married I kept struggling to stop myself saying or doing anything that might be taken as a hint about marriage, until in the end I just got sick of it. We ended up fighting every time we met. And right to the end he went on about nationality. "Your nationality's different, so we can't get married." I did think that since I'd acquired Japanese nationality that was no longer so, but anyway, for some reason that didn't count. He put the blame on his family. He'd say this kind of thing: "I'm the oldest son of a head household,[5] so when I get married all the relatives will want a say in it. As the oldest son I'm supposed to keep the bloodline going, so when I get married it has to be with a suitable partner." He was more bothered about his parents and all that than with the person he was supposed to be in love with.'

'There's more to life than marriage,' says Yoko. 'These days I sometimes think I might not bother getting married at all.'

Unfair examination

In April 1992, Yoko took her studies a step further, going on to junior college to work for a full nursing certificate. She had also applied to two other nursing schools, at one of which she happened to witness an apparent case of racial discrimination.

A few days after our interview I received a letter from Yoko in which she wrote the following:

There's something I forgot to mention at the interview. I actually took the exams for two other schools this spring, besides the one I got into. Something funny happened at one of them. Some people working at the same hospital as me happened to take the same exam, and three of us managed to pass. After the exam you also had to pass an interview, but this was supposed to be formality – the exam was the main hurdle. So all three of us reckoned we'd be OK. By chance we all had our interviews at the same place. I was the second one up, and one of the interviewers asked me 'Why is your father's surname different from yours?' I said, 'Because my father's a Zainichi Korean and my mother's Japanese.' When the third one of us had her interview, she was asked, 'Are you a pure Japanese?' She was, so she said yes.

The reason why that question came up was because my other friend, who had the first interview, *was* Korean. I was the second one, and I had a Japanese-looking name but turned out to have a Korean father. Also they probably thought nearly everyone working at our hospital was Korean because the head of the hospital was.

A few days later I ran into the person who had the third interview, and she said she thought Miss Chung, who had the first interview, might fail. 'The interviewer who asked me that question looked really disgusted about it. So I don't think they'll have Koreans. They'll only let Japanese in.' She didn't know about my own background, which I think was why she mentioned this to me, but until the results were announced I felt very uneasy about it. As it turned out, only the first person failed, and me and the third person passed.

I wouldn't like to think ethnicity had anything to do with it, but after that I got to thinking that a pure Japanese was one with an entirely Japanese family, and that someone like me was maybe kind of impure, you know?

I've said it before, but I don't think I'll stop feeling uncertain about my identity as long as I continue to think that I'm not Japanese, I'm just a person with Korean blood running through her who happens to have acquired Japanese nationality. You told me to take a more relaxed approach to life, but that's very difficult for me.

Sometimes I think I should have talked things over with my father much longer ago, and I regret that I did not.

Not purely Japanese, so not Japanese at all

The following comments, made near the end of my interview with Ogawa Yoko, give some idea of her self-identity at the time.

'I know I'm Japanese now by nationality, but I guess I feel more Korean. And I've actually felt more strongly that way since I got Japanese nationality. When I got it I thought I'd become completely Japanese, but my old identity remained on my registration documents and I found I was reminded of my mixed blood on more and more occasions. Before I changed nationality I didn't exactly accept my Korean identity but, well, I suppose you could say I'd got used to it. Now I wouldn't exactly say I'm stuck half way, but I just don't know what to think. At the time changing nationality didn't seem like such a big deal. My parents told me to go for it, and it seemed like a good idea to me too, but now I think that maybe, if I hadn't done it – you know, looking at myself now, how I seem to have got myself trapped somehow – it might have been better for me. I guess I had unrealistic expectations, and when I realized that they were wrong, I just got more and more...

'Everyone around me thinks I'm Japanese. That just seems to make me even more strongly aware that I'm not.'

At present Yoko speaks virtually no Korean at all. She feels no great attachment to her Korean name, Kang Yang-Ja, and considers herself to have just the one name, 'Ogawa Yoko.' South Korea is a country with some special meaning for her, but she has never been there and does not have any sense that it is her native country. Even so, she insists that she 'feels more Korean' since taking Japanese nationality.

'It's because of the circumstances of my birth, a sort of feeling that because my father is Korean, so am I. My mother's side, the Japanese side, seems to have been sort of rubbed out. I feel, how can I put it, different from my Japanese friends...But I don't have any more worries about jobs, so really marriage is the only thing that still troubles me. I really wonder sometimes if there's any man out there who would understand what it's like to be me.'

Part Two

**Korean Women in Japan:
Their Lives and Struggles**

9 A Dream Is a Dream

The story of Nam Seol-Ji (Nanbara Yukie)

Nam Seol-Ji (not her real name) has two dreams. One is to become an elementary schoolteacher; the other is to marry the Japanese man she has been seeing since her high school days.

Born in 1964, Nam Seol-Ji was 24 years old when I interviewed her on July 27, 1989. She is a third-generation Zainichi Korean holding South Korean nationality. She is the eldest of five siblings, all girls, and goes by the Japanese alias of Nanbara Yukie.

A family history of hardship

Seol-Ji's paternal grandfather, a native of Korea's Kyongsang-Buk-Do province, is in his seventies. Seol-Ji has never been told the full story of how he came to Japan, but he was in his twenties at the time. After wandering around the country for some time, he eventually settled in a small city in the Kansai district of western Japan. There he did various jobs, working at one time as a furniture maker, and at another as a laborer on government unemployment relief programs. His wife, Seol-Ji's grandmother, came to Japan to marry him. She too is still alive.

Seol-Ji's maternal grandfather lives in Kyoto. He too had a hard life working on building sites after coming to Japan.

Seol-Ji's father was born in Japan. He was the oldest of seven brothers and sisters, and managed to work his way through part-time high school. Today he is working as a money-lender. To Seol-Ji, her father is a figure to be feared. Before doing anything, she must get his permission.

Her mother was brought up 'in a sort of filthy old tenement behind the railway station,' and tells Seol-Ji that she still vividly recalls having to go without school lunches because her family could not afford to pay for them. 'My mother told me that at lunchtime she would go and play on the swing in the playground to take her mind off her empty stomach.' She is a kind mother, who protects her daughters from the wrath of their father. On the two crucial questions of Seol-Ji's job and marriage ambitions, however, both parents are opposed to her wishes.

The urge to teach

Seol-Ji knew she was Korean before she even started elementary school, having heard her grandparents speaking the language. Though well-off nowadays, the family was very poor when Seol-Ji was a child, and sometimes had to make do with crusts at mealtimes.

The district where she was brought up was right next door to a settlement of Burakumin (see Preface, Note 10). She went to a small elementary school, with just two classes in each year group. Over half the pupils were Burakumin, and the school attempted to teach them pride and an awareness of their rights. There was just one other Korean child at the school, in the class next to Seol-Ji's. She thinks her classmates knew she was Korean, although she used her Japanese alias, Nanbara Yukie, at school. She was not subjected to bullying or discrimination, but still recalls being constantly aware of how she was different from the Japanese children around her, and how she loathed that difference and longed to conceal it.

It was the teacher who took Seol-Ji's class in the fifth and sixth years of elementary school who instilled in her the burning ambition to become a teacher herself. 'She took care of us just like a mother. She once told us why she had become an elementary schoolteacher: "The children's minds are like white canvases," she said. "The elementary schoolteacher is the first person to put color on the canvas. It's a difficult job, but it has meaning." I listened to what she said, and thought: yes, I want to do that.'

By the time she got to junior high school, Seol-Ji had already abandoned hope of becoming a teacher. 'I thought my nationality would make it impossible. I felt sure it was just a dream.' Even so, when she graduated from senior high school and went on to junior college[1] in Osaka, something made possible by a sharp improvement in the family economy, she made the effort to acquire a teaching certificate.[2] As she put it to me, 'Even if I couldn't become a teacher, at least I would get a couple of weeks' teaching practice. That was the one thing I really looked forward to at college. All the other students used to grumble about having to do teaching practice, but I just couldn't wait to get into the classroom. I really loved it.'

By the time I met Seol-Ji, her 'impossible dream' had taken a surprising step toward realization: she was working at an elementary school in a city not far from the one where her family lived, albeit as a substitute teacher with no security of tenure. She arrived at this job in a roundabout way.

Like most college students, Seol-Ji started job-hunting prior to graduation. 'I thought I didn't have much chance of a job, being Korean, but my teacher said the college would give me a good reference. The people who interviewed me for jobs also said nationality had nothing to do with it…but I didn't get a job. Then in the new year, when I had all but given up,[3] I finally got lucky.'

It was with a large manufacturer of sportswear in Osaka. She worked in the publicity department, as a member of an all-woman project team putting together a newsletter. The commute from home was three hours each way, 'but because the job was so much fun, that didn't bother me at all.'

Even so, Seol-Ji still felt a pang of envy and regret whenever she happened to walk past an elementary school. 'I would try to console myself with the thought that it would have been a tough job if I had got it, that giving up had been the right move, and so on.'

She quit her job at the company after three years, at her parents' behest. They thought it 'shameful' that she should still be unmarried and working at her age. Ironically, however, when she went to the job center to sort out her unemployment insurance, she happened to notice an advertisement for a temporary part-time post at the local city hall. She applied for it, and was pleasantly surprised to find that her nationality did not prevent her getting the job. Nationality is less of a problem for part-time jobs in the public sector. Unfortunately, the work turned out to be extremely dull – making photocopies, recording entries in ledgers, etc.

She also had to adjust to a rather unfamiliar work ethic. 'On my first day, I was given some task to do, and I did it really promptly, handed over the finished article with a bow, and was warned not to put so much effort into my work.'

The city hall staff naturally knew that Seol-Ji was Korean, and would react with a patronizing brand of sympathy when socializing after work. '"What a shame you're going to have a hard time getting married…" they'd say. They knew my grandad and seemed to have a problem with him: "He's a pretty scary guy…" they'd say. At first I laughed it off, but after a while it got on my nerves. "My grandad came to live in this country without speaking a word of the language and without knowing anybody here," I said. "It can't be helped if he's a little rough in his manners." I don't think they understood, though.'

And then Seol-Ji suddenly got lucky again. 'I had previously applied for a job at a private kindergarten. I didn't get it. Didn't have the practical skills, you know. Couldn't play the piano, wasn't much good at gymnastics. But the head of the kindergarten sent my résumé on to the local education committee. And one day I got this phone call out of the blue: "It's the education committee, and we're wondering if you could help us out at such-and-such elementary school." I was ecstatic. I literally jumped for joy.'

And so in July of 1989, just before I interviewed her, Seol-Ji started work at elementary school, filling in for a teacher who was away on maternity leave. 'Now that I'm actually doing it, I find that although it's a tough job, I love it just as much as I thought I would. Now I'm keener than ever to do it on a proper, permanent basis.'

She may yet get the chance. The prefecture where Seol-Ji lives has scrapped the nationality clause in its list of employment conditions for teachers in publicly-run schools, and the first two teachers with Korean nationality have been employed. But the problem of parental consent remains. 'My mother says it's a disgrace to still be working and not married at my age. She keeps on saying "I'm so ashamed I can't even talk to our relatives about it, so please, please quit."'

To marry Mr Right

Seol-Ji's other dream, to marry her childhood sweetheart, is another source of serious family trouble. Like many Zainichi

Korean parents, Seol-Ji's mother and father are very insistent that she should marry a fellow Korean.

'I got this boyfriend when I was in the third year of senior high. We used to walk home from school together, and one day my grandfather spotted us. He told my mother, who was furious with me. "You can't go walking home with a boy! What will the neighbors think?!" I carried on seeing the boy, hiding the fact from my folks. But my mother's got a woman's instincts for these things...she noticed that I kept on turning down promising inquiries about interviews for arranged marriages,[4] and she put two and two together.

'In the end she rang up the boy's parents to ask if they couldn't find a way of breaking up the relationship. The two mothers got me and him sat down at a table with them and argued with us all night. "We're begging you: break it up, break it up, break it up!" Oh, the way they went on at me...I felt like I'd rather die.

'His mother didn't exactly hold back. "There are a lot of high-up people among our relatives," she said. "People with jobs at city hall, people working for the prefecture. I won't be able to show my face in front of them if my son goes and marries a Korean." When we got home, my mother said, "See? You heard what she said. You can't still want to marry into that family. You'd be bullied all the time. They'd be going on like they'd done you a big favor by letting you marry their son despite you being a Korean." She said she'd heard of many such cases. "Mrs So-and-so's daughter married a Japanese, and in the end she got dumped. I just don't want you to go through something like that," she'd say.'

In their arguments, Seol-Ji's mother would sometimes refer to their impoverished past. '"I know I put you through the misery of poverty when you were a kid," she'd say, "so I want to put it right by fixing you up with a real good marriage."' She would also invoke Seol-Ji's responsibility to her younger sisters: 'Marriages between fellow Koreans are always arranged, right?[5] She'd accuse me of letting the family down if I married a Japanese, because then other Korean families wouldn't want their sons to marry my sisters. "Think of the family," she'd say. "You're the eldest, so make a sacrifice for the sake of your sisters."'

Two worlds

Seol-Ji describes South Korea as her 'motherland' (*sokoku*) and Japan as her 'homeland' (*kokyō*). When asked which she considers her 'own country,' she replies, 'South Korea, I suppose. But since I've been brought up here in Japan, and I have no knowledge of anywhere except Japan, I don't think I could live in South Korea.' She hardly speaks any Korean, and she always goes by her Japanese pseudonym except when attending meetings of the local branch of the KYAJ (see Chapter 3, pp. 55-6). 'Somehow I don't feel quite comfortable when people address me as "Nam Seol-Ji,"' she says.

Seol-Ji's commitment to her Korean identity is genuine. She visited South Korea on a Mindan-organized trip during her second year in senior high school. On her return she told her close Japanese friends, through floods of tears, 'I am Korean!' She even used the broken Korean she had picked up to enter a speech contest organized by Mindan.

In the end, however, Seol-Ji's career and marriage ambitions are framed by the Japanese context. She is wholly at ease in a Japanese company: 'I talk away to my heart's content with my Japanese friends. It's lots of fun and I don't have the slightest feeling that I'm in any way out of place with them.' A thoroughly modern woman, she has succeeded in the workplace in the company and school contexts alike. Yet her self-awareness is founded on the Confucian principles of a traditional Zainichi Korean family. In Korean terms it is only natural that high school sweethearts should refrain from walking home together. Daughters who wish to go out must first take care of the household chores, even if that means getting up at 5 o'clock in the morning. Above all, father must be obeyed.

And so Seol-Ji lives in two worlds. One is a world surrounded by Japanese: all her friends, her schoolteachers, her colleagues and superiors at work. The other is a Zainichi Korean world, centered on her family. Whether conscious of the fact or not, she has moved between these two worlds ever since infancy. Her honest, hard-working and friendly character has made her well-liked and fully integrated in both worlds.

Ultimately, however, the great differences between the two worlds make strife inevitable. As Seol-Ji herself puts it: 'Everyone seems free to take the job they want except me. In love and marriage, too, it seems that I'm different from everybody else. Even if I feel like grumbling to my Japanese friends about the problems I'm facing over marriage, I know they won't be able to understand the situation entirely. Sometimes I get to thinking that everyone else is different from me, and that everyone else is happy.'

The discrimination endemic in Japanese society is certainly an element in Seol-Ji's predicament. But the more immediate problem facing her is that of her own parents. 'Somehow it seems that I'm forever being told that I mustn't do this and I mustn't do that, simply because I'm Korean.'

No model to follow

Hitherto, Nam Seol-Ji has maintained a delicate balancing act between her two roles, as modern, self-motivated woman and as obedient daughter. Sooner or later, something has to give. Her parents want only the best for her, which to them means a good marriage to a Zainichi Korean man with prospects, and if Seol-Ji becomes too absorbed in work, that is a threat to the future they have planned for her no less than her relationship with her Japanese boyfriend.

Concerns such as these prompted Seol-Ji's father to order her to quit her job at the sportswear company. Seol-Ji refused at first, leading to a fight that ended with her father saying he disowned her and telling her to get out of the house.

'"All right, then," I said, and I packed my bags. My mother was crying and crying. "Please, don't do that, do anything but not that," she said. "No, it's too late, I'm off," I said. Then my father kicked me. It was the first time he'd ever used violence against me. My mother stepped between us as if she was ready to take the kicks herself to protect me, and, well...' Seol-Ji ended up unpacking her bags and staying.

To Seol-Ji's parents, her two dreams are just two aspects of the same problem: reckless, selfish disobedience. Her decision to take on her temporary teaching post was also seen as an obstacle to her making the right marriage, to the point where her father went in person to see the headmaster and asked him to make his daughter quit.

As she struggles to reconcile her will with that of her parents, Seol-Ji has no model to guide her. Unable to ignore her parents' point of view, all she can do is implore them to change it. She tells them that all other things will be done to perfection, if only she can have her way over the two dreams. 'What I want is absolutely clear to me. In a way it's too clear, which gets me into fights with my parents, but even then I don't give in. If I showed the slightest indecision, they'd take that as a sign that I was about to knuckle under, so I make sure I don't give any such sign.'

But Seol-Ji's parents have had long, hard, first-hand experience of Japanese discrimination. They have no intention of allowing their daughter to flout Korean tradition and marry a Japanese. And so the result is stalemate. Time passes…the matter remains unresolved. The gap between Seol-Ji's perfectly natural desire to do a job to which she is suited and marry a man whom she loves, and her deeply ingrained loyalty to her parents, has widened into a yawning chasm. Nor does she have any example before her to show how such a chasm may be bridged.

Whether or not Seol-Ji finally takes the plunge and leaves home, she must first transform her inner self. The absolute necessity of loyalty to her parents must be changed into something relative. She must learn to question all her values before she can fly the nest.

Seol-Ji's lack of any example as to how to handle her present situation stems from the social isolation of her family. They are surrounded by Japanese, living in an area with virtually no other Korean households. Until recently the only fellow Koreans Seol-Ji ever met were her own relatives. Only since she became involved in the KYAJ has she had a chance to meet other Zainichi Koreans of her own generation. Among them she may yet find a model to deal with her dilemma. Meanwhile, she remains standing at a crossroads. One road leads to abandoning her family obligations in pursuit of her dreams; the other is the more 'realistic' road advocated by her parents.

10 Diplomatic Incidents

The story of Chong Mi-Young-Ja (Soda Mieko)

Chong Mi-Young-Ja (not her real name) was born in Kyoto in 1963, and grew up in Tokyo. When I interviewed her, on May 31, 1989, she was 25 years old. She is the eldest of three siblings, and holds South Korean nationality. Her Japanese alias is Soda Mieko.

Mi-Young-Ja's paternal grandfather never spoke about how he came to migrate to Japan, but Mi-Young-Ja has heard from her father that her grandfather had a tough time. 'Apparently he was a sort of apprentice. He had to run errands barefoot, even when it was snowing, and got frostbite on his feet. He was lucky if he got a bowl of moldy barley to eat.' But he pulled himself up by his bootstraps and ended up as a successful businessman, with his own company making *yūzen* printed silk in Kyoto, and later a small taxi company in Tokyo. Nowadays Mi-Young-Ja's uncle is running the silk company, while her father has taken over the taxi business.

Passing for Japanese

Mi-Young-Ja spent her childhood in a household cut off from Korean influences. It was in an entirely Japanese part of town, her second-generation parents couldn't speak Korean, household conversation was conducted entirely in Japanese and everyone in the family used their Japanese pseudonyms all the time. Even so, Mi-Young-Ja knew she was Korean from an early age. She called her uncle *aje* and her aunt *yimo*, and the family often ate Korean-style meals.

Mi-Young-Ja went by her Japanese alias all the way from elementary school to university. Her mother told her never to mention her Korean identity under any circumstances. 'I believe my mother was pretty badly bullied when she was a schoolgirl herself. My father too. They didn't want me to go through the same thing.' At elementary school there was a girl in another class who got bullied for being Korean, but Mi-Young-Ja didn't give the matter much thought. 'I could pass for Japanese, so I didn't get bullied, so that was alright…by the time I got to senior high, I had become thoroughly Japanese.'

The transformation was never quite complete, however. Sometimes it would bother her when she heard racist anti-Korean comments. Sometimes she and her friends would spot students going to the local Korean school on the train as it pulled into their station. 'Uh-oh, Koreans. Let's not get on.' Mi-Young-Ja would say, 'Why not?' and get right on. She felt uneasy at the racism she sensed in her friends, but she could say nothing. She deliberately avoided thinking deeply about her identity, and in this she was helped by the vocabulary used to discuss Korean matters in Japanese. The subjects of her friends' casual racist remarks were *Chōsenjin* – the term used to describe *North* Koreans. She, by contrast, knew that she was a *Kankokujin* – a *South* Korean. 'I just thought all that stuff about *Chōsenjin* had nothing to do with me.'

First exposure

In senior high school, Mi-Young-Ja began to think it was about time she started to learn a little about her mother country. She considered studying Korean language at university, but eventually followed her teacher's advice and did English literature. At university she made friends with A, a Japanese girl who had lived abroad for many years because of her father's work. 'She told me how she had her hair pulled at an American school in Holland for being "Chinese," and ended up refusing to go to school. Then her family went to South Korea, where she was treated coldly for being Japanese. Only the maidservant who came to her house was kind to her. This maidservant had seen both her parents killed by Japanese colonialists in front of her eyes, but still insisted that "some Japanese are bad, but not all of them." She said that because of all these experiences she'd had, she would never tolerate discrimination against Zainichi Koreans.'

Hearing all this, Mi-Young-Ja decided that at last here was someone she could trust with the truth about herself. She told A that she was Korean. It was a great turning point: the first time in her life that she had mentioned her ethnic identity to anyone. 'She said that anyone who would hate me for being Korean didn't deserve to be my friend anyway. I thought, "She's right..." I started talking about my identity to other close friends. They didn't seem at all bothered, and I started to think that maybe I'd been worrying too much about the thing.'

So Mi-Young-Ja went through university with a triple identity: 'In most Japanese company, I'd be Japanese. At home I'd be Korean. With my close friends, I'd be Zainichi Korean.'

The Korean consulate as foreign territory

Worried by all the talk she heard about the difficulties faced by Zainichi Koreans in the job market, but keen to get a job with an international aspect, Mi-Young-Ja approached her grandfather, who was an influential figure within Mindan, and asked him to fix her up with a job at the South Korean embassy in Tokyo. He duly set her up with a secretarial job in the consular section, which is located in a separate building not far from the embassy itself. However, he insisted that she first spend a token six months studying Korean at a language school. Until then she hadn't spoken a word of Korean.

'The first thing everyone said to me when I started work was "Your name is really weird." Korean given names mostly have one or two characters; mine had three. The family story is that I was supposed to be named "Mie" (equivalent to "Mi-Young" in Korean), but the midwife who registered the birth went and stuck a Japanese-style "ko" on the end.[1]

'I worked at the consulate for just over two years, and experienced culture shock every single day. Except for the interior of the family house, my whole world had been Japanese until I took that job. But at the consulate it was just like being in South Korea. A lot of people over there have the feeling that Zainichi Koreans have somehow betrayed their country, you know. I had some hair-raising conversations. "Can you speak Korean?" – "I'm afraid I can't." "You can't be Korean if you don't speak the language!"...

•

"You're Korean, right? Well, sing the national anthem then!" – "I don't know it. Would the *Kimigayo*² be any good?" – "Who *is* this kid?!" Crazy days. Pretty tough, actually.'

But if Mi-Young-Ja found a few enemies at the consulate, she found far more friends – and quite a few language students. 'Even the first secretary asked me to teach him Japanese. I was always being invited to meals at people's houses. I was surprised to find that the food was totally different to the supposedly Korean dishes I'd had at home. There were all sorts of rare delicacies – including a few that were really hard to stomach.'

She spent her first three months in the consular section processing visas for Japanese nationals. Noticing that Koreans seemed to be fairly open in expressing their wishes to their superiors, she put in a request to be transferred to foreign visas so that she could put her command of English to work. Then six months later, when the consul-general's secretary resigned to get married, Mi-Young-Ja boldly put in for *that* job. She got it, despite her lack of Korean: the consul-general felt that good Japanese was more important, since much of the work entailed dealing with Japanese. He made a deal with her: he'd speak Japanese to her; she would speak as much Korean as possible to him. And so Mi-Young-Ja finally began to pick up her own language.

Her new boss was shocked to discover that she had never been to Korea, and more or less ordered her to go there during the May holiday week. She had a three-day holiday in Seoul, using her newly-acquired language skill to help her younger sister negotiate immigration procedures. 'It was fun...but I must admit I did feel the coldness in the way some of the mainland people looked on us Zainichis.'

Her job at the consulate brought her many Zainichi friends, especially among the staff of the KYAJ headquarters, located as it was inside the consulate building (see Chapter 5, p. 93). She had never had friends who shared her ethnicity before, and there was something comforting in all the shared experience. There was also a certain distance, however: these people took Zainichi Korean issues very seriously indeed, and were constantly arguing about them. In her heart she supported them, but she could not see herself joining their ranks as an activist. These new friendships made her start to realize that she hadn't really been thinking very deeply about her position in society.

After two years at the consular section, Mi-Young-Ja had acquired a reasonable conversational ability in Korean, but the constant emotional tension, along with the long hours of what was a very demanding job, had worn her out. She quit.

'This company does not employ foreigners'

Mi-Young-Ja took it easy for a month or so after leaving the consulate, and then started looking through the recruitment magazines for a job with a Japanese company. 'I thought it would be really interesting to work in a Japanese environment this time. Armed with my experience at the consulate I went looking for secretarial jobs. Employers liked the diplomatic track record, but when they found out about my nationality they would suddenly lose their enthusiasm.

'In the end I tried for about twenty jobs and got turned down for every single one of them. As an experiment, half the time I wrote "South Korea" in the "place of origin" (*honseki*)[3] space on the application form, and half the time I wrote "Kyoto." I never got an interview when I wrote "South Korea"; I always got an interview when I wrote "Kyoto." But later on in the process they would always ask to see copies of documents such as my family register (*koseki*; see Introduction Note 9), which would give the game away, since I don't have a family register, I have an alien registration document. That would be the end of the story. "Our company does not employ foreigners. You're very good, but we can't take you on because you're not Japanese."'

Disheartened by endless rejections, Mi-Young-Ja decided she might as well go for temporary work. She registered with an agency, which sent her to work at the reception desk of a large corporate headquarters. Temps do not have to supply the mountain of documents required when applying for permanent employment, and so Mi-Young-Ja got by as Soda Mieko, Japanese. It had taken her four months of job-hunting to secure this modest temporary position.

For the first time, Mi-Young-Ja wished she were Japanese. 'I wondered why my parents hadn't naturalized. Somehow they seemed terribly indecisive, you know?'

Work at the Japanese company was drastically different from at the consulate. 'I thought, so this is Japanese society, is it? Kind of boring really. At the consulate everyone was really energetic, and keen to show what they could do. But here everyone seemed to be trying to get by doing the bare minimum of work given them.'

For the first time in years, Mi-Young-Ja was pretending to be Japanese. This time, however, it felt different. 'It was just a surface thing. I didn't feel Japanese inside the way I did before. On the contrary, I felt more aware than ever of being a specifically *Zainichi* Korean. In a sense I felt much more relaxed about it. In the old days I'd forever be worrying that I might betray myself by some small slip of the tongue. Now I felt that even if people did find out the truth about me it wouldn't be such a big deal, which was a refreshing feeling.'

'The smell of garlic'

One day, Mi-Young-Ja had an unpleasant experience at work.

'There was this guy in the personnel department, who must have spotted something in my résumé. He was always having a go at people. Anyway, one day he says to me: "I smell garlic when you're around." I'm slightly taken aback. "Oh really," I say, "I must have eaten too many *gyōza* last night." "No," he says. "It's *kimchi* that I smell when you're around."[4] I'll never forgive him.

'It happened one other time too. "You've been talking funny lately," he says. "Gradually reverting to your native tongue, I daresay." "What *are* you talking about?" I reply. He just goes "Huh." I think to myself, so there really are people who'll say things like that. It may be meant as a joke, but all the same you can't forgive it, right?'

The company where Mi-Young-Ja had these experiences has conducted training programs in human rights awareness[5] for its employees for well over a decade. Mi-Young-Ja, however, is unimpressed. 'As far as I could see, even in the personnel department, all the stuff about human rights was just for show. The people there liked to say they were doing that kind of thing, but most of the other employees couldn't have cared less about it.'

Wanderlust

Chong Mi-Young-Ja quit her temporary job as a receptionist in the fall of 1989, having worked at it for one year. These days she is helping out at her father's taxi company. But she is not just marking time while waiting to be fixed up with a marriage partner. Indeed, she is not sure when, or to what kind of man, she might want to get married.

'In my student days, I felt absolutely certain that I'd marry a fellow Zainichi Korean. I would deliberately avoid emotional entanglements, fearing that I might fall in love with some Japanese boy who'd end up turning me away because I was Korean. But now I feel differently. OK, it would please my parents if I married a Korean, but in the end it's me who's got to live with the guy, not them. I wouldn't mind marrying a Japanese, or maybe some other kind of foreigner.'

Her parents are unlikely to make an issue of it. 'They never talk about it. Recently they've got to thinking that they've kept the Korean bloodline going for about as far as it will go. After all, they don't speak the language themselves, and my mother's never even been to Korea. They're South Koreans by nationality, but they don't know the country and they've become almost completely Japanese. So they're hardly in a position to lay down the law and insist that their own child maintain the family's pure Korean bloodline. Lately they've been saying that it's up to me to decide for myself.'

Mi-Young-Ja is in no hurry to tie the knot. 'I don't have the slightest wish to get married right now. I want to get out and see more of the world. Looking at my age and nationality, I suppose my best chance of a job is with a foreign-owned company. I think I'll have to do some studying to improve my English first, though.'

11 This Japanese Is Still Korean

The story of Oh Mika

Oh Mika (not her real name) is a second-generation Zainichi Korean. Her parents acquired Japanese citizenship before her birth in 1961. She has one older brother, and was 28 when interviewed on July 30, 1989. Until 1995 her name was officially registered as 'Takarada Mika.' Her family invented this surname, basing it on the first character of 'Bosong,' the *bonkwan* or district of Korea to which the Oh's trace their ancestral roots (see Chapter 1, p. 6). This character means 'treasure' and reads *takara* in Japanese. The second character, *da* (field), was added to make it sound more Japanese. Today, however, Mika prefers to use the surname 'Oh,' which her father had before he naturalized – this despite the fact that she uses the Japanese reading of her given name, which would read 'Mi-Hyang' in Korean.

Though born a Japanese citizen, Oh Mika insists that ever since she was old enough to think about such matters, she has considered herself entirely Korean.

Work comes first

When she was a little girl, Mika asked her father why he had decided to naturalize. 'So that you and your brother will be able to get jobs in the future,' he replied.

Mika's father was born in 1929, in the southern Korean province of Kyongsang-Buk-Do. Around the age of ten he was taken to Japan by a family friend, to join his father who had already migrated. He was put into the first year of elementary school, alongside children several years younger than him. Helped perhaps by his advanced years, he sailed through the school system at the top of the class. Despite impeccable credentials and a letter of recommendation from his senior high school headmaster, however, he fell victim to anti-Korean discrimination and failed to realize his ambition of getting a job in banking. However, he finally found a company that would employ him despite his nationality, and picked up a university degree by studying nights. He stayed with the same company all the way to retirement.

Mika's paternal grandfather had preceded her father to Japan, and had worked for an association for Korean residents in Japan. After the war he got a new job in local government. When the San Francisco peace treaty took effect in 1952, he was stripped of his Japanese citizenship, as were all Koreans living in Japan, and applied for naturalization to avoid losing his job under the nationality clause. Mika's father, and his four brothers and sisters, all became Japanese citizens at the same time.

Shamanic blood

Although Mika was born into a naturalized family in a district of Kawasaki where no other Koreans lived, she always knew of her Korean ethnicity.

'My grandmother was a *Mudang*, a Korean shaman. She would pray and chant while banging on a large drum. People would come to her with illnesses to be cured or problems to be solved. She'd give them advice that she said she'd got straight from the gods. She'd say things like "Someone's given you a doll recently, right? Move it off the top of the dresser right away."

'My mother didn't believe in all that before she got married. But she nearly died when she gave birth to my big brother: it was a Caesarian section, and she somehow couldn't inhale the oxygen or whatever they were giving her. Just when she was on the brink, she heard a great roaring sound, and a voice talking in Korean, saying "*Nega kugosul masyeoya sanda.*" Apparently *sanda* means 'live' in Korean. When she heard this voice, my mother started inhaling for all she was worth, and she pulled through. Ever since then, her dreams have had a strange habit of coming true.

'When my grandmother got so old and weak that she had to go into hospital, the doctor asked her what her name was, just to see if she was in her right mind. She answered 'Kim Bong-Suk,' much to the consternation of my family, who were trying to pass as Japanese

– ridiculously, if you ask me. In her old age my grandmother spoke 95 percent Korean. My mother could understand her, but the Japanese nurses had no idea what she was going on about.'

The reason why Mika's Japan-born mother could understand Korean was because she'd been brought up in a Korean settlement and had put in a couple of years at an ethnic Korean school. She was born in Tokyo in 1936, to an extremely poor family that only managed to send her to Japanese school for one year – a year scarred by intense racist bullying, which meant that Mika's mother spent most of it at home. To this day she has some difficulty in reading and writing Japanese. Her own father died when she was twelve, leaving her mother to look after 'about ten' children. 'My *halme* (grandma) did all sorts of things to scrape a living. The children all went to work, and the girls all married in their teens. My own mother married when she was sixteen.'

Out of Mika's mother's many siblings, five sisters and one brother are still alive. Mika's mother is the only one who has naturalized.

Korean pride

When Mika was small, her father often spoke of his own childhood in Korea. 'I used to love listening to his stories. That's probably where I got the sense of being Korean myself. For generations his family had been priests at a Buddhist temple on top of a little hill. Before he came to Japan, he used to help his father around the temple, chanting the morning sutras for him, planting ginseng in the temple fields, and so on. He often says he misses his hometown. He's not been back once since he came to Japan.'

With this family background, Mika naturally grew up feeling Korean and proud of it. 'I remember going to look at cherry blossoms with my family when I was very small. There were some Korean people there, dancing around in their *jeogori* (traditional Korean clothing) and banging on a *jang-gu* (Korean drum). I was watching them really intently. Some old man turned to me and said, "Pretty, aren't they?" "I'm Korean too!" I proudly replied. Even after I went up to elementary school, I had no trouble with discrimination for the first couple of years, and I used to tell everyone I was Korean as proud as you like.'

A double life

Mika's family had changed its nationality but not its ethnic identity. And so it happened that they led a double life: Japanese to the outside world, Korean at home. 'We had a tough time at New Year's. We had to lay on Japanese food for my father's friends from work who came to visit, while our Korean relatives were having a great time eating a Korean-style banquet in the next room. When my brother got married, we had two wedding parties – one Korean, one Japanese – with completely different guest lists.'

Mika attended private schools all the way from kindergarten to senior high. Midway through elementary school, she slowly started to sense that it was not a good idea to mention her Korean ethnicity. 'Like, around the third or fourth year I started to notice that if I wore flashy clothes people would say I "looked like a Korean"…in a nasty sort of way. I stopped talking about Korean stuff except to my closest friends.'

She became far more aware of discrimination while at junior high. Some cousins on her mother's side, who had not naturalized, graduated from university but still failed to find jobs and ended up taking over their parents' café for want of better employment. It occurred to Mika that she too might fail to find a job, or indeed a husband, if people knew she was ethnically Korean. She used psychological defense mechanisms. 'I used to go around telling my friends that I wasn't ever going to get married.'

By the time Mika reached senior high, she was thoroughly torn between the desire to forget her Korean origins and the inescapable fact of their existence. 'One incident made a really deep impression on me. We were having a geography lesson, and the teacher wrote "China, Japan, Korea" on the blackboard. One of the kids called out, "Don't put Japan between China and Korea, it's disgusting!" It was a terrific shock. I thought, that's one kid I must never tell.' She also felt her heart pounding with tension whenever Korea came up in history lessons.

'It's not that I doubted my identity,' she explains. 'I've always known that whatever the color of my passport, I'm still Korean. But since my identity spelled nothing but trouble, I wanted to hide it, forget it, get away from it. But time and again, I found I just couldn't. For instance, one of my young non-naturalized cousins lost a point in a test for answering "Japan" to a question where the right answer was "our country." She knew the answer, but she just couldn't write it because she knew Japan wasn't "her country." I imagined myself in her position, and I knew I'd do the same. Being naturalized makes no difference.'

While at senior high school, Mika told two very close friends that she was Korean. 'They just said, "What's that got to do with anything?" That's the kind of standard reply. Although really, being Korean has a lot to do with everything, right? These days I feel kind of funny when people say that to me, because it seems they just don't appreciate the significance of ethnic identity, but at the time it was a great relief to me that they weren't going to change their attitude toward me.'

Self-loathing

Mika failed her university entrance exams. After a year of extra studying, she managed to get on to a correspondence course at a university that did teacher training, but soon dropped out. As a correspondence student she was able to join university clubs, but found personal relations difficult.

'I'd been to an all-girl high school, and I'd never spoken to any boys except for my own brother. I kind of panicked – didn't know how to put the right distance between myself and them. Plus I was always fretting about the Korean thing, wanting to tell people but scared of how they might react, and in the end I was just in a psychological mess.'

For two years Mika attended a club at another university that studied Burakumin issues (see Preface, Note 10). 'I had never heard of anti-Burakumin discrimination until then. I found the activists kind of appealing...since they were campaigning against another form of discrimination, I guessed they wouldn't discriminate against *me* if I told them I was Korean. But in the end, I didn't even tell them. Maybe I'm just a coward...anyway, it was just easier to hide it. If I kept it hidden, employment and marriage would be so much easier...I couldn't escape from it, but I kept trying to all the same.'

She told just one Japanese boyfriend, but the relationship ended badly. 'Since I told no one else, I unloaded all my thoughts and worries on him alone. I'm afraid I made life pretty hard for him.'

And then Mika went through another phase. 'I started telling *everybody* about it. I figured that hiding it had been the cause of all my personal problems. Letting it out made me feel great. Suddenly I could talk to people. Everyone told me how cheerful I'd become.'

Mika went back into education, this time attending a technical school. Now she concealed her ethnic identity once more. 'I was about four years older than the others, who were just out of senior high. The age gap was a problem, and also I heard some of them making racist comments about Koreans – calling us *Chonkō*[1] for instance.'

At twenty-two, Mika had two interviews for arranged marriages (see Chapter 9, Note 4). The prospective partners were both naturalized Koreans like herself. She turned them both down. 'I couldn't stomach the prospect. If I married another naturalized Korean, we'd end up living a life of concealment just like my own parents, just when I was thinking that I couldn't stay in hiding any longer. I figured it would be hell.'

New name, new life

By late 1986, when Mika had completed school and was living off part-time jobs, she made her first visit to the Seikyū-sha,[2] a group based in an ethnic Korean district of Kawasaki, which campaigns for Zainichi rights and conducts ethnic Korean education. She had known of this group for years, but had not felt ready to approach it.

'I was invited to the Seikyū-sha Christmas party. It changed my life. I had thought I was all alone with my problems, but here were lots of people in exactly the same position. I was overjoyed, and started going there all the time. There was just one trouble: no one said it to me directly, but I knew that behind my back people were saying that Koreans who naturalized were traitors.[3] I thought that was pretty unfair. After all, there are plenty of people with South or North Korean nationality who are less Korean than me in their daily lives – people who never do the *Jesa*, for instance – so I was shocked to think that nationality could be such a big deal. Besides, I hadn't even had any choice in the matter. It seemed all wrong.

'I'm still a member of the Seikyū-sha, but I don't go as often as I used to.'

About six months after joining the Seikyū-sha, Mika dropped her Japanese surname and started calling herself by her Korean surname, 'Oh.' In September 1988 she started a temporary job at a workshop run by people with cerebral palsy, and introduced herself as 'Oh Mika.' She also uses this name at the stationery shop where she works today. Her decision was much influenced by Yoon Cho-Ja (see next chapter), who was one of the principal members of another group promoting Korean ethnic awareness, the Society for Winning Back Ethnic Names (see Chapter 3, Note 9). At the time of our interview Mika described this group as more important to her than the Seikyū-sha.

'If you've got Japanese nationality, using a Korean name is the only way to show that you're Korean. I've got a badge with my name on that I use at work, with the character for "Oh" on it and the Korean pronunciation in brackets right after. When people realize what it means, you can see it in their faces. Like one boy saw it and gave his friend a nudge. "Hey, she's Korean, you know!" I hate that kind of reaction. You wouldn't get it without pretty deep-rooted discrimination.

'Advertising my ethnicity like this means everyone treats me as a Korean now. It's tough – there's so much discrimination in Japanese society that they'll turn on you if you just make some small mistake in your conduct. So you try to be perfect all the time, and it's really tiring. Even so, I have no intention whatsoever of going back to calling myself "Takarada."'

As written, Mika's name looks entirely Korean. But even though she uses her unambiguously Korean surname, she still uses the Japanese reading of her given name: Mika, rather than Mi-Hyang. 'Although I'm Korean, I know I'm totally different from mainland Koreans. I'm a specifically *Zainichi* Korean, and I've even got Japanese nationality. I just wouldn't feel right calling myself "Mi-Hyang" in my present circumstances.'

Stuck in the middle

'In the end I've never been able to think of myself as Japanese just because of my nationality. The fact is I'm not Japanese and I've known it from an early age. You can put me in a kimono but my heart will still be Korean. At the same time, because I've always been here in Japan, I just can't feel personally involved in Korean affairs, such as whether the country can be reunified, for instance. I can't even share the pain of Korean nationals in Japan who have to undergo fingerprinting[4] and so on. In that sense I have a kind of guilty feeling that I'm not really a Korean in the true sense of the word either. I really am stuck in the middle, with my Japanese nationality and my Korean surname. That's me. I can't break down my essential self, nor do I want to.'

Oh Mika says that the biggest change after she started using her Korean name was in the attitude of her mother. 'The toughest thing in my mother's life was having to hide her Korean identity. Now she says she's jealous of me. I've come out, and I've still got friends and a job. At first she was dead against it. She didn't want mail coming to the house addressed to someone with a Korean-looking name like "Oh." She told me I shouldn't be making a fuss about living in secrecy. These days, though, she says, "If you really can live without hiding, that's the best way."'

Every year, growing numbers of Zainichi Koreans are acquiring Japanese nationality (see Chapter 2, Note 25). 'Condemning it won't solve anything,' says Mika. 'Calling people who naturalize traitors won't reduce their numbers. It's mostly because people assume that naturalization means hiding your Korean identity that it's seen as betrayal. I think that once people get used to the idea that you can take pride in your ethnic identity even if you've changed your nationality, the meaning of naturalization will change. Otherwise, how are people going to think of themselves?

'I want to see Japanese society develop into one where no one sees anything strange in having Japanese nationality and Korean ethnicity. To help make that happen, I want to preserve the best parts of my ancestors' culture. After all, it's the culture that's made me Korean. Conversely, I don't think I would have had a sense of Korean identity if the culture had not been passed on to me in the home. I think it's really hard if you can't have your own original identity.'

In 1995 Mika won a ruling from her local family court under which her surname was legally changed from 'Takarada' to 'Oh.'

12 Mixed Blood, Mixed Feelings

The story of Yoon Cho-Ja

Yoon Cho-Ja was born in 1951, in Osaka. Her father was Korean, her mother Japanese. When interviewed, on March 22, 1989, she was 37, living in Kawasaki and teaching at a publicly-run elementary school in Tokyo. Cho-Ja was brought up believing herself to be Japanese, with her Japanese name and nationality. But after much inner struggle, she legally adopted her deceased father's Korean surname in April, 1989.

Better illegitimate

Cho-Ja's father was born in Kyongsang-Nam-Do, southern Korea, in 1927. He was brought to Japan at the age of three, following his own father, who had emigrated in search of work and proceeded to 'support the family any way he could: cleaning out night-soil boxes, burning charcoal, brewing *doburoku*,[1] whatever.'

Cho-Ja's father was the eldest son of the family. Desperate to avoid the filthy work he saw his own father doing, he became a musician. He met Cho-Ja's mother and the two planned to marry. However, the plan met fierce opposition from her family. 'She was disinherited, thrown out of the house penniless, and went to live with him.'

Much later, Cho-Ja learned from her mother that her father had begged her, with tears in his eyes, to register the child as her own in order to secure Japanese nationality for her and thereby spare her the miseries of discrimination that he had experienced himself. At the time Japanese law did not yet accord nationality rights to the offspring of a foreign father and a Japanese mother. However, the couple had never registered their marriage, and Cho-Ja's mother was able to register the child under her own name by the humiliating subterfuge of claiming that the father's whereabouts were unknown. He planned to one day naturalize and legally unite the family.

Cho-Ja believed she was entirely Japanese throughout her childhood. 'My father never told me he was Korean, and did not impart any Korean customs to me.'

When she was seven, her parents separated. 'Later I asked a good friend of my mother's why they separated, and she said, "In the end I do think it was the nationality thing, you know." It seems that my mother always felt she had done herself down by marrying a Korean.'

Learning the truth

'When I was about eleven, my mother told me about my father's ethnicity as if it were a deep and terrible secret. "I left your father because he was a Korean and I was thinking of your future," she said. "If people find out you're a Korean, you won't be able to get a job and you won't be able to get married. I left him so I could bring you up as a Japanese and make sure those things didn't happen to you. If you keep quiet about this, no one will ever know. You must never, never tell anyone about this even if they torture you."

'By then I already knew all about discrimination against Burakumin, Koreans and so on, so when I heard that I had some of this despised Korean blood in my own veins, I all but blacked out with the shock. I immediately decided that come what may, I would never breathe a whisper to a soul about this awful secret.'

Not long after, Cho-Ja's mother disappeared, leaving her with an aunt. For Cho-Ja, this was the start of a prolonged internal conflict over her Japanese nationality and Korean ethnicity.

She remembered her mother's dire warning, and kept the secret. In every aspect of her life, she hated and avoided anything that could remotely be considered Korean. When her friends said her hairstyle 'looked Korean' with its center parting, she hastily changed it. She avoided bright green in her clothing, having heard it described as 'so vulgar it's positively Korean.' When she heard the Japanese around her casually belittling Koreans, it chilled her to the bone. 'I knew exactly what I'd get if I let out that I had a Korean father. I did my level best to become Japanese.'

At the same time a determination to show the world that she was worth something motivated Cho-Ja to intense study. 'I felt very keenly that I had nothing at all going for me: I was away from my parents, of mixed blood, half-Korean, and born out of wedlock. I wanted to show the world that despite all this, I did have something.'

In her final year at junior high, however, she learned that her mother, who had disappeared saying that she was 'going abroad to work,' had in fact remarried. 'When I heard that, suddenly there didn't seem to be any point in studying any more. I became a real bad girl. My aunt couldn't handle me any more, and when my mother got the message, she argued my step-father into having me come and live with them in Tokyo.'

The cosmopolitan way

At senior high school in Tokyo, she kept trying to think of herself as not being Korean, only to be sharply reminded that she was not Japanese every time she heard racist comments made about Koreans. Then one day she was given a leaflet at the station, advertising an open day at the local North Korean school.

'It was a sort of cultural festival, with Korean folk-dancing, a get-together to promote friendship between Japanese and Korean high school students. I went there with this hope that I might sort of fit in, being somehow more Korean than I was Japanese. But when I got there, well…the Koreans struck me as having this really rich culture, and they could all speak the Korean language, and once again I got this feeling that I myself had nothing. I couldn't make friends with Koreans any more than I could fit into Japanese society.

'About this time we were given a book called *Cosmopolitan* to read in our English lessons. "This is it," I thought, "the answer to all my problems. Forget all the petty stuff about being Korean or being Japanese – I will live my life in the cosmopolitan way – ignoring ethnicity altogether."'

She first revealed the secret of her birth in the second year of senior high school. 'I was sick and tired of pretending to be Japanese, always scared of letting slip the slightest clue about my real identity, always worrying that I might lose my friends if they found out. I wanted friends that would really understand me. So I decided I had to stop hiding. I picked out six or seven of my friends and told them. "This is just between you and me, OK? As a matter of fact, I'm not a real Japanese…" That was how I put it. They all said it didn't bother them in the slightest, and one of them actually scolded me for my choice of words. "Whisper, whisper! You talk that way because inside, you're ashamed of being Korean yourself." For some reason, those words of hers really hurt.

'After that I got to secretly reading books about Korea. When I read Park Kyung-Shik's book, *Records of Korean Forced Migrant Labor*,[2] a great change of heart came over me. Deep inside me, I really had absorbed the Japanese prejudices against Koreans – that they were dirty, more likely to do bad things, and generally inferior, but when I realized how much Koreans had suffered historically, they seemed somehow pure, almost god-like. I seemed to see my father's face in all the people who appeared in the book, and my feelings changed, they really did.'

Reunion and death

All this happened in 1968, when the era of student protest was at its peak. Cho-Ja went on demonstrations with her friends, and went through another new phase. 'Up to then I'd been very competitive, obsessed with getting ahead of the rest at school so that I'd count for something in a society where education meant so much and thereby avoid discrimination by the great Japanese majority all around me. Now I went right the other way. I dropped out of senior high at the end of the second year, moved to Osaka and continued my schooling part-time.

'That was when I got to meet my father again. I felt at the time that although racism was all wrong, it was also up to Koreans to live their lives boldly and proudly. I asked my father why he always hid himself away. I longed to have a strong, heroic father, but his way of life was so gentle and quiet that it struck me as spineless. I told him off. It must have been awful for him, being spoken to like that by his own daughter, but he twisted up his face and said just one thing: "You lose out if you let them know."

'At the time, I hadn't quite realized how racial discrimination could permeate every single aspect of life. My position was

actually very different from my father's. I had Japanese nationality
and a Japanese name, which put me in a sort of safety zone. He was
not in that safety zone. He never knew when or how he might be
victimized if it came out that he was Korean. Even so, I went and
told him off, my own father, for not showing pride in his Korean
ancestry. Afterwards I started wondering just what gave me the
right to condemn him like that, and I began to analyze my own
behavior and regret it.'

Cho-Ja graduated from part-time high school and went on to
Hokkaido University of Education. She was 23, and had just
completed her third year, when her father died in Kyoto.

'At the wake, I listened to the mourners praising my father,
going on about what a fine character he'd been and all that, and I
got really angry. In order to avoid discrimination, my father had
deliberately ingratiated himself with people so that they'd think
he was an alright sort of fellow, and he'd spent a lifetime
suppressing his real feelings. At any rate, that was the feeling I had
as I looked back on his life. It angered me that they had no idea of
the true reason why he had become such an unassertive person.
What right had they to go on about his sterling character? He didn't
act that way because he wanted to, he only did it to fool people into
liking him. And now he was dead at 47, after a too-short life in
which he never once got to laugh and say, "OK, so what's wrong
with being Korean?" Not once since the Japanese government
forced Koreans to adopt Japanese names had he used his own
name.

'After the funeral, you could sense the relief among my
mother's relatives, and in my mother herself to be honest, that at
last they could put an end to their Korean connection. "No more
trips to Kyoto," she said. I could hardly bear it. It made me think
that I wanted to honestly acknowledge my Korean father even if
no one else did.'

Politicization

Cho-Ja finished university and got a job teaching at a school for
children with handicaps in Tokyo. In her second year at the job she
came across Seikyū-sha, the Kawasaki-based Zainichi group (see
Chapter 11, Note 2), in connection with the campaign over the

Hitachi discrimination trial (see Chapter 3, Note 5). The group was starting to organize children's clubs in the area, and Cho-Ja started helping out as a volunteer.

'The Seikyū-sha totally changed my view of Koreans. Even then I still had some negative values, but they really changed to positive ones. The Korean children who lived in those parts were quite rough. Their wild behavior was a reaction to discrimination. They knew they wouldn't get a job with a posh company or the civil service however hard they studied, so they gave up the effort. Until then I'd thought I could solve the discrimination problem as an individual, simply by becoming "cosmopolitan." Now I strongly felt that I'd like to do something with the children, that I'd like to share sorrows and joys with others like myself.'

Cho-Ja had been pronouncing her name in the Japanese style, as 'Teruko.' Now she started using the Korean reading, though she still retained her Japanese surname. It struck her as a suitable reflection of her mixed origins. But it also drew attention to them: 'One of my fellow volunteers asked me if I got half as much discrimination because of being only half Korean. That made me pause for thought. Actually I think having a Korean father excludes you from Japanese society just as much as having two Korean parents. So after a while I started calling myself Yoon Cho-Ja.' Yoon was her father's surname, unused by her family since the day they were forced to abandon it by the wartime Japanese government.

In April 1981 Cho-Ja got a new job, teaching at an elementary school with a considerable number of Korean pupils. She took the opportunity to start using her fully Korean name at work, somewhat to the puzzlement of colleagues who thought it odd for someone with Japanese nationality. 'I asked the teachers' union to support me in my request to the principal to be known as "Yoon," but they refused. "You've got Japanese nationality, so you're Japanese, right?" When I spoke to the principal, the day before school opened, the first thing he said was: "We wouldn't have given you the job if we'd known about this." Then he banged his fist on the table: "This is a Japanese school!" he shouted. I said: "I know that. I think it's important for Japanese children, too, to be told the truth about Korea." In the end, the principal tried harder than anyone else to understand what I was going on about. I started a little study group to explain the issue, and he came along to every meeting.'

Cho-Ja was qualified to teach children with handicaps, so they became her special responsibility at the school. 'Perhaps because they'd been through a few troubles themselves, I got on very well with the parents.'

One day Cho-Ja had occasion to scold one of the older children. 'He said, "A Chinawoman like you can't tell off us Japanese. Who do you think won the war?!" I was stunned, I must admit – I wasn't ready for it. I went after him, took him to his class teacher and told him, right in front of his teacher, never to say anything like that ever again. Even now people make fun of my name, you know. Like they call me "Yunker,"[3] you know...' She laughs. 'Lately I've got a bit more tolerant about these things.'

Winning back ethnic names

In 1983 Cho-Ja applied to the family court to legally take on her Korean name.

'As I saw it, if it weren't for discrimination my father would have registered his marriage and I would have taken my father's surname, Yoon. Because of discrimination he made me illegitimate so that I could have Japanese nationality. I wanted Japanese society to formally recognize the name that had been stolen from me.'

At the time the move was much criticized by other Zainichi Koreans. 'They had a strong taboo against Japanese nationality, and some people claimed that my action would end up encouraging more people to naturalize.' In the end she lost the court case anyway.

'It made me feel the need for a social movement to change public opinion. In 1985 I got together with some friends in the Kansai region to launch the Society for Winning Back Ethnic Names.[4] Already some people were pointing out that about a quarter of the kids coming to the Korean children's clubs were Japanese nationals, whether through naturalization or mixed marriages, and were calling for the Korean community to take a franker look at the issue. That movement overlapped with ours. Then in 1987 Park Shil in Kyoto and Chong Yang-I in Osaka won their court cases to have their pre-naturalization surnames legally restored.'

In April 1989, Cho-Ja herself succeeded in regaining her surname at the second attempt. The court ruling in her favor was the first ever involving a mixed-blood Japanese national.

The right to mix

'Japan doesn't recognize people of mixed descent. You've got to be one or the other, and I swung between the two like a pendulum. I tried to get over the problem by being "cosmopolitan." Today, though, I'm quite happy to be a mixed-blood person with a Japanese passport and a Korean name.'

Yoon Cho-Ja has been studying the Korean language and learning to play the *jang-gu* – the traditional Korean drum. She used to think that she would have to marry a Korean man in order to maintain the culture, but with her new-found tolerance she eventually married a Japanese teacher also working with Zainichi children. However, Cho-Ja remains convinced that Japan's family register system[5] sustains discrimination against Burakumin, Koreans and illegitimate children alike, so she and her husband have not registered the marriage and maintain separate surnames. They have given their two children names that can be read in Japanese or Korean, and sent them to a nursery run by the Seikyū-sha, under their Korean surname, 'Yoon.' They want their children to live proudly as Korean Japanese.

Cho-Ja's battle continues. 'By the time we get to fourth- and fifth-generation Korean migrants, seventy or eighty percent of them will have Japanese nationality. About three-quarters of Zainichi Korean marriages are with Japanese,[6] and the dual-nationality children of these marriages have to reject one nationality or the other when they reach twenty-two. They will more or less have to choose Japanese nationality because of the great practical advantages it confers in contemporary Japanese society.

'It will be very important to win social recognition for the principle that ethnicity and nationality are two different things. Enabling children of Japanese nationality to freely use Korean names is an important symbolic expression of that principle. It will also generate some constructive social tension: for instance, it will be much more difficult to force every school to display the Japanese flag[7] if some of the children have Korean names.

'Free use of Korean names will be good for Japanese children, too. Right now they have no idea what the Koreans sitting next to them in class are thinking. Do Japanese parents really want their children to be brought up as casual, unthinking racists?'

13 Lifting the Fog

The story of Kang Soon-Ja

Kang Soon-Ja (not her real name) is a spirited, dynamic woman who suffered as a child through intense loathing of her Korean identity. After four years of attending a Japanese elementary school where she used an alias, her parents' decision to transfer her to an ethnic Korean school proved to be a turning point for Soon-Ja.

Soon-Ja was born in Tokyo in 1949. She was 40 at the time of our interview, which took place on March 17, 1990. She is a second-generation Zainichi Korean holding North Korean nationality, and is the second oldest of seven siblings, all but one of them sisters. She used to go by the alias 'Kyomoto Junko.' 'Soon-Ja' is the Korean reading of the Japanese name 'Junko.'

Father's relatives to North Korea

Soon-Ja's father was born in the southern Korean province of Kyongsang-Nam-Do in 1924, and was brought to Japan by his parents at the age of one. His father, Soon-Ja's grandfather, worked as a stevedore, and later went into the scrap metal business. 'My *halabeoji* (grandfather) was quite a gentleman in those days,' recalls Soon-Ja. 'He wore a smart suit and his shoes positively sparkled.' Soon-Ja's father graduated from one of the old-style middle schools,[1] took over the scrap metal business from his father and still runs it most industriously to this day. He has a lot of social relations with fellow Koreans and consequently uses his Korean name most of the time. At work, however, he uses a Japanese alias. Soon-Ja describes him as a serious-minded man who never drinks or gambles.

Her mother was also born in Kyongsang-Buk-Do, in 1923. She was brought to Japan at the age of seven and had a difficult time with her step-mother after her father remarried following the death of her biological mother. The family was very poor and she never had the chance to go to school. She married Soon-Ja's father when both were in their teens. She was a dynamic type and helped him out at work of her own free will.

In the early 1960s many of Soon-Ja's relatives returned to Korea during the first round of the Red Cross repatriation program (see Chapter 2, pp. 38–9). Though born in the southern part of the Korean peninsula, they went to North Korea, which, like many Koreans in Japan at the time, they found a more inspiring place. Soon-Ja's paternal grandparents went, as did four of her uncles and aunts. Soon-Ja was in the first year at a North Korean junior high school at the time, and her family was also planning to make the move. However, one of her aunts, who was already married to a fellow Korean, was unable to go to North Korea because she had acquired South Korean nationality. Soon-Ja's grandfather ordered her father to keep his family in Japan so that the aunt would not be left on her own. He singled out Soon-Ja's father because he was the oldest son and therefore expected to take responsibility for other family members.

Thoroughly depressed

Soon-Ja first became aware that she and her family were not Japanese around the time she moved from kindergarten to elementary school. Her grandparents would converse in Korean, and her mother wore the *jeogori* when she went out. Soon-Ja attended a Japanese elementary school, using her Japanese alias, and became 'thoroughly depressed.'

'If you look at my school reports, you'll see that I'm described as a "lively, talkative child" in the first year, but by the third year the teacher's comments say, "She tends to get dejected, and I wonder what the problem is." Actually I went through my worst period of being bullied during the third year. There were four or five Korean kids in my class. By the time you reach the third year you start to be aware of that kind of thing. In my class people started whispering about it – "So-and-so's a Korean." Even the other Korean kids got into it – they'd tell everyone I was Korean in the hope that they wouldn't get singled out for bullying themselves. So I got the full force of it. Even kids who were good friends of mine started taunting me. "*Chōsenjin!*" (Korean!), they'd say. And then they'd go on about how Koreans get drunk and lie around in the street, or how they're all thieves – anything bad would get pinned on Koreans. I got bullied by everyone. I asked the teacher for help but he was racist himself. Everyone gets a bit noisy sometimes at school, but it was always me who got told off.'

It got to the point where Soon-Ja was actually blackmailed by one of the boys at school. 'He told me to bring him some scrap metal. I filled a bucket with old iron and took it to him. Then I went with him to another scrap metal dealer, who weighed up the metal and gave the boy some money for it. But my mother had noticed my odd behavior and followed us. And that was how my parents first realized that I was being bullied.'

Changing schools

'My class teacher in the fourth year was a very good person. He said, "There's been some taunting of children for being Korean in this class. If I hear of any such thing from now on, I will take a serious view of it." That stopped it, just like that. After school finished for the day, he kept us Korean kids back and told us various things about how our parents' generation came to Japan and so on. He also asked us if we'd thought of going to a Korean school. My dad was very proud of his Korean identity and would have liked to send me to the local Korean elementary school, but it was a long way from where we lived, so he'd decided to wait until I reached junior high school. But when he heard what my teacher had been saying, he said to me and my little sister, "All right, you two, shall we go to the *uri hak-kyo*² tomorrow?"

'I was dead against it – going to a Korean school. Because I hated being Korean. In those days I really wished I could go to sleep and wake up Japanese. We knew we had to learn our Korean names to use them at the new school, and my little sister kept repeating her name, "Kang Yang-Ja, Kang Yang-Ja," so she could memorize it. I was so hostile to the whole idea that I refused to learn the Korean name to the very end. I did learn it just before going through the school gates, so that the teacher wouldn't get cross with me. When the time came to introduce myself, I said "Kang Soon-

Ja." I reckoned I could forget it after that. But later the teacher called me to the staff room and asked me, "What's your name again?" "I've forgotten it," I said. "Well that won't do," said the teacher, and reminded me of my own name. I still hated it though.'

Although she hated the Korean school so much at first, Soon-Ja was to experience a kind of liberation there. 'When I started there, I found it was a relief to be among all Korean people. I started to wonder why I'd hated being Korean so much before, why I'd worried so much about such a silly thing. It felt as if I'd been lost in thick fog, and now the sun was finally shining through it. In the end it's just much more relaxing to be with people who share your ethnicity. I became my old bright and lively self again. And everybody really did their best to help me learn the language.' By the time she reached the sixth year, Soon-Ja was more or less fluent in Korean.

Today she feels deeply grateful to the teacher who encouraged her to change schools. 'I owe what I've got today to that teacher.' It was only when she started studying in a Korean environment that she learned her own ethnic traditions, customs, and most importantly, language. 'If you don't know the language, you don't know your own people,' she says.

Scared of Japanese

Nowadays all girls attending North Korean schools in Japan wear the *jeogori* (Korean dress). It was not always so, and the practice became established around the time that Soon-Ja was a schoolgirl.

'When I was in the first year at junior high school, we were allowed to choose between two school uniforms – the *jeogori* or a blazer and skirt like the ones used at Japanese schools. But in the second year, everyone in my class opted for *jeogori*. We consciously rejected the other uniform in favor of the *jeogori*, and in the end this movement of ours resulted in the whole school going over to *jeogori*.'

The significance of this choice is profound. When a girl wears a *jeogori*, people know at a glance that she is Korean. It is a symbol of ethnic pride, but it can also increase the risk of racist attacks. When Soon-Ja was at senior high school, she experienced numerous unpleasant incidents. 'When I was going to school, and running into kids from Japanese schools, it was pretty scary,' she recalls. 'I'd avert my gaze and look at the floor if they came near me on the train. Some of them would try and tease me, right there in the train. They'd say silly things like "*Cha masireo gaja*" ("Let's go for a cup of tea" in Korean) or something like that. I was scared stiff and I just kept staring at the floor.'

Meeting the race bar

After graduating from senior high, Soon-Ja spent a year learning book-keeping. At the book-keeping school she used her Korean name, albeit with its Japanese reading: 'Kyo Junko.' 'If you don't hide it, they don't feel inquisitive about it. Some of the people I got to know at that period are still friends of mine today.'

Companies would approach the school when they had job vacancies. 'I felt certain that I wouldn't have a chance of a job with a Japanese company, but I put in three applications anyway, just to see what would happen really. I used my real name in the applications, and sure enough they all failed. They told me, "We can't have you because you're a foreigner. We have a principle of not employing foreigners." Basically when they said "foreigners" they meant "Koreans." So my assumption that they wouldn't have me was confirmed.'

From then until she was 27, Soon-Ja worked for the family business. At this point someone from the local Chongryun-affiliated Korean Chamber of Commerce and Industry asked her father to let his daughter work for them, and Soon-Ja found herself in charge of tax-accounting there. She is still there today, advising Korean traders on their tax affairs and helping them compile their annual tax returns. She says that people from Mindan as well as Chongryun come to her for advice. 'At bottom it doesn't matter if they're with Chongryun or Mindan, they're all the same people.'

Unlucky in love

Soon-Ja remains single. 'As it happens, I haven't had much luck,' she says. 'When I was 23 I had an interview for an arranged marriage,[3] which put me off them permanently. I wasn't interested in marrying the guy, but the marriage discussions just carried on regardless. It was awful. In the end I just flatly refused to go through with it, fully expecting to be thrown out of the house for it. Korean parents tend to assume that once a match has been agreed at an interview, you get on with the wedding more or less straight away. Usually there are only two or three months between the interview and the wedding. I really wasn't ready for it, and the pace of events took me by surprise.

'And then of course, the Zainichi Korean world is a small one. I think if I did get married it would probably be better to do it with one of my own people. Regional consciousness is very strong among our people – it wouldn't do to marry someone from Cheju-Do, or Cholla-Do.[4] Someone from our own province, Kyongsang-Do, would be ideal, but of course, if the man's from the same *bonkwan*[5] as me then I'm not allowed to marry him either. So that doesn't leave too many candidates.'

Teaching the *uri-mal*

Since the age of twenty, Soon-Ja has taught Korean language at an informal school run by Chongryun principally designed to keep Korean youths attending Japanese high schools in touch with their native language and culture. She recruits students by visiting Korean households and pointing out the advantages of knowing the Korean language. She has also taught Korean to adults at another Chongryun-run establishment, and subsequently once a week at a culture center run by a Japanese newspaper, *Asahi Shinbun*.

'Because Korea is one country, I don't like to describe the language as *Chōsen-go* (North Korean) or *Kankoku-go* (South Korean). I just call it the *uri-mal* ("our language" in Korean).'

Soon-Ja says that working at the culture center has broadened her horizons. 'Before I only knew the Chongryun way of looking at things. Now I meet other kinds of Zainichi Korean, and Japanese people too, and get to know other points of view.'

Along with the Japanese people who use the culture center, some Koreans come along, often concealing their identity. 'They use their aliases, but usually you can guess from the characters used to write the names. I check them out for a lesson or two, and then I say something like, "Am I right in thinking that you hold North or South Korean nationality?" They say yes, and I say, "Well then, would you mind very much if I called you by your real name starting next time?" – and then I do just that.'

Soon-Ja herself used to have occasional recourse to her Japanese alias. 'It was because I got bored of giving history lessons to Japanese people. If I told them my name was "Kyo" – the Japanese reading of my Korean surname – they'd want to know how come I had such a funny name and I'd end up giving them a long explanation about my personal background. So sometimes, in situations unlikely to lead to a long acquaintance, I just gave my name as "Kyomoto" for convenience. But since I started teaching at the culture center I've dropped "Kyomoto" altogether. I suppose it's because I tend to feel that I'm a representative of Zainichi Koreans there.'

Sympathy with Yoon

For a Zainichi Korean closely involved with the North Korean community and Chongryun, Soon-Ja has had a lot of contact with Japanese. As well as meeting people at the culture center, she is also a long-standing member of an otherwise all-Japanese choral ensemble. She combines the robust ethnic awareness typical of Zainichis who have been to Korean schools with a relatively broad and tolerant view of Japanese society.

'I watched the movie *Yoon's Town*[6] and felt a lot of sympathy for the heroine (a Zainichi Korean woman who has to deal with intense internal conflicts over her ethnic identity). But my niece just said that the girl in the film, and her parents, were stupid. If only they'd sent her to a Korean school from the beginning, all the conflict could have been avoided. I told her that I had had all sorts of worries myself, and she said, "Why? Koreans are Koreans and that's all there is to it, right?" She's been brought up Korean from the start so she doesn't feel the need to question these things. That's the difference between children who've been to Korean schools all along and those like myself who changed halfway.'

Fingerprint feelings

In the summer of 1985 there was a major Zainichi Korean campaign demanding reform of the Alien Registration Law. Many protesters made their point by refusing to give their fingerprint, one of the law's most resented requirements. Kang Soon-Ja was in complete sympathy with them.

'I was first fingerprinted when I was in the third year of junior high, I think. I remember it well. My heart was pounding – I really hated it. Worse still, I lost the alien registration card less than a year after I got it. That meant I had to fingerprint all over again – only this time it wasn't just the usual left index finger, I had to give all ten fingerprints. I asked why and was told, "It's a punishment for losing your registration card." I'd have liked to refuse fingerprinting myself but I couldn't, because the Chongryun line was that we had to obey the Japanese law. Instead I supported the campaign by gathering signatures for petitions and so on.'

Soon-Ja is a busy woman and has never yet found the time to visit North Korea. She insists, however, that Korea is her home country in every sense. 'Not North or South Korea – just One Korea. But my hometown is Tokyo, where I was born and raised.' She longs to see Korea reunified, and fervently believes that it will happen in the not-too-distant future.

Meanwhile, Soon-Ja regards it as deeply unfair that Koreans in Japan are subject to taxation without representation: 'I always feel left out at election time, not being able to participate, but since I'm Korean and they're Japanese elections I don't demand the right to vote. Instead I'd like to see the taxes paid by Koreans returned to the Korean community, to improve the material standards of the Korean schools. I deal with taxation at work and I can tell you the system is riddled with contradictions. For instance, on the back of the tax return form it always says how much of the tax revenue goes toward maintaining schools, but the Korean schools don't get the slightest benefit. All we do is pay. When the school buildings get old and have to be renovated, the entire financial burden falls on the Korean community.'

In teaching the Korean language, Soon-Ja is motivated by a determination to communicate the sense of liberation she felt on encountering her own culture when she changed schools all those years ago. 'I remember something one of my young pupils said to me: "When I studied English I found it very hard, but when I study Korean it doesn't seem that difficult. Maybe it's because it's my own language that it doesn't seem difficult." I thought he really had something there.'

14 'I Hate Japan, but I'll Live Here Anyway'

The story of Park Yang-Ja

Park Yang-Ja (not her real name) lost her father in infancy, and was brought up by her mother. She attended North Korean schools all the way from elementary level to university. She is intensely proud of her Korean identity and regards North Korea as her homeland. Angry at the ignorance and apathy of Japanese youths regarding the events of the past, she does not hesitate to say that she hates Japan. Even so, there is something in her that makes it impossible for her to imagine living anywhere else.

Yang-Ja was born in 1968, in a small city in the Kansai district of western Japan. At the time of our interview, on September 11, 1989, she was 21 years old and attending the Chongryun-affiliated Korea University in Tokyo. She is a second-generation Zainichi Korean holding North Korean nationality, and has an older brother and an older sister.

Japanized relatives

Yang-Ja's father was born in 1926 and came to Japan on his own at the age of seventeen, at the height of World War II. 'I hear that he was planning to study, but I don't think he ever got to school. I believe he worked as a foreman on building sites or something like that. He was killed in a workplace accident when I was one. All his relatives now live in South Korea.'

Yang-Ja's mother, a second-generation Zainichi, was born in Japan in 1936. Both her parents died when she was still in her infancy and so she never heard about the circumstances of their migration. She was the youngest of six children, and the only one who managed to continue her education all the way to a Japanese senior high school – thanks, she tells Yang-Ja, to the hard work of her older sisters.

Two of Yang-Ja's mother's older sisters married Japanese men and naturalized. 'One of them later got divorced, but she naturalized so that her sons could live as Japanese. She also moved house several times, so that she could become completely Japanese and not just a "new" Japanese.'[1]

Although Yang-Ja's other aunts and uncles have not naturalized, she still regards them as having effectively turned Japanese. 'They live under Japanese names, and there's nothing Korean about their lives at all. They're not Japanese, but they're not Korean either. Of the two, they're more like Japanese.'

When Yang-Ja was at kindergarten, her widowed mother took the family to live in a large city elsewhere in the same prefecture. There had only been one other Korean family in the neighborhood where Yang-Ja was born, which had made life difficult for her mother. After the move they had more contacts with fellow Koreans: someone from Chongryun had fixed up Yang-Ja's mother with a job at the organization's prefectural headquarters, and later she opened a *yakiniku* restaurant (see Chapter 2, Note 16).

Influence from the grave

Yang-Ja attended a Japanese kindergarten, going by the alias of 'Akiyama Yoko.' At the time she had no awareness of being Korean. The meals that her mother cooked were Japanese in style. She had never learned Korean cuisine because her own parents had died so early. But things soon changed when Yang-Ja started at a North Korean elementary school. 'I naturally came to know I was Korean. By the time I noticed, I was already learning the language and all the friends around me were Korean.'

It was due to her deceased father's influence that she went to Korean schools. 'He had always said that he wanted the children to go to Korean schools. Apparently my mother had been opposed to the idea, but after he died she decided to respect his wish – almost as if it had been in his will. I think one of the reasons why she moved house was to move us closer to a Korean school.'

Thus Yang-Ja started Korean education in the first year of elementary school, while her older brother and sister had to switch from Japanese schools midway through elementary education. At home they spoke Japanese and Yang-Ja was called 'Yoko.' At school, however, everything was done in Korean. 'There was a movement at the school to use Korean 100 percent of the time. If you let something slip out in Japanese, you'd be criticized, or at least reminded to use Korean, during class meetings.'

For the most part Yang-Ja enjoyed elementary school. 'I enjoyed playing and chatting with my friends, and the lessons were fun, too. The only thing that bugged me was the way they made all us girls join the *kayagum* (Korean zither) club. This was an after-school club, but joining was virtually compulsory.'

Learning to hate Japan

While she was at elementary school, Yang-Ja still sometimes played with Japanese children in the neighborhood. But this stopped when she entered junior high school – in fact, from that time on she had very little to do with anyone living in the neighborhood. Once she started at senior high school, she had to commute to school by train. 'I got some funny looks from Japanese people, but it didn't bother me particularly. I liked wearing the *jeogori*. It gave me a sense of pride. I really did feel that Koreans were superior to Japanese. Like, historically there were times when Korea was more advanced than Japan, and Japan was being taught her culture by Korea, like the Koguryo period, and the time of the Three Kingdoms.[2] I was also proud of how my country had fought to liberate itself from Japanese imperialism. I was pretty patriotic. And I didn't have any trouble with Japanese kids on the train. There were always four or five of us traveling together, and more and more Koreans got on as we approached the school, so we tended to outnumber the Japanese kids and felt like we were the bosses, not them.'

Yang-Ja gradually grew more hostile toward Japan. 'I do bear a kind of grudge toward Japan, if that's the right word. At any rate, I do feel rather angry that the Japanese people, especially the young ones, don't seem to have any sense of having done wrong in the past. I started to feel that way when I was at senior high, from reading the newspapers and so on.'[3]

During senior high, Yang-Ja had virtually no opportunity at all to get acquainted with Japanese of her own generation. The only time she was in the same room as Japanese school students was when her school's brass band played in Japanese schools, which was once or twice a year. 'But even then, I never actually talked with them.'

Korea University

During her second year at senior high, Yang-Ja thought of applying to a Japanese university. 'At the time, I just vaguely thought I'd like to become a writer, so it would be nice to go to the literature department of a Japanese university. I gave up the idea because I figured I wouldn't make it. My academic record had gone way down at senior high and it was too late to get it up again. I'd suddenly gone to a much bigger school, and I was in a very big class as well. None of the other kids had any interest in studying, and they were so noisy that you could hardly hear what was going on in lessons. I kind of got into the atmosphere of it. Within the class I was still near the top, but my actual ability was falling fast.'

Eventually Yang-Ja was persuaded by teachers and friends to apply for a place at Korea University in Tokyo. The decision was not made without considerable hesitation, for which she mentions two reasons: 'Everyone has to stay in a dormitory at Korea University and I'd heard that there were very strict rules there which could be a strain on personal relations. I was also beginning to feel aware of contradictions in the kind of education you got in the North Korean system. There was something unnatural about the aspect of worship for the Great Leader Kim Il Sung, and I did feel that there was a forced imposition of ideas.

'But in the end I feel that although they tend to overdo that aspect of things in North Korean education, without that emphasis it is difficult to have pride in your ethnic identity in this Japanese environment. And I *was* able to have a natural sense of pride in myself as a Korean.

'As for living in a dormitory, it was actually quite tough at first. Now that I've got used to it, though, it's OK. In fact it's more relaxing than staying at home. At home I would have had to think about all kinds of practicalities, about the future, the household and so on. At the dormitory I'm able to escape from all that, and of course I'm with friends.'

One 'practicality' that is of particular concern to Yang-Ja is the question of who will care for her mother in old age. 'I don't think my big brother is going to return to the family house. He's a nice guy but you can't rely on him, and I don't think he's got a proper awareness of his responsibilities as the oldest son. Right now my mother's saying that she'll live by herself, but it looks like either my big sister or I myself will have to look after her sooner or later.

'Not that I'd mind looking after her, or rather living with her, because I like my mother. The only thing is that she does have a tendency to swallow everything she reads in the papers or hears on the TV news, and regurgitate it just like that – North Koreans are no good, Chongryun's no good, North Korea's a scary country and all that. Her way of thinking is exactly the opposite of ours. She says things like, "I'd like to get away from Chongryun, to tell the truth, but it's very awkward because my three kids have all been taken hostage." We have flaming rows about politics every time I go home. Occasionally she even says that Japanese are better than Koreans, but I don't think she really means it.'

Workplace discrimination

Since entering Korea University, Yang-Ja has twice been turned down for part-time jobs on racist grounds. 'At one family restaurant, Fujiya, I was simply told, "No Koreans." And at Ōshō, a chain of *gyōza* restaurants,[4] a friend and I were sent away after one of the staff apparently overheard us talking to each other in Korean. He just gave us one look and said, "You wouldn't by any chance happen to be foreigners?" We said yes, and he said, "We don't take Koreans, so go home! Go on, off you go!" He gave us a real dirty look that made my blood boil.'

Yang-Ja did manage to get a job at Tsubohachi, a chain of Japanese-style taverns, despite announcing that she was from Korea University. Ironically, she ended up having to quit after a week because the university wouldn't give her permission to take the job as she was still only a first-year student. Even that one week was enough to give her a negative impression of her Japanese co-workers. 'We didn't get on. They seemed like a completely different breed of people. Kind of lightweight. Young Japanese these days are just too ignorant. All they talk about is fashion and stuff.'

In Yang-Ja's second year, one of the university lecturers fixed her up with a job working two or three evenings a week at a *yakiniku* restaurant under North Korean management.

Visiting home

The first time Yang-Ja visited North Korea was in her final year at senior high school. 'Mine was one of two "model classes" chosen for the trip.[5] But at the time I wasn't that moved by the experience. We just went round famous tourist sites like Mankyung-Dae,[6] and didn't get to talk to the local people there, the Koreans that is.'

She made a longer visit of two months in the summer of 1989, when she worked as one of the organizers of a youth festival, which made headlines because a female South Korean student called Lim Soo-Kyung attended it without permission from her government and was subsequently arrested on her return to South Korea.

'This time I was working with the local people and had plenty of conversations with them. Getting in direct contact like that made the place feel like my home country for the first time. On the previous trip with the high school, we were all wearing a uniform that marked us out as having come from Japan at a glance. Our facial expressions were completely Japanese, too, and the people there looked on us as foreigners, in a way that I found quite cold. But this time, once I got to talk with them, I found that despite our totally different backgrounds, we did have something in common that made me feel we were fellow Koreans. Everyone was really straightforward and honest, with a goodness that you don't find in Japan. When I left Korea I actually felt quite sad.

'I couldn't actually live there, though. Not now. I really couldn't. I did think that I'd like to, mind you, that it would be a good place to live. But in the end, well, when I think of how low the standard of living is there…I *would* have liked it, if I'd been born there in the first place, that's my feeling.'

Half and half

Yang-Ja sees herself as having a distinctively Zainichi Korean identity. 'The main basis on which I see myself as Korean is blood. Having Korean blood flowing through me. North Korea is my homeland, my motherland, my "own land." Japan is just the place where I happen to have been born and brought up. I hate Japan. But there's some kind of connection between me and Japan that I just can't seem to cut. I suppose I feel it's a place where I have to live, even if I do hate it.'

When Yang-Ja describes herself as a Zainichi Korean, she is also conscious of differences between herself and mainland Koreans. 'Because of my Japanese upbringing, I do tend to think in a Japanese way. My lifestyle, too, is totally immersed in capitalist modes of thought. I really am a half-and-half kind of thing. In my thinking I guess I'm closer to North Korea, but my instincts and lifestyle have become very extravagant, and no different from any Japanese person's. Overall, I'm stuck right in the middle.'

Even so, Yang-Ja's North Korean identity is far more boldly expressed than it is among most Zainichi Koreans of her generation. Her experience visiting North Korea, and her direct observation of the South Korean student movement during the latter visit, have reinforced her desire to somehow contribute to Korean re-unification. Of fellow Zainichis who cannot speak the language, she says, 'They are Koreans of course, but I don't think you can really call them true Koreans. I feel sorry for them. It's not all their own fault. Their parents should have brought them up better.'

Only a Korean will do

Conversation in the dorms at Korea University often turns to future careers and marriage. Park Yang-Ja says she hopes to delay marrying until she is 27 or 28, and to carry on working after tying the knot. 'I won't have any guy who doesn't understand that. My mother has never told me to stay away from Japanese men, she always says she doesn't mind who I marry so long as I get on with it and find someone soon. But I think if I actually told her that I wanted to marry a Japanese man, she would in fact come out against it.'

Yang-Ja herself finds the idea of marrying a Japanese 'unthinkable.' 'At present I have no Japanese friends. It doesn't bother me particularly, and I don't feel any urge to find some. I want my future husband to be someone with a Korean consciousness. I don't think I'd get along with someone who'd been to Japanese schools all along. If I have children, I'll want to send them to Korean schools, and I won't give them Japanese names like mine, either.'[7]

Yang-Ja chose to major in English at the university, hoping to become an English-Japanese translator. Now, as she approaches graduation, she says only that she hopes for 'something in publishing.' She assumes that no Japanese publisher would take her on, and has no inclination to work for them anyway. Instead she hopes to find employment with the Korean-language newspaper run by Chongryun, or with the Chongryun-affiliated wire service. In practice, however, graduates of Korea University are not entirely free to pick a career. They are expected to help out where Chongryun most needs their services, and Yang-Ja says that most of the graduates are sent to teach at Korean schools in the countryside, which are plagued by staff shortages. That, she believes, is her own most likely destination, at least in the first instance. Eventually, however, she believes she will find a way to fulfill her own ambitions.

15 Not Japanese, Not Korean but Zainichi

The story of Kim Myung-Mi (Aoi Akemi)

Kim Myung-Mi (not her real name) attended Japanese schools, using the pseudonym of 'Aoi Akemi.' Her older sister encouraged her to join the Korean Youth Association in Japan (KYAJ; see Chapter 5), and she started attending from her third year at senior high school. After graduation, she went to South Korea for a period of study that helped to convince her that 'We are neither Japanese nor Korean. We are Zainichi Koreans.'

Family history

Myung-Mi was born in 1968, in a large town near Tokyo. Our interview took place on September 3, 1989, at which point she was 21 years old. She is a second-generation migrant, holding South Korean nationality. She is the sixth-born of eight siblings, having two sisters and five brothers.

According to Myung-Mi, her father was born in the northern Korean province of Hamgyong-Buk-Do, in 1925. He came to Japan with three or four friends at the age of sixteen. He was a Catholic, and hoped to become a priest. But although he did some studying at the YMCA, he failed to master Japanese and ended up wandering around the country as a migrant laborer. He never talks about those hard times, but he often does refer to the still harder times he endured before coming to Japan. His parents died when he was still a child, and he was brought up by his older sister. But she in turn died young, leaving him effectively orphaned. There was no medicine for him if he got hurt, and nothing much to eat either. After the war he stayed on in Japan and went into the scrap metal business.

Myung-Mi's mother is a second-generation Zainichi. Her family comes from Cholla-Nam-Do in southern Korea, but she herself was born in Tokyo in 1932. Her own father, Myung-Mi's grandfather, was something of a rarity among early Korean migrants, having learned a fair amount of Japanese before arriving in Japan, where Myung-Mi says he worked as 'something not unlike a public official.' Even during the war, he and his family were able to live fairly well by the standards of the Korean population in Japan.

After the war, all Myung-Mi's mother's cousins returned to Korea. Her own father was also planning to take the family back to Korea, and got as far as completing most of the preparations. But then a Korean acquaintance of his who had already gone home, unexpectedly returned. His message was that South Korea was still virtually impossible to live in, and that however tough life was in Japan, it was still preferable. And so Myung-Mi's mother's family ended up deciding to stay in Japan.

A fiery father

Myung-Mi has been given the following account of how her parents came to get married. 'My grandma (mother's mother) was running a black-market rice operation or something, when she came across my father and a friend of his. They couldn't speak Japanese and they were just hanging around really. My grandma took pity on them and looked after them a bit, and it was at this point that he first set eyes on my mother. He fell in love with her at first sight.'

After her comfortable upbringing, Myung-Mi's mother found married life tough. 'Falling in love is all very well at first, but marriage changes people. Their true character comes through. My old man is a really weird guy – though as he's a first-generation migrant I guess it can't be helped. In his youth he'd get fighting drunk. He'd beat my mother. He'd work and work, and then he'd blow all the money eating and drinking. With that kind of thing going on every day, and more children getting born all the time, it was always tough just to keep the family going from day to day. My grandad and grandma asked her to leave him, but she seems to have thought that if she did that there'd be no one left to look after him…

'I was really frightened of my dad. If you didn't do as he told you right away he'd get into a rage. But he's older now, of course, and I can't hate him. He's still irritable and short-tempered, but now that I'm over twenty I just don't talk to him if he makes me angry. Then he tries to make up to me…and I have to feel sorry for him when I see him looking so miserable, you know?'

What Myung-Mi admires in her father is his determination. 'Once he starts something, he always finishes the job. I remember him painting the house once when I was a little kid. He worked right into the night, in winter, because he wouldn't stop until he'd finished. It was the same with his vices. He quit smoking when he was young and still doesn't touch tobacco, and although he used to drink like a fish, once he made up his mind to quit drinking, he really did stop.

'As for my mother, she's kind of detached. Always cheerful. Seems pretty easy-going, but sticks by her decisions. Doesn't often get angry, but she's possibly even more scary than my dad when she does. When two of my brothers wouldn't stop fighting over some silly thing, she chucked a bucket of cold water over the pair of them, in the middle of winter too. She also got into an incredible fight with my dad. It was his fault, but she put in a really crazy performance. My dad panicked, he got really flustered.'

A mysterious feeling

Myung-Mi's house was one of a little cluster of five occupied by Koreans. She was about five when she became aware of her ethnic identity. 'There were people speaking Korean around the neighborhood, and we had Korean dolls and ornaments in the house. I saw these things and realized we were different, but I didn't feel bad about it for a moment. I just thought it was kind of mysterious. I told my friends I was Korean and felt no embarrassment about it.'

Two of Myung-Mi's older siblings went to Chongryun-affiliated Korean schools before their father decided to switch them to Japanese schools. He had taken against the ideology of Kim Il Sung. After that there was no more talk of ethnic education, and Myung-Mi herself went straight into the local public elementary school. She was very quiet for the first couple of years. 'Because I hadn't been to kindergarten, I wasn't used to being in company.

I avoided talking to people. But I gradually realized that I was going to end up getting bullied if I carried on that way, so I changed – just like that. I figured that if I put myself in a leadership position then I wouldn't get bullied. That's what I did, and sure enough, I wasn't bullied in elementary school.

'But at junior high school, people did start asking me very persistently if it was true I wasn't Japanese. Nearly everyone in my class knew I was living in a Korean settlement. But one kid didn't know I was Korean. He heard a rumor about it and asked me if it was true that I wasn't Japanese. I was going to say yes, because I wasn't ashamed of it, but the boy sitting next to me flashed me a warning look and I shut up. I was really pleased that he bothered to look out for me. When I was asked the same question by one of the older kids in an after-school club, another friend stepped in and said, "What's the big deal if she is?"'

Into hiding

Myung-Mi continued to a private girls' senior high school. 'I failed to get into a public one. I'd missed a lot of lessons through illness. I think that damaged my school report. I don't think I did too badly in the tests themselves. There was no one else from my junior high school there, and I took the opportunity to conceal my identity. I hated the very thought of it up till then. I didn't want to be friends with anyone who'd smile at me and then dump me for being Korean. I was planning to be open about it at senior high, too, but I gradually realized that I couldn't. Although it was an all-girl school, it was a really bad one, with lots of hooligans. My old idea of staying away from people who despised my identity wouldn't work any more, because they were nearly all like that. So I covered up. It was my own decision.'

Concealment may have spared Myung-Mi trouble, but it caused other problems of its own. She found it difficult to express herself and lost self-esteem. She had to endure listening to Koreans being casually insulted by people who did not know they were in the presence of one. And on a few occasions, people saw through her disguise anyway.

'In junior high it felt really good, being honest about it. But in senior high I started hating myself. We'd pass Korean school kids in the street, and everyone would be shouting out, "There go the *Chonkō*."[1] I'd be pretending to agree with all the abuse, while inside I was on fire. Because you do get angry.

'People often pointed the finger at me. In my second year someone said, "You're a Korean, right?" I was in a sweat. I tried to laugh it off. I said, "Yeah, that's right. I just love hot food." It happened again in the third year. My dad mentioned it to a teacher whom he'd mistaken for my class teacher. The next day one of the kids asked me about it. Apparently this teacher had told some kids, though he wasn't supposed to. I admitted it this time, as it happened to be a friend of mine who asked, but I hated the teacher for it. I still do.'

A voyage of discovery

When Myung-Mi was approaching graduation from senior high school, her father persuaded her to take an examination for a South Korean government-financed study trip to South Korea. Much to her surprise, she passed.

'At the time I couldn't manage more than a few greetings in Korean. I'd been to a few classes run by Mindan, but only because my dad made me. I wasn't interested. Korean writing looked like some kind of code that made my eyes glaze over. I quit after a year and a half.'

Armed with this modest command of the language, Myung-Mi proceeded to spend two whole years studying in South Korea. One of her older sisters went with her on the same program, and her father accompanied them to Seoul to put them at their ease.

'When we arrived at Kimpo airport, I was disappointed because everything looked just the same as in Japan. But I began to warm to it looking through the taxi window at the *han-gul* (Korean script) on the billboards, and then supper on the first night was another big moment. It tasted really Korean.'

Myung-Mi found that her feelings swung between intense enjoyment and homesickness for Japan at roughly three-month intervals, starting in the positive phase. She stayed with her older sister at a succession of boarding houses in Daehak-ro, or 'University Street,' in Seoul. They moved often, mainly because of problems with food and the use of the bath. 'They'd make something that would keep, and then serve up the same thing for breakfast, lunch and supper. We could stand it for the first three days but after that it was too much. And because water is quite a precious commodity there, they'd only have a bath once a week in winter. We got into a lot of disputes about bathwater.'

Myung-Mi says the best thing that came out of her study period in Seoul was that she made lots of friends who were also Zainichi Koreans on study trips. 'We understood each other and didn't have to keep any secrets. I made friends with some mainland Korean people as well, mostly businessmen and students who I taught Japanese as a home tutor, but in the end they don't really accept you. There's always an awareness of difference. You'd tell them you were a *kyopo*,[2] and you could see their faces change. I got to understand how they feel about us very well. At first I tried really hard to get on with them, but at bottom they think we're quite simply Japanese. Since they won't accept us, however hard we try, I don't see much point in struggling to be Korean. And since we're not Japanese either, though we live in Japan, we might as well get used to thinking of ourselves as Zainichi Koreans and concentrate on getting along with each other. That's the only way, I think.'

And so Myung-Mi did not find a place in her mother country where she could fit in. Concluding that her long-term future lay back in Japan, she abandoned the thought of going to a Korean university and concentrated on her language studies with a view to possibly finding employment with a Korean company operating in Japan. Since returning to Japan, however, she has found herself occasionally feeling homesick for South Korea.

'Though I say all these negative things about the place, I have to admit that in some ways it was incredibly easy, living there. For instance, when Japanese people go to a public bath, they wouldn't dream of walking home afterwards, in broad daylight, with their hair still wet. But in Korea they just do it up, wet as it is, and stroll off home. That kind of thing I found relaxing. There was something really easy-going, almost American about the people. So it was really easy to live there. If only they had a few more…things…'

Back in Japan

Myung-Mi returned to Japan in May 1988. From the job-hunting point of view, this was poor timing, since in Japan the vast majority of new permanent jobs start in April and are arranged some time before that. She got a part-time job at a photographic studio for a few months. 'I used my Japanese alias, but this was near where my family lived and I think they spotted me for a Korean right away. Sometimes Korean people would come in to have their pictures taken and I would chat with them in Korean. The boss was over 80 years old, and he looked kind of surprised when he heard it. I just said I happened to have studied Korean a bit. It turned out he was president of the Parent-Teacher Association at my old junior high school, and I believe he checked up on me and found out that I was in fact Korean. But he didn't show any particular change in attitude toward me.'

The following November Myung-Mi got a job with a Korean trading company through an introduction from Mindan. There she naturally used her Korean name. Then in August 1989 she moved on to an office job with the KYAJ.

The Zainichi way

Kim Myung-Mi has known of her two names ever since she was at elementary school. She almost exclusively went by 'Aoi Akemi' until the last year of senior high. 'When people at the KYAJ started calling me by my Korean name, I felt kind of detached – like it wasn't really me. But these days I hardly ever use the Japanese name. I have to make a conscious effort to avoid saying, "Hello, Myung-Mi here," when I ring up Japanese friends. I tell my Korean name only to my best Japanese friends. To me, both names are me. I don't feel any big difference depending on which one I use, and I like both of them. I do think, though, that if I have children in future I'd like them to use their real names at school, if they're strong enough. While they're too young to understand I might give them an alias to use. But if they want to change to their real names when they get bigger, that'll be fine with me.'

One of Myung-Mi's older sisters has married a fellow Zainichi Korean; one of her older brothers has married a Japanese. 'My parents were totally opposed to my brother's marriage. He brought the girl to meet them, but they said she wouldn't do for him because she was too quiet and he would only get on with someone a bit more lively. Also, one of my uncles on my mother's side had married a Japanese, and things didn't go well for him. I hear that her parents were also against the marriage, but my brother went to see them and finally managed to win their consent. After the wedding he was effectively disowned by our parents, but once he had children of his own – grandchildren of our parents – they finally gave up their opposition. Only my grandmother doesn't see a problem with intermarriage. She says, "Since we're living in Japan, an *Ilbon-saram* (Japanese person) is OK." She has quite a youthful sort of outlook.'

Myung-Mi herself hopes to marry a Korean when the time comes – for her own sake rather than her parents'. But the choice is rather limited: 'It can't be a mainland Korean, and I won't marry a Zainichi who's naturalized. I don't think I'd marry someone with North Korean nationality either – they may be the same ethnic group, but their way of thinking is different. I *might* consider marrying someone from the same *bonkwan*,[3] if I really fancied him. If we're the same Korean people, I don't think one's ancestral origins matter particularly.' As Myung-Mi's statement indicates, her choice of marriage partner will be governed by the principle of 'similar way of thinking,' rather than more traditional Korean considerations.

Myung-Mi has a well-established identity as a specifically Zainichi Korean. 'I've never regretted being one, and I've never worried about it. So long as you make it something to be proud of, there's no problem. My mother country is Korea; "my country" is Korea; my home is in Japan. It's not something I've thought about deeply, but when I hear words like "homeland" (*sokoku*) or "native place" (*kokyō*) I tend to think "Japan" – or rather, I think of the town and district in Japan where I was brought up. I like Japan. I'm glad I was born here.'

As for politics, Myung-Mi is not overly concerned with the reunification of Korea, which she regards as practically impossible because of profound differences in thought that have been instilled in the people of North and South over the years. What does matter to her is the treatment of Koreans in Japan, especially the issue of electoral participation: 'Whenever there's an election in Japan, I feel a deep sense of grievance. We pay taxes, so why aren't we allowed to vote?'

Myung-Mi never feels more relaxed than when in the company of her Zainichi Korean friends. 'I used to knock around mainly with Japanese people, but these days most of my friends are Korean. It's a completely different kind of relationship. With my Japanese friends there are still some things I can't talk about. About my dad, for instance. I just don't know how they'd react. Their upbringing is completely different from mine, and there are some things they won't understand even if I tell them. But when I discuss those things with my Zainichi friends, it turns out they've had the same experiences and the same thoughts. So there are no taboos between us.'

Despite her strong emphasis on Zainichi social relations, Myung-Mi returned to a Japanese working environment about a year after our interview, leaving her job at the KYAJ to work as an instructor at a Japanese-run day-care center for school-children.

16 In Search of Self-Fulfillment

The story of Kim Jung-Mi

Kim Jung-Mi (not her real name) attended a South Korean high school, but found English more attractive than Korean as a language to study. She later spent extended periods working and studying in New Zealand, Britain and the United States. She says, 'I like being with European and American people because they treat me as an individual. When I'm accepted for what I am, I feel a sense of liberation.'

An old-style dandy

Jung-Mi was born in Tokyo in 1949 and was 40 years old when interviewed on December 26, 1989. She is a second-generation migrant holding South Korean nationality. She has four sisters and one brother, being the third oldest of six siblings.

Her paternal grandfather came to Japan from Kyongsang-Nam-Do in southern Korea, 'some time in the Taisho period' (1912–26). 'He seems to have been a landowner over there, but he used to say that he squandered his assets away on pleasure and ended up coming to Japan out of hardship. I remember him always being impeccably dressed, walking along with a western-style hat, a smart coat and a cane. He really was a gentleman of leisure – very good at playing the *jang-gu* (Korean drum), extremely know-ledgeable, and always singing lovely Korean songs.'

Jung-Mi's father was born in Kyongsang-Nam-Do in 1916, the oldest son among eight children. He came to Japan with his father, Jung-Mi's grandfather, when he was a small child, and had a Japanese education which, however, went no further than element-ary school. 'After that he supported the entire family single-handed. He worked as a laborer for the occupation army, he worked as a taxi-driver, and several times he tried to set up his own business – but he failed every time. He had TB. Running a business would weaken his constitution and he'd soon have to give it up. My father had an extremely quiet nature, and he understood children.'

Jung-Mi's mother was also born in Kyongsang-Nam-Do, in 1924. She came from the same district as Jung-Mi's father, and married him at the age of eighteen. Although all the relatives on Jung-Mi's father's side came to Japan, none of her mother's kinsfolk came. One of her older brothers died fighting in the resistance against the Japanese occupation of Korea. The only education she got was at elementary school in Korea, and to this day she cannot read or write Japanese. Moreover, Jung-Mi's mother has had mistrust of the Japanese drummed into her through experiences in the course of her life.

'Sib-won juseyo'

Jung-Mi always knew she was Korean. 'There were just a few other Zainichi families in the neighborhood where I was brought up, but my mother would wear her *jeogori* to go cherry blossom-viewing, and she also attended Mindan-sponsored trips to the seaside. My grandfather never got on with my mother and they were always fighting, but he doted on his grandchildren. From when we were very small, we knew that if we said "*Sib-won juseyo*" ("Please give me ten yen" in Korean) to him, his face would break into a smile at the sound of us using the Korean language and he'd give us the coin.

'The nameplate by our door said "Yamamoto," but everyone knew we were Korean. The house facing ours belonged to a dentist, and he had a girl the same age as me, but no way would they let her play with me. My mother used to tell me, "Those people won't let you play with their children because they're prejudiced against us. So don't you go playing with her." We did play with the other Japanese kids, though…and the dentist's girl would look on enviously.'

Jung-Mi went off to elementary school, using the name 'Yamamoto Masami.' Most of her schoolmates didn't know she was Korean. She never had any trouble from them. 'I was quite a self-conscious child, and I tended to think of myself as different from all the kids around me, not just from those who were Japanese.'

Jung-Mi was a quiet girl and her schoolwork was good. Even so she recalls being beaten by her teacher for no apparent reason. 'Once my teacher asked me when my birthday was and I answered with the date my mother had taught me, based on the old lunar calendar. She was furious. "You stupid girl! You don't even know your own birthday!"'[1]

Poor = Korean

In the household, Jung-Mi developed a negative image of her Korean identity. 'It was because we were poor. Even as a small child, I sensed that our poverty had something to do with our being Korean. My father had to go into hospital with his TB. We were living on welfare, and piecework that we did at home. We used to fold the pieces of paper used to wrap precooked food sold at a *sōzaiya*.[2] My mother was extremely strong-willed, determined to do the right thing, and she always told us to have pride in ourselves. She'd say: "Although we're poor, the reason we're poor is because we haven't borrowed money. We're not living the kind of life where we have to bow and scrape to anybody." I believe that as soon as we'd got ourselves back on our feet, my mother stopped claiming the welfare payments. She was that kind of person. So we never really found it that tough being poor. In the midst of our poverty, we were an incredibly mutually protective family. I almost feel nostalgic for the poverty we went through in those days.'

Jung-Mi went on to a Japanese junior high school. Though she hated being poor, she never hated being Korean. 'I didn't like being spoken about in a negative way because of being Korean, but I didn't hate the fact of being Korean in itself.

'Our teacher used to make us sit in order of academic achievement. I never made Number One, but I did get to sit in the Number Two seat. After that everybody paid a bit more attention to me. I thought, "Hey, people notice you if you work at your studies!" and I enjoyed the taste of it. After that I was made a class representative as well.'

However, when Jung-Mi was in her second year at junior high school, the family moved to a densely-populated Korean district of Kawasaki, the large industrial city between Tokyo and Yokohama. There the family ran a *yakiniku* restaurant (see Chapter 2, Note 16).

Learning English at a Korean school

When Jung-Mi's parents told her they'd be sending her to a Mindan-affiliated Korean senior high school, the move struck her as perfectly natural. 'I'd never known anything other than family discipline, so it never occurred to me that I might make my own choice in such matters.' At the school she reverted to her Korean name, Kim Jung-Mi.

'Senior high is a kind of blank period in my personal history. I think I had a funny sort of superiority complex, and I rather think I used to make fun of my classmates. You see, I never did much studying, but I was always top of the class.

'We had Korean classes every day, but I never bothered to study. The one thing I did study, very intensely, was English. I was in love with the West. I suppose it was a sort of escape from reality for me. I didn't really understand anything about my own personal situation – I just knew I hated it. I suppose I tended to feel that there was nothing wrong with me, but there *was* something wrong with my circumstances. If I could only change the circumstances I could make things better for myself. So I took the pragmatic view that mastering Korean would never help me put food on the table, but mastering English would.

'The one thing that I had figured out was that I needed to make myself independent at all costs. I looked at my mother and realized that her personal fortitude was a response to her oppressive surroundings. To escape those surroundings I had to make myself independent. Although as I say my father had a kindly side to him, at the same time he did believe in his own authority as head of the household. If we women ever tried to express an opinion, he'd say, "Women should be seen and not heard."'

Escape from Japan

Jung-Mi graduated from senior high school and for a while she helped out at the family *yakiniku* restaurant. 'But I really, really wanted to learn more English. I tried going to a language school, but I soon realized that I wasn't going to learn English that way. So I worked for a while as a live-in nanny with an American family in Yokohama, and then I got jobs with foreign-owned companies. The first one was with a Canadian company. Secretarial work. It was fantastic, meeting up with Western people. What was really nice was how they looked on me as an individual. They would accept me for what I was, on my own terms.'

At the time, however, Jung-Mi was using her Japanese name.

'When I was 23, I made my first attempt to escape from Japan. I went to New Zealand and worked in a bank there for a year. A New Zealander acquaintance of mine fixed up the job. What a great sense of liberation I felt in New Zealand! Ah, how suffocating it had been, living in Japan! How full of life I felt now! Of course I was escaping from my family, as well. Always had to be a good girl in front of my parents. Always knew that if I were going to get married, it would have to be with a Korean – those were the rules. But away from the country...well, no one was watching me, so I could do as I pleased.'

Jung-Mi came back to Japan and once again got a job with a foreign company. But still constrained by the tenets of her strict Confucian upbringing, she gave in to family expectations and quit the job to help out at another *yakiniku* restaurant run by some relatives who found themselves short-handed.

'I made my next trip abroad when I was 26. This time I went to Britain. Again for a year. They have this au pair system. You get to live in some family's house for free, in exchange for looking after the children and doing the cleaning. Again I felt really comfortable living abroad. I felt as if I could sort of construct my own personal identity, and it felt really good. Not having it given to me, but making it myself.'

Resisting paternalism

After returning from Britain, Jung-Mi continued to work for foreign-owned companies, still changing jobs about once a year. She started to get involved with the Seikyū-sha (see Chapter 11, Note 2). 'I was very much attracted by the Seikyū-sha's principle of looking at Zainichi Koreans in the Japanese context, without any involvement with Mindan or Chongryun. I got together with some friends to form a group for Zainichi and Japanese women involved with Seikyū-sha. I also started showing up at meetings of the Asian Women's Association.[3] It was around this time that I started questioning my own feelings, and began, little by little, to understand them. I started to be aware of myself as a woman. Then I became one of the editors of an English-language feminist newsletter.

'The starting point of my feminism is opposition to the subordination of women symbolized by the men-only *Jesa* ritual.[4] I had one uncle whom I couldn't abide. He was a kind of living embodiment of patriarchy, and he'd push the women of the family around like pawns on a chessboard. The family was everything to him, and if one branch of it were short-handed in some enterprise, he would simply order a few of us to go and help out. He would issue these orders when the family got together for the *Jesa*. I myself had to quit several jobs that I'd managed to get with foreign companies because of that uncle. At the time I was still unable to resist. I'd never seen any other lifestyle model, so I thought there was no alternative to living in this family-centered environment. I think I was about 27 when I first rebelled against that uncle. Once I'd gone to a few meetings of the Asian Women's Association, it was only natural to answer back.'

It was also around the time she came back from Britain that Jung-Mi started using her Korean name as a matter of course. 'It made my self-perception change completely. When you're using an alias, there's always that guilty feeling that you're living a lie. That you're not living as yourself. When I started using my real name, I came to understand that very well.'

To the States for study

'I entered a university at the age of 34. An American university. I majored in sociology and graduated in three years. I did it partly because I'd developed an occupational disability that meant I wouldn't be able to work for a while.[5] Also I was kind of irritated that I didn't have my feet properly on the ground. I was aware of all sorts of problems, but it bothered me that I couldn't seem to relate them to each other systematically. I wanted to study things properly, put them in some kind of order. When I told one of my friends at the Asian Women's Association that I felt like doing some studying in the United States, she said, "If you're going to do it, you might as well do it properly and get yourself a degree."

'I wouldn't say I got a totally clear picture of the structure of discrimination while I was there, but I think I did manage to relativize the problems of us Zainichi Koreans by going to an American university. Seeing the similarities and differences with the problems of black people in the US, for instance. Looking at gender discrimination, too. In that sense the activities of black women gave me many hints. They have to fight against gender discrimination within the black community at the same time as working alongside black men to fight racial discrimination in the broader society. You have to aim that high when you're dealing with discrimination, otherwise you'll never achieve liberation in the true sense of the word. However hard you fight against racial discrimination, if that's all you can see then ultimately you can't become liberated.

'I also got talking with lesbian women. I saw with my own eyes that it was OK for people to live the way they wanted. I saw that like them, I might be discriminated against by other people, but I could still choose my own way of life. That was a liberating realization. I now take the view that so long as you take responsibility for yourself, you can do whatever you like.'

Jung-Mi returned to Japan once more. She took a job with a Japanese corporation, at the same time looking around for a suitable outlet for her activist impulses.

Relativizing state and ethnicity

Jung-Mi's experiences have led her to see concepts such as state and ethnicity in relative terms. 'I feel a resistance to words like "homeland" and "motherland." I can't take them at face value. Or rather, I just can't tell you what my own country is. I feel equally uncomfortable with "ethnicity." It's a word that includes concepts that I don't want included. That's something I've felt since coming back from the States. I have the feeling that my own individualism has really widened because of going to America.'

Relativizing the frameworks of state and ethnicity does not point Jung-Mi in the direction of assimilation. She says she has never

211

once felt like acquiring Japanese nationality. Nor does it mean that
she has no interest in Korea and Japan, the places of her ethnic
roots and birth and upbringing respectively.

'I can't ignore Korea any more than I can ignore Japan.
Wherever I may be living, I always want to know what's going on
in South Korea. On that point I'm just like everyone in my family.
It's in my make-up, and I couldn't get rid of it even if I wanted to.
Japan and Korea – they're both things that go beyond choice for
me. They were given to me at birth. America is my place of choice.'

Jung-Mi has visited South Korea three times to date. The first
was on a high school trip. The second time was a business trip,
when she was working as a secretary for a Japan-US-Korean joint
venture. The third time was a stopover in Seoul en route for the
US. On the first of these trips, she met some of her Korean
relatives. 'The moment I met them, I burst into uncontrollable
sobbing. My whole body was just racked with homesickness and
I was in quite a state,' she recalls.

A voyage of self-discovery

Today, Kim Jung-Mi defines herself as follows. 'First there's my
ego. That's the basis of my thinking. The fact that I'm a Zainichi
Korean, and a woman – these are just happenstance. My self-
awareness as a Zainichi Korean is founded on the experience of
discrimination. When I look for an apartment, I get turned down
because I'm Korean. When I go for a job, if it's a European or
American who interviews me, there's no problem – I get offered
the job 99 percent of the time. But if I'm interviewed by a Japanese,
even when the job is with a foreign company, I get turned down 90
percent of the time. So you have to call it discrimination, right?

'One thing that's changed in me since coming back from the US
is that I now understand that ultimately people only do things for
themselves. I no longer feel much attraction to established groups.
I'm not really interested in tackling Zainichi Korean problems "for
the sake of Zainichi children." People don't do things for the sake
of others. I think you have to live at least once as an out-and-out
individual. For my own part, I'm much more interested in changing
my own situation, in changing things that I think are tough on *me*.
That's where I put the energy I've got. Because I believe that if I

carry on concentrating on my own individual self for long enough, I'll start to understand things.

'What I want to deal with now is my own lack of clarity as to what the real problem is. I never seem to have my feet on the ground. I'm always rushing around, sticking my nose into this, that or the other problem. But I'm never quite sure what I really want to do. Always indecisive. I've had that indecisiveness for a long time, and now I want to make it clear what it's all about, and how I should go about expressing myself.'

'Self-fulfillment' is a kind of personal motto for Jung-Mi. Japanese discrimination has given her no negative feelings about herself as a Korean in Japan; she insists that it is the situation that is wrong, not herself. If the environment can be changed, self-acceptance will be that much easier. In the course of her personal voyage of discovery, she has consistently stressed her identity as a Zainichi Korean and as a woman. She says: 'The people with whom I want to work now are Zainichi Korean women.'

17 Looking for a Way Out

The story of Sung Soon-Ja (Sugiyama Junko)

Sung Soon-Ja (not her real name) had a purely Japanese education, all the way from kindergarten to university. Up to senior high school she went by the name of 'Sugiyama Junko,' and she only realized she was Korean slowly, as she went through school. As the realization dawned, she became intensely depressed. However, at university, attendance at a seminar on discrimination problems helped her to accept her ethnic identity.

Soon-Ja was born in 1970, in a large city in the central part of Japan's main island of Honshu. When interviewed, on September 19, 1989, she was nineteen years of age and in her first year at university. She holds South Korean nationality and describes herself as a fourth-generation migrant. Certainly it is the case that her father's side of the family has been living in Japan since the great-grandparental generation, though whether her paternal grandfather was born in Japan was unclear from our interview. She has an older brother and a younger sister.

The misty past

Soon-Ja says she has 'no idea' how her paternal great-grand-parents and maternal grandparents came to migrate from Korea to Japan. She can recall addressing her great-grandmother as *halme* (a Korean term that strictly speaking means 'grandma'), but knows only Japanese names for her family relations. She does not know whereabouts in Korea her family *bonkwan* (ancestral homeland) may be located.

Her paternal grandfather worked in the city of her birth. Just after the war he was 'doing some kind of job like clearing up the remains of burned-out houses.' Later he worked as a dealer in scrap metal from discarded vehicles. Until recently, when he quit, he was involved with Chongryun. Soon-Ja's father grew up in poverty, but nonetheless managed to graduate from the agriculture department of a national university. He worked as a researcher in a chemical factory for some time, before taking over the family business from his own father. Soon-Ja describes her father as 'sickly, withdrawn, diffident and shy, but given to occasional terrifying explosions of anger, which he would take out on his children. I wasn't beaten myself, but my little sister was.'

Her mother's family lived in another city in the same prefecture. They had their own confectionery factory and were reasonably prosperous. Soon-Ja's mother had two years of higher education at a junior college. However, she sometimes tells Soon-Ja of an unpleasant incident that happened when she was at elementary school: she was playing in her own garden, when someone threw a rotten watermelon at her. It hit her, and however many times she washed herself she could never seem to get rid of the smell. To this day, Soon-Ja's mother cannot eat watermelon. Unlike her husband, however, she is a clear-speaking, energetic person.

School days of despair

It was a long time before Soon-Ja became fully aware of her nationality and ethnicity. 'When I was in the fifth year at elementary school, I read *Madogiwa no Totto-chan*[1] and I asked my mother, "How come the people in this book have such a good time and we don't?" She said, "We're different. So you'll just have to put up with it." "Different in what way?" I asked, but she didn't reply.' Soon-Ja recalls this conversation as the first time either of her parents mentioned that the family was different from others. She had already noticed that the religious rituals that were often performed in her house seemed somehow different from those conducted at other households, and that there was a different atmosphere about the place at New Year. But her family had almost no social relations with Japanese families in the neighborhood and so Soon-Ja had few opportunities to realize that these cultural differences stemmed from differences in ethnicity.

'When Korea was mentioned in my lessons at elementary school, I listened without thinking it had anything whatever to do with me.'

Soon-Ja lived in an area where everyone else was Japanese, but the name-plate next to the front door at her house said 'Sugiyama' with the character for 'Sung' in brackets right next to it. But she assumed the character for 'Sung,' which means 'star,' was to be read in the Japanese style, as 'Hoshi.' 'I just thought that "Hoshi" was an extra name that my father used for some reason.' She did not realize that it was a Korean surname. She recalls an incident regarding that second surname, just after she'd gone up to junior high school. She was taken on a family visit to see a friend of her father's from a company he used to work for. She was shocked to find that she herself was addressed as 'Miss Hoshi' by this person. 'The hospitality was Korean-style, too...' She recalls thinking that she didn't want to visit that household again. Meanwhile, it finally began to dawn upon her that her own family was Korean.

During her first year at junior high, Soon-Ja was taken ill with a heart complaint, which forced her to go into hospital. 'I kind of grew weary of life. I used to say there was no point in studying because I wouldn't live to see my twentieth birthday anyway, and things like that.'

The gradually strengthening awareness of her ethnicity only made things worse for Soon-Ja. 'I was old enough to understand about it, I did know it really, but at the time I just hated to admit it. I hated even to think about it, and the thought that I was different from everyone else made me feel extremely insecure.' Her Japanese friends did not know that she was Korean and she had no direct experience of discrimination. She just felt 'vaguely insecure.'

By the second and third years of junior high, Soon-Ja's feelings had crystallized into outright rejection of her Korean nationality. She and her younger sister would implore their father, with tears in their eyes, to rid them of the hated Korean nationality by naturalizing. Their self-hatred had been deepened by trouble at the family company, which had brought many of their relatives to the house and led to angry confrontations.

At the time, there was nothing particularly Korean about family meals. 'We used to have the usual sort of stuff – spaghetti, hamburgers, fried vegetables and so on.' When Soon-Ja had been younger, her mother had also served up Korean dishes, garnished with garlic, but once Soon-Ja had become aware of the ethnic association she had developed an intense loathing for garlic. She refused to eat it, and her mother had stopped putting it on the food. Her father liked to eat *kimchi*, but this too she flatly refused to swallow. Even now, Soon-Ja will not eat spicy foods, and even avoids the quintessentially Japanese-style *wasabi* paste that is generally used to spice up *sushi*.

At senior high school, Soon-Ja was 'an ordinary student who liked to keep everything clean and tidy.' She got onto the school library committee and 'read books like crazy.' 'I read Akutagawa, straight through. Then on to Dazai. I read everything by Dazai. Then on to somebody else. Whatever it was, I read obsessively. Around the third year I got into Hashimoto Osamu.[2] I also used to tear through books on psychology and psychoanalysis. I loved books so much, I wanted to become a librarian.'

Outwardly, Soon-Ja was 'showing up for school with a smile on my face every day.' Inwardly, she was drowning in a swamp of depression over her otherness. Now when Korean matters were mentioned in the course of a lesson, she felt physically sick. She started thinking that her nationality would prevent her from ever becoming a librarian.

Soon-Ja didn't want to go to university. She hoped to go straight into employment on graduation from senior high. She hated the atmosphere at home and longed to save enough money to leave home and live independently, as fast as she could. But she was shocked when the first employer she tried turned her down, telling her that they'd never employed Koreans at that company. That one racist rejection was enough to make her promptly abandon the search for work. Looking back at that period, she remembers being plagued by insomnia even before the awful thing happened.

'And so I became depressed. Well, I don't know if what I suffered from would technically be called depression, but it was incredibly hard to bear anyway. I made the decision to go to hospital myself. At first I didn't say much, and they thought I was a bit weird so they just gave me medicine to put me to sleep. It was quite a while before I started talking properly. The counseling sessions started with my problems at home, and only right at the end of the treatment did I start coming out with bits and pieces about how I wouldn't be able to become a librarian, and about being a Zainichi. Anyway, one way or another I got better.'

At this point, one of Soon-Ja's senior high-school teachers introduced her to a Zainichi woman who had graduated from a university where she had attended a special seminar on discrimination problems.

'When I went to see her, I found that although she was a Zainichi, she seemed to have an incredibly dynamic lifestyle. Being a Zainichi didn't seem to bother her at all, she just seemed to be having fun. Anyway, the moment I met her I felt this sense of security, and although it was the first time we'd met I told her all sorts of stuff. Honestly, I felt so relieved I nearly cried. When I was about to go home, she told me, "Ms Sugiyama, if you try for that university, I'm absolutely certain you'll get in." That gave me lots of confidence.'

Thus Soon-Ja started to recover from her depression. Up to then, she had hated the fact of being Korean, and even the very fact of having been born. Many Zainichi Koreans report that once they reach a certain age they receive lectures from their parents on the importance of marrying a fellow Korean. However, Soon-Ja didn't wait for her parents to broach the subject. 'I told them, without being asked, that there was no way I would marry a Korean, so they might as well forget about it. I told them I couldn't bear even to look at a Korean guy. My father said, "I think you'll find there are some good Koreans too," and stuff like that. But I just kept saying, "I hate them, I hate them, I hate them!"

'Actually I didn't particularly want to marry a Japanese either. I wanted to stay single. I figured that if I got married I would have to have children. I kind of felt sorry for any kids that I might give birth to. And so on.'

Aided by a recommendation from her head teacher, Soon-Ja duly got into the university that the Zainichi woman had told her about. Liberated from the need to study for exams, she took a part-time job as a dentist's assistant. On previous occasions when forms had to be filled in, Soon-Ja had always written the name of the prefecture where she was born and raised in the section on 'legal domicile' (*honseki*), but now, for the first time, she wrote 'South Korea.' 'I said, "I've got South Korean nationality – does that matter?" The dentist said it didn't matter.'

Right at the end of her final year at senior high, she finally told a particularly close friend of her Korean identity. 'She'd been a friend of mine since junior high school, and I think she was just about to take her university entrance exams. We were just having some spaghetti together in a restaurant, and for some reason I suddenly blurted out, "I'm Korean." She said, "It's OK. You don't look that way at all. I don't pay any attention to that kind of thing." Hearing her say that I felt kind of sad. What did she mean by "looking that way"?'

Political awareness

In April 1989, Soon-Ja entered university. 'When I started at university, my dad said, "Do whatever you like, only stay alive." He seemed to think I might commit suicide. It was kind of sad, but that's what he said.'

Going to university raised the awkward question of Soon-Ja's name. She had used her usual pseudonym, 'Sugiyama Junko,' to take the examination, but once she came to tackle the paperwork entailed in matriculating, she gave her name as 'Hoshi Junko,' using the character of her Korean surname but pronouncing it in the Japanese way in the section on each form where the name was to be written out phonetically. 'My father looked at the papers and said, "Uh-oh, that won't do." In the phonetic section he crossed out "Hoshi" and wrote "Sung" in its place.' This was how Soon-Ja first discovered the Korean pronunciation of her Korean surname. However, her father left her forename unchanged. 'Soon-Ja' is written with the same characters as 'Junko' and looks like a Japanese name rather than a Korean one. But at the time when she entered university, Soon-Ja was neither 'Sung Soon-Ja' nor 'Hoshi Junko' (much less 'Sugiyama Junko'), but 'Sung Junko.'

At her matriculation ceremony, Soon-Ja was presented with her student identity card. Naturally, it had 'Sung Junko' written on it. 'The moment I saw it, I knew I had to change it somehow. I hated it. After all, it was different from the name I'd been using up till then. It wasn't my own name.' She went to the university's administrative office and asked for the card to be changed. 'They drew two lines through "Sung," stamped a big red seal over it, and neatly wrote "Sugiyama" in the little space just above it. It was so obvious that it had been changed that I felt there hadn't been much point in having it done.'

Soon-Ja went along to the seminars on discrimination problems, which were given by a prominent Zainichi literary critic who was a visiting lecturer at the university. 'I just wanted to see what they were like. At first I thought of chucking it in, but in the end I decided to stick it out for six months and see how I felt. Now I feel quite at home with it.'

It was at one of these seminars that Soon-Ja was taught how to pronounce her personal name in the Korean style. '"You are Sung Soon-Ja," said the teacher.'

Just over thirty students attended the seminar, including four Zainichis besides herself. For Soon-Ja, who had had very little experience of meeting other Zainichi people outside her own family, this was a new sensation. 'I was just amazed to find that there were other Zainichis as well as me. I discovered that there were various different kinds of Zainichi, and it was interesting to listen to them talk. The one that amazed me most was a student who'd been to a Korean school. Then there was one who had mixed Japanese-Korean parentage and Japanese nationality, and another who was active in the ethnic Korean movement. I realized that some of them were using their Korean names. Amid all these surprises, I gradually found I was becoming part of the team.'

Sugiyama Junko vs Sung Soon-Ja

At the time of our interview, Soon-Ja was wavering between her two names – 'Sugiyama Junko' and 'Sung Soon-Ja.'

'I first introduced myself at the student dormitory as "Sugiyama Junko." Right at the end I said, "Oh, and by the way, I happen to be a Zainichi Korean," but this was a drinking party and I don't think too many people were listening by then. Still, I wanted to say it. I wanted to change everything from my time at senior high.

'Revealing my Zainichi identity has been a relief. But I still find that there are situations where it feels strange to suddenly start using my Korean name. I call myself "Sugiyama" with some of my friends, "Soon-Ja" with others.[3] Sometimes relationships don't develop just because you want them to, right? Like people you get to know just because you happen to be in the same dormitory. They know me as "Sugiyama" because that was the name I used when I entered the dorm. But I think most of the people whom I've got to know out of choice know that I'm Korean. They tend to mention it quite casually. And I just say, "I'm called Sung Soon-Ja or Sugiyama Junko." I don't try desperately to hide it the way I did at senior high school, though.'

Soon-Ja says she currently feels comfortable with both her names. 'The first time I heard the name "Soon-Ja," I thought it was kind of cute. It had a nice ring to it. I feel that something of Soon-Ja has now entered into the old Sugiyama Junko. Sometimes I think I ought to choose one or the other and stick to it, but when I think of going back to being Sugiyama Junko all the time, I know I can't do it. Then I imagine myself saying "I'm Sung Soon-Ja" all the time, and I know I can't do that either. I somehow think it would be wrong to the people who know me as Sugiyama. Still, the other day somebody told me it would be better for me to give up thinking of my real name as Number One and my Japanese name as Number Two, and I thought that was probably right. I think I'd like to go with the one that feels least uncomfortable in each situation.'

Three months as a Zainichi

Sung Soon-Ja is studying Korean in her language classes at university. She had never come into substantial contact with the language before. 'I didn't even know that eomeoni means "mother" until I went to university. I told my parents I was studying Korean in a letter. Then my father got ill and had to go into hospital. I went to see him, and when I popped into the sickroom, he started jabbering away in Korean. I knew it was Korean, but I couldn't get what he was going on about. Was I working hard at my studies, maybe, or something like that. I don't know. Anyway, I kind of sat there with my jaw sagging, and he said – in Japanese, this time – "This won't do! You're not working hard enough."' Laughing, Soon-Ja remarks that this was the first time her father had revealed to her that he could speak Korean.

At university Soon-Ja attended a single meeting of a strongly political Chongryun-affiliated student group called *Ryuhakdong*.[4] 'It was a good experience, but I won't be going anymore. They kept on talking about Korean reunification, but as soon as anyone expressed a slightly unorthodox opinion one of the older students would cut in and say something like, "Ahem! I'd just like to correct that observation," and then go on for ages and ages, until somehow the talk got right back to where it was before the unorthodox comment was made.

'They asked questions like, "What do you honestly think reunification of the homeland would mean to you personally?" Then they all took it in turns to go on about how brilliant it would be, but when it was my turn I said, "Suppose they achieved reunification tonight, I might wonder how things were going and have a look in the paper tomorrow and think 'Oh, that's good,' but that's about it – I don't think it would affect me at all." Then they all started shaking their heads and tut-tutting about the corrupting influence of Japanese schools. You see, apart from myself, they'd all been to ethnic Korean schools. They were all nice kids, and fun to be with, but on certain subjects they'd all show exactly the same reaction, and I came away thinking that it was kind of scary, or creepy, you know?

'They have a special way of talking, too. Like, "That video *juseyo*." That's "please give me" in Korean. They'd stick Korean words on the end of sentences like that, or use Korean greetings when they met. It was that kind of world.'

Soon-Ja was impressed when she met students of her own age who could speak Korean, 'but no more than if they could speak English, or use a word processor.' She thinks of Japan as her motherland, and the city where she was brought up is home to her. 'I'm connected to Korea whether I like it or not, so I do think it's a special country for me, but I can't call it my homeland. Maybe I will feel that way about it in future, who knows?' She has never been to South Korea, but hopes to visit one day, 'when I'm more clear in my thinking.'

At the time of our interview, Soon-Ja's feelings about her ethnic identity were confused – she had only come out in the open about it three months before. 'It's what I'm mainly interested in, but I can't seem to say confidently, "I'm a Zainichi," unfortunately. I'm a Zainichi but it's hard to think of myself as a Zainichi, which troubles me, or confuses me. How can I put it? I kind of feel that I shouldn't go around boasting or putting on airs about being a Zainichi. And then again, I've only been one for three months! Until three months ago, I really didn't think I was a Zainichi. I thought of myself as Japanese! One of the older students at the seminar told me, "Real Japanese people don't think of themselves as Japanese!" I said, "But I'm not at all like a Zainichi!" He said, "Some Zainichis are like that!" I felt like I was in Zainichi hell. I know that sounds strange, but it was like, whichever way I went, I couldn't get away from it. These days I don't think it's that bad, really, being a Zainichi. But I still couldn't say I was *happy* to be a Zainichi, not even if you tried to force me at gun-point.'

At this very delicate point in Soon-Ja's personal development, her parents have suddenly started talking about naturalization. 'This summer my father suddenly said, "We're thinking of getting naturalized." I'm against it. My kid sister wants to naturalize, though, and so does my big brother. I'm not against it in principle. If people get naturalized because they think it's best for them, I've got nothing against it. But in my own particular case I just don't fancy it right now. I'm right in the middle of studying about all this stuff, and it wouldn't feel right to just quietly take Japanese nationality at this point. I'm just asking my folks to give me a little more time to study, so that I can make an informed decision, to naturalize or not to naturalize, that I can feel comfortable with.'

18 Making Japan a Place Where Koreans Can Be Themselves

The story of Kim Jung-Yi

Kim Jung-Yi is the daughter of a Korean father and a Japanese mother. She attended a Korean elementary school but continued her education, all the way to university, in Japanese schools. At university she became a student activist for Zainichi Korean rights, continuing in the movement after graduation. Today she is still engaged in the battle to make Japan a country where Koreans can freely live as Koreans.

Kim Jung-Yi was born in 1959. When interviewed, on March 19, 1989, she was 29 years old. She is a third-generation Zainichi Korean holding North Korean nationality. She has no Japanese alias. Her only sibling is a sister two years her senior.

'*Tanabata* is for the Japanese'

Jung-Yi's paternal grandparents came to Japan from Cheju, the island off the south coast of Korea from which so many people migrated to Japan. All that Jung-Yi has heard from them about the move is that they came to Japan 'because life was hard.' Jung-Yi's father was born in Japan and fought his way through the education system all the way to university graduation. He and Jung-Yi's mother got married despite considerable opposition from both families. He worked as a teacher at North Korean schools and then as an official with North-affiliated ethnic Korean organizations, before finally quitting later in life.

Jung-Yi knew she was Korean from an early age. Her older sister got some unfriendly comments about her name at kindergarten. Her father got angry with her sister for asking if they could celebrate the *Tanabata* summer festival at their house, because it was 'a Japanese thing.' So early in her childhood Jung-Yi got the vague impression that her family was not Japanese. She recalls visits to the hospital: 'When it was our turn to be seen and they called out our name, "Kin",[1] everyone would turn and stare at us, so I got to realize that ours was definitely not a Japanese-sounding name.'

Jung-Yi's father wanted his daughters to receive an ethnic Korean education, and sent them to North-affiliated Korean schools until Jung-Yi's big sister was in her first year at junior high school and Jung-Yi herself was in her last at elementary school. Jung-Yi never experienced blatant discrimination during these years, but there were certain occasions when she recalls feeling uncomfortable. 'I would go to school, with my satchel on my back, on Japanese public holidays. People would ask me if my school wasn't closed, and I'd explain that it was a Korean school. But that was a bit of a hassle, so in the end I got to wearing my *jeogori* just on those days, so that people would know without asking.

'I also remember talking with the local Japanese children and thinking how utterly different they were from me. We were learning totally different things at school. We were learning about Korean geography and history and they weren't. We all studied *kokugo*,[2] but ours was Korean and theirs was Japanese.'

During the summer and winter holidays, the sisters would be taken to their mother's family home in Osaka. Their father would tactfully stay behind on these occasions. But their maternal grandparents, who had opposed their daughter's decision to marry a Korean, kept the Korean connection secret from Jung-Yi's cousins. So Jung-Yi would be addressed as 'Sei-chan'[3] at her Japanese grandparents' house, reverting to 'Jung-Yi' when she got back home from the visit. 'I always felt kind of guilty at the grandparents' house,' she recalls.

'Your *eomoni* is a Japanese'

Jung-Yi was also made to feel uncomfortable in Korean company. Her mother being Japanese, the family usually ate almost entirely in the Japanese style. 'When we took lunch-boxes to school, the contents were totally different from everyone else's. All the other kids had *kimchi* or *namul*, and we had *umeboshi*.'[4]

Jung-Yi's classmates at the Korean school knew that her mother was Japanese, but did not discriminate against her for it. She did, however, feel a certain coldness in her teacher's attitude toward her. 'Once, when it was going to be parents' day, the school gave out notices about it in Korean. In my first couple of years I still couldn't understand everything myself. My father often came home late, too. "Even if I take this home, my mother won't be able to read it," I said. "Why can't she read Korean?" asked the teacher. "Because she's Japanese," I said. "Well she may be Japanese but you'd better get her to study Korean," said the teacher.

'I also had trouble with the children of certain executives from the organization my father worked for, because he'd taken a critical stance toward it. They'd taunt me: "Oy, you've got a Japanese *eomeoni* (mother)."'

Jung-Yi's father's decision to switch the girls into Japanese schools met with a cynical response from his Korean relatives. Their view was that it was just what you'd expect from a family with a Japanese mother.

Inner conflict and the wish to assimilate

Jung-Yi's father moved his daughters into Japanese schools for two main reasons. One was that he had become critical of North Korean-style education; the other was that he hoped eventually to send the girls to Japanese universities, which might not recognize a Korean high school graduation certificate.

'My six years of North Korean education entirely convinced me that I was Korean. I still feel that way today. I had also learned to thoroughly hate Japan – for the things she had done historically, and for the fact that she was still helping to perpetuate the division of Korea to the present day. So when I was told to go to a Japanese junior high school, it was a terrible shock to me. I refused outright, and honestly, I was crying every night.'

She could not, however, resist her father's will. 'I was really tense when I started going to the Japanese school. I was determined to behave like a model Korean, even in a Japanese school. I was incredibly self-conscious, because I thought all the Japanese kids would be forming their impressions of Korean people by watching me, so that I had to behave well at all costs. Then I was hit by intense culture shock. They had a test to decide which classes we'd go into, and believe it or not, all the questions were in Japanese! Everything was different. At the matriculation ceremony we were made to sing the Japanese anthem and they put up the Japanese flag. That was a first for me.

'I was also surprised at the emphasis on competition at the Japanese school. One of the good things about the North Korean style of education is the importance they place on the group. If there was something that you alone could do, you'd be really sharply criticized for it. If there were kids who couldn't do something, then the ones that could do it were supposed to look after them. In the Japanese school only a certain percentage of the children in the class were allowed to get top grades, but in the Korean school if everyone worked hard and got good results, they could all get top grades. In the Japanese school, if there was some kid who couldn't keep up with the lessons, the teacher and the other pupils couldn't care less. I wanted to be a model student, so I studied really hard. Then there were some kids who couldn't keep up. I thought to myself, at my old elementary school I'd have had to help those kids catch up…and I felt really guilty about it.'

Jung-Yi's teacher at junior high school called her 'Kin Seii' – the Japanese reading of her Korean name. 'The other kids didn't know I was Korean, and said what a weird name it was. Once they did find out I was Korean, some of them would abuse me in various ways, saying that I stank of garlic and all that. That sort of thing made me build a wall around myself – I was determined not to have a close relationship with any Japanese kid. But as time passed, and I got used to the Japanese school, I did start to make efforts to fit in with the kids around me.

'At the same time as moving toward assimilation with them, I also developed a complex. I just hated writing my Korean name on my school shoes, and I wished and wished that I too had a Japanese name. By the time I finished my first year, I got to hate being Korean so much that I often used to tell my mother: "If I were you, I would never have married a Korean man."

'I was worried sick, and in my second year at junior high I told one of my best friends, "I'm really bothered about being Korean." She said "Kin, if it weren't for your Korean name, you'd seem just like a Japanese." That gave me a real big shock. She was trying to comfort me by saying that I was alright because I seemed Japanese. In the end that implies being Korean is in itself something to worry about, right?'

Jung-Yi's friends started talking about which of the boys they liked. Once again Jung-Yi felt isolated. 'Even if I did happen to fancy some boy, no way would I have let on. I felt certain that any Japanese boy would despise me if I told him I was Korean, and I was absolutely determined not to let that happen. Even if I did come across one who struck me as kind of nice, I'd automatically apply the emotional brakes.'

History lessons were another source of grief. 'In the Korean school we'd been taught that we had this magnificent 5,000-year-old cultural heritage, but in the Japanese school Korea only ever got mentioned as a weak country that was always getting conquered by Japan. They never taught anything about how come we Zainichi Koreans came to be in Japan. When I knew Korea was going to come up in a history lesson the next day, I really didn't want to go to school. I knew I'd blush to the roots as soon as the word "Korea" even got mentioned in the lesson. I'd just look at the floor.'

Jung-Yi accounts for her excessive self-consciousness at this age as follows: 'I was mistrustful of Japan, I hated myself, and I had a grudge toward my parents. I thought I was truly pathetic because I'd abandoned everything I learned at the Korean school so quickly, and I blamed my father for being the source of the blood that made me Korean.'

Politicization

Jung-Yi went on to a prefectural girls' senior high school.

'However much I might worry, I made sure I never showed it in front of the Japanese kids. When it was time for self-introductions, I came straight out and said, "I'm Kin Seii, I'm Korean." I still felt inferior, but in my case there was no way I could hide it, so I just had to brazen it out.' At senior high school Jung-Yi's classmates showed what she calls 'a strange kind of sophistication.' None of them ever so much as mentioned her ethnicity, though she felt convinced that they remained very much aware of it.

At the end of the first year, Jung-Yi got to study Ishimure Michiko's book, *Kugai Jōdo (Paradise in the Sea of Sorrow)*.[5] This is a work of reportage, dealing with the lives of people suffering from Minamata disease, the methyl-mercury poisoning caused by industrial pollution of the coastal waters at a town in Kyushu. The book made a huge impact on Jung-Yi. 'I got intensely angry about the pollution issue. But as for my own problem to do with my ethnicity, I still couldn't confront it head-on. I still felt guilty about it, my friends still didn't mention it, I was still just drifting cozily along. But around this time I finally realized that if I didn't resolve my own problem, I wouldn't be able to say anything about any other problems. And that was why I started studying Korean history again.'

After that, Jung-Yi started talking to her friends about her problem, began to show up at a social problems study circle, and generally became active on the Korean issue.

Student activist

In 1978 Jung-Yi entered a women's university. She had planned to join Ryuhakdong, the Chongryun-affiliated Korean Exchange Students League (see Chapter 17, Note 4), but it soon became obvious that she would not fit in. Her years at Japanese schools had given her a considerably more critical stance toward Chongryun and North Korea than was to be found within Ryuhakdong. Instead, she attempted to work alongside Japanese activists within the student union. This didn't last long, however. 'I talked with them quite a bit, but in the end I felt that after all, I couldn't really get on with them. They were all very factional, belonging to one Communist sect or another, and they totally rejected nationalism in the name of "internationalism."[6] This meant that things like the democratization movement in South Korea and the issue of Korean reunification meant virtually nothing to them.'

At the start of her second year, unable to find any other outlet for her activist instincts, Jung-Yi paid her first visit to *Hanhakdong* (the South Korean Students League in Japan). The reason she had not approached this organization earlier was because 'I assumed that the organization must be faithful to South Korean government policy, and hence anti-Communist. When I actually showed up, I found that sure enough they were displaying the South Korean flag and singing the South Korean anthem. With my North Korean-style education, I viewed the Republic of Korea as a puppet of American imperialism and strongly rejected the whole process by which it came into being, so I naturally couldn't handle the flag and anthem.'

Half a year later, however, Jung-Yi gave Hanhakdong a second chance. 'Anyway, somehow or other I wanted to work with other Korean students.' Once she got talking to the other students in Hanhakdong, Jung-Yi learned that although Hanhakdong had originally been affiliated to Mindan, it had actually been expelled for criticizing Mindan's support for the Park Chung-Hee regime that had crushed the South Korean democratization movement. This fact enabled Jung-Yi to take a positive role in Hanhakdong's activities.

Jung-Yi's activities with Hanhakdong took her away from her studies, but she just about managed to graduate in the usual four years. She had never thought properly about a career and had no idea what to do with herself after graduation, but happened to pick up a part-time job at a publishing house. She was still doing that job at the time of our interview. 'Part-time work suits me fine. It leaves me free to get on with my activism and all the other things I want to do.'

Against fingerprinting

In 1984 Jung-Yi joined with some friends to launch a movement against the fingerprinting requirement included in the Alien Registration Law (see Chapter 1, p. 19). 'It just so happened that the people who got together to discuss fingerprint-refusing seemed different from the Korean friends I'd met up until then, and their thinking seemed much closer to my own.'

Jung-Yi first had her fingerprint taken under the Alien Registration Law at the age of fourteen. 'My father had told me that in Japan they had this sort of registration system under which you had to give your fingerprint, so I was ready for it. Of course I didn't like being fingerprinted, but I just thought that this kind of harassment was exactly what you'd expect in a country like Japan.'

In September 1980 a first-generation Zainichi travel agent called Han Jong-Seok hit the headlines when he refused to be fingerprinted. 'At the time I had an oh-so-clever student-type argument against fingerprint refusing. You'd never solve the problems of Zainichi Koreans just by refusing one fingerprint; the problem was the Alien Registration Law itself, that and the Immigration Control Act,[7] under which Koreans could be deported if they engaged in political activity – the problem was inherent in the system itself! That sort of thing.'

But then people started getting indicted and arrested for refusing to be fingerprinted. 'I couldn't justify continued compliance with the fingerprinting requirement, which I did see as unjust, while other people were getting that kind of treatment for refusing. I was moved to find that high school kids were refusing fingerprinting, not for some theoretical reason but really out of pure intuition. It also occurred to me that refusing fingerprinting would enable me to meet various kinds of Korean people and work with them on a particular issue.'

In 1985, Jung-Yi refused fingerprinting along with several fellow protestors. In June 1988, a half-hearted reform of the Alien Registration Law removed the obligation for foreign nationals to give their fingerprint more than once, by stipulating that the initial fingerprint could be transferred to the new alien registration card when registration was renewed. Since then, Jung-Yi and her comrades have continued campaigning, now refusing to have their fingerprints transferred.

Double isolation

Jung-Yi says she feels like an outsider in Japanese and Korean company alike. 'Some politically aware Zainichis think the answer is to "return to the homeland." They believe that the way for a Zainichi Korean to achieve liberation is to go to South Korea and join in the pro-democracy movement there. But I want to stay in Japan and tackle Zainichi problems here. Many Koreans involved in ethnic activism tend to ignore problems not directly related to the ethnic issue. They say that anything else is "a problem for the Japanese" and nothing to do with them. They want to get rid of every last vestige of Japaneseness that they may have absorbed through living here, and learn to be Korean. But I think that as long as we're living in Japan we are also affected by Japanese problems, and I think it's probably necessary to put those problems in the picture when we think about the future of the Koreans in Japan.

'Meanwhile, the proportion of Zainichi Koreans marrying fellow Koreans is now less than half. Whatever the fine print of the law may say, their children are effectively turned into Japanese nationals. Most of the people who marry Japanese end up naturalizing. And whether they naturalize or not, all Zainichi Koreans are exposed to discrimination and pressure to assimilate. The Ministry of Justice operates a policy that assumes the ideal thing is for Koreans to naturalize of their own accord. I just want to say that that's wrong. Why have you got to create the sort of society that makes Koreans want to become Japanese? What on earth is wrong with Koreans living here in Japan as Koreans?

'For instance, they say stuff like, "Only Japanese people get sentimental when they look at cherry blossoms. Koreans can't be expected to understand that kind of emotion. So it wouldn't do to let Koreans teach in Japanese schools." But there are in fact some Japanese who couldn't care less about cherry blossoms, just as there are some Koreans who've been born and raised in Japan and who *do* get sentimental about cherry blossoms. That's why I hate arguments that assume people have some kind of essential ethnic character – whether Japanese or Korean – with which they are endowed before they're even born. Look at me – I call myself Korean, but I wasn't brought up there and so I haven't acquired Korean culture and customs. Maybe you could say I'm a Korean with a head but no body. I call myself Korean because the history by which Zainichi Koreans were created, and our present circumstances, matter to me. It's not because I mind about blood that I don't naturalize, it's because I can never forgive Japan for what it has done.'

Against gender discrimination

Another big issue for Kim Jung-Yi is the gender discrimination which she sees as endemic within Zainichi Korean society. As with Kim Jung-Mi (Chapter 16), her gender awareness started with discomfort regarding the Korean *Jesa* ceremony (see Chapter 2, Note 22). 'It's always the men who say the ritual prayers and greetings first at a *Jesa*, and the women last. It's only the men who get to sit and feast. The women always gather in the kitchen and do all the preparations. That's what the *Jesa* looks like, and I can't stand it.

'Korean men have a really strong feudalistic mindset. There are various types among the Japanese guys too, of course, but with Koreans, the *Jesa* is the sort of foundation on which they construct their ethnic identity. So I think there are an awful lot of cases where they mistake feudalism for nationalism.'

Jung-Yi's father is rather hoping that she'll soon get married. But having learned to mistrust so many institutions already, Jung-Yi is also extremely skeptical about the institution of marriage. 'I don't think I'll ever get married,' she says. 'I want to be able to love freely forever.'

19 Japanese Nationality Not Good Enough to Beg for

The story of Cha Yuk-Ja

Cha Yuk-Ja had a Japanese education, and went by the name 'Yasuda Ikuko' until she reached senior high school. She married a Japanese man and wanted to acquire Japanese nationality, but when she encountered the naturalization system, under which she would have to humbly request the privilege of being allowed to become Japanese, she sensed a contradiction and withdrew her application.

Yuk-Ja was born in Tokyo in 1953. She was 35 years of age at the time of our interview, which took place on September 17, 1988. She is a second-generation migrant holding South Korean nationality. Her three children all have Japanese nationality. Her husband, Kishi Yuji, 36 (born 1952), was also present at the interview.

From weakling to tomboy

Yuk-Ja's paternal grandmother was born in 1911, and came to Japan in 1938 in order to marry a Korean man who had already migrated. It was her second marriage, and she took with her a seven-year-old son who would one day become Yuk-Ja's father. Yuk-Ja recalls addressing her grandmother as *halme*, the Korean term for 'grandma,' when she was very small. Thus she very early became aware of her Korean ethnicity.

Her father was a quiet man who made his living as a shoemaker. Her mother, a second-generation Zainichi, helped the household finances by working at a bookbinder's.

'I was a very weak, almost sickly child up to the early years at elementary school, but after that I gained strength remarkably fast, and at the same time I became quite a cheeky kid. Sometimes my parents would scold me but I would insist that I'd said nothing wrong. Then my father would punish me, for instance by burning moxa on my hand.[1] Even then I wouldn't apologize, and I got quite a reputation as an uncontrollable child among our relatives.

Yuk-Ja brought this self-willed determination to the issue of her ethnicity. In her fourth year at elementary school she was denounced as a *Chōsenjin* (Korean) by a mixed-blood boy with Japanese nationality who hoped to avoid bullying for his own half-Korean ethnicity by using her as a scapegoat. Determined not to share the boy's sense of fear and inferiority over his ethnicity, she told her best friend in class that she was indeed Korean. 'She had worries of her own, because her parents were getting divorced, and I think that was one reason why we became friends. After that I gradually told the other pupils, one by one. I would figure out the likely reaction of each one before talking to them about it. In the end, everyone in the class got to know about it.'

Yuk-Ja never suffered any discrimination from her classmates. She did, however, have a problem with her class teacher in the sixth year. 'He was getting on in years, and I think he did have some prejudice. You'd glimpse it occasionally. Like when it was time to go home, and everyone was making a bit of a row, and not listening to what he was saying, he'd shout out "Yasuda! Aren't you Japanese? If you were, you'd understand what I'm saying!"'

Negative Korea

As Yuk-Ja moved from elementary school to junior high, she developed a powerful prejudice of her own against Koreans, and particularly against Korean men.

'There was this couple in my neighborhood. Later they went to North Korea on one of the repatriation ships. The husband was really far gone. He'd be on the booze from first thing in the morning, he'd beat his wife. The Korean men I met when I was a child were mostly pretty simple men without much education. At the time I had no idea how difficult it was for a Korean man to go out and make a proper career for himself in Japanese society. All I saw was a bunch of lazy bums getting drunk all day and not doing a stroke of work. I despised them, because I thought that if only they made an effort they could actually make a prosperous living for themselves. I felt that especially strongly during junior high. When I went on to senior high I just thought "they're different from me" and deliberately distanced myself from them.'

These factors contributed to a strong desire on Yuk-Ja's part to become Japanese. 'I literally dreamed of it. I had dreams where I was Japanese. I felt I wouldn't even mind being in a one-parent family, if only it were a Japanese one. I thought that I would give my right arm to become Japanese. I guess that was the toughest period of my life.'

Own name at senior high

At senior high school Yuk-Ja used her Korean name with its Japanese reading, 'Sha Ikuko.' A number of experiences had made her determined to overcome her anxieties and live openly with her Korean identity. One was a memorable lesson with a progressive social studies teacher who told the class that 'The Korean peninsula is the mother of Japan. Japan was brought up suckling at the breast of Korea.' Another was her first experience of registering as an alien, at the age of fourteen. 'I was bothered by the sight of my finger, dirty with ink from the fingerprint. But rather than feeling bad about it, it was almost the opposite. My main feeling was one of confirmation. Yes, I really was Korean. And since I really was Korean, I might as well live my life as a Korean.'

Her parents did not oppose her decision to use her real name at senior high school, but they did worry about it. 'My parents spent their youths sheltering from the storm of Japanese oppression, and they had very strong instincts of self-defense, I suppose you'd call it. So I think they were quite worried, that I might be bullied and so on.'

However, Yuk-Ja herself found that the change took a load off her shoulders. 'I'd got sick and tired of it. All the inner conflict I'd been through at school. I felt guilty about hiding my identity from my friends. Although I'd told some of them at elementary school, I'd carried on with the alias and so a lot of people didn't know I was Korean at junior high. But I was always being driven on by this urge to tell people I was different from them. In the end I just couldn't bear using that name, "Yasuda," to hide myself away any more. I actually hated being mistaken for a Japanese. I wanted to proclaim to all that even here in Japan, there were Koreans living proper lives.'

Yuk-Ja entered senior high school in 1969, at a time of intense campus struggle. In her first year she did virtually no studying, spending the whole school day in classroom debates. 'We put barricades up in the school grounds. It was fantastic. It was fun. Because we were free.' Perhaps it was partly because of this special atmosphere that none of her friends showed any discrimination toward the openly Korean Yuk-Ja.

Different at work

Yuk-Ja was in the basketball club at senior high, and hoped to become a teacher of physical education. She even had a place all but lined up at university, but her parents wouldn't have it. 'My parents said it was outrageous for a woman to go to university. "If you get any more cheeky than you already are, we'll never find anyone to marry you" – that's what they said.'

The reason why the strong-willed Yuk-Ja gave in to her parents on this occasion was because she reflected that 'the nationality clause would stop me getting a job at a publicly-run school in Japan anyway, so there wasn't that much point fighting a big battle to go to university.'

The teacher in charge of career advice at her school was not optimistic. 'He said that as I wasn't Japanese, and as I'd missed the main recruiting season on account of planning for university, no one would give me a job except maybe in a factory. But I got lucky. Someone who'd graduated from my high school was launching a new company and was recruiting office staff. I got one of the jobs. It was a very small company – there were just five of us.

'I wanted to use my Korean name, but the boss asked me to call myself "Yasuda" again, because he said it was "easier to say." Since I'd just seen my dream for the future go up in smoke, I thought what the hell, it doesn't really matter.'

A year later, a personal connection helped Yuk-Ja to get a new job at a travel agency. 'I called myself "Yasuda" there as well. I told them I'd used that name at my previous company, but I'd like to call myself "Cha" this time. But the boss said, as if doing a little act of kindness, "I think you'll find that it's easier to get along with 'Yasuda,' so why don't you stick with it?'"

Yuk-Ja's job involved foreign travel. 'I asked Mindan to have a passport made for me.[2] The first couple of times there was no problem, but the third time I was summoned to the South Korean embassy. The official who interviewed me gave me a funny look and said, "You're South Korean, right?" I said, "Yes." "Can you speak Korean?" he asked. "No I can't." "Why not? Don't you want to learn it?" "Sure I want to," I said. Then he said, "You've been to places like Hawaii and Guam, right?" "Yes I have," I said. This time he got really angry with me. "If you're buzzing around foreign countries like that, how come you never think of visiting your own native country?!" I was being preached to, that's what was happening. He thought I was an insolent little Zainichi who never bothered to learn her own language and went playing around in Hawaii and Guam without ever paying a respectful visit to her motherland – something like that. It was a terrific shock to me. How dare he go on like that, without having the slightest idea of how we Zainichis felt about things?'

Marrying a Japanese

Cha Yuk-Ja married Kishi Yuji when she was 23. The couple explained how it happened as follows:

Yuji: We went to a noodle restaurant together one evening, and then carried on to a bar. And then suddenly…

Yuk-Ja: I said, 'I want to get married!' I didn't mean with him particularly. I'd just lost out in a love affair with another Japanese man, actually. There'd been various problems…when the subject of marriage came up, his family was against it. Right from the word go. I just felt really tired of it. The guy wasn't showing much fighting spirit either. Looking back, I don't think he loved me enough to defend me himself. Seeing his attitude I just thought, I've had enough of this.

Yuji: So I just blurted out, 'Why not get married to me?' I kind of had a good feeling about her, and she seemed like an interesting person, and the words just popped out somehow. She accepted me right away, and then she said, 'I'm Korean. Is it still OK?' I said, 'Yeah, sure it's OK.' In the fraction of a moment it took to say it, I had this instinctive feeling that we were two of a kind. I know it sounds kind of pompous, but I felt that the two of us were fellow members of the weaker element within society.

Yuji's mother was born in Peru. Her parents were Japanese people who had migrated there. She returned to Japan when she was sixteen, because her parents thought it would be good for their children to study in Japan. She got married in Japan, but her husband, Yuji's father, died when Yuji was just three years old. She supported Yuji and one other child by working as a maid for an officer at one of the US military bases, as a cook at the Peruvian embassy, or at Latin-style restaurants. Yuji himself got a job with an advertising agency after graduating from senior high school.

Yuk-Ja quit her job at the travel agency 'without any regrets' after marrying Yuji. Today she says she is pleased she married a man of different nationality to her own. 'I wonder whether couples of the same nationality talk together as much as we do. How can I put it? Because we're different, we want each other to understand, and so we talk. We can't communicate without talking,[3] and so we do talk, even when we have a row about something. From that point of view I kind of think it was a good move.'

Too high a price for Japanese nationality

In 1979, at the age of 26, Cha Yuk-Ja responded to a reader survey on ethnic identity in a small-scale Zainichi-run magazine called the *Jan-so-ri Quarterly*[4] as follows: 'I now think that I'm neither Korean nor Japanese but a citizen of the world.' She also wrote: 'I want the right to participate in politics. Recently I have been considering naturalization. Naturalization used to be a form of escapism, but I don't think that is the case any more.' Here's how Yuk-Ja explains her feelings at that time of her life:

'I felt that although I was Korean, I wasn't so by choice. Not that I disliked being Korean, I just felt that nationality was a matter of random chance. I had the feeling that fundamentally human beings could live anywhere and it was all the same, so I didn't want to be imprisoned by a concept like nationality.

'So at the time I *was* inclined to naturalize. I wanted to take Japanese nationality and secure my civil rights. It was clear that I was going to live in Japan for the duration. I couldn't go over to Korea and start afresh. In America they talk about Korean Americans and so on, right? That kind of thing. If I could become a Korean Japanese then I thought it would be OK to naturalize. I thought there ought to be room in Japanese society for something like a Korean Japanese.'

Yuk-Ja and her husband recall that period as follows:

Yuji: I checked out the naturalization process with a lawyer. He said the first thing you had to do was write a formal request. I asked him what sort of thing one was supposed to write, and he said, 'Something like "I have been brought up exclusively in Japan, and have no intention of residing in South Korea. I have married a Japanese national, we have children...and I love Japan."' But when Yuk-Ja wrote out her request, it came out something like 'I don't like Japan, but from the point of view of everyday convenience that just can't be helped. So I will do you the favor of becoming Japanese.' I thought, 'Uh-oh, this ain't going to work.' You're supposed to *request* naturalization, and although you may have mixed feelings about it, the application form is not really the place to express them. I put that to her, and she just said, 'Well in that case I'm not going to get naturalized' – to cut a long story short.

Yuk-Ja: To put it in a nutshell, I didn't want Japanese nationality badly enough to beg for it. The only reason why I hold South Korean nationality despite being born and raised here is because Japan happens to be a country that bases its nationality law on blood-line rather than place of birth. I feel that very strongly. I just can't write something that conceals my true feelings. I think the whole naturalization system is wrong in the first place.

One reason why Yuk-Ja feels this way is because of what she has seen happen to some relatives on her mother's side who naturalized as a family many years ago. 'I invited my uncle and his wife and oldest son to my wedding. When the boy saw me wearing my *jeogori*, he said, "What!? I didn't know Ikuko was Korean! What does that make us?" And my uncle said, "Ikuko's mother married a Korean, and became a Korean herself." This was a lie, of course. I guess he plans to hide the truth away forever.'

Resistance and pride

In March 1987, when Yuk-Ja had to renew her alien registration, she refused fingerprinting. She had made up her mind after getting to know some members of the anti-fingerprinting movement and studying the issue at some length.

'The fact is, the fingerprinting system was first devised when Japan was building the Manchurian Railway, as a way of controlling the Chinese who lived in the area. I didn't think it was right for one group of humans to control and oppress another like that. I didn't think such a system had any place in a society that respected human rights. I had already been fingerprinted many times, and I wondered whether there was really much point in refusing this time round, but I thought about the next generation of children, and in the end I thought that we should try and create a situation in Japan where those children would not be confined by such a system.

'What the fingerprinting issue made me think was that up until then I'd been looking upon Japanese society rather objectively, as something that Japanese people had made. In fact, Japanese society wasn't made by Japanese people alone – we helped make it, too. So even if it was just some tiny little thing, we had to do what we could to make that society better, that's what I thought.'

In April 1987, when her second child entered elementary school, Yuk-Ja attended the entrance ceremony wearing her *jeogori*. She did it because she wanted to communicate Korean culture to her children as much as she could. Her children's friends immediately knew that the Kishi children had a Korean mother. As far as she knows this did not result in her children being bullied.

'My older child's in the fourth grade now. She's a very interesting kid, and she's always going on about her Korean mother. She gives me a hard time for not knowing the Korean language, and tells me I've got to study it.'

Yuji says that the household has quite an international atmosphere these days. 'My Peruvian-born mother lives with us, so there are Peruvian decorations up all over the house, and when Yuk-Ja's grandmother went to South Korea she brought back some Korean dolls as souvenirs. So when we had the *Hina* festival,⁵ we got out all the different dolls we had around the house and displayed them all together. Talked about where they all came from and so on. We didn't particularly intend it to be an educational experience, but I guess you could say it was. At least it was educational in the sense of encouraging the kids not to have any prejudice.'

Changing name again

Nowadays Kishi Yuji has his own advertising agency and Cha Yuk-Ja is working there, too. When I met Yuk-Ja, she was just in the middle of having some business cards made up with her Korean name on them.

'Since I got involved in the anti-fingerprinting movement, I've been subtly dividing up the social contexts where I use my two names. When I meet Zainichi people, I'm "Cha." I used to be "Kishi" – though I knew it wasn't really very good, calling myself "Kishi." Now I think the time has come to expand the range of social situations where I call myself "Cha." That's my big thing at the moment – being "Cha" from now on. I'm just at the stage of thinking that it's time to stop instinctively judging each individual before deciding which name to use with them, and to try and create a society where I can call myself "Cha" in front of anybody. When I call myself "Kishi," it feels as if I'm disguising myself. I want to stop doing that, and live my life in a way that allows me to be myself.'

20 Floating on the Tide of Assimilation

The story of Kim Yang-Ja (Kanai Yoshiko)

Kim Yang-Ja (not her real name) attended Japanese schools all the way from elementary school to nursing college. She has always used the Japanese pseudonym 'Kanai Yoshiko,' and still uses it in all situations today. I will accordingly refer to her as 'Yoshiko' throughout this chapter. 'I think that once we reach the third generation we're no different from Japanese,' says Yoshiko. 'In my own case especially, my friends never say or do anything about my nationality, and in that sense I guess I'm lucky.' Yoshiko refers to Korea, the land where her grandparents were born, simply as 'over there.'

Yoshiko was born in 1968, and lives in the Kanto region centered on Tokyo. She was 21 years old when interviewed, on August 9, 1989. She is a third-generation Zainichi, holding South Korean nationality. She has a younger brother and a younger sister.

Hating her own name

Yoshiko's paternal grandfather is still alive and well at the age of 90. He has told Yoshiko that he came to Japan because of war-induced poverty and unemployment in Korea. His wife, Yoshiko's grandmother, is also alive and is 81.

Yoshiko's father is 60. He graduated from a Japanese university and went on to work for Shōgin Bank, a Mindan-affiliated financial institution (see Chapter 5, Note 12). He recently retired, having reached the stipulated age. He has made many visits to South Korea and speaks Korean. Yoshiko describes him as 'a quiet man.'

Her mother is 47, and is also a second-generation Zainichi. She quite often talks to Yoshiko about her experiences of ethnic discrimination. 'She says that in one of her music lessons, when she put up her hand to ask to be allowed to play an instrument, the teacher said, "Koreans aren't allowed," right in front of the whole class. She says she was so humiliated that she went home in tears. She tells me lots of things like that.'

On the other side of the family, Yoshiko's maternal grandfather lost his eyesight in an industrial accident at a glass factory where he worked in his youth. His wife had to go out to work as well as raising seven children. Yoshiko's mother was only able to pursue her education as far as junior high school. Yoshiko describes her mother as 'a real Mother Courage.'

Among Yoshiko's cousins on her mother's side is a singer who has achieved considerable popularity among young people in Japan. 'But that's something I don't even mention to my friends.'[1]

Yoshiko knew about her ethnic identity very early. While her father worked at the Shōgin bank, her mother ran a noodle shop, and made no secret of the fact that she was Korean. But Yoshiko tended to feel embarrassed about it. 'When I was in elementary school, we sometimes had to give the school copies of our social insurance certificates in case of accidents on school trips and the like. On the certificate my name was given as "Kin Yoshiko," the Japanese reading of my Korean name. When the class monitors returned the copies to us, I noticed that the teacher had crossed out "Kin" and replaced it with "Kanai" in pencil. I wasn't particularly bullied about it or anything, but as a kid I really hated it. The fact that I was Korean I thought of as a kind of guilty secret, or as meaning I was different from everybody else, and I resisted it like crazy. So when I was at elementary school I never told any of my friends about it.'

Learning to be open

In each of her last three years at elementary school, Yoshiko attended Mindan-organized summer schools, along with her younger sister. 'My father got a letter about it because his job at the Shōgin bank brought him into contact with Mindan people. He said, "I'll pay the fees, so you go along." At the summer school the instructors were from the KYAJ,[2] and they would call me by my Korean name, Yang-Ja. But all the kids who took part behaved exactly the same as at school, and talked in Japanese. They got us to draw pictures of the South Korean flag, and taught us some Korean songs. That was about as far as it went. Us kids just made a big rumpus together, and made friends among ourselves. It was fun. We went three years running. It was nice, not having to hide our identity, being open about it, you know?

'When I went on to junior high, things changed a bit. I would practice at the table tennis club every day, and I gradually stopped worrying about it as I got to know the other kids better. I started telling my friends at the club, just like that: "By the way, as a matter of fact…" They'd say "Oh really? I never knew!" or something like that. They didn't change their attitude toward me after that, it was just the same really. After all the fears and bad feelings I'd had about it at elementary school, that was all that happened: "Oh really?" It made me wonder why I'd made such a fuss about it.'

Later on, when she was at senior high school, Yoshiko and some friends of hers secretly took some lessons and acquired moped licenses – something strictly forbidden under the school rules. 'The school found out about my friends, suspended them for a week and confiscated their licenses. One of the teachers must have gone along to the police and checked out the license records.[3] Mine must have gone unnoticed because it was registered under my official, Korean name. I was kind of pleased that it had actually worked in my favor for once. My friends asked me how come I was the only one who got away with it, and I said, "Well, as a matter of fact…" and told them. "That's not fair!" they said. It would have taken a bit of guts to stick my hand up in class and state that I was Korean, but in a playful situation like that it wasn't any problem.'

However, Yoshiko often heard her classmates make insulting remarks about students at the local North Korean school. 'It was all rumor that had got more and more exaggerated with each retelling. Like, they'd come and beat you up if you just let your eyes meet theirs. Or they kept razors in their pockets and they'd slash your face for nothing. At times like that, I'd just listen to the conversation and say "Really?" I didn't feel particularly good about it, but somehow I felt it didn't have much to do with me. My mother always said, "We're different from that lot."'

What her mother meant, of course, was that South-affiliated Koreans like themselves were different from the North-affiliated Koreans who sent their children to the North Korean school.

Choosing to be a nurse

When the time came for Yoshiko to pick a career, she dashed her father's hopes that she would follow him into Shōgin Bank, and chose instead to become a nurse. 'I was dead against getting a job at the bank. I didn't want to work in a place where everybody else was Korean too. I decided to become a nurse while I was in the second year at senior high. I thought that if I could get a qualification, it would be easier for me to find employment, despite my different nationality, and even if I got a bit older. I want to work all my life, you see. I think it's kind of a waste, or a bore, if you just work to fill the time for a while.'

Yoshiko started to think carefully about employment after hearing of troubles experienced by her cousins who'd been to Korean schools when they tried to get work. 'My father's younger sister married a man with North Korean nationality, and their children can't get jobs, not in Japanese society. The best the boys can hope for is to become truck drivers or construction workers, and the girl couldn't even get a job as an ordinary office lady, so she ended up becoming a beautician. Whenever my aunts or uncles mentioned the subject, they always said, "If only the kids had at least gone to Japanese schools..." So I thought that had to be part of the problem.'

At nursing school, Yoshiko again told a group of close friends that she was a Zainichi Korean. When she reached the age of twenty, which is considered to mark the start of adulthood in Japan and Korea alike, she attended two different coming-of-age ceremonies – a Japanese one and a Mindan-sponsored Korean one. Her own inclination was to attend only the Japanese ceremony, and she even wore an elegant *furisode*⁴ for the occasion.

'At first I didn't plan to attend the Mindan ceremony, but a lot of my folks said since I was Korean it would be good to go, as a way of marking a milestone in my development. If it had just been my parents I would have objected, but my uncles and aunts were going on about it as well, so...it didn't seem right to be secretive about it, so in the end I did the whole thing properly, right down to the *jeogori*. One of my relatives bought it for me on a trip to South Korea. My little sister didn't like it: "Yuk, that's gross!" she said. But some of the Japanese housewives who lived in the neighborhood saw me wearing it and said, "Oh, how pretty you look!" There were sixteen of us girls at the ceremony, and we were all wearing *jeogori*. We had the ceremony at a hotel, and then moved on to a restaurant for the banquet. We went right through the streets in our *jeogori*, cool as you like. We were very open, and somehow it didn't seem to bother anybody.'

This was the first time Yoshiko had met any fellow Koreans outside her family since the summer camps of her elementary school days, but she didn't make much effort to mingle with the other Koreans at the coming-of-age ceremony. 'When people tried to talk to me, I just said, "Yeah, you're right," and stuff like that. I didn't dish out my address much. I kind of thought it would be a hassle if I got invited to meetings and so on long after the event.' From junior high school on, Yoshiko had become increasingly absorbed in Japanese society and had placed a considerable psychological distance between herself and Zainichi society.

Yoshiko completed a two-year course to obtain her auxiliary nursing qualification, but failed the exam to continue her studies toward a full nursing certificate.[5] After graduating, she spent a short time working part-time at the campaign office of the local mayor, who was seeking re-election. A Japanese acquaintance tipped her off about the job. She concealed her Korean identity, along with the irony that she herself would be unable to vote for the mayor, or any of his rivals, because of her nationality.

After that Yoshiko got a nursing job at a national hospital. 'I went along for my interview, and the first thing I did was show them my auxiliary nursing certificate, which had my official Korean name and nationality on it, and ask them if it mattered that I was Korean. They said it didn't matter. Well, after all, I was only going for a temporary position until the following March, when I was hoping to have another try at getting in to the full-certificate course. If there were plenty of nurses, if there were so many nurses around that you could pick and choose, they wouldn't employ people like me at national hospitals, I'm absolutely sure of it. It's just that there happens to be a shortage of nurses right now. If I'd chosen to be a nursery teacher, or a dictician – any profession with more qualified people than jobs – I wouldn't have got a job, I'm sure of it.'

No naturalizing

Yoshiko's father has five brothers and sisters, of whom three have married Japanese spouses and acquired Japanese nationality, 'to avoid leaving the children in limbo.'

'My aunt is so happy that she can vote in elections and all that. She sometimes asks my dad why he doesn't naturalize too, since he's got three children to think of. But he hasn't got the slightest intention of doing any such thing, so he just laughs it off. My brother and sister both want to do it, though. My kid sister's just started going for driving lessons, and she says she hates being called "Miss Kin" by her instructor. I don't think she tells anyone about her Korean identity. My little brother, too, was saying how he hated filling in the forms to go to senior high school, because he had to put his nationality on them.

'Personally, I've no intention of naturalizing. I've thought that way ever since I was seventeen, when my grandmother died. My grandmother looked after me when I was at elementary school, because my parents were both working. In those days I used to go with her to the hospital occasionally. When they called out her name – "Sai Bunnin"[6] – I asked her if it didn't embarrass her, using such a non-Japanese-sounding name. "What's the point getting embarrassed about things at my age?" she said. "I'm more embarrassed about your grandfather going around getting called Kinnosuke by people." That was the Japanese alias that my grandfather was using, you see.

'After all, it's not that bad being a Zainichi Korean. It's not as if people refuse you service in shops, or that you can't get any kind of job, or that you can't eat. It seemed to me that I was living pretty much the same way as the kids next door, so there wasn't really a problem.'

Different for kids

When interviewed, Yoshiko was in a relationship with a Japanese man whom she got to know in her third year at senior high school through a part-time job she did at a supermarket.

'I told him about the Zainichi thing as soon as I knew him well enough to talk to, and he said he already had some Zainichi Koreans among his friends. It didn't seem to bother him at all. After all, I guess it's different if you've been to a Korean school, but the rest of us are exactly the same as Japanese. He even thought I was joking when I said I was Korean. He didn't really believe me until I showed him my driving license with my real name on it. I go and visit at his house all the time. I've shown his mother pictures of me wearing the *jeogori* and so on, and I'm quite open about it. His father died when he was in junior high, so it's just him, his mother and his kid sister. He and I often go out to restaurants as a foursome with his sister and her boyfriend. All quite ordinary and open.'

Yoshiko recalls that when she was at senior high school her aunts used to advise her to marry a fellow Korean. 'They said it would be easier for me than marrying a Japanese, because of differences in customs and so on. But I don't feel that way at all. It's just the opposite: I don't know what I'd do if I married a Korean man from a family that took it really seriously. What if my mother-in-law spoke Korean all the time and I couldn't understand her? What if there were all sorts of things I didn't know? I haven't been brought up to know all those Korean customs and manners and all that, you see. I feel much more bothered about that kind of thing than about getting along with Japanese in-laws.'

Despite rejecting naturalization for herself, Yoshiko feels strongly that she would like her children to have Japanese nationality. 'It's incredibly awkward and inconvenient having South Korean nationality. You have hassle every time you need to fill in a form. Like when I applied for my nursing certificate, they wouldn't let me use my "Kanai" seal, and I had to have one urgently made up with "Kim" on it.[7] And when I made the application I had to check extra carefully to make sure I had the same personal details on each one, because that kind of thing is always spread over a period of time. OK so it's no big deal, but it's the kind of hassle you can do without. So I'd like to marry a Japanese if possible...that way my children can freely choose Japanese nationality even if I don't naturalize myself.'

Japanese name sounds right

Yoshiko also says that she feels more at home with her Japanese name than with her Korean one. 'My parents only gave me a

Japanese name. I should have had a Korean name too, really, same as my father, but they just named me "Yoshiko" and used the same name with a Korean reading, "Yang-Ja," for the other one.[8] Everyone calls me Yoshiko, and if someone calls me "Kim Yang-Ja," I don't even react. "Kanai Yoshiko" just seems to fit better, or to be more natural somehow. If possible I'd like to have that name on all my licenses and everything.'

Although Yoshiko had her Korean-speaking grandmother living with her for some years, she says that she herself cannot speak a word of the language. 'Just this year, when I went to the coming-of-age ceremony, I listened to some high-up from Mindan giving a speech in Korean, but it might as well have been double Dutch. I tend to think it would do me more good to learn English than Korean, at least that's the way I've been brought up to think. Even if I did speak Korean, I'd have no one to use it with.'

Yoshiko views Japan as her homeland, her motherland, and as 'her country' in general. She has never been to Korea, though she says she would at least like to visit the district where her ancestors came from one day. She says she feels only a distant concern with the reunification issue. 'When I hear it mentioned, I just nod my head and say yeah, yeah.'

Conclusion:
Towards a Society of Peaceful Coexistence

'Coexistence' as a slogan

Since the later 1980s, the word *kyōsei*, meaning 'coexistence' or 'living together,' has come into common use in Japanese society. It is used in all sorts of contexts: to speak of coexistence between humankind and nature, for example, between people with and without disabilities, and indeed between Japanese and Zainichi Koreans.

I happen to believe that if fundamental changes are to be made to society, then a slogan is needed that will appeal to the great masses of the people. In the Japan of the late 1960s and 1970s, the word *kyōtō*, meaning 'joint struggle,' had a certain degree of power to arouse people. However, if we examine this word in the context of improving majority/minority relations, it is evident that we cannot expect members of the majority to participate in joint struggle, except for a small number of radicals. Another word that has recently been used as a rallying call in social movements is *jinken* (human rights). Within Japanese society, however, this term tends to carry the patronizing implication that 'we fortunate members of the majority must do those poor victims of discrimination the favor of looking after their human rights.' To the members of the majority, then, 'human rights' are thought of as being somebody else's problem.[1]

I believe that the limitations of 'joint struggle' and 'human rights' as organizing concepts for social change leaves 'coexistence' as the best paradigm currently available to concentrate efforts toward a solution of the Zainichi Korean problem that has been the theme of this book. The term implies the question of whether and how it might be possible to construct a system of social relations under which the majority and minority can live together in peace. It is a term with the latent ability to involve members of the majority as well as the minority.

However, the more frequently such an emotion-charged word like this is used, the more varied and widely scattered do its meanings and implications become to the people who use it. Already there are those who fear that the word 'coexistence' may be in danger of becoming soiled by overuse. On November 8, 1997, I was invited to serve as a panelist at a Mindan-sponsored symposium in Nagoya. The title of the symposium was 'Towards the Realization of a Society of True Coexistence.' The striking use of the adjective 'true' is indicative of a concern that the term 'coexistence' is already beginning to lose its meaning.

But here is what I think about coexistence. When a word or turn of phrase appeals to a lot of people, it becomes a potent weapon for the advancement of social movements. There is no easy way of avoiding the dilution and distortion of meaning that the word undergoes during that process. But that fact makes it all the more imperative to stick to the task of constantly clarifying the meaning of the catchphrase.

Very well – how would I myself define the meaning implied by the term *kyōsei*, or 'coexistence'? It is of course more than just a matter of inhabiting the same space; it means creating a society in which people can live together in mutual recognition of their differences.

Now it is all very well to speak about 'mutual recognition of difference,' but we need to clarify this term, too, lest it convey no more than vague liberal good intentions. As I see it, there are three key aspects to 'mutual recognition of difference,' as follows:

(a) Not attaching a negative meaning to difference

Hitherto the Japanese majority has always attached negative connotations to the ethnic differences of the Korean minority, and this has underpinned the discriminatory treatment inflicted upon Koreans. We must overcome the discriminatory relationship and create a new relationship where difference does not imply discrimination.[2]

(b) Difference should be accentuated, not diluted

Once the majority Japanese stop attaching negative meanings to ethnic difference, Zainichi Koreans themselves can be expected to shed the negative associations that many of them hold regarding their own ethnicity. However, whether they like it or not, Zainichi Koreans are becoming increasingly assimilated to the host society with each succeeding generation that lives in Japan. What is needed here is not a *laissez-faire* spirit of resignation to the steady dilution of Korean ethnicity, but a serious attempt to think of ways of restoring vitality to that distinctive ethnic identity.

(c) Majority and minority must get in touch

To promote the relationship of coexistence practically, Japanese and Zainichi Koreans have got to see more of each other, get to know each other better, and expand their mutual relations whenever and wherever possible. The Korean minority has been an invisible presence in Japanese society. The problem here is what concrete steps might be taken to bring the two groups together.

I would now like to discuss these three issues in greater depth.

(a)   Not attaching a negative meaning to difference

Is there any prospect of an end to ethnic discrimination in Japan? There are some signs that the foundations of institutionalized racism may be starting to weaken. The following incident may give some idea of the state of play.

One night in September 1997, I received a telephone call from the *Asahi Shinbun*, one of Japan's biggest newspapers, asking me to comment on the fact that all Japan's national universities refuse to recognize students of ethnic Korean high schools in Japan as qualified to take their entrance exams. Our 30-minute conversation resulted in a short article in the morning edition of Sunday, September 21. I was quoted as describing the case of a Zainichi Korean student at the national university where I work, Saitama University. This student had managed to enter the university by a roundabout route: by first entering a private two-year junior college that recognized her Korean high school graduation certificate, and then transferring to Saitama as a third year student. I suggested that in view of all the talk one hears these days about the need for 'domestic internationalization,' i.e., for good relations with foreign nationals living in Japan, it was about time the Ministry of Education stopped forcing Zainichi Koreans to make this kind of elaborate detour in order to attend national universities. The national universities should open their doors to graduates of Korean schools in Japan.[3]

Alongside my own comment, the newspaper carried another by an official at the Ministry of Education. Far from showing any sign of flexibility, he criticized those universities that had already started to recognize Korean high school qualifications: 'I have heard it rumored that some private, prefectural and municipal universities are allowing students from Korean senior high schools to take their entrance examinations, but this is being done on the basis of a mistaken interpretation of the School Education Law and the school education system. We want to instruct all of these institutions not to allow these people to take their entrance exams.'

The official's comment showed a remarkable degree of inflexibility. However, as I mentioned earlier (Chapter 2, Note 8), the *Asahi Shinbun* survey, to which these comments were appended, shows that whether the Ministry of Education likes it or not, more than half of all private and public universities in Japan do now recognize the right of students from Korean senior high schools to take their entrance exams. Only the national universities continue to comply with the Ministry line. In October 1997, eight Korean students made the first formal test of the national universities' resolve by applying to several of them (my own included) for authorization to take their entrance exams. All eight applications were rejected.

However, the attempt has heightened awareness of the issue among teaching staff, many of whom share my own opposition to the closed-door policy. The tide of opinion for admitting Korean high school graduates to national universities is rising and will surely not be held back much longer. On February 20, 1998, the Japan Federation of Bar Associations presented an advisory to the Japanese government in which the refusal of national universities to allow graduates of ethnic schools to take their entrance examinations was condemned thus: 'The systematic unfairness of the present policy represents a serious violation of human rights.'

Finally, on August 31, 1999, the Ministry of Education amended the Enforcement Ordinances appended to the School Education Law. By issuing this notification, the Ministry of Education made the qualifications needed for admission into graduate schools more flexible. That is, even 'graduates of junior colleges, colleges of technology, special training colleges, miscellaneous schools and other educational institutions' and 'those who have reached the age of 22' are able to sit for graduate school entrance examinations.

Increasing demands that the qualifications of Korea University graduates be appropriately recognized is considered a key factor in the Ministry's decision to amend the ordinance at this particular time. There was no request for the graduates of junior colleges etc. to be misleadingly treated in the same way as university graduates. The Ministerial notification referred to junior colleges etc., which are not four-year tertiary institutions. Yet, it placed Korea University, which is a four-year tertiary institution, in the category of 'other educational institutions.' Although the amendment allows Korea University graduates to take Japanese graduate school entrance examinations, it should be pointed out that the Ministry of Education was most reluctant to grant this recognition.

At the same time, the Ministry of Education announced that if graduates of Korean high schools sit for and pass the *Daiken* (university entrance qualification examination), they will qualify to sit for the national university entrance examinations. Previously, graduates of Korean high schools were not even able to sit for the *Daiken*, because of two requirements; the applicant must be at least 18 years of age and also a junior high school graduate. However, as the Ministry of Education would not recognize the academic records of the Korean school students, they could not sit for the *Daiken* without concurrently attending a Japanese high school. No longer having to attend both Korean and Japanese schools is certainly a step forward. However, this only qualifies them to sit for the *Daiken*, which Japanese high school students are not required to sit, and not the university entrance exams. There is no doubt that educational reform has taken place. However, it must be stressed that the Ministry of Education has adopted a rather half-hearted and discriminatory approach in this endeavor.

There have also been developments recently on the related issue of employing foreign residents as public officials. On May 13, 1996, the city of Kawasaki scrapped the nationality clause that had until then applied to 'general administrative staff.' This was a direct challenge to a long-held government policy that barred foreign nationals from 'any form of public employment entailing the exercise of public authority or participation in the formation of the public will.'

Admittedly, the 'Kawasaki formula,' as it has come to be known, is only a half-measure. The city's policy includes a proviso to the effect that foreigners employed under the new policy will not be placed in certain positions 'entailing the exercise of public authority,' nor will they be promoted to 'positions with decision-making power.'

On November 8, 1996, the Home Affairs Minister of the day, Shirakawa Katsuhiko, expressed central government approval of the Kawasaki formula. 'Opportunities for foreign residents to be employed as public officials in local government may be expanded. Provided that it is made clear which posts relate to public authority and are not available to foreigners, and what the limitations are on the personnel front, we will leave the question of employment of foreign nationals to each local authority.'

Even this very partial opening of the door was criticized in the Diet, Japan's parliament, by Matsunaga Hikaru, a member of the House of Representatives from the ruling Liberal Democratic Party. In a speech on November 26, 1996, he argued that if foreign nationals wished to become public officials, even at the level of local government, they should acquire Japanese nationality. Public officials must be motivated by patriotism, he said, and someone who does not hold Japanese nationality cannot be expected to love Japan.

Though Matsunaga is the only member of the Diet to have publicly attacked the Kawasaki formula to date, it is fair to assume that there are plenty of other conservative politicians who share his views. Despite conservative objections, however, a growing number of local authorities are adopting the Kawasaki formula or some variation of it. As I write, three major cities have followed Kawasaki's lead: Kobe, Yokohama and Osaka.[4] Two prefectures, Kochi and Kanagawa, have done likewise. In 1997 four foreign nationals actually passed employment examinations and were promised jobs as public officials in general administration: three in the Kawasaki city government and one in Kanagawa prefecture (in which Kawasaki and Yokohama are located).

On November 26, 1997, there was another breakthrough in the battle against employment discrimination. Chung Hyang-Kyun, who had been working for the Tokyo metropolitan government since 1988 as a public health nurse, won a law suit she had brought against her employer for refusing to let her take an examination for promotion to an administrative position. The verdict handed down by the Tokyo High Court stated that a blanket refusal to allow people to apply for promotion to any administrative post, simply on grounds of their nationality, was a violation of the constitutional guarantees of equality under the law and freedom of choice of occupation.

The campaign to abolish the nationality clause in employment of public officials still has a number of hurdles to overcome. However, it seems fair to say that the campaign is making steady progress, at least in local government. (Abolition of the nationality clause for public officials in central government remains an altogether more distant objective, with many hurdles still to be crossed.)

We have also seen rapid advances recently in a parallel campaign to secure the right to political participation for foreigners holding permanent residence in Japan, of whom the great majority are Zainichi Koreans. In September 1993, the city assembly of Kishiwada, in Osaka prefecture, responded to calls from Korean residents and adopted a resolution calling on the central government to guarantee the human rights of foreign permanent residents, including the right to participate in local elections. To date, over 1,300 local assemblies, including some prefectures, as well as cities, towns and villages, have followed Kishiwada's lead and adopted similar resolutions.

The battle to win political rights has also been fought in the courts by a group of second-generation Zainichi Koreans holding South Korean nationality.[5] Their campaign to get the Japanese courts to confirm their constitutional right to participate in local elections ended in defeat at the Supreme Court in March 1995. However, there was some consolation in the text accompanying the verdict. Though the court denied that the Constitution of Japan positively guaranteed the right of foreign nationals to participate in local elections, it also found that 'the Constitution does not forbid the establishment by law of a measure granting foreign nationals the right to participate in elections for governors, mayors or members of regional assemblies.' Thus, the verdict means that there is no constitutional bar to reforming the Local Officials Act in the Diet to allow foreigners to participate in local elections. However, as I write, there are few signs of any positive activity within the Government or the Diet to undertake the necessary legislation.

Inactivity at the national level has not stopped some regional assemblies from finding their own ways to give foreigners a voice in their affairs. On December 1, 1996, the city of Kawasaki launched the Kawasaki City Representative Assembly for Foreign Residents, on the basis of a city ordinance that had been passed earlier. Members of the assembly are selected, by a panel of academics and other professionals, from among all the foreign residents who apply to join. The assembly started off with thirty-five members representing twenty different nationalities, including South and North Korea, China, Brazil, the Philippines, etc. Under the ordinance the city government promises to give serious consideration to proposals emanating from the Representative Assembly when planning city administration.

Then, on November 26, 1997, the Tokyo Metropolitan Government held the inaugural meeting of the Foreign Advisory Council of the Tokyo Metropolitan Government. This body, launched with twenty-five members of sixteen nationalities, has the legal status of a private consultative body to the governor of Tokyo.[6] The metropolitan government appoints twelve of the twenty-five members directly and selects the other thirteen from among foreign residents who send in applications.

Due to the pioneering initiatives of Kawasaki and Tokyo and, in particular, the Zainichi Koreans themselves, the Diet has finally begun to grant foreign permanent residents the right to participate in local government. An October 1999 agreement by the three coalition parties (Liberal Democratic Party, Liberal Party and Komeito) clearly stated that foreign permanent residents should be granted the right to vote in local government elections. However, as there was strong opposition within the Liberal Democratic Party to this bill, only the Liberal Party and Komeito issued a joint proposal in January 2000.

However, the bill was unsatisfactory. Firstly, those foreign citizens over the age of 20 who have permanent residency are able to vote for candidates but are unable to run as candidates themselves. Regarding this point, I recall a discussion at the aforementioned Mindan-sponsored symposium held in November 1997. One of the panel members, Fuyushiba Tetsuzo (Secretary General of Komeito), stated 'we are going to prepare a bill recognizing the voting rights of foreign citizens in local government elections.' In response, I argued that we should not only recognize voting rights but also the right to run as a candidate, which is the basis of democracy. My statement that Fuyushiba should not be stingy on this issue drew a loud applause from most of those who attended. What the Zainichi Koreans seek is not only the right to vote but total political rights.

Secondly, the bill only recognizes those who give the name of their country when filling out an application for Alien Registration. This means that North Korean nationals are excluded as the Japanese government has not only failed to apologize or provide compensation for its past colonial rule, but also does not recognize the Democratic People's Republic of Korea. Therefore, when North Koreans in Japan give the name '*Chōsen*' (the Japanese expression for Korea) on their Alien Registration applications, it is not considered to be the name of a country but only the 'symbol' of a region. To the Zainichi Koreans, this is seen as another attempt by the Japanese government to divide the Korean peninsula. A major factor contributing to the bill is not so much a desire to grant permanent foreign resident equal political rights but political ideology. A considerable distrust of communism within the government continues to impede the rights of North Korean citizens in Japan.

To sum up, the developments I have just described suggest that although much steadfast campaigning is still required, there is good reason to hope that the worst excesses of institutional discrimination against foreign residents in Japan will eventually be swept away.

But of course, discrimination is not just an institutional problem. There is also the question of discrimination at the personal level, in everyday life. When it comes to 'attaching a negative meaning to difference,' the problem is perhaps even more fundamental at this personal level. I will discuss this point in section (c) below.

(b) Difference should be accentuated, not diluted

If Korean ethnicity is to be revitalized in Japan, the issue of how to guarantee and carry out ethnic education is of prime importance.

The 1993 KYAJ survey conducted by Kim Myung-Soo and myself, mentioned above, covered South Korean youths aged 18 to 30, most of whom were third-generation migrants. We found that most of our respondents had grown up without any opportunity to receive ethnic education. The overwhelming majority of them had not mastered the Korean language (see Chapter 2, Note 14), and as this implies, the general level of ethnic awareness among South Korean youths is steadily falling.[7]

However, multivariate analysis of the data in the 1993 KYAJ survey produced an extremely interesting discovery in regard to the possibility of revitalizing Korean ethnicity. As my research partner, Kim Myung-Soo, puts it, 'Ethnicity can be divided into two ethnic orientations, one of which is based on emotional ties with fellow members of the ethnic group, while the other is based on instrumental behavior related to ethnic issues' (Fukuoka and Kim 1997:119). In other words, our data reveals an 'expressive orientation,' under which the subject feels a spirit of comradeship with other members of the ethnic group and seeks to preserve that spirit; and an 'instrumental orientation,' under which the subject seeks to acquire mastery of the ethnic language and various kinds of knowledge relating to the ethnic group. Analysis of the data indicates that the biggest factor influencing the formation of expressive orientation toward ethnicity among the Zainichi South Korean youths is 'degree of contact with ethnic tradition within the family,' while the biggest influence on formation of instrumental orientation toward ethnicity was 'degree of ethnic education received' (Fukuoka and Kim 1997:103–19).

Among Zainichi Koreans who play an active part in ethnic movements, there are some who believe that ethnic identity is strengthened by the experience of being discriminated against, and that although of course it would be a good thing if discrimination disappeared, the attendant decline in ethnic awareness would be a problem. But is there really a cause-and-effect relationship between the experience of discrimination and the development of ethnic awareness? Analysis of the 1993 KYAJ survey of young South Koreans suggests there is no direct influence. True, Kim Myung-Soo did find that 'experience of discrimination' had the effect of strengthening 'feeling of relative deprivation,' and this feeling in turn had the effect of heightening ethnic awareness as a reaction against Japanese society. On the other hand, he also found that 'experience of discrimination' had the effect of strengthening 'feeling of ethnic inferiority,' which in turn had the effect of *weakening* ethnic awareness as the subject attempted to distance himself or herself from the ethnicity perceived as inferior. Both these indirect influences were weak, however, and they tended to cancel each other out in the population as a whole. We concluded that experience of discrimination did not have any significant effect on formation of ethnic awareness.

The reason why these findings are so important is because they imply that there is nothing natural or inevitable about loss of ethnic identity as generations succeed one another in the host country. Ethnic identity can be maintained or revitalized by human effort.

The first responsibility for ethnic education lies, of course, with Zainichi Korean families themselves. It is impossible to overemphasize the importance of passing on an ethnic lifestyle in the household. As for ethnic schools, there has been a striking difference in approach between the two ethnic Korean organizations: Chongryun has enthusiastically promoted ethnic education while Mindan has not.[8]

The Japanese government should support organizations that attempt to provide ethnic education. The United Nations Convention on the Rights of the Child, which Japan ratified on March 29, 1994, clearly states that ethnic education must be guaranteed. The Government of Japan is thus under a moral obligation to give up its oppressive policy toward ethnic schools and replace it with one of positive support.

Ethnic education outside the school framework, as provided by organizations such as Chongryun, Mindan (including its youth association, the KYAJ), and independent groups like the Seikyū-sha in Kawasaki, the Takatsuki Mukuge Society, and the Tokebi

Children's Club in Yao,[9] are also of great significance and need to be given greater moral and financial support by local authorities than has hitherto been forthcoming.

However, the fact remains that nowadays the vast majority of Zainichi Korean children are attending regular Japanese schools. This means that the teachers at those schools also bear a measure of responsibility for providing Zainichi children with ethnic education. Otherwise, Japan will be failing to meet her commitment to provide ethnic education.

How do things stand at present? After Japan signed its treaty on the treatment of South Korean nationals with the Republic of Korea in 1965 (see Chapter 1, p. 19), the Ministry of Education issued a circular to all prefectural education committees, stating that Zainichi Korean children were to be given the same education as Japanese children. The Ministry has stuck firmly to that position ever since. In other words, Japanese schoolteachers are not supposed to provide any kind of special treatment for Zainichi pupils. How does this policy translate into classroom reality? Let me give an example from one of my own interviews, this one with the late Chung Wol-Soon, a second-generation Zainichi born in 1949 and interviewed on September 6, 1992:

'It has been nine years since the elementary school that my children attended started to conduct multiethnic education. These days there are plenty of teachers there who are making an effort to deal with the issue on the basis of respect for ethnic difference, but when my oldest daughter started there, they hadn't yet launched the program. It was terrible in those days. My daughter was bullied, just for being Korean. She was using her real name, and was bullied just for having a funny-sounding name. When I brought the problem up with her class teacher, the first thing she said was, "We treat all the children the same in school, whether they are Korean or Japanese." She also said, "Japanese children get teased for having funny-sounding names too, you know." These two comments struck me as enormously problematical and deeply wrong. I kept telling her that the two cases weren't the same, but she just wouldn't get it. I would tell her,

"My child is not Japanese. She is a Korean who lives in
Japan. She may have been born and raised in Japan, but
even so her background is different from that of the
Japanese children." But however many times I told her, it
was no good. She just couldn't see the difference. She
wasn't even trying to recognize the difference.'

These days some publicly-run schools in Osaka, Kyoto and Hyogo
prefectures, and in metropolitan Tokyo, are attempting to provide
ethnic education outside regular school hours by putting together
'ethnic classes' for their Zainichi pupils. A number of schools in
Kawasaki city have gone a step further, by adopting a multiethnic
education policy under which they attempt to foster mutual
understanding between Japanese and Korean students inside
regular school hours. This policy, known as *fureai kyōiku*, literally
'contact education,' was what Chung Wol-Soon was referring to
at the start of the passage just quoted.

However, the great majority of Japanese schools still take the
same view of ethnic difference so roundly criticized by Chung. The
overwhelming majority of teachers believe that if there are any
Korean pupils in their class, they should simply be treated the same
as the Japanese pupils. In other words, the fact of their presence is
ignored. This means not only that there is no attempt to guarantee
ethnic education, but also Zainichi Korean children are effectively
abandoned to the dangers of discrimination.

At the same time, there are quite a few conscientious teachers,
who sincerely want the best for the Korean children in their classes
but believe that if ethnicity is no longer an issue for the children
then it would be wrong for themselves, as Japanese teachers, to try
and force awareness of Korean ethnicity on children who may not
particularly want it. What these teachers do not realize is that they
themselves are partly responsible, however unintentionally, for the
Korean children's lack of interest in their own ethnicity. It is a sin
of omission. Not providing ethnic education produces ethnically
unaware pupils just as surely as providing it produces ethnically
aware pupils.[10]

I have stated that in order for Zainichi Korean ethnic awareness
to be revitalized, there is a need for Zainichi Korean households
to pass on ethnic lifestyles to younger generations, for more

education in ethnic schools, for increased educational activities by ethnic Korean groups, and for Japanese schools to guarantee ethnic education to a far greater extent than at present. However, I am not trying to insist that every Zainichi Korean child should master the Korean language and internalize a powerful ethnic consciousness.

To bluntly state my own point of view, the kind of society that I personally would like to see is one where each individual can freely choose his or her own favored way of life. In other words, I do not think it is necessarily desirable for the individual to be constrained in choice of lifestyle by *any* pre-existing external framework. In a sense, questions of how to live in relation to one's nationality or ethnicity are themselves no more than external frameworks constraining individual freedom. Nationality, and even ethnicity, are historically and socially constructed concepts. In the particular case of Japanese society, where mixed marriages between Japanese and Koreans are rapidly on the rise, it is desirable that the offspring of these marriages should be free to choose whether to live as Koreans, as Japanese, or as people who combine elements of both cultures.

As the case studies presented in this book demonstrate, there are many, many ways for a Zainichi Korean to live in contemporary Japanese society. Between the extreme positions – mastering the Korean language, absorbing Korean culture, keeping North or South Korean nationality; and becoming Japanese in legal, cultural and linguistic terms – there are countless compromise positions, many of them demonstrated by the subjects of this book. For example, one may keep one's Korean name, even if one absorbs relatively little of the Korean language and culture. It is most desirable that each individual should be able to freely choose which course to take.

At the same time, certain necessary conditions must be fulfilled if people are really to have something resembling that ideal freedom of choice. There must be adequate opportunity to acquire the various forms of knowledge needed to make an informed choice. Under the present circumstances many Zainichi Koreans are being asked to make a choice with virtually no knowledge of one of the possible options (that of maintaining a Korean identity). Under these circumstances, the choice to adopt a Japanese identity is not really a choice in the true sense of the word at all. I believe that many Zainichi Koreans think they are making a positive choice to assimilate to Japanese society when in fact their abandonment of Korean identity is effectively forced upon them because they have been deprived of educational opportunities to acquire knowledge of their own ethnicity.

Accordingly I am arguing that all Zainichi Korean children should be guaranteed the chance to learn what it actually means to live as a Korean, so that they can make an informed choice of lifestyle. It is for that purpose that the revitalization of ethnic education is so important.

(c) Majority and minority must get in touch

Let us now consider what is required to break down the invisible wall of consciousness between Japanese and Zainichi Koreans as individuals.

At Saitama University I teach a course called 'Contemporary Social Theory' in which I deal with Zainichi Korean issues and other minority problems in Japan. Every year I start the course by asking my new students to write an essay. One of the topics I set them is this: 'If there were a Zainichi Korean person living near you, how do you think you would behave toward that person?'

Reading the essays elicited by this question, one is first struck by how few of the students have actually knowingly come into contact with Zainichi Koreans. As I have mentioned (Chapter 2, p. 38-9), Zainichi Koreans, including those who have naturalized, may reasonably be put at 1 percent of the overall population of Japan. The number of students who report having encountered Zainichi Koreans is extremely small in view of that figure. No doubt many more of them have met Zainichi Koreans without being aware of it, since so many of them assume Japanese names and identities. One only wishes that more of them would use their real names and be more open about their ethnic origins. However, there are problems on the part of the Japanese majority, too. I believe that there is a mechanism in the Japanese consciousness that avoids contact with Zainichi Koreans.

What is this psychological obstacle on the Japanese side that prevents a true meeting of minds with Zainichi Koreans? A look at some passages from my students' essays may be revealing. I do occasionally come across students who are blatantly prejudiced against Koreans, but they are few enough in number to be called exceptional. Far more students display a sincere wish to 'do the right thing,' accompanied, however, by a tendency to avoid dealing directly with difference when faced with it in another person. Here are a few characteristic examples:

> I think I would behave normally if there were Zainichi Koreans close to me. When I say 'normally,' I mean I would relate to them in the same way as with other (Japanese) people.

> I wouldn't want to look at them in a special way, or deliberately pay special attention to them. I might be confused at first if I met people like that. But I would want to behave in a normal way.

> It would not bother me particularly if there were a Zainichi Korean person around. You could say it's easy for me to say that since I haven't actually come across such people as yet, but I would want to behave normally without paying any special attention to it.

> If there were a Zainichi Korean in my class, I guess I'd be slightly surprised, but it wouldn't bother me. I've been taught that it shouldn't bother me, and I myself would never change my attitude because of something like that.

> In my head, this is what I believe: we're all humans, just the same. But how my heart and body would react at that time (when meeting a Zainichi Korean) – well, that's a problem.

> If there were a Zainichi Korean somewhere around me, I would try to relate to him or her just the same as usual. But I have a feeling that I would be more careful about it than I needed to be, so that it would be rather an awkward relationship.

Even if I knew (that a certain friend of mine were a
Zainichi Korean), I think I would behave as if I didn't
know. But I lack the confidence to say I could really forget
about it completely in my feelings. I think I would always
be thinking 'Ah, she's one of them,' in some corner of my
heart. I don't know whether that's good or bad. It may be
a bad thing, but it's my honest feeling.

If I met some Zainichi Koreans, I think I would do my best
to act as normally as possible, but the thought that they
were different from me would always be there at the
bottom of my heart. And if I kept on consciously trying to
get rid of that thought, I'm afraid it would actually show
up all the more in my attitude, and I'd end up hurting the
other person.

Of course I would want to treat Zainichi Koreans, or any
other people, as friends just like my other friends. But I
think my awareness that I had to treat them as 'ordinary
people' would actually work too strongly. Until this
consciousness disappeared, I wouldn't be able to have a
genuine relationship with them, nor would they be able to
trust me, I guess.

And so on. Certain terms recur endlessly through these essays, like
a kind of mantra: 'ordinary,' 'normal,' 'the same,' 'without
consciousness of difference.' These students are well-intentioned
young people who have been repeatedly taught that ethnic
discrimination is a Bad Thing. Yet they are bewitched by the idea
that the way to deal with difference is to pretend it does not exist.
My own observations suggest that this is a deeply ingrained
attitude, inculcated through many long years of what used to be
known as 'post-war democratic education.'
    The message that Japanese teachers at the great majority of
schools in Japan have been giving their students is that people are
all the same and that this is the reason why it is wrong to discriminate
against people. With the exception of a tiny minority of schools with
a special commitment to human rights education, schools have
ignored the existence of Zainichi Koreans attending classes under

Japanese pseudonyms, just as they have ignored the presence of Burakumin children in their classes, while preaching the wickedness of discrimination as a kind of abstract moral principle.

Now the idea that 'all people are the same' ought to mean that all people deserve to be respected equally as individuals. A precondition for that kind of respect is that people must have a solid *knowledge* of each other, including the various differences between them. This equality of respect is essential to the concept of human rights as understood in modern society.

So when Japanese teachers ignore the presence of Korean and Burakumin children in their classes and tell their pupils that 'people are all the same,' the message that the pupils get is that people all *look* the same, that where differences do exist they must not be mentioned, and ultimately that it is *good* for people to be the same – a very different message to one that insists on respect for each individual as a human being. Thus the students emerge from this kind of education burdened with the illusion that there is somehow something wrong even in being conscious of some difference between themselves and another person. They must not be aware of difference. At least on the surface they must relate with other people 'normally,' or 'in the same way as with everyone else.' That, they erroneously believe, is what it means to show a non-discriminatory attitude.

Nevertheless, the fact remains that there *are* differences between Japanese people and Koreans who live in Japan. As I have tried to show in this book, they are placed in very different social positions. Their cultural background, too, though similar in many respects, has clearly different aspects. As the case studies presented in this book show, many young Zainichi Koreans suffer conflicts of identity as they struggle to reconcile their ethnic background with their social environment. Attempts to ignore these differences, to suppress consciousness of them and treat all people as 'the same,' however well-intentioned they may be, will never lead to any meaningful meeting of minds between majority and minority. On the contrary, this approach effectively destroys any chance of Japanese youths understanding and sympathizing with the conflicts endured by Zainichi Korean youths.

As I hope I have just shown, the first step toward establishing a society where people of differing ethnicity can live together in peaceful mutual respect is to overturn the prevalent tendency to avert the eye from any kind of difference.

The process has to start with a drastic change of consciousness within the teaching profession. We are a very long way from achieving that change, but at least, I believe, the direction in which we need to move is clear enough.

Rather than bringing this book to a close with a polished summation of my own, allow me to finish with two last quotations from Zainichi Korean informants of mine. I tend to think that whether or not Japan can achieve the transition to a society of peaceful coexistence will depend on whether Japanese people can respond to the challenges posed in these two statements.

The first is something that my good friend Kim Haeng-Yi (second-generation Zainichi Korean, born 1951) said to me when we first met back in August 1980:

'What I want to say is this: Don't discriminate; Do distinguish. Many people have the mistaken notion that pursuing assimilation is the way to achieve liberation. I rather think that what is needed now is the courage to be distinguished, the courage to make distinctions. Because after all, each and every one of us lives under different conditions and inhabits a different internal world.'

The second quotation comes from an interview I conducted on February 17, 1990, with Kim Soo-Il (second-generation Zainichi Korean, born 1961, member of the Kawasaki Seikyū-sha). Here Kim recalls his feelings when, as a student at senior high school, he decided to abandon his Japanese pseudonym and use only his ethnic Korean name, as he has done ever since:

'It's tough living under a pseudonym, and it's tough living under your real name, but if they're both equally tough, then the kind of toughness that comes from presenting yourself honestly is the easier to bear. When you're using an alias, the very fact that you're Korean is taboo, right? So in a funny sort of way, Japanese people end up taking special care over you. When you use your real name, and you can talk about all sorts of things with the other fellow…well, there really isn't anything that's taboo, and the human relationship has creativity.'

Notes

Preface

1 Throughout this book I refer to my subjects as *young* or *younger* ethnic Koreans. By this I do not mean children or teenagers. Most of my subjects were in their twenties and a few were in their thirties. I emphasize their relative youth mostly to make it clear that they belong to generations that were born and raised in Japan, as opposed to older first-generation migrants who actually made the big move from Korea to Japan.

2 The word *Zainichi* literally means simply 'resident in Japan.' It is used adjectivally with *Chōsenjin* (North Korean) and/or *Kankokujin* (South Korean), or more informally as a noun on its own, to indicate members of the Korean minority in Japan. For the purposes of this book I define 'Zainichi' as including (1) ethnic Koreans who came to Japan around the time of World War II, or earlier, and have lived here ever since; and (2) their offspring, who have been born and raised in Japan and basically look upon Japan as their permanent place of residence.

3 To date, there has been only one instance of a local authority list of foreign residents being made available for an academic survey, namely the list from Kanagawa prefecture on which Kimpara *et al.* 1986 is based. This was a highly exceptional case in which the use of alien registration documents was permitted.

4 *Mindan* is officially known in Japanese as *Zai-Nihon Daikanminkoku-min-dan* and in English as the Korean Residents Union in Japan. It is an ethnic Korean organization, founded in October 1948, which supports the government of

the Republic of Korea (ROK; South Korea). The abbreviation *Mindan* happens to be the same in Korean and Japanese.

5   *Chongryun* is officially known in Japanese as *Zai-Nihon Chōsenjin Sōrengōkai* (*Sōren* for short) and in English as the General Association of Korean Residents in Japan. It is an ethnic Korean organization, founded in May 1955, which supports the government of the Democratic People's Republic of Korea (DPRK; North Korea).

6   In 1993 Kim Myung-Soo and I conducted a large-scale quantitative survey of South Korean youths in Japan (Fukuoka and Kim 1997). This was carried out at the request of the Mindan-affiliated Korean Youth Association in Japan (KYAJ), and stemmed from the friendly relationship I enjoyed with the then president of KYAJ, Kim Kyung-Pil, which was established during the preparation of the present volume. Without this kind of special connection, it is very difficult to gain access to the lists of names held by Mindan or Chongryun.

7   *Mintōren* was launched in 1975. It is a group campaigning for the rights of Koreans and other ethnic minorities in Japan. The official English name adopted by Mintōren was the National Council for Combating Discrimination against Ethnic Peoples in Japan. In 1995 Mintōren changed its name to *Zainichi Korian Jinken Kyōkai*, officially translated as the Human Rights Association for Koreans in Japan. At the same time the group's informal networking style of organization was replaced by one with a strong central executive. Some members were unhappy with these changes, and are now hoping to rebuild the old Mintōren. Thus Mintōren has effectively split into two different groups.

8   In an attempt to at least partially offset the weaknesses of the qualitative approach, I have occasionally made use of the quantitative data generated by the 1993 survey on the consciousness of young South Koreans, mentioned in Note 6 above and published in Fukuoka and Kim 1997. I refer to this survey as 'the 1993 KYAJ survey.' The population targeted by this research was 'people born in Japan, with South Korean nationality, aged from 18 to 30.' We selected 1,723 people at random from a list of some 70,000 names held by

the KYAJ. The research was carried out by interviewing over a period of three months, from July to September 1993. We obtained exactly 800 valid replies, a response rate of 46.4 percent.

However, the reader should be aware that this is not a case of quantitative data covering the entire subject population while qualitative data focuses on sub-sections within the population. On the contrary, although my intensive interview data covers only 150 respondents, against 800 in the questionnaire survey, it does include ethnic Koreans of North Korean, South Korean and Japanese nationality, whereas the 1993 KYAJ survey is restricted to young people of South Korean nationality. The two populations are fundamentally different, and as such the 1993 KYAJ survey data should be viewed strictly as supplementary to the qualitative data on which this book is based, and not as part of the same project.

9   One of these cases concerned a woman born and raised in a district with a large Zainichi population. She used an assumed Japanese name but said that she lived a normal life, making no attempt to conceal her Korean identity, which was known to all around her. She went to a college far from her hometown and continued to use the assumed name. She insisted that even at college she made no particular attempt to conceal her ethnicity. However, from the overall tone of our conversation I had the feeling that using an alias had a different meaning for her when surrounded by Japanese people at the college rather than among fellow Koreans in her hometown. I accordingly titled the case study 'The trouble with aliases.' This infuriated her. 'A Japanese like you has no right to be criticizing me!' she said, and refused permission to publish.

The other case where permission was refused was that of a Mintōren activist, who said: 'When I want my life story in print, I'll write it myself. I don't want anyone else writing it for me.'

10   *Burakumin* literally means 'hamlet people.' The term is a euphemism for people traditionally made to live in desig-nated outcaste settlements. These settlements are known today as *hisabetsu buraku* or 'discriminated hamlets.' Burakumin are Japanese people, ethnically identical to other

Japanese but subject to intense discrimination as the present-day descendants of outcaste groups with their origins somewhere in the middle ages. Today there are thought to be up to 6,000 Buraku districts and over 3 million Burakumin in Japan.

It used to be widely accepted that the despised outcaste group from which the Burakumin are descended, known as *Eta* (a word literally meaning 'full of impurity'), was created by the ruling authorities during the early years of the Edo period (1603–1868), as part of a divide-and-rule policy toward the masses. In the last twenty years, however, historians have increasingly come to question this account of Burakumin origins, and the whole issue is being comprehensively reviewed. As I write, no new consensus has yet emerged from the various competing hypotheses.

What is clear, however, is that in the course of the Edo period the outcastes known as *Eta* were placed in the lowest position in society. Some were put to work as executioners or junior policemen, others worked in transportation, yet others were singers and dancers, who conducted ritual performances to ensure good harvests etc. Many more worked in manufacturing industry, tanning leather or making whetstones, lamp wicks, bamboo parts for looms, etc. These industries were official outcaste monopolies, and appear to have ensured a minimal standard of living for the outcastes.

Following the Meiji Restoration of 1868, the government issued the so-called 'Emancipation Edict' in 1871. This officially abolished outcaste status and re-designated the former outcastes as commoners (*heimin*). Ironically, this edict had a negative impact on the outcastes. On paper the category no longer existed, but in reality discrimination persisted; meanwhile abolition of the category also meant the end of the outcaste monopolies and designated jobs, depriving many former outcastes of their means of support.

Notwithstanding the rural connotations of 'hamlet people,' modern-day Burakumin do not live in places remote from the rest of society. During the Edo period some of the Buraku were located on the outskirts of castle towns, others by the side of major highways or rivers (reflecting the traditional outcaste role in road and river transportation). Today it remains the case that there are both urban and rural Buraku.

For myself as a sociologist, anti-Burakumin discrimination ranks alongside the Zainichi Korean issue as a major research theme. Among my Japanese-language publications are a research survey reconstructing the lifestyles of people living in a discriminated hamlet (Fukuoka *et al.* 1987), research focusing on the people who do the discriminating (Fukuoka 1985, 1992), and a project combining quantitative and qualitative approaches to the issue of attitudes to the use of discriminatory language among people working in the mass media (Isomura and Fukuoka eds 1984).

Introduction: 'Japanese' and 'Non-Japanese'

1   For example, in 1979, after much delay, the Japanese government finally ratified the International Covenants of Human Rights. The following year the government submitted a report on Article 40 of the International Covenant on Civil and Political Rights, in which it stated that in Japan minorities as defined in the covenant 'did not exist.' As a result the report was roundly criticized in the United Nations Human Rights Committee, by members pointing out that it ignored the existence of Korean residents, Ainu, Okinawans, and Burakumin.

2   *Yamato* is a word used to describe the Japanese as a race. The word has been mythologized, as in expressions such as *Yamato-damashii* (the Japanese spirit) or *Yamato-nadeshiko* (a comely Japanese maiden).

3   See also Hirowatari 1994. Japanese nationality is defined principally by blood inheritance, in a modification of the Nationality Law first enforced in 1899, which simply stated that 'children born of Japanese nationals are also Japanese nationals.' As Hirowatari points out, 'this definition is logically open-ended, because even if we went back into history applying it backward from one generation to another endlessly, we would never get a clear-cut definition of a Japanese national' (Hirowatari 1994:3–4).

4   Law No.147 (1950) amended by Law No.268 (1952) and by
    Law No.45 (1984). All quotations from the government's
    official English translation (Ministry of Justice 1985).
5   'A child shall be a Japanese national: (1) When, at the time
    of its birth, the father or the mother is a Japanese national.'
    (Ministry of Justice 1985:1)
6   It is virtually impossible to question the issue of Japaneseness
    without using terms that in turn give rise to further questions.
    If we look at the history of 'the Japanese' we find there is no
    such thing as a single, clearly defined ethnic group that has
    inhabited the Japanese archipelago since antiquity.

    These islands were peopled, over many thousands of years,
    by people who came across the sea from the Korean penin-
    sula, from the Chinese mainland, and from other regions to
    the north and south. In more recent history, too, there have
    been large-scale migrations to Japan that cannot be ignored.
    For example, according to one early ninth century document,
    the *Shinsen Shōji Roku (A Newly-Compiled Record of
    Aristocratic Families)*, one-third of all the aristocratic
    families then living in the region of present-day Kyoto, Nara
    and Osaka were of overseas origin. At risk of stating the
    obvious, let me make it plain that there is nothing 'pure' about
    the concept of the Japanese race itself: we are talking about
    a grand mixing of ethnic strains here.

    As for 'Japanese culture,' again we are talking about a
    conceptual construct rather than a ground-level reality.
    Japanese culture varies considerably from one region of
    Japan to another, and, like the blood-stock, has absorbed
    countless foreign influences over the centuries. Hence my use
    of inverted commas for these terms.
7   Article 14 of Japan's Nationality Law permits the holding of
    dual nationality up to the age of 22, at which point the holder
    must choose whether to retain Japanese or foreign nationality
    (Ministry of Justice 1985:5).
8   In an attempt to resolve the contradiction between its need for
    imported unskilled and semi-skilled workers, and the long-
    standing ban on issuing working visas to such people, the
    Japanese government in 1989 loosened its visa restrictions
    for foreign nationals of Japanese descent (cf. Hirowatari

1994:23). The length of stay permitted is in direct proportion to the percentage of Japanese blood that the applicant can be proved to possess. This has encouraged a wave of temporary reverse migration from *émigré* Japanese communities for work purposes.

9   The family register (*koseki*) is a Japanese system of social control. Unlike, say, an ID-card system, it pertains to families rather than individuals. The place where one's family is registered is called the *honseki*. Often the *honseki* is not the registered person's actual address at all. Rather it is deemed to be that of the 'main household' (*honke*) of the person's family. This may be the address of the individual's parents, grandparents, siblings, etc. There may even be no one living at the address at all.

Ｗhen Japan annexed Korea, the conflicting desires to absorb her people, and yet remain distinct from them, were reflected in changes to legal institutions. Koreans were now 'Japanese nationals' (*Nihon kokumin*); but even if they lived in Japan, their family register would be kept in Korea. This was called 'Korean registration' (*Chōsen koseki*). Meanwhile, the original Japanese people were described as having 'domestic registration' (*naichi koseki*).

10   In the Ainu language, *Ainu* simply means 'people,' while *Moshiri* means 'peaceful land.' Hence *Ainu-Moshiri*, the term used for the Ainu homelands, literally means 'the peaceful land where the people live.'

11   *Utari* is an Ainu word meaning 'comrade,' applied only to fellow Ainu. The Utari Association's efforts brought a partial victory on May 9, 1997, when the 1899 Law on the Protection of Former Indigenous People of Hokkaido (*Hokkaido Kyū-Dojin Hogo Hō*) was finally abolished and replaced with a new law that established a government foundation for the promotion of Ainu culture. The old law was designed to legitimate the Japanese invasion of *Ainu-Moshiri*, confining the Ainu to 'agricultural reservations' and effectively outlawing their traditional hunter-gatherer lifestyle.

The new law drops the discriminatory word *dojin* (an insulting term for an indigenous person) but refrains from using the more neutral term *senjū minzoku* (aboriginal people), since the wording literally means 'people who lived somewhere before' and could imply a Japanese government responsibility to recognize Ainu land rights. Inadequate though the new law is, however, it at least holds out some hope for a revival of the *Ainu-puri* (Ainu lifestyle) and the Ainu language.

12 During the boom years of the 1980s, many political and business leaders appeared to believe that Japan's economic success *vis-à-vis* the multiethnic USA was due to her ethnic homogeneity. On August 22, 1986, then-prime minister Nakasone Yasuhiro famously remarked that 'Japan, with her high level of education, has become a pretty intelligent society – far more so than America. In America there are quite a few blacks, Puerto Ricans and Mexicans, so that the average level is still extremely low...' Again, on July 24, 1988, Watanabe Michio, then head of the Liberal Democratic Party's Policy Research Council, remarked that while Japanese took bankruptcy very seriously, the many black people in America simply laughed at it because they no longer had to pay their debts.

13 The practice of pressuring people to change their name when they naturalize is an especially clear example of this mindset at work. If someone becomes a Japanese national, he or she is supposed to have a Japanese-sounding name, too. To many Japanese, and especially immigration officials, there is something intrinsically wrong about a Japanese person with a foreign-sounding name. Nationality and culture must match. Not that there is anything to this effect in Japan's immigration laws. It simply used to be common knowledge among Zainichi Koreans that one's application for Japanese nationality would not be accepted if one did not write a Japanese-sounding name in the relevant section of the form.

Having said that, there is some evidence that in recent years immigration officials have been exerting less pressure on people to adopt Japanese-sounding names when they acquire Japanese nationality. According to Kim Chan-Jung (personal communication), some five or six Zainichi Koreans known to him personally have recently naturalized while keeping their Korean names. Strictly speaking, however, these people have not quite kept their names unchanged: the Japanese government insists that names of Japanese nationals be written in Chinese characters that are in general use, as defined and listed by itself, or in one of the two Japanese syllabaries, *hiragana* and *katakana*. For Koreans this means that they may have to change one or more of the characters in their name if they are not on the government lists, and that they cannot officially register their names in *han-gul*, the Korean script, or in Roman letters for that matter.

It is impossible to say what percentage of people who naturalize are keeping their original names these days, for the naturalization announcements carried in the *Kanpō* (the official gazette published daily by the Japanese government) only record the pre-naturalization name.

However, the 1993 KYAJ survey found that among young South Korean nationals living in Japan, there was a strong correlation between 'strength of desire to naturalize,' on the one hand, and 'sense of ethnic inferiority' (Pearson's correlation coefficient $r = 0.56$), and the opinion that 'there is no need to make a fuss about one's ethnicity' ($r = 0.38$), on the other (Fukuoka and Kim 1997:96). This amounts to suggestive evidence that most Zainichi Koreans who adopt Japanese nationality do, in fact, use a Japanese-style name after naturalization – typically the same name they have been using as an alias prior to naturalization. One also hears frequently of the practice whereby Japanese employers automatically give Japanese nicknames to their foreign workers from Asia and Latin America in the workplace.

14 The expression *Zainichi* was first adopted by members of the Korean minority themselves, shortly after the end of World War II. The usage reflects the fact that at the time they themselves tended to believe that their stay in Japan would only be temporary. The word is still used by Japan's ethnic Koreans to describe themselves, but it has taken on a rather different significance. Rather than implying temporary residence, it is now used by some ethnic Koreans to make a distinction between themselves, the Japanese, and mainland Koreans of North and South alike.

Part One Identity Formation in Japan's Korean Minority

1 The History of Japan's Korean Minority

1   As in the case of Korean migration to Japan, there had been some migration to Northeast China before Japan's annexation of Korea. But the process was greatly accelerated by the destruction of livelihoods caused by Japanese colonialism. The Koreans who fled to China and their descendants today number some 1.9 million people according to Chinese government statistics. Although Koreans are an ethnic minority in China as they are in Japan, they have not been subjected to nearly such harsh policies. They hold Chinese nationality, but have retained their Korean identity. In the area around Yanpian, in Jilin province, the Koreans have been granted their own 'autonomous prefecture,' and Korean-language school education is also guaranteed. Ethnic Koreans make up 61.5 percent of the population in Jilin province.

2   At the war's end, another 40,000 Koreans were working as migrant or forced laborers on Sakhalin, a Russian island in the Northern Pacific of which the southern half was seized by Japan after the Russo-Japanese War (1904–05) and subsequently reclaimed by the Soviet Union after World War II. The 300,000 Japanese citizens on Sakhalin were repatriated to Japan after the war, but the Koreans were simply abandoned to fend for themselves. They were not permitted to visit family in South Korea until 1990, when the Japanese and Korean Red Cross commenced charter flights (Ohnuma 1992).

3   Until very recently this prohibition was enshrined in South Korean law as well as custom. On July 16, 1997, the Constitutional Court of the Republic of Korea ruled that the law forbidding *dongseong-dongbon* marriage, i.e., marriage between members of the same clan, was unconstitutional. Under Korean law, the court's verdict carries the force of law from 1998, even if the parliament does not amend the legislation. It follows that same-clan marriage is now legal in South Korea.

4   The 1993 KYAJ survey found that only 35.3 percent of the young South Korean respondents could name their *bonkwan* (Fukuoka and Kim 1997:38–9). To mainland Koreans, this constitutes shocking ignorance.

5   It is of course very hard to generalize on this point. For example, some of my informants told me that their migrant antecedents had traveled frequently between Korea and Japan rather than residing permanently in the latter.

6   Consider for example the following extract from an interview I conducted on August 3, 1989, with the late Chung Wol-Soon (1949–94), a second-generation Zainichi who used to teach at a day-care center for Japanese and Korean children in the ethnic Korean quarter of Kawasaki city. She told me the following story of how she acquired her Japanese alias, 'Kuroi Emiko': 'My father's older brother had two Japanese friends called Kurokawa and Inoue, who gave him shelter at the time of the Great Kanto Earthquake. So when the order came to adopt Japanese names, we took the first character of each of their names to create the improvised name, "Kuroi."'

   In mentioning cases like this, I do not in any sense mean to minimize the wrongs inflicted on the Koreans under Japanese colonialism. On the contrary, the historical fact of these acts of kindness by some Japanese toward some Koreans should serve as a reminder that none of us can blame force of circumstance for our deeds. Ultimately, the circumstances themselves are no more than the outcome of myriad personal choices.

7   During the occupation period (1945–52), Japanese government policy was of course subject to approval by the allied occupation authorities, and was sometimes even dictated by GHQ (the General Headquarters of the Supreme Commander for the Allied Powers, General Douglas MacArthur). Sorting out the Japanese-inspired elements from the elements imposed by GHQ is a very tough task for historians. However, it is a fact that at the start of the occupation the allies defined Japan-resident nationals of Japan's former colonies as 'liberated peoples,' but changed this policy in November 1945 under a directive from the US federal government.

Under the new policy, the Koreans and Taiwanese were to be 'treated as liberated peoples so far as military security will permit. However, these people were citizens of the Japanese empire, and where necessary are to be treated as citizens of an enemy country.' Thus Koreans and other former colonial subjects were treated neither as allies nor as enemies, but as 'third-country nationals.' The Japanese equivalent of this term, *Daisangoku-jin*, became a term of abuse. For their part, the Koreans viewed themselves as 'liberated people' and used this perceived status to take control of the black market etc. They thereby inspired jealousy and more hatred among the Japanese.

8   For more detail on how the Koreans were cheated of war reparations, see Mintōren ed. 1989.

9   I include voluntary repatriation in this category, since that was the desired option of the majority of Koreans after the war.

10 Please note that in picturing these imaginary scenarios I have not taken account of the various constraining factors stemming from the international and domestic political situation at the time. To demonstrate why a particular scenario was or was not adopted would be a job for a historian, who would have to analyze the complex power relationships of the day between the Japanese government and the various decision-making bodies of the occupation. All I am attempting to do here, as a sociologist, is to broadly outline the options that were available and give an idea of the basic character of the policy that was, in fact, adopted.

11 This obligation is stipulated in the current Alien Registration Law.

12 There is nothing in Japanese law which says that foreigners may not become public servants, yet the Japanese government still does not permit it in principle. When challenged, the government defends its position on the grounds that it is an 'indisputable legal principle' that foreigners should be barred from public office. Over the years, some progress has in fact been made in opening up public employment to non-Japanese nationals: the government has gradually come to accept the employment in public positions of foreign

nationals with specialized skills, such as doctors and nurses, for example. Some low-prestige public work that does not involve 'the exercise of public authority or participation in the formation of the public will,' such as delivering the mail, has also been opened up to non-nationals (see the account of Lee Chang-Jae in Chapter 4). However, the government still refuses to admit non-nationals to the administrative grade of the Civil Service (*ippan-shoku*), effectively refusing them any role, however small, in public administration.

In some cases local authorities have hired non-nationals as public officials in posts that the central government still denies to them. However, local defiance is usually tempered by some show of deference to the center: the non-national tends to be given a contract that rules out promotion to senior posts, restricts his or her activities to a certain specialized field, or in some other way ensures inferior status and bars access to real influence.

13   When Japanese children reach six, the age when compulsory education commences, their parents are sent a school attendance notice by the local authority, telling them which elementary school their child should attend. Until 1991, this document was not sent to the parents of foreign children, who had to apply to the local education committee themselves if they wished to send their children to publicly-run Japanese schools. Only since 1991 have school attendance notices been sent to all non-Japanese families as a matter of course.

There is a difference between the letters sent to Japanese and non-Japanese parents. The former are *instructed* to send their children to a certain school; the latter are *informed* that they *may* send their children to a certain school. This reflects the fact that elementary and junior high-school education is compulsory only for Japanese nationals.

14   For more detail on the legal measures discussed in this section, see Hirowatari 1994.

15   Applications had to be made during the five-year period starting on January 17, 1966.

16   The law was renamed the Immigration Control and Refugee Recognition Act. It created a new category of permanent residence, called 'exceptional permanent residence,' for

Koreans who had not been eligible to obtain permanent residence under the 1965 treaty between Japan and the Republic of Korea. In effect, nearly all the people covered by this legal revision were North Korean nationals. Applications for permanent residence under the new rules had to be made during the five-year period starting on January 1, 1982.

17   Japanese full-time teachers are called *kyōyu* while non-Japanese are termed *jōkin kōshi*. Traditionally, *kyōyu* has been used to mean full-time teachers and *kōshi* to mean part-timers. Since *jōkin* literally means 'full-time,' it follows that the new job designation created by the Ministry of Education in 1992 literally means 'full-time part-time teacher.' This insidious bureaucratic paradox eloquently conveys the fact that non-nationals may work full time but will still be excluded from promotion, participation in staff-meetings, etc., just as part-timers are.

Before 1992, the education committees at a number of local authorities were already employing non-nationals as *kyōyu* in defiance of ministry policy. For these rebel authorities, the 1992 reform was a powerful call to abandon their defiance and redesignate their non-Japanese teachers as *jōkin kōshi*.

18   Only when the present volume was close to completion did I have a chance to read Kim Chan-Jung's new history of the Korean minority in Japan, *Zainichi Korian Hyaku-nen-shi (A One-Hundred-Year History of Koreans in Japan)*. This book is only available in Japanese at present (Kim 1997), but I recommend it to anyone who wishes to know more of Zainichi history.

2   Japan's Korean Minority Today

1   As of the end of 1996, there were 548,968 ethnic Koreans registered as 'special permanent residents' by Japan's Ministry of Justice. This category signifies Koreans who came to Japan during the colonial period and settled permanently, plus their descendants, assuming they have not naturalized. In addition there were 23,596 'general permanent residents' who had acquired permanent residence in the

same way as other foreign nationals: by applying to the Ministry of Justice under Article 22 of the Immigration Control and Refugee Recognition Act. These people had all been in Japan for a considerable number of years, though not from the pre-war period.

2   The Japanese government does not publish statistics on numbers of ethnic Koreans affiliated to North and South Korea. Japan maintains diplomatic relations with the ROK but not with the DPRK; consequently nationals of the former are registered as such (*Kankoku*), but the latter are simply recorded as being from 'Korea' (*Chōsen*), with the Japanese government insisting that this is simply a geographical descriptor and not a recognition of nationality. Koreans affiliated to the ROK can get a South Korean passport; those affiliated to the DPRK cannot be issued with a passport and carry only a re-entry permit issued by the Japanese government when traveling abroad.

3   Mintōren is a group campaigning for the rights of Koreans and other minorities in Japan (see Preface, Note 7). It is described in greater detail in Chapters 3 and 4. Takatsuki is a small provincial city between Kyoto and Osaka. The *mukuge* is a flower, known in English as the rose of Sharon or althaea, which symbolizes Korea much as cherry blossom symbolizes Japan.

4   The Burakumin are briefly described in Note 10 of the Preface.

5   In the 1993 KYAJ survey, one question asked 'In the household where you were born and raised, how much was the Korean language spoken?' Only 9.2 percent responded that 'conversations were sometimes carried out in Korean,' while another 5.0 percent responded that 'daily greetings were sometimes made in Korean' (Fukuoka and Kim 1997:40).

6   It has not been possible to obtain more recent data, because the North-leaning schools do not publish enrollment statistics. The figures given here were located in issue No.8 of *Human Report*, a small circulation magazine edited by Mindan member Suh Hae-Seok, published in December 1987. The 1986 figures are ascribed to Mindan Central

Headquarters, and it is unclear how the 'North' Korean figures were derived. Note also that all these figures apply only to those ethnic Koreans who still hold South or North Korean nationality. With a very small number of exceptions, those who have acquired Japanese nationality are not covered.

7 By 1992, only 127 of the 809 students at the South Korean school in Tokyo were the children of long-term residents of Japan. Figures for all four 'South' Korean schools showed Zainichis accounting for 799 out of 1,757 students – less than half (Source: personal communication from Choi Hee-Sup, president of the KYAJ).

8 Generally speaking, the Ministry of Education continues to exercise strict control over the prestigious national universities. The other universities, run privately or by local authorities, have been able to get round the problem of Korean schools not being recognized under Article 1 by applying Article 69, Clause 1, Item 5 of the Enforcement Ordinances appended to the Japanese School Education Law. This permits universities to allow candidates to take their entrance exams 'if they have reached a suitable age and are recognized as having attained an educational standard equivalent to, or higher than, a high-school graduate.' The reason the national universities have refused to apply this to graduates of Korean schools is because the Ministry of Education has not allowed them to do so.

In another instance of how bureaucratic thinking denies Zainichi Koreans the rights of Japanese and foreigners alike, the Ministry of Education also has refused to allow graduates of the Korean schools to take exams as 'foreign exchange students,' though this is permitted to graduates of schools overseas who have at least twelve years of schooling behind them.

On September 21, 1997, the *Asahi Shinbun* reported on a survey of university admissions policy conducted by Zainichi Korean students and others. It showed that 219 out of 422 private universities surveyed did allow graduates of ethnic Korean schools to take their entrance exams, along with 30 out of 53 public universities run by prefectures and municipalities. Roughly speaking, just over 50 percent of universities in both sectors now recognize graduation certificates from the Korean schools. This figure has risen sharply in the 1990s after slower progress in the 1980s: from about 10 percent in 1977, to 20 percent in 1985, 25 percent in 1991, and 30 percent in 1994. Only the elite national universities refused to defy the Ministry of Education's insistence that the qualification should not be recognized: for them, the recognition percentage remained at zero.

9 The Korean language has always exhibited wide regional variations. Since partition, the governments of South and North Korea both have attempted to standardize the language, basing the national versions on the Korean spoken in Seoul and Pyongyang respectively. There are major differences in pronunciation, the main reason being deliberate changes enforced by the government of North Korea as part of its linguistic reform program. Thus for example the popular Korean names pronounced in South Korea as Yi (often spelled 'Lee' in English), Yu, Yang and Im (often spelled 'Lim' in English), are written with the same characters in North Korea but are pronounced Ri, Ryu, Ryang and Rim.

10 Until very recently, 'North' Korean schools also used to teach a thoroughly North Korean political agenda, including worship of Kim Il Sung and strict adherence to his ideology of *Juche* (self-reliance). The basic principle was to run the school in just the same way as if the pupils were living in North Korea. However, the curricular reform carried out by the schools in 1993–95 was designed to recognize the reality that they were in fact living in Japan. I am indebted to Sonia Ryang (personal communication) for much of the material on 'North' Korean schools and their pupils. Far more detail may be found on the subject in her book (Ryang 1997).

11 Source: personal communication from Choi Hee-Sup, president of KYAJ.

12 Japan's public broadcaster, NHK (Japan Broadcasting Corporation) has run Korean-language courses on TV and radio for many years. There is no politically neutral way of describing the Korean language in Japanese, and NHK feared criticism from South-leaning Koreans if it described the

language as *Chōsen-go* ('North' Korean), or from North-leaning Koreans if it called it *Kankoku-go* ('South' Korean). Accordingly the programs refer to the language as '*Han-gul*' – the name of the script in which Korean is written, and not strictly speaking the name of the language itself. Such are the delicacies which attend host-nation relations with this politically divided community.

13 For example, on my trip to Korea with the Takatsuki Mukuge Society, we were joined for part of the journey by Mukuge representative Lee Kyung-Jae, along with his parents, wife and children. His father, Lee Kang-Chae (an elderly first-generation Zainichi), got into a conversation with the bus driver, and it was noticeable that Hong In-Sung (a second-generation Zainichi who spoke pretty good Korean) kept his mouth tightly shut. He told me later that he would not have been able to use the correct polite forms in a conversation where the bus-driver was showing respect to Lee Kang-Chae as an elder by using highly respectful language. His up-bringing meant that Hong In-Sung only knew the kind of Korean used by parents toward their children.

14 In the 1993 KYAJ survey, we asked young South-affiliated Zainichi Koreans 'What level of conversation can you conduct in your mother tongue?' Only 1.9 percent of respondents said they knew enough Korean to 'engage in complex debate.' Another 6.9 percent said they could manage 'simple everyday conversation' (Fukuoka and Kim 1997:41). One would naturally expect higher figures among young Zainichis with North Korean nationality, since far more of them attend ethnic Korean schools. It is consider-ations such as these that lead me to conclude that, very roughly speaking, about 20 percent of young Zainichi Koreans have some command of the language.

15 Kanagawa prefecture adjoins Tokyo; Yokohama is the prefectural capital. This questionnaire survey covered random samples of Koreans and Chinese aged over twenty. The response rate was 48.0 percent, with 1,028 valid responses, made up of 866 from Koreans, 161 from Chinese, and one that did not state nationality.

In striking contrast to the Korean figures, over 80 percent of the Chinese respondents turned out to have no Japanese alias. Ishida Reiko, author of Chapter 6 of the Kimpara collection, which focuses on the use of aliases, offers the following explanations for the low usage of aliases among ethnic Chinese in the Kanagawa survey: (1) A large proportion (43%) were first-generation migrants, three-quarters of whom came to Japan after the end of World War II. (2) Reflecting their historical background, none of the Chinese respondents had ever been *obliged* to use an alias, whereas 13.1 percent of the Koreans surveyed were old enough to have been forced to adopt a Japanese name during Japan's colonial rule over Korea. (3) Many of the children were attending ethnic Chinese schools, at least to the end of junior high school, and therefore had no need of a Japanese name for school purposes (Ishida in Kimpara *et al.* 1986:175–9).

16 *Yakiniku* is a Japanese word simply meaning 'cooked meat' and used to denote a grilled meat cuisine found in Korean restaurants in Japan. The mainland Korean equivalent is *bulgogi* but the two cuisines are not entirely the same. *Yakiniku* is a variant of *bulgogi* that has been modified by Zainichi Koreans to appeal to Japanese tastes. For example, the pieces of meat are cut much smaller and neater in *yakiniku* than in *bulgogi*. *Yakiniku* cuisine was invented by Zainichi Koreans shortly after the war, initially as a way of making the internal organs of cows more appetizing at a time when widespread poverty meant that most people could not afford more expensive kinds of meat. It eventually caught on with Japanese as well as Koreans and today is an extremely popular dish in Japan.

Pachinko is a form of pinball played on an upright table and with a strong gambling element.

Yakiniku restaurants and *pachinko* halls are the two businesses most closely associated with the Korean minority in Japan. In some cases these small businesses are no longer small at all. *Pachinko*, in particular, has become a massive and highly profitable industry with some very sizable companies in it.

17   In the 1993 KYAJ survey, 72.6 percent of the young ethnic Koreans who responded said they had 'never' been called by their Korean name in the household and another 13.9 percent said they had 'seldom' been called by that name (Fukuoka and Kim 1997:79).

18   'Takayasu' strikes the Japanese ear as a rare surname, but then again, there are many rare surnames in Japanese. 'Keisai' also sounds slightly unusual to the Japanese ear; a likely reaction would be to wonder whether the holder is the son of a Buddhist priest, since the characters are read in the Chinese-derived style (*on-yomi*) and such names are common in the priesthood.

19   This appears to be part of the recent trend for Japanese men living in rural districts to seek brides in other Asian countries because of the unwillingness of Japanese women to marry men who are obligated to take over the running of family farms. An obsession with the supposed attractions of city life in Japan, along with a fear of having to look after elderly in-laws with traditional expectations regarding the oldest son's wife, has created this trend. The economic gap between Japan and other Asian countries has made it possible for Japanese men to attract brides from Korea, the Philippines, etc. Cultural and language barriers often cause these marriages to break down (Shukuya 1988).

20   The Zainichi Koreans who came to Japan before and during the war often lived together in ethnic Korean settlements, referred to as *Chōsen Buraku*. This reflected the extreme difficulties they faced in winning acceptance in Japanese communities. (The Burakumin communities were an exception: see Chapter 4, Note 9.) These *Chōsen Buraku* often developed because Koreans were gathered together under the forced labor policy and located close to their workplace; or because they took up residence in locations where the residential conditions were so bad that Japanese would not live there. These latter cases included some where Koreans illegally occupied land officially deemed unfit for residence, such as riverside locations on the wrong side of flood barriers.

      However, as Kim Chan-Jung points out, some of these settlements disappeared after the 1960s (Kim 1997:216–18).

The 1993 KYAJ survey asked 'About how many fellow Koreans lived in the area where you were resident at the age of twelve?' To this, 15.5 percent selected the response, 'It was an area with many Korean residents.' Another 10.1 percent selected the response, 'It was not a Korean district as such, but there were ten or more Korean households' (Fukuoka and Kim 1997:179). These rather low figures probably reflect the growing tendency for Zainichi Koreans to disperse into Japanese society as their living standards have risen through the years of high economic growth.

21 The 1993 KYAJ survey found that 22.3 percent of respondents had 'six or more' fellow-Korean friends, while 42.5 percent had 'one to five.' Fully 35.1 percent said they had no Korean friends at all (Fukuoka and Kim 1997:188). In addition, only 14.2 percent said they had a Korean boyfriend or girlfriend, against 42.2 percent who said they had a Japanese one (Fukuoka and Kim 1997:190).

22 The *Jesa* is a traditional Korean rite of ancestor-worship, typically conducted at the house of the eldest son of the family. If strictly observed, it is held on the night before the death anniversary of ancestors of the last four generations, continuing through the night until dawn of the anniversary itself. Large-scale *Jesa* dedicated to the spirits of all deceased ancestors are held on New Year's Day and at *Chuseok* (August 15 by the lunar calendar). Families will also gather at their gravesites on a fixed day of the year to hold a *Jesa* for the spirits of ancestors of five and more generations ago. Only men may participate in the ritual itself; women prepare the ceremonial food which is eaten by everyone afterwards.

These days it is becoming less common to stay up all night for the *Jesa*, and there is a tendency to hold the ceremony less frequently in the course of the year. However, it remains an integral part of life for Koreans, including those in Japan. Only 12.3 percent of respondents in the 1993 KYAJ survey said they had never participated in a *Jesa* (Fukuoka and Kim 1997:37–8). Besides its religious and cultural significance, the *Jesa* is also an important chance for relatives to get together.

23   Attitudes toward intermarriage among young Zainichis themselves also vary, but those that do not object appear to be in a majority. The 1993 KYAJ survey asked young Zainichi Koreans with ROK nationality whether they would insist on marrying a fellow Korean, and got positive responses from only 35.0 percent of the sample. There was no statistically significant difference between male and female respondents on this question (Fukuoka and Kim 1997:190).

24   It may be worth noting that a similar trend may be observed in patterns of intermarriage between mainstream Japanese and another discriminated minority group, the Burakumin (cf. Preface, Note 10). Despite deeply ingrained prejudice, there has been an unmistakable increase in the incidence of marriages between young Burakumin and non-Burakumin in recent years. However, when visiting Burakumin districts I have often been told that love marriages between Burakumin women and non-Burakumin men are on the increase, but that it is still rare for an outside woman to 'marry into the Buraku.' My informants in these communities say that consequently there are many male Burakumin still unmarried in their thirties and over.

25   The number of Koreans who had naturalized stood at 204,622 as of the end of 1996. Naturalization proceeded at a rate of about 5,000 cases a year in the 1970s and 1980s, but rose rapidly going into the 1990s. There were 8,244 cases in 1994, 10,327 in 1995 and 9,898 in 1996 (Source: Ministry of Justice, *Hōsō Jihō* (legal bulletins)).

26   On September 19, 1997, the ROK Ministry of Justice announced a reform of the Nationality Law that discarded the previous principle of recognizing descent only through the paternal line and enabled the offspring of marriages between South Korean women and foreign men to acquire South Korean nationality. The reform bill duly completed its passage through the South Korean parliament on November 18, 1997. The law was promulgated on December 13, 1997, to take effect six months later.

This South Korean reform effectively means that all the offspring of legal mixed marriages between Zainichi Koreans and Japanese will now hold dual nationality. The South

Korean legislation establishes the same principle that is applied in Japan: dual nationality is permitted up to the age of 22, at which point the holder must choose one or the other.

However, as mentioned in Note 27 below, that freedom to choose is constrained in reality by the Japanese practice of registering the children of mixed marriages in the Japanese parent's family register and giving legal status to the Japanese surname unless specific legal measures to the contrary are taken by the parents. Thus as I argue in the Conclusion to the present work, unless and until the right to ethnic education is established in Japan, the legal availability of dual nationality will not in itself prevent the onward march of 'Japanization' among the Zainichi minority.

27   It is possible for children of mixed marriages to keep their Japanese nationality but change from using the Japanese parent's surname to using the foreign parent's surname, even after the child has been entered in the Japanese parent's family register (which automatically entails taking the Japanese parent's surname). Changing the surname entails obtaining permission from a family court. The child is removed from the Japanese parent's family register and a new family register is established with just the child in it. Some people do undergo this procedure. For instance, Kim Soo-Il (mentioned earlier) married a Japanese woman. Their daughter has her own family register in her ethnic Korean name. However, such cases amount to a very small minority of the total.

3   A Typology of Zainichi Identities

1   In the 1993 KYAJ survey, we asked 'Have you ever felt bad about being a Zainichi Korean?' Of our 800-strong sample, 11.7 percent replied 'very often,' 15.7 percent 'often' and 36.3 percent 'sometimes.' Thus 63.7 percent of the young ROK nationals surveyed had experienced negative feelings about their ethnicity to some degree (Fukuoka and Kim 1997:50–1).

2   The Alien Registration Law was promulgated on April 28, 1952. Article 14 stated that 'he (the alien) shall have his

fingerprints taken on the registration card and fingerprint card.' The fingerprinting measure met with powerful opposition from many of the Koreans residing in Japan at the time, and the government was not able to enforce the fingerprinting measure until 1955. The law required even those foreign nationals who had been born and raised in Japan to be fingerprinted within thirty days of their fourteenth birthday and at three-year intervals thereafter. The law was revised in 1982, raising the age for initial fingerprinting to sixteen and the subsequent intervals to five years. Hence nearly all the people interviewed for the present study were fingerprinted at least once, on their fourteenth or sixteenth birthday. The only exceptions were those who had Japanese nationality at birth, represented here in Chapters 11 and 12.

In 1992 the Alien Registration Law was amended so that people classified as 'special permanent residents' (*tokubetsu eijūsha*) or 'permanent residents' (*eijūsha*) would no longer have to be fingerprinted. The great majority of ethnic Koreans are in one of these two categories and hence are now exempt from fingerprinting.

3 The 'differential impulse,' is a rough translation of *ika shikō*, a Japanese term that I have coined myself in contradistinction to *dōka shikō*, the assimilatory impulse.

4 Nimmi Hutnik has proposed a schema to categorize the identity of second-generation Indian immigrants in Britain that shows interesting similarities and differences to the one outlined here. His subjects are at once British citizens and of Indian ethnic origin, and he schematizes the range of identities using a pair of axes indicating 'Degree of identification with the minority group' and 'Degree of identification with the majority group.' This produces the four-part paradigm for 'strategies of ethnic identity management' (Hutnik 1986:153) shown in *Figure N.1*.

Hutnik labels the first of these four states of consciousness *assimilation*, which he defines as abandonment of ethnicity in favor of total identification with the majority group. The second state he labels *acculturation*, in which 'the minority becomes more akin to the dominant group although it continues to exist as a separate entity.' People in this group,

Figure N.1 Hutnik's classification of ethnic identity

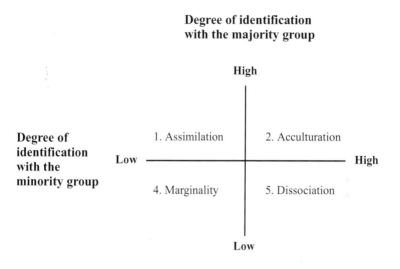

he says, 'identify with *both* the ethnic minority group and the majority group.' The third state he labels *dissociation* and defines as deliberate distancing from the majority group and association with the minority group. Finally the fourth state is *marginality*, where the individual is caught in a dilemma in which he can identify with neither the majority nor the minority.

Certain interesting problems arise if one attempts to apply this theory-driven model to young Zainichi Koreans.

One problem arises with the axis labeled 'identification with the majority group.' Many ethnic Koreans feel an affection for the Japanese neighborhood in which they were born and brought up, but hardly any of them have such positive feelings for the nation-state, Japan, which has consistently subjected them to oppressive policies.

The second axis, 'identification with the minority group,' is no less problematical, since ethnic Koreans in Japan are divided along political lines reflecting the division of their motherland. Some identify with South Korea, others with

North Korea, yet others with neither. When the 'ethnic minority group' itself is so resistant to definition, the axis becomes a far less effective tool.

Yet a third problem stems from Hutnik's treatment of the fourth quadrant, 'marginality,' which he implies to be a problem category with this reference to an earlier work on the American Oriental: 'He belongs neither to America nor to the Orient. He cannot identify himself completely with either civilization. There is no easy road for him out of this dilemma.' (Stonequist 1937:105, in Hutnik 1986:153) But can there not be more positive ways of living, which are not constrained by concepts of nationality and ethnicity? The appearance of theoretical consistency of the Hutnik model is tarnished by the fact that this one quadrant is labeled as a condition of involuntary failure while all the other three imply volition, or in Hutnik's terminology, 'strategy.'

5   This trial arose after Park Chong-Seuk, a second-generation Korean born in 1951, applied for a job with Hitachi, the major consumer electronics company. He took the Hitachi employment examination under his Japanese alias and was informally offered a job. However, when the company learned of his Korean identity, it abruptly withdrew the offer. In December 1970, Park filed suit against Hitachi at the Yokohama District Court for wrongful dismissal.

Park's argument was that being highly assimilated to Japanese society he was no different to a Japanese person, so that Hitachi had no grounds to refuse him employment just because of his non-Japanese nationality. He was not supported by either Mindan or Chongryun, both organizations believing that employment with big Japanese corporations was just another step toward assimilation. However, Park did get support from various ethnic Korean and Japanese youths, and won a complete victory when the verdict was finally announced in 1974. Meanwhile, some of his supporters helped to launch Mintōren.

It is worth mentioning that Park is still working for Hitachi today, and using his Korean name. The trial proved to be a learning experience for him, from which he emerged with a stronger sense of his ethnic identity. This suggests that fears among the Korean community that the trial represented a step toward assimilation were groundless.

6　This case arose from an incident that occurred in Osaka in January 1989, when Bae Keun-Il, a second-generation Korean born in 1950, tried to rent an apartment in Osaka. He told the real estate agent that he was a South Korean national and was told this was not a problem; he paid a deposit and signed a provisional contract. However, when the landlord learned that his prospective tenant was Korean, he refused to accept him. Negotiations broke down and in April 1989 Bae filed suit against the landlord and the real estate agent at the Osaka District Court, alleging unfair discrimination and demanding that the contract be recognized as valid and compensation paid. He also sued the Osaka prefectural government, for negligence in failing to meet its obligation to issue administrative guidance against discrimination in tenancy agreements. The verdict, handed down on June 18, 1993, recognized that cancellation of the provisional contract because of the tenant's Korean nationality constituted discrimination. The landlord was ordered to pay compensation to Bae, although the real estate agent and prefectural government were absolved of responsibility.

　　I interviewed Bae Keun-Il on December 17 1989. He subsequently died in 1995.

7　Many assimilation-minded ethnic Korean parents give their children Japanese personal names. However, for legal purposes they are obliged to keep their Korean surnames. On their alien registration documents the Korean surname is entered as the official name with the Japanese surname added as an alias. These documents do not specify the pronunciation of the characters used to write the name. Hence an ethnic Korean child could be given a Japanese personal name, such as 'Kazuko,' but if she later applied for a South Korean passport the same name would be entered with its Korean pronunciation ('Hwa-Ja').

8　It may be worth noting that whereas naturalized Korean-Japanese are in principle excluded from nationalist-type groups associated with Chongryun, the KYAJ does allow them to participate, but only as associates, not as full members. There could be no clearer indication of how this organization positions itself between the nationalist and pluralist positions. Hence my use of the fifth term, 'ethnic solidarity,' to describe its position.

9 The *Minzoku-mei wo Torimodosu-kai* (Society for Winning Back Ethnic Names) was formed in December 1985, by some Zainichi Koreans who had Japanese nationality as a result of naturalization or being the offspring of mixed marriages, but wanted to have their ethnic Korean names recognized as their legal names. Until that time at least, it was clearly stated in the *Handbook on Applying for Naturalization*, published by the Ministry of Justice, that people should adopt a 'Japanese-style name' after naturalizing, meaning that the concept of holding Japanese nationality but having a foreign-sounding legal name was not accepted. The Society was formally disbanded in September 1994 on the grounds that it had successfully achieved its original goal.

Between 1987 and 1994 there were ten cases in which members of the Society applied to family courts to legally change their forenames, all of which succeeded. Nine of the cases involved Koreans and one Chinese. Three more Korean-Japanese have succeeded in legally restoring their Korean names since then.

These thirteen cases covered a considerable variety of personal circumstances: cases where the applicant had naturalized; where the applicant had been born of naturalized parents; Japanese nationals who were the offspring of Korean-Japanese mixed marriages; and one Japanese woman who had married a Zainichi Korean husband. The woman in this last case had continued to use her Japanese surname after marriage, before deciding many years later that she would prefer to legally take on her husband's Korean surname. By this time her husband had already died, so that she had to fight the case on her own.

4 Learning to Live with the Japanese

1 'Cholla-Nam-Do' means South Cholla province, while 'Cholla-Buk-Do' means North Cholla province. Because

Cholla-Do covers a wide area, it is divided into these two regions for administrative purposes. However, in terms of lifestyles and emotional affiliation, there is no difference between the two provinces. The same applies to Kyongsang-Do, and several other regions of South and North Korea that are also divided into north and south provinces.

2   According to Lee Kyung-Jae, the derivation of this name is as follows. His father, Lee Kang-Chae, was a member of the Lee clan of Chonju. The Chonju Lee claimed royal descent from the Lee dynasty that ruled over most of Korea from 1392 to 1910. One member of this royal dynasty adopted the pseudonym 'Koan' on becoming a commoner. The Japanese reading of this name is 'Takayasu.'

3   As mentioned elsewhere in this case history, several other leading figures in the Mukuge Society have taken posts in the Takatsuki city government. Kyung-Jae mentions two reasons why he himself has avoided that course: The first is that people with an interest in the movement, whether friendly or hostile, might draw the conclusion that he had only become an activist in order to secure a good post for himself later on; the second is that if he were to be employed by the city, it would make it far harder for him to press demands with the authorities in his other role as a Korean civil rights activist.

4   On the official level, Mindan and Chongryun are in permanent conflict with each other because of their support for the South and North Korean governments respectively. However, as Kyung-Jae suggests, there is a considerable amount of fraternization at the informal level. At events such as the *Jesa* (cf. Chapter 2, Note 22), it is not uncommon for ethnic Koreans holding South Korean, North Korean and Japanese nationality to mingle and drink together quite freely.

5   There is a movement demanding the right to political participation for Zainichi Koreans. However, at present the mainstream of this movement is calling only for voting rights in local elections. People like Kyung-Jae who demand national-level political rights are in the minority among Zainichi Koreans.

6   I say that Chang-Jae's grandmother 'returned' to North Korea, but strictly speaking this was not a 'return' in the full

      sense of the word, since she hailed from a district that is now in South Korea (cf. Chapter 2, pp. 38–9).

7   The Japanese government's forced migrant labor program did not start until 1939.

8   Marriages between fellow Japan-resident Koreans of the first or second generations were often arranged between families, in keeping with traditional Korean practice. It was not uncommon for bride and groom to see each other for the first time on the day of the wedding.

9   There have been many cases, all over Japan, of Korean communities forming in Burakumin districts. While mainstream Japanese have instinctively avoided such places, to people who are themselves struggling economically they have appealed as places with a friendly atmosphere within which the necessities of life are freely borrowed and lent. Another major factor in the tendency for Zainichi Koreans to live in Burakumin communities has been the extreme difficulty faced in winning acceptance in non-Burakumin districts (see Chapter 2, Note 20). Nowadays the borrowing and lending lifestyle has all but disappeared with improvements in Burakumin living standards and the erosion of communal spirit in the places where they live. However, the geographical association between Burakumin and Zainichi Koreans remains strong.

10   'Katchan' is the diminutive form of 'Katsuo,' Chang-Jae's Japanese pseudonym.

11   See Chapter 2, Note 22.

12   The *Buraku Kaihō Dōmei* (Buraku Liberation League) is an organization created and staffed by Burakumin (see Preface, Note 10), dedicated to liberating the Burakumin from discrimination. The Buraku liberation movement effectively started on March 3, 1922, with the formation of the *Zenkoku Suihei-sha* (National Levelers Association). The movement lapsed during World War II, but was relaunched in 1946 under the name of *Buraku Kaihō Zenkoku Iinkai* (National Committee for Buraku Liberation). The name was changed to its present form, the Buraku Liberation League, in September 1955. The BLL is the biggest organization in Japan devoted to combating social discrimination and demanding human

rights. Membership is restricted to people of Buraku origins and their spouses.

13 Publicly declaring one's real Korean name is considered a crucial rite of passage in the ethnic Korean educational movement. It is a climactic moment in the lives of many Zainichi Koreans.

14 It is a sign of the changing times that Chang-Jae's school, located in a Burakumin district and with two different discriminated minorities attending it, was well enough equipped to have closed-circuit television. Just a few years before, such a thing would have been inconceivable. Burakumin children had always attended poorly-built, under-equipped schools. The improvement in the 1970s was a result of intense campaigning, mainly by the Buraku Liberation League and especially in districts like Osaka prefecture with large Burakumin communities.

15 In fact it was only partially abolished. Jobs at the post office are divided into two types, 'internal' (*naimushoku*) and 'external' (*gaimushoku*). The former covers work done by clerks inside the post office, the latter covers mail deliveries. It was this latter category for which Chang-Jae and Soo-Gil applied, and for which the nationality clause was lifted in 1984. The nationality clause for 'internal' jobs is still in place today.

16 'Lee-kun,' 'Son-kun.' *Kun* is a title used for younger men and boys. Custom varies from place to place, but in the post office kun is not normally used when addressing younger workers.

5   For the Sake of Our Fellow Zainichis

1 Like many Zainichi Koreans affiliated to the KYAJ, Kim Dae-Won tends to sprinkle his speech with Korean words, especially when referring to family relations.

2 The Ginza is the most glamorous shopping district in Tokyo. To have a shop there, however small, constitutes a major commercial success.

3 Within Korea, women from Cheju island have a reputation for selfless devotion to their husbands. Although Dae-Won's mother was born in Japan, he believes that her Cheju-born parents' influence is still strong.

4   Dae-Won's father's change of allegiance followed a change of nationality, from North to South Korean. From 1965, when the Japan-ROK treaty of that year granted 'treaty-based permanent residence status' to ROK nationals, to 1981, when reforms to immigration laws granted 'exceptional permanent residence status' to DPRK nationals, there was a period of some sixteen years when there were great practical advantages to be had from choosing South Korean nationality. One got guaranteed permanent residence in Japan, plus the right to an ROK passport that would allow freedom of international travel. These substantial practical considerations, sometimes allied to an unease about the ideology of Chongryun and its sponsor, the North Korean government, led large numbers of Zainichi Koreans to switch from DPRK to ROK nationality during the 1970s when Dae-Won was growing up.

5   *Shiragi* and *Kudara* are the Japanese pronunciations of Silla and Paekche, names of kingdoms that used to exist on the Korean peninsula in ancient times. For more detail, see Chapter 14, Note 2.

6   Kim Yang-Ki (born Tokyo, 1933) is a second-generation Zainichi Korean who is a professor at the University of Shizuoka, specializing in Korean-Japanese comparative folklore studies.

7   Sukiyabashi is in Tokyo. The '1991 question' refers to negotiations between Japan and the Republic of Korea on revising the 1965 Japan-ROK Agreement on the Legal Status and Treatment of Nationals of the Republic of Korea, which were due to be completed in 1991, twenty-five years after the original agreement came into force. Members of the KYAJ staged a hunger strike to put pressure on the Japanese government to make further concessions on the rights of Zainichi Koreans. Cf. Hirowatari 1994:17–18.

8   The *samul nori* is a traditional Korean folk performance combining music and dance. Four kinds of traditional musical instrument are used. Participants dance and play the instruments simultaneously.

9   As mentioned earlier (Chapter 3, Note 8), the present situation is that naturalized Korean Japanese are allowed to become associate members, but not full members, of the KYAJ.

10 'Kong-Ja' and 'Kyoko' are Korean and Japanese readings of the same characters. The character *Matsu* in *Matsui* has been deliberately selected because of its similarity to the character for 'Park.' Using the latter character itself would have betrayed the family's ethnic identity, since it is very common in Korean names but never used in Japanese names. The character *i* has been added to create a typical two-character Japanese surname, as opposed to a typical one-character Korean name.

11 The Japanese educational system includes two main types of school for the approximately 96 percent of junior high school graduates who continue to the senior high school level. Students with university in mind usually attend *general* senior high schools. But there are also *vocational* senior high schools, including industrial, commercial, agricultural and nursing senior high schools. These mix general education with vocational training.

12 The Shōgin Bank mentioned here is one of a group of Mindan-affiliated financial institutions. Like all of them, in strict legal terms it is a credit union rather than a bank. There are Shōgin Banks in various large cities, known as Tokyo Shōgin, Yokohama Shōgin, Osaka Shōgin, etc. These are independent institutions, not branches of an overall institution.

13 Most Korean names have three characters – one for the surname and two for the forename (Cf. Chapter 1, p. 8). Japanese names tend to have four characters – two for the surname and two for the forename – although there are numerous exceptions to this general rule.

14 A kind of savory pancake. The dictionary definition of *monja* is 'a thin, flat cake of unsweetened batter fried with various ingredients.' It resembles the Japanese dish known as *okonomi-yaki*.

15 As Kong-Ja says, it is fairly common for Japanese people, especially young women, to refer to themselves by their personal names rather than with the first-person pronoun *watashi*.

16 Some mainland South Koreans have a negative image of Zainichi Koreans. As they see it, they have endured Japanese colonialism and then rebuilt their shattered and divided

country after the Korean War (1950–53), while their Zainichi counterparts have had an easy time living in a wealthy country, Japan. This view is based on a total absence of knowledge of what Zainichi Koreans went through before and during the war, and what they have been through since.

6   Living as Overseas Nationals

1   *Chōgin* is short for *Chōsen Ginkō or* 'Bank of Korea.' The name is applied to a group of financial institutions – technically credit unions rather than banks – having close institutional links to Chongryun. There are Chōgins in every Japanese prefecture with a substantial ethnic Korean population, named Tokyo Chōgin, Hiroshima Chōgin, etc. Structurally, each one is an independent institution.

2   Cf. Chapter 2, pp. 38–9. Notwithstanding the use of the word 'repatriation,' Jae-Soo's uncle went not to the land of his birth and ancestry, which was in South Korea, but to a place where he had probably never set foot before, in North Korea. The same applied to nearly all the Zainichi Koreans – over 90,000 of them – who 'repatriated' to North Korea during the period 1959–84. Kim Chan-Jung has an account of how these people made the decision to pursue their dreams in North Korea (Kim 1997:198–203).

3   In answering questions about himself, Jae-Soo often drifts into the plural, talking of 'we' rather than 'I.' This is probably because of the intense feeling of solidarity engendered among the students at North Korean schools in Japan. He is not unusual in saying (later in this chapter) that he has no Japanese friends. People who attend North Korean schools, and then proceed to work for Chongryun-affiliated companies or organizations, form what may reasonably be called a 'closed society' within Japan.

4   Readers may find it odd that Jae-Soo speaks of having no awareness of discrimination or persecution, despite the fact that he himself reports having racist insults hurled at him as a schoolboy, being forced to give his fingerprint, and feeling that he had no chance of getting a job at a Japanese company.

Objectively there can be no doubt that Jae-Soo has been subject to discrimination. His insistence that he has no subjective 'sense' (*jikkan*) of discrimination probably reflects the strength of ethnic pride instilled in him at the North Korean schools he attended – a pride that robustly shrugs off Japanese racism as something only to be expected. This may account for the absence of anger in Jae-Soo's attitude toward Japan.

5   Mah-jongg is a gambling game of Chinese origin, for four players. It involves collecting certain combinations of patterned tiles, of which there are 136 in all.

6   On *pachinko*, see Chapter 2, Note 16. In many popular models of *pachinko* machine, hitting certain targets activates a spinning digit counter that pays out a jackpot if it stops on three sevens. Repeated jackpots will clean out a machine, so that it has to be reset by attendants. This state is called uchi-dome. Nowadays *pachinko* machines will pay out 100,000 yen or more before they go *uchi-dome*.

7   Some students at North Korean senior high schools go on study trips to North Korea in their final year. Selection is made on a class basis, with teachers evaluating the behavior and educational attainment of each class before deciding which ones will be allowed to make the trip.

8   Il-Hun says 'unfortunately' because Kyongsang-Buk-Do is in present-day South Korea, making it difficult to visit as he holds North Korean nationality.

7   Going It Alone

1   Dae-Son attended a six-year private high school that combined the junior and senior high schools, which usually take up three years each of secondary education in Japan.

2   The practice of recent recruits setting up informal contacts between their employers and junior students still at university is a well-established aspect of graduate recruitment in Japan.

3   *Shichigosan* is a Japanese rite of passage for young children. The word literally means 'seven-five-three' and the ceremony is held on November 15 during the third and

seventh year of age for girls and third and fifth year for boys. The rite is conducted at Shinto shrines and there is no such custom among Korean people.

4   The Nara era lasted from AD 710 to 784.

5   This much-heralded piece of legislation was passed in 1985 to enable Japan to comply with the United Nations Convention on the Elimination of All Forms of Discrimination Against Women, previously ratified by Japan. The law obliges enterprises to 'make efforts' to achieve sexual equality; however, it only offers guidelines and is not legally binding.

6   These are meetings at which representatives of companies explain the company's business and the kind of vacancies available to university students who might contemplate applying for jobs. Sometimes they also entail a simple test, which functions as a kind of preliminary employment examination.

7   It only took Hwa-Mi two years to get her US degree, because her Japanese degree counted for two years' worth of credits.

8   This is of course yet another variation on Hwa-Mi's name, since the romanized version on her Korean passport puts the surname last instead of first, as in the Korean or Japanese versions.

8   Turning Japanese

1   *Chon* is a common term of anti-Korean racial abuse used by Japanese.

2   The film *Yoon's Town* has a Zainichi Korean district of Osaka as its setting and a young third-generation Zainichi woman as its heroine. It was directed by Kim Woo-Seon and released in 1989.

3   The Japanese nursing profession recognizes two qualifications. One can become an auxiliary nurse (*jun-kangofu*) by passing an examination after a two-year course of study at a nursing school; or one can become a full-qualified nurse (*sei-kangofu*) by attending a three-year nursing school, or by studying nursing at a three-year junior college or a four-year university. People who obtain the auxiliary nursing cert-

ificate can then acquire the full certificate by attending nursing school or junior college for just two years. This was the path followed by Yoko.

4   As well as being traditional clothing in Korea, the *jeogori* is also used as uniform for girls at North Korean schools in Japan. Much as in the case of the Japanese kimono, there are male and female versions, but the latter is more commonly used today.

5   The head household, or *honke*, is part of the traditional Japanese *ie* system. The head family of an *ie* would aim to practice inheritance through the oldest son, while younger sons would sometimes be allowed to set up branch households (*bunke*). Issues of marriage and succession would tend to be more intense in the *honke* than in the *bunke*. The concept is largely outdated in contemporary Japan, although it still survives, on paper at least, in the family register system (see Introduction, Note 9).

Part Two Korean Women in Japan: Their Lives and Struggles

9   A Dream Is a Dream

1   Japanese higher education is broadly divided between two institutions: the university, where most degree courses take four years to complete, and the junior college, where courses last just two years. The overwhelming majority of junior college students are female.

2   It is remarkably easy to acquire a teaching license in Japan. Most teachers pick up their qualification by taking a few education-credits as one small part of a university or junior college course. The 'training' includes teaching practice that, as in Seol-Ji's case, need last no more than two weeks.

3   Junior college and university students graduate in March. The recruitment season tends to start in summer of the previous year or even earlier, and students are generally considered to be in serious difficulties if they have not secured employment by the turn of the year.

4   These interviews, known in Japanese as *Omiai*, are arranged
     by the parents or by a go-between who is usually a family
     friend or relative. Unlike arranged marriages in some other
     countries, there is usually relatively little obligation on either
     party to accept the match, and it is quite common for either
     party to decline. Many first-generation Zainichi Koreans
     were effectively forced into marriages with fellow Koreans
     arranged by their parents, but in recent years the element of
     coercion has largely disappeared.

5   In point of fact there are many cases of love marriages
     between fellow Zainichi Koreans. However, they normally
     occur between couples who have been to Korean schools,
     participated in ethnic solidarity organizations, and gen-
     erally been part of the Korean scene in Japan. For people
     like Seol-Ji, who are cut off from the Zainichi network, an
     arranged marriage tends to be the only way of marrying a
     fellow Korean. Mindan often organizes parties to enable
     marriage-minded youths to meet members of the opposite
     sex.

10   Diplomatic Incidents

1   The last character in Mi-Young-Ja's name reads 'ja' in
     Korean and 'ko' in Japanese. It is a standard ending for a
     Japanese girl's name, but not for a Korean girl's name.

2   The *Kimigayo* is the Japanese national anthem. It celebrates
     the reign of the emperor and is detested by many Koreans
     who associate it with Japanese colonial rule over their
     country.

3   In Japanese law, the *honseki* is a person's 'legal permanent
     domicile,' which is not necessarily their current place of
     residence (see Introduction, Note 9). In the case of Zainichi
     Koreans, the *honseki* is officially 'South Korea' or just
     'Korea' (see Chapter 2, Note 2), even if the individual has
     never set foot on the Korean peninsula.

4   *Gyōza* are small fried dumplings stuffed with minced pork.
     A staple of Chinese cuisine, they are also very popular in
     Japan and do not carry very strong racial associations.
     Kimchi is spicy pickled vegetables. The word itself is

Korean and the dish is one of the representative icons of Korean culture.

5   The company was a member of the *Tokyo Dōwa Mondai Kigyō Renraku-kai* (Industrial Federation for Equality Problems, Tokyo). The word *dōwa* (a coinage roughly meaning 'equality and harmony') is a modern euphemism for any issue to do with the human rights of the Burakumin outcastes (see Preface, Note 10). The Federation was founded in 1979, following a series of incidents in which companies had been attacked by the Buraku Liberation League for discriminating against Burakumin in their employment policies. In 1990 it changed its name to the *Tokyo Jinken Keihatsu Kigyō Renraku-kai* (Industrial Federation for Human Rights, Tokyo), effectively signaling a broadening of scope to cover the human rights of ethnic Koreans and other minorities as well as Burakumin.

As of 1994 the Federation had 123 member companies, divided into eight groups, each of them attempting to raise the standards of company staff with responsibility for human rights.

During the nine-year period from 1986 to 1994, I myself conducted annual workshops for members of companies in Group No.3 of the Federation, entailing field trips to a Burakumin community in Tochigi, a rural prefecture not far from Tokyo. Generally speaking, attempts to eradicate discrimination are more advanced in the Kansai region around Osaka than in the Kanto region centered on Tokyo. However, I had the impression that this corporate grouping was considerably more committed to fighting discrimination than other groups in the fields of education and government.

It was therefore revealing to me personally to hear Mi-Young-Ja roundly criticizing the company that employed her for its hypocritical approach to discrimination. The company happens to be a member of Group No.3 of the Federation, and her experiences show that establishing formal structures to heighten human rights awareness cannot in itself be expected to eradicate the deep-rooted prejudice and discrimination within Japanese society.

11 This Japanese Is Still Korean

1 A traditional term of abuse used by Japanese against Koreans. See also Chapter 8, Note 1.

2 The Seikyū-sha is one of the most influential groups within Mintōren (see Preface, Note 7). The group is based in Kawasaki, the large industrial city between Tokyo and Yokohama, and remains very active today. Its origins date from 1969, when the South Korean Christian church in Kawasaki opened a day-care center that catered to both Zainichi Korean and Japanese children. The Seikyū-sha itself was launched in 1973, by a group of activists centered on Lee Yin-Ha, a first-generation Zainichi Protestant minister born in 1925 and holding South Korean nationality. It was legally recognized as a social welfare organization by the local government. The 'Seikyū' in Seikyū-sha literally means 'Blue hills,' and this is a word that traditionally symbolizes Korea.

In 1988 the Seikyū-sha prevailed upon the Kawasaki City government to build the *Fureai-kan* (Encounter Hall), which is managed by the Seikyū-sha. This Hall, now managed by Bae Jung-Do, a second-generation Zainichi, serves as a venue for ethnic education for Zainichi children and for various activities designed to bring Zainichi and Japanese children together.

3 The notion that Zainichi Koreans who naturalize are 'traitors' used to be widespread within Zainichi society. However, this attitude appears to be on the wane. The 1993 KYAJ survey asked respondents to react to the statement that 'People who naturalize have lost their ethnic pride.' Only 5.7 percent said they agreed with the statement, against 65.6 percent who disagreed and 28.7 percent who were neutral (Fukuoka and Kim 1997:100).

4 See Chapters 1 and 3, esp. Chapter 3, Note 2.

12 Mixed Blood, Mixed Feelings

1 *Doburoku* is illegal unrefined *sake*.

2 Park Kyung-Shik, a first-generation Zainichi historian, was born in 1922. He was tragically killed on February 12, 1998, when a car ran into him. Park was a pioneer of Zainichi

historical research, who investigated the issue of Korean forced migrant labor long before any Japanese scholar took any interest in it. His book was published in Japanese as *Chōsenjin Kyōsei Renkō no Kiroku* (Park 1965).

3   The brand-name of a popular Japanese health drink, which happens to sound slightly similar to Cho-Ja's surname, 'Yoon.'

4   The Kansai is the region of western Japan centered on Osaka, Kyoto and Kobe. Cho-Ja lives in the Kanto region in eastern Honshu, centered on Tokyo, Yokohama and Kawasaki. The two regions are Japan's biggest population centers. On the Society for Winning Back Ethnic Names, see Chapter 3, Note 9.

5   *Koseki seido*. See Introduction, Note 9.

6   For details, see Chapter 2, pp. 34–7.

7   The government's attempts to enforce display of the Japanese *Hinomaru* (Rising Sun) flag at formal school events have been widely opposed by the Japan Teachers Union and others for many years. To many people the flag is still associated with Japan's pre-war colonialism. Refusal to display the flag has been especially common in Okinawa. The anti-flag movement has tended to weaken in recent years.

13   Lifting the Fog

1   The old-style middle schools of the pre-war Japanese education system broadly corresponded to the senior high schools of the new system launched in 1948. However, only a small fraction of the population was able to attend them.

2   *Uri hak-kyo* is the Korean term used by Chongryun-affiliated Zainichi Koreans to describe 'North' Korean schools. It literally means 'our school.'

3   See Chapter 9, Note 4.

4   These are regions adjoining Soon-Ja's home district of Kyongsang. There is said to be a powerful sense of regional rivalry between Kyongsang-Do and Cholla-Do, while people from Cheju island (coterminous with the province of Cheju-Do) are generally subject to discrimination within Korean society.

5   See Chapter 1, pp. 6–7 and Note 3.

6   See Chapter 8, Note 2.

14 'I Hate Japan, but I'll Live Here Anyway'

1 Foreigners who acquire Japanese nationality have the fact of naturalization recorded on the new family register (*koseki*) that is drawn up for them, making it easy for them to be identified as 'new' Japanese (see Chapter 8, p. 136). However, if the holder of the register subsequently moves house, and transfers the register to the new address, then the fact of naturalization is deleted from it. Hence moving house is an effective way of concealing one's ethnic origins.

2 Koguryo was a large state, extending from northeast China across the Korean peninsula, that flourished from 37 BC until AD 668. It was one of the Three Kingdoms, the others being Paekche (18 BC to AD 660) and Silla (57 BC to AD 935). The Three Kingdoms period tends to be roughly defined as lasting from the early fourth until the late seventh century AD. All three kingdoms were important sources of advanced culture for Japan.

3 An example of the kind of news story that angered Yang-Ja would be the so-called 'textbook controversy.' During the mid 1980s there was a protracted debate, including lengthy battles in the law courts, about the Ministry of Education's insistence that Japan's invasion of her Asian neighbors during her imperialist adventure should be described in school history books as an 'advance' (*shinshutsu*) rather than an 'invasion' (*shinryaku*).

4 On *gyōza*, see Chapter 10, Note 4.

5 On graduation trips to North Korea, see Chapter 6, Note 7.

6 Mankyung-Dae is a well-known North Korean beauty spot.

7 The name 'Yang-Ja' is not a typical Korean name. It is simply the Korean reading of the very common Japanese girl's name, 'Yoko.'

15 Not Japanese, Not Korean but Zainichi

1 See Chapter 11, Note 1.

2 *Kyopo* is the Korean term for a fellow countryman living abroad.

3 See Chapter 1, pp. 6–7 and Note 3.

16   In Search of Self-Fulfillment

1   The lunar calendar is still used for certain aspects of life in Korea and Japan alike. However, its use is far more wide-spread in Korea. For example, both countries conduct festivals of remembrance for the ancestors on the fifteenth day of the eighth month in the year, but whereas the Japanese version (*Bon*) falls on August 15 by the solar calendar and is thus a mid-summer event, the Korean version (*Chuseok*) is held on the fifteenth day of the eighth lunar month, which usually puts it in early fall. Celebration of the lunar New Year is also quite widespread in Korea but not in Japan. Nowadays people of both countries define their birthdays by the solar calendar, but until quite recently the lunar calendar was used for birthdays in Korea.

2   A *sōzaiya* is a shop selling precooked croquettes, tempura and other simple boiled and seasoned foods for use as side dishes with meals taken at home.

3   The Asian Women's Association was launched in 1977, with Matsui Yayoi as its representative. Most of the members are Japanese women. It started out as a pressure group against 'sex tourism' in South Korea by Japanese men, and has since taken on various other issues involving the exploitation of Asian women, including the 'comfort women' issue. In 1995 the organization formally changed its name to the Asia-Japan Women's Resource Center.

4   See Chapter 2, Note 22.

5   Jung-Mi said she suffered from paralysis of the hands and arms.

17   Looking for a Way Out

1   *Little Totto by the Window*. A best-selling childhood memoir by popular Japanese media personality Kuroyanagi Tetsuko.

2   Akutagawa Ryunosuke, Dazai Osamu, Hashimoto Osamu. Well-known Japanese novelists. Akutagawa and Dazai are both established as great figures of modern Japanese literature. Hashimoto is a contemporary writer, popular with teenagers.

3   Soon-Ja uses her surname in Japanese mode and her forename
     in Korean mode. This reflects general practice. Forenames are
     used far more often in Korean than in Japanese society. This
     may be partly because a few surnames are so common in
     Korea that using them is likely to cause confusion.

4   *Ryuhakdong* is known as *Ryūgakudō* in Japanese and as the
     Korean Exchange Students League in English. Despite the
     name, the members of Ryuhakdong are not exchange students
     visiting Japan from North Korea – something that is virtually
     impossible to do at present. They are North-leaning Zainichi
     students at Japanese universities. Because they view them-
     selves as North Korean citizens who happen by chance to be
     resident in Japan, they style themselves 'exchange students'
     though they may never have set foot on Korean soil.

18   Making Japan a Place Where Koreans Can Be Themselves

1   'Kin' is the Japanese pronunciation of the Korean name
     'Kim.'

2   *Kokugo* literally means 'national language.' It is the word
     used to describe Japanese lessons in Japanese schools.

3   'Sei' is the Japanese reading of the character 'Jung' in Jung-
     Yi. 'Chan' is a diminutive suffix often attached to the names
     of children.

4   *Kimchi* are spicy Korean-style pickles; *namul* are Korean-
     style boiled greens; *umeboshi* are Japanese-style pickled sour
     plums, traditionally put with rice in a lunch-box.

5   The full title of the Japanese original read by Jung-Yi is *Kugai
     Jōdo: Waga Minamata-byō* (Ishimure 1969). The English
     translation is entitled *Paradise in the Sea of Sorrow: Our
     Minamata Disease* (Ishimure 1990). The story of Minamata
     disease is a tragedy of capitalist industrialization. In 1908 a
     chemical fertilizer factory was built at Minamata. Waste from
     the factory, including methyl-mercury, was pumped straight
     into the sea, resulting in a steady accumulation of poisonous
     pollution. By 1925 local fishing boats were already coming
     back to port with noticeably smaller catches, and by 1950
     there were dead fish floating in the sea, cases of cats going

mad from eating poisoned fish, etc. In 1954 the first human victims of the poisoning were identified (Harada 1972). Both the company that ran the factory and the Japanese government gave higher priority to economic development than to public health, with disastrous consequences for the people of Minamata. Today the legal battle over compensation is finally over, though many people continue to suffer from the effects of methyl-mercury poisoning.

6   At the time virtually all Japanese student activists considered themselves to be Marxists. The 'internationalism' mentioned here by Jung-Yi is shorthand for the Marxist stress on international proletarian solidarity. Ethnic discrimination was viewed as one of the many problems that would naturally wither away come the revolution, and was therefore given no attention whatsoever.

7   The full name of this piece of legislation is the Immigration Control and Refugee Recognition Act (see Chapter 1, Note 16).

19   Japanese Nationality Not Good Enough to Beg for

1   Yuk-Ja's father was practicing moxibustion, an East Asian therapy known in Japan as *kyū*. The word *kyū* is also used to mean 'chastisement,' reflecting the fact that moxibustion is a traditional way of punishing wayward children in Japan, albeit one seldom used today.

2   According to Yuk-Ja, the reason why she made her passport applications via Mindan rather than directly to the South Korean consulate was as follows. When Zainichi Koreans apply in person for South Korean passports, they have to obtain documentary evidence of their family registration in South Korea. This entails filling out forms in Korean, which in many cases, including her own, is impossible. If one applies through Mindan, one has to pay a substantial fee, but Mindan will handle the Korean-language bureaucracy. At the time when Yuk-Ja was working for the travel agency, multiple-use passports were not yet available, meaning that she had to apply for a new passport every single time she went abroad.

3   It is widely believed in Japan that fellow Japanese can understand each other without talking. They are supposed to understand each other instinctively. This cultural belief leads to many all-too-avoidable misunderstandings occurring in Japan.

4   *Jan-so-ri* is a Korean expression meaning 'to grumble.'

5   The *Hina* festival is a Japanese festival, held on March 3, when girls are given traditional-style dolls and display them on special shelves in their homes.

20   Floating on the Tide of Assimilation

1   Yoshiko says the reason why she does not tell anyone about her celebrity connection is because the singer in question is generally known to be a Zainichi Korean, so that telling people about the family link would reveal her own Zainichi identity.

2   The Korean Youth Association in Japan. This organization is described in some detail in Chapter 5.

3   This incident occurred in Chiba prefecture, which borders on eastern Tokyo. Chiba has a reputation for maintaining especially strict social controls in its education system. Under Japanese law, anyone who has reached the age of sixteen is entitled to acquire a moped license, so Yoshiko and her friends were not doing anything illegal. However, schools in Chiba not only ban their students from coming to school on mopeds but even forbid them from acquiring licenses. The police cooperate with this policy by divulging license records, though the legal justification for all this is far from clear.

4   A *furisode* is a long-sleeved kimono, considered the height of elegance in formal wear for young unmarried women in Japan.

5   For a brief account of the Japanese system for training and qualifying nurses, see Chapter 8, Note 3.

6   This is the Japanese reading of her Korean name, Choi Moon-Yim.

7   Personal seals, rather than signatures, are the standard means of written personal identification in Japan. People with

common Japanese names can easily buy cheap, ready-made seals, but rare or foreign names have to be carved to order, a process that usually takes a few days and costs a little more money.

8 'Yang-Ja' is not a usual Korean name. It is simply a transliteration into Korean of the Japanese name 'Yoshiko.'

Conclusion: Towards a Society of Peaceful Coexistence

1 I do not intend for a moment to belittle the value of the concept of human rights itself. I merely believe that it has come to carry an unhelpful set of associations in the Japanese context.

2 One reason why it is so imperative to wipe out ethnic discrimination is because of the sense of inferiority it engenders among members of the minority. In the 1993 KYAJ survey of young South Korean nationals in Japan, which I carried out with Kim Myung-Soo, 63.7 percent of the respondents gave positive answers to a question asking whether they felt a sense of ethnic inferiority while growing up. Using multiple regression analysis, Kim examined the effects of the following variables on engendering a sense of ethnic inferiority: gender, age, educational attainment, concentration of fellow Koreans in place of upbringing, strength of parents' ethnic awareness, level of ethnic education received, degree of discrimination experienced, degree of involvement in ethnic organizations, and father's occupational status. The results showed that 'degree of discrimination experienced' was the most influential factor (the standardized partial regression coefficient *beta* was 0.341) (Fukuoka and Kim 1997:51).

3 For an explanation of the distinctions between the different types of Japanese universities and their policies toward admitting students from Korean senior high schools in Japan, see Chapter 2, esp. Note 8.

4 Among smaller cities and towns there are many more that have abolished the nationality clause in their policy on employing public officials. One of them is Takatsuki City in Osaka Prefecture (see Chapter 4).

5   The campaign for political rights for Koreans in Japan is not supported by those holding North Korean nationality, or at least not by those involved with Chongryun. See 'the nationalist type,' Chapter 3, pp. 51–53.

6   By one of life's little ironies, the Foreign Advisory Council of the Tokyo Metropolitan Government was launched on the very same day that Chung Hyang-Kyun won the suit mentioned earlier against the Tokyo Metropolitan Government for its racist refusal to consider her for promotion. Aoshima Yukio, the former comedian and novelist who was then governor of Tokyo, announced two days later that he would appeal the verdict to the Supreme Court. One has to conclude that despite all the fanfare about the Foreign Advisory Council, the Aoshima administration did not show anything like the consistent respect for foreigners' rights exhibited by neighboring Kawasaki.

7   We asked our respondents, 'Up to now, have you received an ethnic education in the broad sense?' The question was designed to include informal education in the home or at ethnic youth clubs, etc. as well as formal attendance at ethnic Korean schools. Responses were as follows:
    'A very substantial amount of ethnic education' .. 4.9%
    'A substantial amount of ethnic education' 6.9%
    'A little ethnic education' 26.9%
    'Almost no ethnic education' 23.7%
    'No ethnic education whatsoever' 37.7%
    (Fukuoka and Kim 1997:30)

8   Mindan has hitherto taken the view that ethnic education is something for each Zainichi household to take care of itself. However, results of the 1993 KYAJ survey make it clear that there are limitations to what can be achieved with an approach that leaves the matter entirely to the household.

9   These groups are all discussed in earlier chapters: the KYAJ in Chapters 3 and 5; the Seikyū-sha in Chapters 11, 12 and 16; the Mukuge Society in Chapters 2 and 4; and the Tokebi Children's Club in Chapter 4.

10 A major reason for the importance of ethnic education is that it enables children of ethnic minorities to live without any sense of ethnic inferiority. The multiple regression analysis

cited in Note 2 above also found that receiving higher levels of ethnic education tended to reduce feelings of ethnic inferiority (*beta* = -0.227) (Fukuoka and Kim 1997:51).

References

Fukuoka, Y. (1985) *Gendai Shakai no Sabetsu Ishiki* (*Discriminatory Consciousness in Contemporary Society*), Tokyo: Akashi Shoten.

.... (1992) *Gendai Wakamono no Sabetsu-suru Kanōsei* (*Discriminatory Potential among Contemporary Youths*), Tokyo: Akashi Shoten.

.... (1993) *Zainichi Kankoku-Chōsenjin: Wakai Sedai no Aidentiti (Japan-Resident Koreans: The Identity of the Younger Generation)*, Tokyo: Chūōkōron-sha.

Fukuoka, Y. and Kim, M. (1997) *Zainichi Kankokujin Seinen no Seikatsu to Ishiki (The Life and Consciousness of Young South Koreans in Japan)*, Tokyo: University of Tokyo Press.

Fukuoka, Y. and Tsujiyama, Y. (1991a) *Dō-ka to I-ka no Hazama de: 'Zainichi' Wakamono Sedai no Aidentiti Kattō (Caught Between Assimilation and Differentiation: Identity Conflict in the Younger Generation of Japan-Resident Koreans)*, Tokyo: Shinkan-sha.

.... (1991b) *Hontō no Watashi wo Motomete: 'Zainichi' Nisei Sansei no Josei-tachi (In Search of My Real Self: Japan-Resident Korean Women of the Second and Third Generations)*, Tokyo: Shinkan-sha.

Fukuoka, Y., Yoshii, H., Sakurai, A., Ejima, S., Kanegae, H. and Noguchi, M. (1987) *Hi-Sabetsu no Bunka, Han-Sabetsu no Ikizama (Discriminated Cultures and the Anti-Discriminatory Way of Life)*, Tokyo: Akashi Shoten.

Harada, M. (1972) *Minamata-byō (Minamata Disease)*, Tokyo: Iwanami Shoten.

Hatada, T. (ed.) (1987) *Chōsen no Kindai-Shi to Nihon (Korea's Modern History and Japan)*, Tokyo: Yamato Shobō.

Hirowatari, S. (1994) 'Foreigners and the "foreigners question" under Japanese law,' *University of Tokyo Institute of Social Science Occasional Papers in Law and Society*, 7.

Hutnik, N. (1986) 'Patterns of ethnic minority identification and modes of social adaptation,' *Ethnic and Racial Studies* 9(2): 150–67.

Ishimure, M. (1969) *Kugai Jōdo: Waga Minamata-byō (Paradise in the Sea of Sorrow: Our Minamata Disease)*, Tokyo: Kōdan-sha.

.... (1990), translated with an introduction and notes by L. Monnet, *Paradise in the Sea of Sorrow: Our Minamata Disease*, Yamaguchi: Yamaguchi Publishing House.

Isomura, E. and Fukuoka,Y. (eds) (1984) *Masukomi to Sabetsu-Go Mondai (The Mass Media and the Problem of Discriminatory Language)*, Tokyo: Akashi Shoten.

Kim, C. (1997) *Zainichi Korian Hyaku-Nen-Shi (A One-Hundred Year History of Koreans in Japan)*, Tokyo: Sango-kan.

Kimpara, S., Ishida, R., Ozawa, Y., Kajimura, H., Tanaka, H. and Mihashi, O. (1986) *Nihon no Naka no Kankoku-Chōsenjin, Chūgokujin: Kanagawa-kennai Zaijū Gaikokujin Jittai Chōsa yori (Koreans and Chinese Inside Japan: Reports from a Survey on Foreign Residents of Kanagawa Prefecture)*, Tokyo: Akashi Shoten.

Ministry of Justice (1985) *The Nationality Law*, Tokyo: Civil Affairs Bureau, Ministry of Justice.

Mintōren (ed.) (1989) *Zainichi Kankoku-Chōsenjin no Hoshō-Jinken Hō (The Law Regarding War Reparations and Human Rights Protection for Japan-Resident Koreans)*, Tokyo: Shinkan-sha.

Miyata, S., Kim, Y. and Yang, T. (1992) *Sōshi-Kaimei (Make a Surname, Change the Forename)*, Tokyo: Akashi Shoten.

Nomura, S. (1996) *Korian Sekai no Tabi (A Journey Round the Korean World)*, Tokyo: Kōdan-sha.

Ohnuma, Y. (1992) *Saharin Kimin (Abandoned on Sakhalin)*, Tokyo: Chūōkōron-sha.

Park, K. (1965) *Chōsenjin Kyōsei Renkō no Kiroku (Records of Korean Forced Migrant Labor)*, Tokyo: San'ichi Shobō.

Ryang, S. (1997) *North Koreans in Japan: Language, Ideology, and Identity*, Boulder, Colorado and Oxford: Westview Press.

Shukuya, K. (1988) *Ajia kara Kita Hanayome: Mukaeru Gawa no Ronri (Brides from Asia: The Logic of Those Who Take Them)*, Tokyo: Akashi Shoten.

Simpson, G. E. and Yinger, J. M. ([1953]1972) *Racial and Cultural Minorities: An Analysis of Prejudice and Discrimination*, 4th ed., New York: Harper & Row.

Stonequist, E. V. ([1937]1961) *The Marginal Man: A Study in Personality and Culture Conflict*, New York: Russell & Russell.

Takagi, K. (1992) *Jūgun Ianfu to Sengo Hoshō (Military Comfort Women and Post-War Compensation)*, Tokyo: San'ichi Shobō.

Takara, K. (1993) *Ryūkyū Ōkoku (The Ryukyu Kingdom)*, Tokyo: Iwanami Shoten.

Tomiyama, I. (1990) *Kindai Nihon Shakai to 'Okinawajin': 'Nihonjin' ni Naru to iu Koto (Modern Japanese Society and 'Okinawans': The Matter of Becoming 'Japanese')*, Tokyo: Nihon Keizai Hyōron-sha.

Utsumi, A. (1982) *Chōsenjin BC-kyū Senpan no Kiroku (A Record of Korean B- and C-grade War Criminals)*, Tokyo: Keisō Shobō.

Yamawaki, K. (1994) *Kindai Nihon to Gaikokujin Rōdōsha: 1890 Nendai Kōhan to 1920 Nendai Zenhan ni okeru Chūgokujin, Chōsenjin Rōdōsha Mondai (Early Modern Japan and Foreign Workers: The Question of Chinese and Korean Workers in the Late 1890s and Early 1920s)*, Tokyo: Akashi Shoten.

Yoshimi, Y. (1995) *Jūgun Ianfu (Military Comfort Women)*, Tokyo: Iwanami Shoten.

Glossary

Korean

abeoji	father
aje	uncle
ban-chokbali	'half cloven hooves' – insulting term for Zainichi Koreans
bonkwan	ancestral place of origin
bulgogi	cooked meat
chokbali	'cloven hooves' – insulting term for Japanese
chokbo	documents of a clan
Chosun-saram	Korean people
Chuseok	Korean festival held on August 15 by the lunar calendar
dduk	Korean rice cake
dongseong-dongbon	same surname and same ancestral land
eomeoni	mother
eoseo osipsiyo	welcome
haleoboji	grandfather
haleomeoni	grandmother
halme	grandma
han-gul	Korean script
Ilbon-saram	Japanese people
jang-gu	traditional Korean drum
jan-so-ri	grumble
jeogori	traditional Korean dress
Jesa	Korean rite of ancestor worship
kayagum	traditional Korean zither
kimchi	very spicy vegetables
Kyopo	a Korean living abroad
Mudang	Korean shaman

namul	boiled greens
samul-nori	traditional Korean mode of song and dance
sangnom	commoner
sudkarak	spoon
uri hak-kyo	our school
uri mal	our language
yangban	Korean aristocracy
yimo	aunt

Japanese

Chon	term of abuse for Koreans
Chonkō	term of abuse for Koreans
Chōsenjin	Korean or North Korean
Daiken	university entrance qualification examination
Daisangoku-jin	third-country nationals
doburoku	unrefined *sake*
Eta	insulting term for Burakumin
furisode	a long-sleeved kimono for a young unmarried woman
gaijin	'foreigner'
gyōza	small fried dumplings
Hina matsuri	Japanese traditional doll festival for girls held on March 3
Hinomaru	Japanese national flag
honke	the main household
honseki	official domicile
ie	Japanese traditional household
jinken	human rights
Kankokujin	South Korean
Kimigayo	Japanese national anthem
kokugo	national language, hence Japanese
kokyō	one's old home
koseki	household registers

kyōsei	coexistence
kyōtō	joint struggle
kyū	moxa treatment
mochi	Japanese rice cake
monja	a thin flat cake
okonomi-yaki	pancake-like food eaten as a light meal
omiai	formal meeting arranged by a go-between for a man and a woman each seeking a marriage partner
pachinko	a kind of pinball game
sake	a brewed alcoholic beverage made from fermented rice
Shichigosan	a rite of passage for young children
sokoku	motherland
soroban	Japanese abacus
Sōshi-Kaimei	make a surname and change one's forename
sōzaiya	a shop selling precooked foods
tabi	Japanese-style socks
Tanabata	traditional Japanese festival held on July 7
tatami	Japanese traditional flooring mat
umeboshi	pickled sour plums
yakiniku	cooked meat
yūzen	a textile dyeing method

Index

Mintōren (National Council for Combating Discrimination Against Ethnic Peoples in Japan), xii, 22, 50, 52, 58, 61–83, 272n7, 285n3, 296n5

Mudang (Korean shaman), 163

Mukuge Society See Takatsuki Mukuge Society.

names, **xxi**, **5–9**, **27–33**, 51, 53, 54, 55, 64f, **68f**, 74f, 79ff, 87f, **91**, 97f, 100f, 104, 106, 109f, 114–9, 125, 131, 138, 140, 157, 162, 163, 168f, 175ff, 181f, 184f, 202, 216, 219ff, 225, 227, 236f, 242, 244, 248, 249f, 278–9n13, 281n6, **287n9**, **290nn17,18**, **293n27**, **297n7**, 298n9, 299n2, 301nn13,16, 303nn10, 13, 308n1, 312n7 See also alias.

nationalist type, **51–3**, 56ff, **101–12**

nationality, **xxixff**, **38ff**, 125f, 177, 239f, **285n2**, 292-3n26

Japanese, xxviiif, 12, 70, 129, 137ff, 162, 168f, 170, 177, 256, 275n3, 276nn5,7, 293n27

North Korean, 22, 101, 105, 129, 179, 188, 224, 246, **302n4**, 305n8, 318n5

South Korean, 22, 61, 71, 83, 93, 113, 119, 134, 147, 155, 180, 196, 205, 214, 234, 243, 257, **292-3n26**, **302n4**

nationality clause, 14, 19, **77ff**, 80, 148ff, 237, **256f**, **282–3n12**, 284n17, **301n15**, 317n4, 318n6

Nationality Law, **xxviii**, 39f, 117, 134, **137**, 170, 275n3, 276nn4,5,7

naturalization, xxxii, 39, 54f, 71, 81f, 92, 104, 119, 120, 127, **133f**, 137ff, 162f, 169, 189, 216, 223, 234, **239ff**, 248, **278–9n13**, **292n25**, 298n9, **310n3**

naturalizing type, **54f**, 57ff, **129–43**

North Korea (DPRK), 22, 51ff, 104, 111, 180, 188, 193f, 285n2, 304n9, 305n7

Okinawa See Ryukyuans.

overseas nationals, 51, 101

pachinko, 29, 108, 110, **289n16**, 305n6

pluralism, 13

pluralist type, **50f**, 56ff, **61–82**

political rights, 70, **257f**, 299n5, 318n5

pseudonym See alias.

repatriation program, **39**, 71, 101, 180, 299-300n6, **304n2**

Republic of Korea See South Korea.

research ethics, **xv–xvii**, xix

reunification of Korea, 51f, 69, **105**, 133, 186, 194, 203